Half the people in Hollywood are dying to be discovered and the other half are afraid they will be.
Lionel Barrymore

BOOKS BY TROY TAYLOR

DEAD MEN SO TELL TALES SERIES
Dead Men Do Tell Tales (2008)
Bloody Chicago (2006)
Bloody Illinois (2008)
Bloody Hollywood (2008)

HAUNTED ILLINOIS BOOKS
Haunted Illinois (1999 / 2001 / 2004)
Haunted Decatur (1995)
More Haunted Decatur (1996)
Ghosts of Millikin (1996 / 2001)
Where the Dead Walk (1997 / 2002)
Dark Harvest (1997)
Haunted Decatur Revisited (2000)
Flickering Images (2001)
Haunted Decatur: 13th Anniversary Edition (2006)
Haunted Alton (2000 / 2003 / 2008)
Haunted Chicago (2003)
The Haunted President (2005)
Mysterious Illinois (2005)
Resurrection Mary (2007)
The Possessed (2007)
Weird Chicago (2008)

HAUNTED FIELD GUIDE BOOKS
The Ghost Hunters Guidebook
(1997/ 1999 / 2001/ 2004 / 2007)
Confessions of a Ghost Hunter (2002)
Field Guide to Haunted Graveyards (2003)
Ghosts on Film (2005)
So, There I Was (with Len Adams) (2006)

HISTORY & HAUNTINGS SERIES
The Haunting of America (2001)
Into the Shadows (2002)
Down in the Darkness (2003)
Out Past the Campfire Light (2004)
Ghosts by Gaslight (2007)

OTHER GHOSTLY TITLES
Spirits of the Civil War (1999)
Season of the Witch (1999/ 2002)
Haunted New Orleans (2000)
Beyond the Grave (2001)
No Rest for the Wicked (2001)
Haunted St. Louis (2002)
The Devil Came to St. Louis (2006)

STERLING PUBLICATIONS
Weird U.S. (Co-Author) (2004)
Weird Illinois (Barnes & Noble Press) (2005)
Weird Virginia (Co-Author) (2007)
Weird Indiana (Co-Author) (2008)

BARNES & NOBLE PRESS TITLES
Haunting of America (2006)
Spirits of the Civil War (2007)
Into the Shadows (2007)

HISTORY PRESS TITLES
Wicked Washington (2007)

STACKPOLE BOOKS TITLES
Haunted Illinois (2008)

DEAD MEN DO TELL TALES SERIES

BLOODY HOLLYWOOD
History & Hauntings of Tinseltown Crime & Unsolved Mysteries
BY TROY TAYLOR

- A Dark Haven Entertainment Book from Whitechapel Press -

When I was a kid, I spent many Saturday afternoons in front of the television watching a show that aired on our local PBS station called "Matinee at the Bijou". The theme song for it still runs in my head and I'll never forgotten my first introduction to classic films, vintage newsreels, comedy shorts, weekly serials and the magic of the movies. I have no idea who created the show, but whoever it was... this one's for you!

And to Betty, sorry that your fame came too late.

© COPYRIGHT 2008 BY TROY TAYLOR & DARK HAVEN ENTERTAINMENT, INC.

All Rights Reserved, including the right to copy or reproduce this book, or portions thereof, in any form, without express permission from the author and publisher

ORIGINAL COVER ARTWORK DESIGNED BY

©Copyright 2008 by Michael Schwab & Troy Taylor
Visit M & S Graphics at http://www.manyhorses.com/msgraphics.htm

THIS BOOK IS PUBLISHED BY:

Whitechapel Press
A Division of Dark Haven Entertainment, Inc.
15 Forest Knolls Estates - Decatur, Illinois - 62521
(217) 422-1002 / 1-888-GHOSTLY
Visit us on the internet at http://www. dark haven entertainment. com

First Printing -- September 2008
ISBN: 1-892523-60-4

Printed in the United States of America

BLOODY HOLLYWOOD

I always thought the real violence in Hollywood isn't what's on the screen. It's what you have to do to raise the money.
David Mamet

If only those who dream about Hollywood knew how difficult it all is.
Greta Garbo

Hollywood is an extraordinary kind of temporary place.
John Schlesinger

It's said in Hollywood that you should always forgive your enemies - because you never know when you'll have to work with them.
Lana Turner

Strip away the phony tinsel of Hollywood and you'll find the real tinsel underneath.
Oscar Levant

Fame is no sanctuary from the passing of youth... suicide is much easier and more acceptable in Hollywood than growing old gracefully.
Julie Burchill

TABLE OF CONTENTS

INTRODUCTION - PAGE 8

1. HOLLYWOOD EXPOSED - PAGE 10
The History of Crime & Horror in Los Angeles

Hooray for Hollywood - 14
Booze & Broads - 16
The "Jesus Racket" - 18
L.A. in the 1930s - 19
After the War - 20
The Mob in Hollywood - 22
Hollywood's Favorite Gangster: Bugsy Siegel - 23
The Hollywood Extortion Case - 27
Hollywood's Underworld - 29
Mickey Cohen: America's Most Shot-At Gangster - 29
Hollywood Hookers - 32
Hollywood's Preachers, Cults, Kooks & Crazies - 34
"Fighting Bob' Shuler - 35
Sister Aimee - 36
The Blackburn Cult - 38
Mankind United - 39
Heaven's Gate - 39
Fountain of the World - 40
Process Church of the Final Judgment - 41
Four P Movement - 43
The Manson Family - 44
A Rogue's Gallery of Killers - 59
L.A.'s Bluebeard - 59
The "Ghost in the Garret" - 61
The "Tiger Woman" - 63
"Fate", "Death" & "The Fox" - 65
The "Rattlesnake Murderer" - 67
Death of the "Red Light Bandit" - 69
The Hillside Strangler - 71
The Sunset Slayer - 73
The "Night Stalker" - 75

TABLE OF CONTENTS

2. HOLLYWOOD'S HAUNTED HOTSPOTS - PAGE 81
Where the Stars Still Linger
Hollywood's Haunted Movie Studios - 81
Universal Studios - 83
Culver Studios & The Mysterious Death of Thomas Ince - 88
Paramount Studios & Hollywood Forever Cemetery - 92
Hollywood's Haunted Movie Theaters - 100
Grauman's Chinese Theater - 100
Warner Pacific Theater - 102
Pantages Theater & The Mystery of Howard Hughes - 103
Hollywood's Haunted Hotels - 109
Knickerbocker Hotel - 111
Alexandria Hotel - 122
Hollywood Roosevelt Hotel - 123

3. SEX, SIN & SUICIDE - PAGE 126
Hollywood Scandals and The Restless Spirits Left Behind
Olive Thomas: The First Hollywood Scandal - 127
The Fall of the "Funny Fat Man": The Fatty Arbuckle Scandal - 130
Haunts of the Sheik: Remnants of Valentino - 138
Drugs & Death: The Tragedy of Alma Rubens - 146
Peg Entwhsitle & The Haunted Hollywood Sign - 149
The Lonely Death of Lupe Velez - 153
"In Like Flynn": The Scandals of Errol Flynn & His Lingering Spirit - 156
James Dean: Too Fast to Live - 164
The "Sweater Girl" & The Gangster: The Murder of Johnny Stompanato - 172
Ghost of the Pink Palace: Jayne Mansfield's Death Curse - 179

4. NO REST OF THE WICKED - PAGE 188
Hollywood's Murders & Unsolved Mysteries
William Desmond Taylor: Hollywood's Original Unsolved Mystery - 188
The "Creepy Little Man": The Strange Death of Paul Bern - 195
"Hot Toddy": The Mysterious Death of Thelma Todd - 204
Who Killed the Black Dahlia? The Tragic Life & Death of Elizabeth Short - 212
Vanished! The Unsolved Disappearance of Jean Spangler - 221
The Unsolved Murder of Helene Jerome - 224
Faster Than A Speeding Bullet? The Mystery of George Reeves - 228
Birth of a Legend: The Mysterious Death of Marilyn Monroe - 236
"Fall of a Hero": The Unsolved Murder of Bob Crane - 244

INTRODUCTION

Los Angeles, the fabled City of Angels, home to the rich and famous, to palm trees, sandy beaches, orange groves, Disneyland and most of all, to that wonderful place of the American Dream known as Hollywood.

Like many readers, I have always been fascinated by the glamour, the glitter and the decadence of old Hollywood. I have walked the Hollywood streets, searching for the names of my favorite celebrities along the Walk of Fame. I have stared in awe at the elaborate facade of the Chinese Theater and have pressed my own palms into the solidified handprints of film greats like Humphrey Bogart. I have always been intrigued by tales of movie stars and by the secret inner workings of the great film studios.

But like the city of Hollywood itself, the legends of the place have a dark side. About the time that I got interested in ghosts and hauntings I got interested in the less glamorous side of Hollywood. I learned that the bright photographs of its sunny streets hid whispers of crime and corruption and that the lavish homes and splendid architecture hid tales of spirits who did not rest in peace. There are many unsolved mysteries connected to Hollywood, as well as tales of scandal, depravity, murder, and, of course, ghosts.

The lure of Tinseltown has been a part of America since the first silent film makers came west to the small town of Los Angeles in the early 1900s. What began as a scheme for moviemaker Mack Sennett to make some extra money with a low-cost housing development called Hollywoodland became a movie colony for artists, writers and actors who came west to make it big.

Today, Hollywood remains not so much a place as a state of mind. In fact, it has not even been incorporated as a city since 1910, when in joined Los Angeles to share its water supply. However, it still retains that strange allure for those of us who have an interest in history, hauntings, and American crime and for those who have lived their lives against the backdrop of the mythical silver screen.

Of course, to understand how Hollywood earned its starring role in the hearts and minds of America, we have to first look at the history of the city of Los Angeles, the place that actually invented the Hollywood we all know.

The history of the region is a dark journey

through sordid tales of crime, corruption, death, murder and, of course, Hollywood-style scandal. Nearly every tale of ghosts and hauntings in Hollywood involves a terrible crime or an unsolved murder. Why is this? We don't know for sure, but perhaps there is something about the region itself that attracts both the brightest lights and the darkest shadows to its streets.

The tales that follow will introduce you to the bloody history of the place that became Hollywood, along with accounts of some of the most terrifying crimes ever committed in the United States.

Ghost researchers and enthusiasts find that locations earn a designation of "haunted" because of violent crimes that took place there that remain unsolved. There is something about unfinished business, especially the bloody kind, which prevents the dead from crossing over to the other side. You will find many such stories within the pages of this book. Hollywood is a place where crime has always been commonplace and where many of the victims (and sometimes the perpetrators) refuse to rest in peace.

But keep in mind that not all of the stories in this book will be related to ghosts. Some of them were simply so strange, so mysterious and so horrifying that they had to be included. They may not be about ghosts but you won't find them to be any less terrifying and scandalous. As it has been said in the past, it's not always the dead that we need to be afraid of, sometimes it's the living.

I dug through my files of Hollywood crimes and chose a number of my favorite stories. I think you will find all of the tales ahead of you, whether familiar or strange, to be about events that have left a bloodstained mark on the haunted landscape of Hollywood. Many of them will frighten you, some will disturb you and others will undoubtedly have you looking over your shoulder as you read. These are not tales for the faint of heart but they are all part of the rich and textured landscape of this unusual place.

Ahead of you lies a strange, perplexing, and sometimes stomach-churning, journey so sit back, relax and prepare yourself for an encounter with a side of Tinseltown that few ever live long enough to see.

Welcome to the dark side of Hollywood.

Troy Taylor
Summer 2008

1. HOLLYWOOD EXPOSED
THE HISTORY OF CRIME & HORROR IN LOS ANGELES

Los Angeles, the so-called "Wonder City of the West," captured the imagination of the American public in the late 1800s and early 1900s in a way that no other place in the country ever had before. There was great natural beauty with mountains, beaches and orange groves, but the architecture was modern, borrowed, or bizarre in ways that went beyond any Midwesterner's imagination. It was the land of film stars, both real and imagined. There was Hollywood and Vine, movie star mansions, movie premieres, nightclubs, and carefully sculpted images that created the fantasy. There were kooks, nuts and cults and cemeteries for pets. The frequent fires, earthquakes, and mudslides reminded the residents that little here was permanent. There was a lack of history, but there was also the chance to leave everything in the past behind and to re-invent and re-imagine.

And there was crime. The horrors visited on Los Angeles were just as real as in any other big city, but in a place that was larger than life the crime seemed a little bigger and bit more skewed. The murders, prostitution, gambling, and drugs, when filtered through pen, paper and celluloid, became the noir that would make men like Raymond Chandler and James Ellroy famous.

Almost from its founding, Los Angeles had a bad reputation. The once-sleepy Spanish mission had been stolen from its rightful Mexican owners during the American quest for Manifest Destiny and soon, immigrants from the East were pouring out to the West Coast. The Eastern newspapers promised sunshine, warm weather, easy living and, of course, an elusive fortune that could be obtained in the California gold fields. What many of the immigrants found instead was poverty and death. The majority of them returned home with nothing to show for their travels and hard work. Many of them never returned home at all.

By the mid-1800s, Los Angeles (dubbed the "City of Angels" by the original founders) was literally filled with murderers, thieves and

The beginnings of Los Angeles in the 1800s (Los Angeles Public Library)

prostitutes. The streets were nothing more than rutted dirt paths where animals roamed and where garbage was dumped. With murders, robberies and kidnappings becoming commonplace, the primitive court system could only handle a small percentage of the cases filed by police officers, allowing scores of criminals to go free. This led to the formation of vigilante committees, which stepped in to take care of criminals on their own, often with the complete approval of the city's mayor.

In 1854, the Los Angeles Rangers were formed and were financed by some of the city's leading judges, lawyers, and businessmen, including Phineas Banning, a California tycoon and founder of the Banning Railroad. Other groups included the Los Angeles Home Guard, another paramilitary group of bloodthirsty citizens and the feared El Monte Rangers, a group of Texas immigrants who specialized in killing Mexicans.

The vigilantes had no regards for suspects' rights, some of whom were dragged from their homes, jail cells, or even churches, then beaten, horsewhipped, tortured, mutilated, castrated, and then hanged from the nearest tree. In 1854 alone, 22 men fell victim to one vigilante group or another.

One of the most shocking cases of vigilante justice in California took place in Los Angeles' Chinatown in 1871. The massacre of Chinese immigrants was reported in newspapers all over the country and led to many people referring to the city as "Los Diablos" from that time on. The massacre took place near the old city plaza on the Calle de los Negros, which was commonly mistranslated in those days and called "Nigger Alley." The narrow street was a block of saloons, gambling parlors and dance halls. It was said that three or four men were murdered in the alley every weekend.

At the time, the Chinese were competing with the Mexicans for most of the hard labor that was being done in the area and, consequently, suffered from all manner of racism and injustice. A typical front page article in the newspapers of the time stated: "Not only do the Chinese revel in crime, but they delight to draw the detested white race down to their level." Not surprisingly, the "celestials," as

Calle de Los Negros ("Nigger Alley") in downtown Los Angeles -- the site of the 1871 Chinatown Massacre (Los Angeles Fire Department)

the Chinese often were called, were unable to vote, own property, or run legitimate businesses. As a result, many of them were forced into prostitution, narcotics, and gambling to earn a living.

By the 1860s, two rival gangs had established themselves among the Chinese: the Hong Chows and the Nin Yungs. Both gangs kept their activities within the Chinese community, but managed to make city officials very nervous. In 1870, the chief of police began making regular raids on Chinatown, which only ratcheted up the tension being felt in the city. Finally, in 1871, these tensions exploded into a massive, citywide insurrection.

No one knows for sure how the riot started, but one version states that a Los Angeles police officer, Robert Thompson, went to issue a warrant to a Chinese gang member who worked in Nigger Alley. But rather than allow the warrant to be served, the gang member produced a gun and shot and killed the policeman. That, in turn, led to a chain reaction that ended with the slaughter of dozens of innocent men and women. Another version claimed that a drunken Chinese man began firing his gun and accidentally hit a white man. Within minutes, an inebriated and enraged mob swarmed through the streets, lynching, burning, stabbing and beating any Chinese they could get their hands on.

However, historian Horace Bell, in his book *On the Old West Coast*, claims that the riot began not because police officer Thompson went to Nigger Alley to serve a warrant, but rather to steal money from a Chinese man. Thompson had seen the money days earlier when Ah Choy, the "gang member" in question, had taken him to his shop to prove that he could make bail. Apparently, Choy had been arrested when a rival merchant had issued a complaint against him. The police chief refused to allow him to go free because he didn't believe the man could pay his bail. So Choy took Thompson to his shop and showed him a box filled with $7,000 in cash. Choy was given a court date and let go – while Thompson schemed with another officer to break into Choy's store and steal the money.

Horace Bell claimed that Choy caught Thompson with his hand in the till and shot him in self-defense. Thompson's partner, meanwhile, was apprehended by some of Choy's friends and held inside the building until Choy could figure out what to do. When word spread that Chinese "gang members" had killed a police officer and had taken another hostage, a mob began to form outside. Choy tried to turn himself in, but it was no use. Bullets began to be fired at the shop and all hell broke loose. Choy's friends returned fire as vigilantes from all over the city, commanded by the chief of police himself, descended on Chinatown and attacked every Asian they could find. Eventually, 19 of them were killed.

A Grand Jury indicted 156 men in the affair, with only six of them actually going to jail. Several days later, the six were released for lack of evidence. These were the first charges of corruption

IMAGES OF OLD LOS ANGELES

(Left) The L.A. Courthouse & the Hall of Records (Right) Downtown Los Angeles

(Left) Downtown Los Angeles in 1890 and (Right) A Scene from downtown L.A. in the early 1900s

1910's Bathing Beauties at Venice Beach

leveled against the city government, but they would not be the last. Corrupt officials and a police force of dubious reputation plagued the image of Los Angeles for decades to come – and some would say that that taint has never really gone away.

In the early years of the 20th century, a new flock of immigrants arrived, and many of the new arrivals found plenty of sunshine in California, but not much else. Water, a necessary staple that was brought to the area under questionable circumstances and made millions for the privileged few, transformed the desert into a phony paradise of fake vegetation and fantasy architecture. Fortunes began to be made in oil and land and, as a matter of course, graft and petty crime became commonplace. The population explosion brought not only the upright citizens but also the scam artists, con men and nut cases who tried to take advantage of the rapid growth. To fill the subsequent voids, many newcomers joined clubs for the lonesome or sought solace with healers of the soul, from evangelists to psychic mediums, who comforted the lonely in return for money.

Like most other cities in the country, corruption and vice came with the territory but Los Angeles was different. It was new and fresh and the geography of the area, the automobile and the glamour of Hollywood all combined to create a unique combination. Other cities had grown up around horse-drawn carriages, railroads, and trolley cars, but Los Angeles was born at the beginning of the automobile age and with over 450 square miles of roads, the city had plenty of room to grow. The motorcar was the principal form of transportation and this created a boomtown mentality for new arrivals.

HOORAY FOR HOLLYWOOD!

Of all of the reasons for the rapid growth, Hollywood was undoubtedly one of the biggest ones. The mere mention of the name guaranteed readers for any newspaper story in the nation. In just a few short years, thanks to stars like Mary Pickford, Douglas Fairbanks and many others, Hollywood had managed to set itself apart from the rest of the world, as everything there seemed larger than life. The city within a city had seemingly come from nowhere to become one of the most recognizable places on earth.

In 1853, only a single adobe hut stood at the spot that would someday be Hollywood. By 1870, a farm community had started to flourish and some believe the name of the community came from the ample stands of California holly that covered the hillsides with bright red berries each winter. But, as with everything else in Hollywood, every legend has at least two versions, if not more.

The name "Hollywood" was coined by H.J. Whitley, the man considered the father of Hollywood. He and his wife, Gigi, allegedly came up with the name while on their honeymoon. As they stood on a hill (which is now in the center of Hollywood) admiring the view, they spotted a rickety old horse-drawn wagon driven by a Chinese man. As he approached them, the man stopped his

H.J. Whitley, his wife, Gigi, and their family. Whitley has been called the "Father of Hollywood" and Gigi all;agedly coined the name of the town when they visited the area on their honeymoon. Whitley platted the town and later built the legendary Hollywood Hotel.

wagon and Whitley asked him what he was doing. In broken English (and of course, with a "Chinese laundry" accent), he replied, "I up sunrise. Old trees fall down. Pick up wood. All time haully wood." With an epiphany, Whitley declared that he would name his new town "Hollywood," or so this racist legend goes.

Another version of the story about the name of the town is connected to Harvey Wilcox, who bought land in the area for the development of homes. His wife, Daeida, met a woman on a train who mentioned that she named her Ohio summer home Hollywood. Daeida, who liked the name, gave it to the new development and it first appeared on Wilcox's map of the subdivision in 1887.

However, the name really gained its popularity thanks to filmmaker Mack Sennett, who created a low-cost subdivision called "Hollywoodland" when he came to California. The subdivision later vanished into the depths of Hollywood, but the advertising sign's tall white letters remain, still watching over the community from the Hollywood hills.

However the city gained its name, it was beginning to thrive in 1900. With a post office, newspapers, hotel, two markets, and a population of about 500, it lay about seven miles east of Los Angeles, nestled in the fruit groves. Contact with the larger city was sparse in the early days. Only a single-track streetcar connected the two and service was infrequent and took nearly two hours.

The first section of the famous Hollywood Hotel, the first major hotel in the city, was opened in 1902. Its creator, H.J. Whitley, was eager to sell building lots among the lemon groves that lined the foothills. Located on the west side of Highland Avenue, the hotel fronted Prospect Avenue, which was still a dusty, unpaved road at the time.

Hollywood was incorporated as a municipality in 1903 but it was still little more than a country town. Among the town ordinances at the time was one that banned the sale of liquor, except by pharmacists, and one that prevented ranchers from driving cattle through the streets, except in herds of 200 head or less. In 1904, a new trolley car track running from Los Angeles to Hollywood up Prospect Avenue was opened. The system was called "the Hollywood Boulevard." It drastically cut down the amount of time needed to get to Los Angeles and opened the city to even greater development.

By 1910, because of an ongoing struggle to secure an adequate water supply, Hollywood voted to be annexed by the city of Los Angeles. By this time, the Los Angeles Aqueduct had opened and was piping water down from the Owens River in Owens Valley. Hollywood gained not only a water supply, but access to the larger city's sewer systems, too. When the community was annexed, the name of Prospect Avenue was changed to Hollywood Boulevard and all of the street numbers in the new district changed, as well.

Around this same time, America's fledging motion picture industry discovered Hollywood. Before California, moviemakers had flocked to Chicago. In the early 1900s, filmmakers were abandoning the East Coast, hoping to stay one step ahead of the stringent copyright rules that were being imposed on the industry by Thomas Edison. Chicago was just far enough west to stay under Edison's radar, at least for awhile. The harsh winter weather in the Windy City soon had performers

The Hollywood Hotel was built in 1902 by H.J. Whitley

D.W. Griffith

looking for a new location on the sunny West Coast.

In early 1910, the Biograph Company sent director D. W. Griffith to California with his crew and acting troupe, consisting of Blanche Sweet, Lillian Gish, Mary Pickford, Lionel Barrymore and others. They started filming on a vacant lot in downtown Los Angeles. The company began looking for other locations and traveled a few miles north to the small community of Hollywood. Griffith then filmed his first movie in Hollywood: "In Old California," a melodrama that was set in Mexican California in the 1800s. The company stayed there for months and made several films before returning to New York. However, Biograph, along with many others, would be back.

The first movie studio to be established in Hollywood was the New Jersey-based Centaur Company, which thought California would be perfect for low-budget westerns. They rented an empty roadhouse on Sunset Boulevard and converted it into a movie studio in October 1911. It was dubbed Nestor Studios, after the name of the western branch of their company. The first feature film made in a Hollywood studio was "The Squaw Man," directed by Cecil B. DeMille and Oscar Apfel in 1914.

By 1915, the majority of American films were being produced in Hollywood and the city became a household word almost overnight. Hollywood began to set itself apart from the rest of the world and soon, residents began believing their own press that everything there really was larger than life.

BOOZE & BROADS

At the start of the 1920s, Prohibition came along and created a new set of problems for Los Angeles. As with just about everywhere else in the country, the demand for illegal liquor was high in Los Angeles and there were dozens of hoods who were happy to bribe the cops to get the kegs and bottles in the right hands. Perhaps the most famous L.A. hotspot for booze was Culver City, known as the "Heart of Screenland." This town was home to M.G.M., Hal Roach and a number of other studios and its main street, Washington Boulevard, played host to dozens of speakeasies, gambling parlors and gin

An L.A. liquor raid in 1931 (Los Angeles Herald-Examiner)

joints. The town's "open" reputation also attracted gambling and prostitution rackets and soon added a racetrack, a boxing arena and a dog racing track to its list of dubious attractions. All of them served as magnets for local gangsters. In addition, the Culver City Police Department was well known for looking the other way, losing evidence and bungling their investigations (as long as cash landed in the right pockets.) Thanks to this, crime operated there undisturbed.

The Rex, Santa Monica's most famous gambling ship, is raided by police officers in 1938. The ships anchored off the coast for nearly a decade before being closed down by the authorities. (USC Regional History Collection)

Of course, Culver City was not the only place to find booze, gambling and broads; the rest of southern California had a thirst for illegal liquor and vice, as well. And Hollywood could always be counted on for more than its share of corruption and scandal. The film industry, which was the largest business in the area by the 1920s, provided more than enough money for both excess and debauchery. A series of scandals rocked Hollywood in the early 1920s: the alleged rape and murder of Virginia Rappe by America's beloved funny man, Fatty Arbuckle, the drug-related death of Wallace Reid, the murder of director William Desmond Taylor and others.

All of this gave America a front row seat to the scandals of the movie colony and its shining stars. There was no doubt about it, with orgies, drugs, illegal hooch, scandals and sex Hollywood had officially arrived!

One of the best places to find gambling in Los Angeles was not in the city, but about three miles off the coast. The first gambling ship arrived in 1928 to entertain and lighten the pockets of residents and visitors who were looking for action. The various refitted barges that anchored off the coast for the next decade became a lucrative venture. Flaunting legal jurisdiction, they operated openly until the late 1930s, when a series of raids finally put them out of business.

With the kind of newspaper headlines and scandal sheet stories that were pouring out of Southern California, it was a natural progression to see gangsters and crime bosses across the country heading to L.A. to set up shop. Bootleggers and gamblers like Tony Cornero, Dominic DiCiolla, and Albert Marco controlled the business. Mobsters like Guy McAfee, Nola Hahn, Jack Drgna, and Bob Gans ran numbers rackets, prostitution, gambling, and slot machines. In return for their share of the profits, local cops were expected to keep any eastern concerns from muscling in on the territory. When Al Capone came calling in 1927, he was met by a couple of detectives who made it clear that the Chicago mob boss was not welcome in Los Angeles. After this little visit, Capone headed back to the Windy City, ending his "vacation" in sunny California. It would be a few more years before any serious organized crime muscle would come to L.A. to stay.

The cops in Los Angeles weren't just keeping eastern gangsters from setting up operations in the area. Chief of Police Ed "Two-Gun" Davis and his cronies in City Hall were also making sure that the graft continued to flow into the pockets of the cops who would take it. Their operations culminated in 1938 with the car bombing of an ex-LAPD private investigator named Harry Raymond. He was in the process of exposing the widespread corruption in the police department and uncovered a lot of information that no one wanted publicized. The

Dead Men Do Tell Tales: Bloody Hollywood - Page 17

bombing was traced back to the LAPD's Intelligence Squad and the public outrage that followed managed to oust Mayor Frank Shaw, while Chief Davis, along with 23 police officers, was forced into resigning.

L.A. was also the scene of several sensational crimes by the late 1920s. They would be the first of many to come. In 1927, the case of Edward Hickman and the kidnapping and dismemberment of 12-year-old Marion Parker would make headlines as would the 1929 gun battle between Jack Hawkins and Zeke Hayes and the L.A. police within the courthouse elevator. The two men had long records, which included the alleged torture death of a San Francisco cop. When they were discovered in southern California, they found themselves set up for L.A. sheriff-style revenge.

These crimes were just a foreshadowing of bloody things to come.

THE "JESUS RACKET"

The unsavory reputation of Los Angeles and Hollywood became a favorite topic for sermons across America. Those who came west into this "den of iniquity," found evangelists and preachers like Aimee Semple McPherson and "Fighting Bob"

Shuler waiting to save their souls -- as long as the collection plates were always full.

Occasionally, as in the case of Reverend Shuler, their investigations into civic affairs sometimes exposed the graft and corruption that was an indelible part of the city. In other cases, as with Aimee Semple McPherson, their own scandals captured national headlines.

It was during this time that Los Angeles began to earn its reputation as a landing spot for cults and the fringe element. According to novelist Nathaniel West, who used the dark side of L.A. for atmosphere in several of his books and stories, some of the local churches included the "Church Invisible," where fortunes were told; the "Tabernacle of the Third Coming," where a woman in male clothing preached the Crusade Against Salt and the "Temple Moderne," where 'Brain-Breathing, the Secret of the Aztecs" was taught.

One of the most famous cults, the Church of I Am, was founded in 1932 by Guy and Edna Ballard. The "religion" was based on the worship of the questionable deity, St. Germaine, who supposedly gave off a violet ray of supernatural power. The Ballards accepted "love offerings" at their temple near downtown L.A., which was topped by a glowing neon sign that read "I AM." It was said that they gained tens of thousands of worshippers while selling products like "New Age Cold Cream." Their son, Donald, claimed to have the ability to become invisible as well as being in possession of a psychic power (derived from ascended spirits) so powerful that it enabled him to sink several Nazi submarines. The Ballards were eventually indicted for mail fraud although the charges were later overturned. By this time, however, the cult had collapsed and the pair vanished into obscurity.

All sorts of kooks, nuts, and crazies flocked to Los Angeles in the 1910s, '20s and '30s -- all offering spiritual enlightenment, redemption and even passage to the stars aboard UFO's.

(Left) A so-called "Eastern Seer" awaits his following at a Hollywood stage show, designed to convert those with money in their wallets.

Dead Men Do Tell Tales: Bloody Hollywood - Page 18

L.A. IN THE 1930S

Los Angeles continued to expand in the 1930s. Newcomers arrived on a daily basis. There were "Okies" looking for work, scavengers looking for a quick buck and of course, dream-seekers who came to California looking for their big break. Hollywood continued to serve as a beacon for would-be starlets and dreamers, but death and scandal sometimes shadowed even the brightest aspects of Tinseltown.

This was definitely the case with the death of film celebrity Thelma Todd, who was brutally murdered in 1935. Though plenty of suspects and theories have been floated over the years, her murder remains unsolved. Combining the elements of gangsters, gambling, and a beautiful corpse, it was purely a Hollywood-style killing.

Another sensational case was the bizarre "Rattlesnake Murderer," which may have inspired James Cain's noir novel *Double Indemnity*. In this real-life story, Robert James was a man who loved women, kinky sex, and taking out insurance policies. He had already left a couple of dead wives behind him when he settled in Southern California. He opened a downtown barbershop and developed a noisy (according to neighbors), violent habit of lovemaking with his newly insured wife. When cash started running low, he killed his wife by thrusting her foot into a box that contained two rattlesnakes.

As mentioned, 1938 was a turning point for Los Angeles crime. After private investigator Harry Raymond was killed while looking into reports of police corruption, the ensuing investigation revealed proof of bribery and vice throughout the police department and among city officials. L.A. Mayor Frank Shaw was implicated and he was eventually replaced by Fletcher Bowron. After that, raids increased on nightclubs and gambling spots and as many mobsters lost their political connections, they headed out of town to Las Vegas.

While the heat was undeniably turned up for awhile, it did not bring an end to crime and corruption in the city. As World War II loomed closer, reports of overseas fighting began to replace newspaper headlines about sensational crime. But the war began to expose other problems in L.A., namely the situation with gangsters and the black market. Soon, readers were introduced to the king of the Los Angeles underworld, Mickey Cohen.

He was the most recognizable of the city's gangsters and he always dressed and acted the part, hanging out in all the right places and making enemies of all the right people. Connected to almost every type of vice in the city, he was constantly in the newspapers and was trailed by both the LAPD and the sheriff's department, who busted him for small infractions that inevitably

Dead Men Do Tell Tales: Bloody Hollywood - Page 19

revealed larger crimes. Rival mobsters made several attempts on Cohen's life, but it would be the FBI who would get him in the end. They eventually put him in prison on charges of tax evasion. Apparently, Cohen didn't learn much from the public trials of Al Capone on the very same charges.

AFTER THE WAR

Los Angeles and Hollywood changed after World War II. By this time, the "star system" and the stranglehold the studios held on their stars' lives began to collapse. The big studios began to see increased competition and they began to lose much of their earlier influence.

In L.A., the end of the war saw the collapse of the black market and a decrease in crime. The rise of Las Vegas after the war emptied many of the nightspots of their big-name talent. Some of the larger venues closed down and smaller, "hip joints" became popular. The smaller clubs prospered and were joined by a few larger places like Ciro's, Mocambo, and the Crescendo on Sunset Boulevard. One district that matched the popularity of Sunset Boulevard was on Central Avenue, the heart of L.A.'s African-American community. Called "Darktown," the place was a hotbed of juke joints and jazz clubs. Whites and celebrities who went there looking for authentic jazz were never disappointed.

In unincorporated parts of Los Angeles County, strip clubs, burlesque theaters, and gambling parlors also added to the tawdry nature of the region. In the late 1940s, the Monterey Club, the Normandy, the Horseshoe, and several other lesser spots, provided a small, Vegas-style area where illicit activity was allowed to operate in obscurity. In addition, beachfront communities like Long Beach, Venice, and Santa Monica hosted "games of chance" (including bingo and keno) that were just another form of illegal gambling. These small-time gambling parlors flourished after the war, but faded by the 1950s.

Other nearby locations also offered assorted criminal activity. Palm Springs catered to both Hollywood stars and L.A. gangsters. The Dunes, a private gambling club run by former Detroit mobsters, was one of the swankiest places in town. Up in the mountains, film star Noah Berry ran a guest resort that offered illegal booze in an isolated location that kept out the authorities. In nearby counties, those who went looking could find cockfights, dog racing, nudist colonies, and just about any other sort of

(Above) The legendary Follies, Main Street's immensely popular burlesque club.

(Right) The club's full orchestra and an entire runway filled with dames. (Wesselman Collection / The William's Partnership)

vice imaginable. Small beach communities up and down the coast were favorite places to rendezvous for those trying to stay away from cops and photographers.

Even though L.A. lost a lot of its crime after the war, the sex trade continued to operate uninhibited. In the late 1940s, Brenda Allen, one of the city's most notorious madams, faced a series of raids on her bordello. The case turned into a full-blown scandal when it was learned that a member of the vice squad was in Allen's pocket and that a lot of money had changed hands to keep the house of ill repute open. Scandal ran rampant when it was learned that scores of movie stars and film studio executives were listed in Allen's "black book." The case turned seamy and complicated and in the end, Allen was jailed, the police chief resigned and a number of vice cops were demoted. As for the celebrities and movie executives who were caught using hookers – no one cared.

Several sordid and unsolved murders made headlines in the late 1940s. In June of 1947, a rifle bullet to the head ended the life of Benjamin "Bugsy" Siegel, Hollywood's most notorious gangster celebrity. He had been killed while visiting girlfriend Virginia Hill's Beverly Hills home. There was much speculation as to who had "whacked" Siegel but it was considered to be a mob hit. Apparently, Bugsy had been skimming money from the construction of the Flamingo Hotel, the gambling mecca that would put Las Vegas on the map. Like most mob hits, Bugsy's murder has never been solved.

Even more mysterious, and much more gruesome, was the January 1947 murder of Elizabeth Short. Her dismembered and bloodless body was discovered in a vacant lot in L.A. and would go on to become one of the most famous murders in the city's history. Dubbed the "Black Dahlia" by the local press, Short was the epitome of the small town girl who came to Hollywood to seek stardom. Her final months were traced back through the darker side of Hollywood and her mysterious and haunting murder remains unsolved.

Also that same year was the murder of former aviatrix Jeanne French, whose battered nude body was found in a vacant lot in the Mar Vista section of L.A. The case was quickly coined the "Red Lipstick" murder when her torso was inscribed with an obscene message and signed with the words "B.D. - Tex Andy." Police guessed that the words might have been a mysterious reference to the Black Dahlia murder that had taken place about a month before. The search for the killer ended with no solutions and remains unsolved.

So-called "Red-Light Bandit" Caryl Chessman went on a crime spree that included robbery, kidnapping, and rape, preying on lovers' lane couples who told police that they had been approached by an attacker who used a red spotlight as a ruse to get them to open their windows. After weeks of mayhem, Chessman was captured in east Hollywood. Although he claimed that his confession was beaten out of him, he was sentenced to death after 17 convictions. He managed to stall for over a decade, acting as his own attorney, but he was eventually executed in the gas chamber in 1960.

Although never a high-profile drug, marijuana got a boost in popularity when actor Robert Mitchum and a young starlet were busted for reefer possession in a Laurel Canyon bungalow. Mitchum's photograph was splashed across the scandal sheets when his trial went public, but it only enhanced his bad-boy image when he served two months in the L.A. County Jail.

Post-war Los Angeles was rocked by the scandal that involved "Sweater Girl" Lana Turner and Mickey Cohen muscle Johnny Stompanato. Their torrid affair was trumpeted by the newspapers and got even more press when Lana's daughter, Cheryl Crane, stabbed Stompanato to death when he got rough with her mother.

By the 1950s, the noir reputation which L.A. had earned, thanks to books and films, was starting to come to an end and by the 1960s it was gone altogether. Los Angeles had grown into an urban sprawl of concrete and freeways, devouring the small communities and suburbs that were once scattered among the hills and citrus groves. The real gangsters had fled to Las Vegas, where murder and mayhem was easier to commit.

But, in spite of this change, the darker element still managed to rear its ugly head, as witnessed by the brutal Manson family murders, the Night Stalker killings, the Hillside Strangler, and others. Los Angeles remains a city that is filled with magic – and stained by the sins of the past.

HOLLYWOOD CRIME BEAT: THE MOB IN HOLLYWOOD

Most crime writers tend to discount the effect that organized crime had on the movie industry, downplaying the amount of mob activity in the Los Angeles area during the first few decades of the 20th century. Few chronicles of Hollywood life make much mention of the influence that gangsters had on the daily operations of the movie studios and how mobsters rubbed shoulders with celebrities by night and terrorized studio executives during the day. While actors and actresses were facing the "studio system" and the iron wills of their bosses, gangsters were intimidating the movie moguls into lucrative compliance. It was a situation that never really came to light until years after the mob's influence had diminished in the movie industry.

Organized crime's infiltration of the film business began when movies were still silent and existed through Hollywood's "Golden Age" (1920s-1950s), when most of the industry's power was held by a handful of major studios and their tight-fisted bosses. Thanks to this, the mob had well-defined targets to threaten and shake down and of course, they regularly did so.

By the 1920s, Hollywood was no longer just a second thought for the dominant East Coast movie business. The major studios were now all located in L.A. and were thriving during the years of Prohibition, when organized crime was growing in leaps and bounds all across America. The swanky movie colony was a rewarding marketplace for bootleg liquor and mob syndicates were making a fortune peddling narcotics to the film crowd.

With the repeal of Prohibition in the early 1930s, organized crime in New York and Chicago began looking for new ways to bleed cash from the movie industry. As they worked to control the movie business, they sought out contacts in the industry and one of the most famous was George Raft.

Born in 1895, the future movie star grew up in Manhattan's infamous Hell's Kitchen, where one of his childhood pals was Owney Madden, who grew up to be one of New York's most vicious bootleggers and killers. Madden's rackets made him a feared and respected member of the New York underworld and his old friend, George, rubbed shoulders with gangsters for years. When Madden decided to distance himself from a brewing gang war in New York, he traveled to California in 1930 and brought George along. Raft had made an earlier trip to L.A. under mob orders to chaperone nightclub hostess Texas Guinan, who was about to make a Hollywood film. This time, Raft was ordered to stay in Hollywood. Madden wanted to protect this friend from underworld rivals in Manhattan and he also believed that his good-looking pal had screen star potential.

George Raft

In films like "Quick Millions" and "Scarface," Raft quickly established his movie persona as a slick, well-dressed gangster. It was a part that he knew well. In addition, movie studio bosses appreciated a star with real-life mob affiliations playing a gangster. That way, organized crime would be tolerant of his celluloid representations and the studios would not be held responsible.

Although Raft had been married to Grace Mulrooney since 1923, the marriage fell apart. Being a staunch Catholic, Raft refused to divorce her. However, he had no qualms about carrying on torrid affairs with Hollywood starlets. With his almost-single status and his agility on the dance floor (he had a brief career as a dancer on Broadway), the handsome and mannered actor was in constant demand on the Hollywood social scene. Film people were always intrigued by his connections to the underworld and they loved the idea of brushing up against real danger. Raft's array of escorts over the years included Carole Lombard, Lucille Ball, Betty Grable, Norma Shearer and others. However, his greatest love was socialite and fledging actress Virginia Pine, with whom he unofficially shared a house in the late 1930s.

Raft circulated on the Hollywood scene with, among other underworld characters, Pasquale "Pat" DiCicco, who was affiliated with New York kingpin Charles "Lucky" Luciano. DiCicco was sent to L.A. posing as a manager and talent agent, but was, in reality, a front man of the rackets. From 1932 to 1934, he was married to movie actress Thelma Todd, who died mysteriously in 1935. Her death was reportedly ordered by Luciano when she turned down his offer to turn her beachside restaurant into a gambling club. Later, DiCicco turned to film producing, which would some would stay is barely a step above gangster.

HOLLYWOOD'S FAVORITE GANGSTER

Another of George Raft's close pals was Benjamin "Bugsy" Siegel.

Ben Siegel grew up on New York's Lower East Side and by the age of 14, he was already running his own criminal gang. He formed an early alliance

Benjamin "Bugsy" Siegel

with a youth named Meyer Lansky and by 1920 they had formed a gang that specialized in bootleg liquor, gambling and auto theft. On occasion, Siegel and Lansky hijacked liquor shipments from other operations, before realizing that there was more money to be made by hiring out their gang as protection for the other outfits. Soon they were connected to rising Italian mobsters like Charles Luciano, Frank Costello, Joe Adonis, Albert Anastasia and others. After Luciano and Lansky created a national crime syndicate, they often assigned Spiegel to carry out murders that were used to gain control of various operations. He relished the blood and was so enthused by it that he was dubbed "Bugsy," although he was never called that to his face.

In the 1930s, Siegel was sent to California to run the syndicate's West Coast operations, including the lucrative racing wire service for bookmakers. It was here that he found his niche.

The handsome gangster loved the Hollywood nightlife and rubbing shoulders with movie stars who undoubtedly enjoyed "slumming it" with a real-life gangster. Siegel was suave and entertaining and became friends with Hollywood celebrities like Jean Harlow, Clark Gable, Gary Cooper, Cary Grant, and especially George Raft.

When Siegel arrived in L.A., Southern California was being run by Jack Dragna, whom local papers called "the Al Capone of Los Angeles." However, Dragna's operation (which was later laughingly referred to as the "Mickey Mouse Mafia") was never well organized and was easily taken over by Siegel and his associates.

Soon after Siegel's arrival in Hollywood, he and Raft began to be seen everywhere together, from the Santa Anita Racetrack during the day to the Tinseltown party circuit at night. The two good-looking men attracted beautiful starlets and Siegel easily found girls who were thrilled to be dating a real-life mobster.

One of Siegel's most frequent girlfriends was actress Wendy Barrie, who hoped to someday marry the volatile and elusive gangster. Another of his steady dates was Marie "The Body" McDonald, a voluptuous movie personality who made several forgettable films in the 1940s. However, Siegel was smitten with Virginia Hill, a crime syndicate bagwoman. This hard dame's career including dancing in a carnival and being a bed partner to various underworld characters, including Frank Costello, Joe Adonis, and Frank Nitti. Siegel probably met Virginia for the first time in New York but their relationship heated up when she came to Hollywood in 1939, hoping to make it in pictures – or at least that's what she told Bugsy. She had actually been dispatched to California by the New York Syndicate, with orders to keep an eye on the erratic Siegel. Virginia attended all of the best Hollywood parties, was a fixture on the nightclub scene and was usually seen in the company of Siegel and his buddy, George Raft.

During World War II, Siegel began to have dreams that would take him away from Hollywood and into the Nevada desert, where he planned to turn a sleepy watering hole called Las Vegas into a legal gambling paradise. With Siegel already in California, it was not hard for him to convince Syndicate pal Meyer Lansky of the potential in Las Vegas. Gambling had always been a huge moneymaker for the mob and in Nevada, legalized gambling had a much lower overhead than anywhere else. There were no politicians or police officers who had to be paid off and legal gambling would be the perfect arrangement for laundering money.

The land that would later be the site of Siegel's iconic Flamingo casino was owned, in 1944, by Billy Wilkerson, owner of the *Hollywood Reporter* and several nightclubs on the Sunset Strip. Wilkerson had hired George Vernon Russell to design a hotel that was more in the European style than the so-called "sawdust joints" that were located on Fremont Street. Russell planned a hotel with luxurious rooms, a spa, showroom, golf course, nightclub and upscale restaurant. Due to high wartime materials costs, though, Wilkerson began to run into financial problems almost at once, running almost $400,000 short. He began looking for new financing.

In late 1945, Siegel convinced Meyer Lansky to invest in Las Vegas. He first purchased the El Cortez on Fremont Street for $600,000 and later sold it at a hefty profit. At the same time, Siegel learned that Wilkerson had run out of money for his grand hotel and casino. Using the profits from the sale of the El Cortez, Siegel influenced Wilkerson into accepting new partners. With Lansky's blessing, Siegel talked the Syndicate into investing $2 million in the new property. Wilkerson was allowed to keep a nominal interest in the casino and, on the surface, would retain operational control. Everyone knew, however, that it was actually Bugsy Siegel who was running the show.

Siegel took over the final phases of construction and convinced more of his mob associates to invest in the project. The problem was that Siegel had no experience in construction or design and the cost quickly spiraled out of control. Things were made worse by price gouging from construction firms and suppliers, as well as companies who delivered by day, stole their materials at night, then re-sold them to Siegel again the next day. Rumors of such things ran rampant, as well as claims that Siegel was actually in on the scam, which allowed him to skim part of the construction money into his own accounts. The project ran into delay after delay, falling far behind schedule.

Siegel finally opened the Pink Flamingo Hotel & Casino on December 26, 1946 at a total cost of $6 million – triple the budget that he had promised the Syndicate. He named the resort after Virginia Hill, who loved to gamble and whose nickname was "Flamingo," which Siegel had dubbed her due to her long, skinny legs. Virginia allegedly helped Siegel skim money from the construction project and made frequent trips to deposit money for the mobster in Swiss banks. Hill may have been Siegel's favorite mistress, but she was not his only one. At one brief time after the casino opened, Siegel had four of his favorite girlfriends lodged in separate hotel suites. They were Virginia Hill, Countess Dorothy di Frasso and actresses Marie McDonald and Wendy Barrie, who frequently announced her engagement to Bugsy and never gave up hoping. Whenever she saw Wendy in the hotel, Virginia Hill would go wild and once she punched the actress so hard in the face that she nearly dislocated her jaw.

Unfortunately for Siegel, women trouble soon became the least of his concerns. The Syndicate began getting restless when, a year after the official groundbreaking, the resort had produced no revenue and had become a drain on the resources of the investors. Then, charges were made at a mob meeting in Cuba that either Siegel or Hill was skimming the resort's building budget, an accusation that seemed to be substantiated when Hill turned out to have a $2.5 million bank account in Switzerland, where the skimmed money was believed to be going.

Charles Luciano and the other mob leaders in Havana asked Meyer Lansky what to do. Distressed because of his longtime ties to Siegel, who he loved like a brother, Lansky nevertheless agreed that if someone was stealing, he had to go. However, he was willing to give Siegel a chance to come clean and make good on the investments. He persuaded the others to wait for the Flamingo's casino

The original Flamingo Hotel, opened by Ben Siegel

opening and if it was a success, then Siegel would have a second chance. Luciano agreed to the plan and so the others followed along with him.

The splashy opening -- with a roster of stars present that included, George Raft, George Jessel, Rose Marie, Jimmy Durante, Clark Gable, Lana Turner, Cesar Romero, Joan Crawford, and others — was a disaster. Even these big names did not seem to be able to lure the customers and gamblers to the Nevada desert. Lansky managed to persuade the other mob chiefs to give Siegel one more reprieve and allow the Flamingo a little more time. In January 1947, the resort was closed until the hotel could be finished and Bugsy knew that he was in big trouble.

However, the Flamingo re-opened in March and, despite the hotel not being complete, things began to change. Crowds flocked to the new resort and by May, the place was reporting a $250,000 profit. Lansky could finally show the others that Siegel had been right about Las Vegas all along, but it still wasn't enough to save Bugsy's life.

On June 20, Siegel was sitting in the living room of Virginia Hill's Beverly Hills home. She was away in Europe at the time. He was reading a newspaper when two steel-jacketed slugs tore through the front window. One of them shattered the bridge of his nose and exited through his left eye, while the other entered his right cheek and blew out the back of his neck. Authorities later found his right eye on the dining room floor, more than 15 feet from his body. Siegel was dead before he hit the floor.

Siegel likely knew that he was a marked man by the time he died and so did everyone else. Only five people --- all members of Siegel's family – attended his funeral. His friend Meyer Lansky was nowhere to be found and Virginia Hill was conveniently out of the country. His movie star pal, George Raft, was sick at home with asthma. All of Hollywood stayed away and their "golden boy" went to the grave at the age of 41.

Even the eventual success of the Flamingo was not enough to save Siegel's life. He was murdered in Virginia Hill's Beverly Hills mansion -- and is believed to haunt the place today.

But have we really seen the last of Bugsy Siegel? Virginia Hill's former home, which is a private residence on Linden Drive in Beverly Hills, is reportedly still haunted by the panicked presence of Ben Siegel as he scrambles for cover, attempting to hide from the bullets that killed him. His stark fear, as he spotted his killer and knew that the game was up, has left an indelible impression on the house. According to reports, witnesses have been startled for years by the apparition of a man running and ducking across the living room, only to disappear as suddenly as he came. A psychic who was brought in to investigate the house claimed that the image was the residual presence of Bugsy Siegel, imprinted on the place in his last desperate moments before death.

As the years have passed, Bugsy's ghostly energy here may have faded somewhat, but it has been suggested that his actual spirit may not rest in peace either.

After Siegel was assassinated, the mob continued to support the Flamingo Hotel and eventually saw it grow and prosper. They poured millions of dollars into Las Vegas and it became the gambling mecca that Siegel envisioned in the early 1940s. Siegel had pioneered the luxury casino in Vegas and the popular performers that began playing at various resorts in town did much to make the city – and gambling – appear respectable. Meyer Lansky took over the running of the Flamingo and within a year, had made a profit of $4 million. He also had shares in the Sands Hotel, along with singer Frank Sinatra, who with the "Rat Pack," put Vegas on the map.

Siegel left an enduring legacy here in the desert and it is said that his spirit still resides at the Flamingo Hotel today. His phantom has been seen here on a number of occasions, wearing a smoking jacket and slacks as he wanders about what he still feels is his hotel. He appears to guests and employees alike and only when he vanishes do they realize that what they have seen is no longer a living person. His wide smile may put them at ease but the eeriness of his disappearance terrifies many, including one custodian who, after a run-in with Bugsy, immediately quit her job.

The 1940s and 1950s were the heyday of Las

Vegas as a Mafia-run enterprise. The casinos were incredibly lucrative but as time went on, it became more and more difficult to conceal illegal activities, and in the 1970s and 1980s, the mob presence in Vegas began to wane. At that point, many of the casinos were sold off to legitimate companies. In 1972, the Hilton Hotel chain acquired the Flamingo. Las Vegas is a place of perpetual progress and as the city grew, so did the Flamingo. In 1993, the last remnant of the original hotel, which many claim was Bugsy's personal suite, was demolished to make way for a new rose garden. In 1999, the hotel split from the Hilton chain and was taken over by Caesars Entertainment, which still operates the Flamingo today. Even after all of these changes, Siegel simply refuses to leave, spending his time loitering in the hallways and startling young women with his chilling good looks.

Bugsy is often encountered in the rose garden, near a plaque bearing his name but most unsettling are his frequent appearances in the hotel's presidential suite. Although it was built many years after his death, there are those who say that this suite bears a striking resemblance to Bugsy's own beloved rooms. Guests in this suite had reported a number of strange encounters with his spirit from eerie, moving cold spots to items that vanish or move about from place to place. Bugsy's apparition has also been spotted in the bathroom and near the pool table.

Those who have seen him all state that he always appears the same. He is never distressed or upset, but always content and happy to be around. Perhaps Bugsy is simply having the last laugh from the other side. As he looks around, he can say that he told them so: Las Vegas turned out exactly the way the always knew that it would.

Siegel's pal, George Raft, was distraught over his friend's death, but he was smart enough to keep his mouth shut about any details or suspicions that he had concerning the murder. In the years that followed, at the request of the mob, Raft became involved as a front man and greeter in casinos in Cuba and Las Vegas and, later, at the Colony Club in London. At each casino, he talked up the high rollers, danced with their women, and signed autographs for those who were still impressed by the fading star.

George Raft died in 1980, still remembered as the big-screen gangster that he almost was in real life.

THE HOLLYWOOD EXTORTION CASE

During the Great Depression, one of the only thriving industries in America was the movie business. This was enough to attract the attention of organized crime, specifically, the Chicago Outfit. When Al Capone was convicted of income-tax evasion and sent off to prison, the Outfit expanded in a number of directions. Prohibition was over and the mob began looking toward gambling, prostitution, and extortion as major rackets. One extortion scheme stretched all the way to Hollywood.

In the early 1930s, two minor labor racketeers, Willie Bioff and George E. Browne, began extorting money from Chicago theater owners. Under the guise of donating money to area soup kitchens to feed the city's Depression victims, the two men hit up one theater chain for $20,000. They bragged about this score in front of the wrong people and soon ended up as "employees" of the Outfit. Soon, the entertainment industry in the city was under the Outfit's control, which they achieved by taking over trade unions like the Motion Picture Operators' Union. They also set up a protection racket on movie theater chains, often demanding up to 50 percent of the take. Bioff and Browne ran the local racket and another Chicago gangster, Johnny Roselli, broke into Hollywood as a result of the 1933 strike by the International Alliance of Stage Employees (IATSE). The studios went to Roselli to break the strike, which he did by hiring thugs to intimidate the strikers.

Meanwhile, in Chicago, the Outfit had summoned George Browne to a meeting. Browne was a candidate for the next president of the IATSE and the Outfit guaranteed his election in return for control of the union. Browne, already in trouble with the Outfit for running a protection racket in their territory, agreed. He was quickly elected president and, in fact, no other candidate was even nominated to run.

Browne and Bioff were sent to New York, where they were introduced to Luciano and Costello, who had reluctantly agreed to an alliance with Chicago, for a cut of the racket, of course. Soon afterward, Browne was able to demonstrate his power by calling for a strike against the RKO and Loews theater chains. He then went to the chairman of RKO and offered to call it off for the sum of $87,000. It was quickly handed over. The president of Loews, Nick Schenk, then paid Browne and Bioff $250,000 for a no-strike deal that would last for a period of seven years. In exchange, Browne agreed to reduce worker wage increase demands by two-thirds.

Bioff was put in charge of the Hollywood branch of the IATSE in 1936. He and Browne then levied a two percent surcharge on paychecks as "strike insurance." This levy generated more than $6 million, a hefty percentage of which went directly to the Outfit.

With the major unions under control, the mob then moved against the film studios. By controlling the unions, they could cripple any studio that refused to pay protection against strikes. They could close down all of the theaters in the country with a single telephone call. They went to Nick Schenk first and demanded $2 million, finally settling for $1 million before they started making the rounds to other studios.

The Outfit was soon in control of Hollywood, but it was not meant to last. Unfortunately for them, Bioff was the weak link in the organization. He made a down payment on piece of property using a $100,000 check from Twentieth Century Fox, run by Nick Schenk's brother, Joe. The check proved to be Bioff's undoing. A breakaway organization from the IATSE, the International Alliance Progressives, was determined to remove the underworld control of the union. They began to convince workers to defy Bioff. At the same time, Bioff tried to take over the Screen Actor's Guild, which started to investigate Bioff's activities. The California state legislature became interested in him, as well. The $100,000 check and Bioff's past history as a Chicago pimp came to light. The case against Bioff was put on hold but Joe Schenk was prosecuted, and his explosive testimony began to unravel the mob's Hollywood operation. Even worse was to come. The press discovered from Chicago police files that in 1922, Bioff had been convicted of beating a prostitute. He was still wanted on that charge and a warrant was issued for his arrest. He ended up serving five months in jail.

In New York, Joe Schenk was indicted for fraud. In returned for a suspended sentence, he agreed to tell everything that he knew about Bioff and Browne. There were indicted in 1941 for tax evasion and racketeering. Desperate to keep their names out of the case, the Outfit sent lawyer Sidney Korshak to Hollywood. He told Bioff to confess to being Schenk's bagman, but to admit nothing else. To Korshak's dismay, Bioff entered a "not guilty" plea, which meant that he could be questioned – the last thing the Outfit wanted. Bioff was sentenced to 10 years in prison and Browne to eight.

During the trial, Bioff let slip a reference to Chicago. This was the lead that the government had been waiting for. Terrified of being murdered for this error, Bioff decided to cooperate with the authorities. On March 18, 1943, a New York City grand jury handed down indictments on Frank Nitti, Paul "the Waiter" Ricca, Louis "Little New York" Campagna, Phil D'Andrea, and other members of the Chicago Outfit. Nitti, rumored to be despondent at the possibility of returning to prison, committed suicide the day after the indictments were announced.

Once he was freed from prison, George Browne vanished without a trace. In 1955, Bioff, who was living under an alias in Las Vegas, was discovered by his old mob enemies and was blown up with a car bomb. Johnny Roselli, who had gotten Browne and Bioff hooked up in Hollywood in the first place, spent a few years in prison as a result of Browne and Bioff squealing to the authorities. He had married actress June Lang in 1939 and after his release from prison, began producing films. Later, he moved to Las Vegas and handled underworld investments in the city.

HOLLYWOOD'S UNDERWORLD

It was not just a rumor that Frank Sinatra enthusiastically counted a number of underworld figures as his close friends. In the 1930s, Sinatra was a struggling newcomer and Willie Moretti, a northern New Jersey racketeer who had an associate related to Sinatra's first wife, helped the singer get important bookings. The two men became friends and stayed in touch until Moretti's murder in 1951.

During the 1940s, Joseph Fischetti, a Chicago gangster, also became friends with Sinatra and the two men met occasionally in New York and Miami. In early 1947, Sinatra accompanied Fischetti and his brother to Cuba, where they got together with deported gangster Lucky Luciano. It was Fischetti who helped Sinatra gain bookings in Chicago and Miami in the early 1950s, when Sinatra's career was experiencing a temporary downturn.

In the late 1950s, Sinatra became friends with Sam Giancana, who was then the head of Chicago's Outfit. In 1962, when Giancana was operating the Villa Venice Supper Club (part of an illegal gaming operation), Sinatra arranged for himself, Dean Martin, Sammy Davis, Jr., and Eddie Fisher to perform at the venue, which was located in Wheeling, Ill. Meanwhile, Sinatra was given a partnership in the Cal-Neva Lodge on Lake Tahoe, a casino club where he had previously appeared. During a 1963 investigation, the Nevada State Gaming Commission revoked Sinatra's gaming license, based on his unsavory associations with gangsters.

Jean Harlow was another Hollywood figure who mingled with the underworld. In the early 1930s, Jean was starting her career at MGM Studios. She went on a promotional tour and while in New York, her stepfather, Marino Bello, introduced her to a longtime pal named Abner "Longy" Zwillman, who, along with Willie Moretti, ran the rackets in northern New Jersey. Bello, not exactly an outstanding parental figure, pushed for an association between Jean and Zwillman, hoping to be rewarded for his efforts. Harlow and the love-struck gangster became intimate and, for a time, he

One of the most mob-connected Hollywood personalities was singer and actor Frank Sinatra. He made no secret of his friendships and connections with underworld characters, especially Sam Giancana.

sent monthly checks to help support her relatives and to maintain a lavish Hollywood lifestyle. The relationship ended when Harlow wed producer Paul Bern in 1932.

MICKEY COHEN: AMERICA'S MOST SHOT-AT GANGSTER

Los Angeles gangster Mickey Cohen had the dubious distinction of escaping more attempts on his life than perhaps any other mobster in American crime history. Cohen became sort of a cult hero in L.A. during the 1940s and 1950s. He rose through the ranks as Ben Siegel's bodyguard and made himself scarce on the day that Bugsy was hit in Virginia Hill's Beverly Hill mansion. Cohen had abandoned his beloved mentor under orders from Meyer Lansky but it soon turned out that while he might bow to pressure from the National Crime Syndicate, he wouldn't back down to any other gangsters in Los Angeles. Cohen began building his

(Above) Jack Dragna, the so-called "Al Capone of Los Angeles" was no threat to eastern gangsters who came to take over L.A. Ben Siegel dismissed Dragna's operation as the "Mickey Mouse Mafia".

(Right) Mickey Cohen, who became L.A.'s most famous gangster, thanks to his love for attention and affinity for the press.

own empire within days of Siegel's removal with gambling, prostitution and extortion rackets and never paid a dime to any of his L.A. superiors. The Syndicate had stated that Cohen would inherit Siegel's numbers operation, but that was all. In spite of this, Cohen set up his own operations, drawing the ire of Jack Dragna, the aforementioned "Al Capone of Los Angeles."

Dragna was an old school Mafioso. He had moved into L.A. at the start of Prohibition and had pushed out the loose outfits of organized crime that already existed there. He began a bloodbath that resulted in numerous deaths, including 30 men who were gunned down along Darwin Avenue in 1925 alone. This stretch of roadway became known as "Shotgun Alley."

Dragna was an immigrant from Sicily and the president of the Italian Protection League. He was the unofficial mayor of the Italian neighborhood in L.A., dispensing wisdom, settling family disputes, and enforcing his own set of rules. He muscled in on the bootleg liquor market and gained the leadership of the first Italian crime family in Los Angeles. He and his gunmen managed to gain national prominence for the L.A. mob. Dragna's power was compromised with the arrival of Ben Siegel in the 1930s. Siegel dismissed Dragna's operation as the "Mickey Mouse Mafia" and soon took over control of the region. Siegel arrived with the blessings of Meyer Lansky and Dragna understood that if he wanted to stay in business at all, he was going to have to turn over his bookmaking operations, casino interests, racetrack betting, and gambling ships to Siegel. In this way, Bugsy, who had made his presence known by assassinating Les Bruneman, a key member of the original L.A. operation, had solidified his control of the rackets by 1937. Dragna remained the head of the L.A. family, continued to settle disputes, arrange hits, and oversee drug trafficking throughout the region.

Mickey Cohen never paid any respect to Dragna, even when he had to occasionally work with him under Siegel's orders. The animosity between the two men was mutual. Dragna refused to let Jews into his outfit, just as his Mafia predecessors had done in the past, and Cohen hated him for it. He also imitated the disdain that Siegel had for Dragna, further exacerbating the situation. Once Siegel was taken out, Dragna expected to inherit the operation that had been left behind, but Cohen had other plans. Soon, the two mob operations were at war.

Fortunately for Cohen, Dragna's attempts on his life were as ineffectual as his operation had been when Bugsy Siegel had taken it over. Cohen managed to cheat death at least five times. Twice, Dragna's hit men tried dynamiting Cohen's home, once with a homemade torpedo and once with straight dynamite. The torpedo never exploded and the dynamite went off, but it had been placed directly under a concrete floor, causing the explosion to travel downward and sideways instead of up. The blast shattered windows throughout the neighborhood, but left Cohen, his wife, his dog, and the family maid unharmed. What upset Mickey the most was that more than 40 $300 suits had been shredded to rags in the explosion. Neighbors jokingly dubbed him "Public Nuisance No. 1" after the bomb blast.

On another occasion, a Dragna gunman let loose with both barrels of a shotgun one night as Cohen was driving home. His Cadillac was peppered with holes but, incredibly, not a single slug touched him.

Another attack occurred in front of Sherry's Restaurant on Sunset Boulevard. Cohen was there, drinking and enjoying the entertainment, until he left the club at about 4 a.m. As he and his men walked out, a storm of gunfire erupted from across the street. Just as the gunmen opened up on them, Cohen had noticed a scratch on his shiny new Cadillac and bent down to examine it more closely. A bullet flew right past his head and killed Neddy Herbert, one of Cohen's closest friends.

After that, Cohen's attorney, Sam Rummel, made sure that he notified the LAPD of Cohen's whereabouts, which gave him a veil of police protection. Dragna refused to back down and ordered hits on Cohen's lieutenants. Two men named Frank Niccoli and Save Ogul disappeared a short time later and their bodies were never found. Then, the next week, two assassins ambushed attorney Sam Rummel outside of his home and he was shot dead.

Cohen finally got the message and made overtures of reconciliation. However, he never

Mickey Cohen loved his press -- one of his most famous photos shows him surrounded by his favorite headlines.

offered to relinquish any of his territories or give any money to Dragna. This infuriated the Italian even more. A year after Rummel's death, Dragna sent Sam Bruno, a veteran hit man, to wait outside of Cohen's house with a high-powered rifle. Cohen arrived home just after 4 a.m. and Bruno opened fire on him. He blazed away at Cohen and left after three minutes, believing the mobster was finally dead. Somehow though, once again, Cohen emerged without a scratch.

Dragna never did get Cohen. Even after Cohen was convicted on a tax rap and sentenced to serve five years in prison, a major corruption probe cost Dragna the police protection that he needed to take over his rival's operations.

Cohen became a nationally known mob figure and was probably the most-quoted gangster of his day. In 1950, he appeared before the Kefauver Committee's hearings on organized crime. He was asked to explain why a Hollywood banker had given him a $35,000 loan without any sort of collateral. Cohen quipped, "I guess he just likes me."

Cohen was twice convicted on tax violations, serving four years of a five-year sentence on one occasion and 10 years of a 15-year term on the other. When he was released from prison in 1972, he declared his intention to go straight. It wasn't really a matter of choice by that time. He was partially paralyzed as the result of a head injury that he received at the hands of another convict in Atlanta in 1963.

Mickey Cohen died – of natural causes – in 1976.

HOLLYWOOD CRIME BEAT: HOLLYWOOD HOOKERS

Prostitution in Los Angeles dates back to the city's very beginning but it did not became an organized vice until just after the turn of the 20th century. It was at that time, in 1906, that members of the Good Government League, and Deputy District Attorney Thomas Woolwine, attacked L.A. Mayor Arthur C. Harper for conspiring with the chief of police and a notorious gangster to control prostitution in the city. Woolwine's investigation revealed that Harper, who was well acquainted with brothels, had repeatedly sold phony stocks to madams as a method of hiding monthly payments, bribes and extortion fees. The news caused a sensation at the time, yet it failed to cause many problems within the police department. After all, it was no secret that the LAPD had helped to set up the city's first red-light district a few years earlier, designed to cater to visiting investors, politicians, and businessmen.

Hollywood's connections to prostitution in Southern California began only a few short years after the establishment of the movie colony. One of the rumors that dates back to that time was that there was a West Hollywood brothel that had prostitutes who were made up, or even given plastic surgery, to make them resemble famous movie actresses. James Ellroy's book, *L.A. Confidential* (and the movie that was based on it), added veracity to the story since Ellroy is famous for weaving factual information from the city's lurid past into his novels. The book contains a subplot about an exclusive call girl service that catered to men who wanted to bed girls who looked like Rita Hayworth, Ava Gardner, Veronica Lake and others. How much of this was truth, and how much was fiction?

In 1993, author Charles Higham wrote a biography about MGM boss Louis B. Mayer and in it, he described a whorehouse that could have come right out of Ellroy's novel. He claimed that Mayer financed the house in Hollywood and that it was well known in the industry. The madam, Billie Bennett, accommodated visiting exhibitors and executives with prostitutes who were exact doubles of the stars. There is no other record of Billie Bennett in the annals of L.A. crime, but it's certainly possible that such a place existed.

But high-priced call girls and fancy bordellos were always a part of Hollywood history. One of the first Hollywood madams was Pearl Morton, who was a notorious purveyor of girls in the movie colony. During the 1920s and 1930s, Lee Francis was the city's premier madam and she boasted an influential clientele of important businessmen and, of course, important people in the movie business. Francis had at least four bordellos under her management and she always kept a fresh supply of chilled imported champagne and Russian caviar at every house. That way, whenever the vice squad showed up for one of their scheduled "raids" – and there was no one in the house to arrest – she could make sure the diligent lawmen were served some refined refreshments.

Lee's brothels each had its own swimming pool, tennis court, full-service restaurant, fully-stocked bar, and, of course, dozens of girls to choose from. The brothels were not used only for sexual purposes, but also provided men with a place to conduct business meetings, play cards, or even go for an afternoon swim when they were supposed to be at the office and couldn't go home. Movie stars were common at the houses because Francis maintained a strict code of secrecy, which allowed them to come and go as they pleased with no worries about photographers or fans.

After Lee Francis was jailed for 30 days on a morals charge, Ann Forrester (known as the "Black Widow") stepped in and became Hollywood's top madam in the late 1930s. It was said that Forrester's operations grossed more than $5,000 every week. By 1940, though, Ann had been jailed for her illegal activities. This occurred despite Mayor Fletcher Bowron's request that she be given a light sentence because "her information was of great value in determining the identity of those police department members whose honesty was questionable."

The Black Widow's protégé, Brenda Allen, took over her operations in the 1940s. Allen became known as Hollywood's most famous madam. Using a series of elaborate houses located above the Sunset Strip, Brenda catered to the city's wealthiest clients, including many notable Hollywood personalities. Allen was reported to gross more than $9,000 a day, one-third of which was earmarked for bribes, physician and attorney fees, and bail bondsmen.

Brenda maintained secret client files in case she ever got into legal difficulties and had to call on one of her clients for help. As an added insurance policy, she had an ongoing affair with LAPD Sergeant Elmer Jackson of the vice squad. Allen's luck ended in 1948 after telephone tapes captured a revealing conversation between her and Jackson.

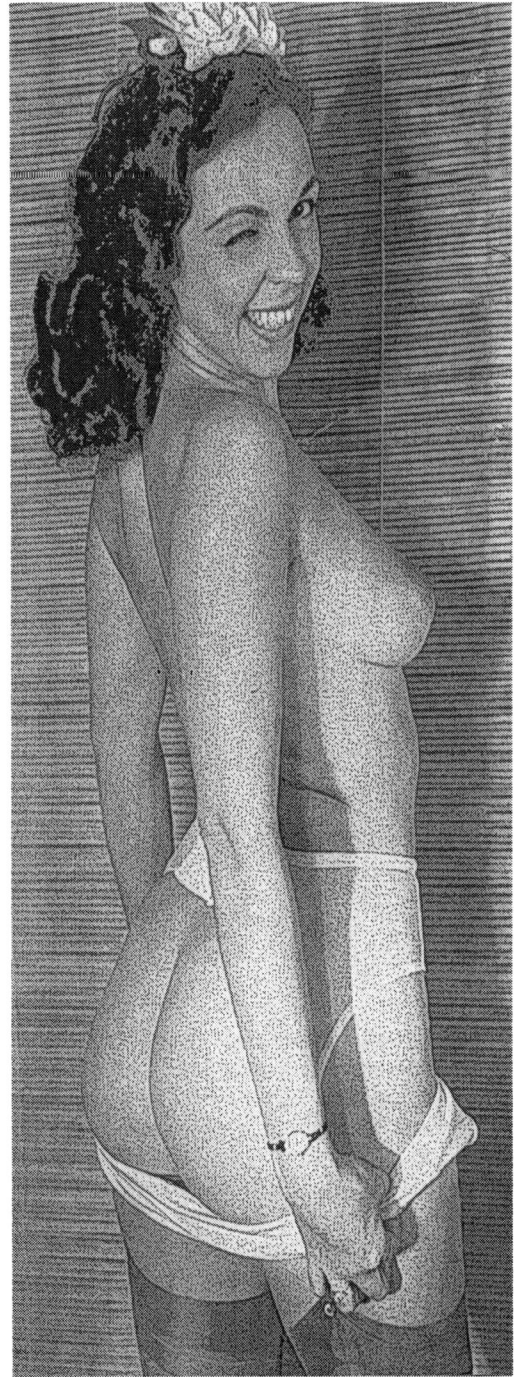

Famous Hollywood madam Brenda Allen
(Los Angeles Times)

Her arrest caused a scandal, not for the list of Hollywood clients that were in her black book, but because it became clear that her operation depended on the cooperation of several corrupt vice cops, including Jackson. When her bordellos were shut down, the stink from the whole mess resulted in the retirement of Police Chief Clemence B. Horrall.

But the fall of Brenda Allen was certainly not the end of brothels in Hollywood. In the 1950s, a protégé of Allen named Barrie Benson began operating from an lavish, 13-room, Moorish castle on Schuyler Road, north of the Sunset Strip. One of her protectors was mob gunman Sam Farkas, a bodyguard and friend of Mickey Cohen. Benson's tenure ended under the regime of hard-nosed Police Chief William H. Parker, the first honest cop that L.A. had seen in years.

Tinseltown brothels were far from a thing of the past and into the 1970s, 1980's and beyond, they operated under the organization of Elizabeth Adams (Madam Alex) and Heidi Fleiss, whose eventual arrest revealed that she really did earn the nickname of "Madam to the Stars." Among the celebrities in her black book (actually four red leather Gucci day-planners) were film executives like Robert Evans, actors like Charlie Sheen, and rock stars like Mick Jagger and Billy Idol. In January 1997, she was convicted and spent the next two years in prison.

HOLLYWOOD CRIME BEAT: HOLLYWOOD'S PREACHERS, CULTS, KOOKS & CRAZIES

Somewhere around 1510, a mystical Spanish author named Garci Rodriguez de Montalvo wrote a novel about the son of Amadis of Gaul and his wanderings and exploits. In the book, he described a mythical island that he called "California" and located it somewhere "west of the Indies." He described it as a "terrestrial paradise" that was populated by women, with no men among them.

The story (not surprisingly) motivated many Spanish explorers, including Hernán Cortés, to go in search of this magical place. They were seeking "paradise" – just like millions of others who have followed in their wake over the centuries.

California has seen more than its share of paradise-seekers and has witnessed a tidal wave of cults and communes – more than any other place in the world, in fact – ranging from the Theosophical Society to Marxist co-ops to some of the strangest collections of people in history. In 1917, the *Los Angeles Times* referred to some of the early communes as "spookeries" or "fairy farms" and did anything to undermine their success. While such disparaging comments may not have been true about all of the religious movements and communes in Los Angeles at the time – they would soon start to live up to their reputations.

"FIGHTING BOB" SHULER

The 1930s brought the Great Depression and a mass exodus of "Okies" from the Dust Bowl region, hoping to make a new life in sunny California. No one knows how many people came west, hoping to find the glittering promise of the region, but the impact of these new arrivals, who were mostly poor, white, Protestants, was tremendous. A new wave of churches, cults and sects sprang up in response. Simple, welcoming and often "fire and brimstone" in theology, the new sects, along with the traditional churches of charismatic fervor, attracted huge followings. Unfortunately, bigotry was usually a part of the Sunday morning message and Hollywood was traditionally an easy target.

Bob Shuler (or "Fighting Bob," as he became known) was a preacher from Corner's Rock, Va., who arrived in Hollywood in 1920 after a stint as a rural preacher in Texas. He took over the congregation of a failing Methodist church in downtown L.A. and soon began offering spellbinding, electric sermons that blamed everyone but his poor congregation for their problems. His message began to spread, appealing to the new arrivals, and soon his church attendance had increased to almost 3,000 people. He also began a radio ministry that reached tens of thousands more. Like many preachers at the time, he hated Catholics, Jews, Hollywood, movies, and the theory of evolution. He was also, not surprisingly, a supporter of the Ku Klux Klan, which believed that it was necessary for white Protestant men to preserve their heritage., often violently.

In 1926, a member of Shuler's congregation gave him his own radio station as a present, which started him on the road to becoming America's first broadcast evangelist. He began spreading his message to greater audiences, but it was not long before he went too far. He accused Los Angeles Mayor Charles Cryer of being on the take, the police chief of spying on him, city officials for allowing pornography in the movie houses, and the

The Reverend "Fighting Bob" Shuler, who landed in jail for the trouble that he caused in L.A. in the 1920s and 1930s (Library of Congress)

newspapers of conspiring to silence him.

In 1929, Shuler spent 15 days in jail for claiming on his radio station that theater owner Alexander Pantages and his wife, both of whom were about to go on trial (he for the rape of a showgirl named Eunice Pringle in a broom closet at his theater; she for drunk driving and manslaughter), would bribe their juries. Later that year, however, a Shuler congregation member and Klan supporter, John Porter, became mayor and for a time, Shuler could do and say just about anything that he wanted.

In 1932, Shuler ran for U.S. Senate on the Prohibition ticket. After losing an earlier political run, Shuler had placed a curse on the entire state and then took credit for several subsequent earthquakes. Apparently, his predictions of dire catastrophes if he lost again were not enough to sway the voters. He came in second to Woodrow Wilson's son-in-law, William McAdoo.

Shuler's popularity was beginning to fade and it was reported that William Randolph Hearst spent $1 million in an effort to destroy the preacher.

Soon, Shuler's radio station was taken away from him and the FCC called him a "public nuisance." A magazine that he edited, espousing his prejudiced views, folded in 1933. After thousands of new war industry jobs arrived in L.A. in the early 1940s, Shuler's ministry base, the poor and the unemployed, declined. Shuler died in 1965, a forgotten relic of a stranger time.

"SISTER AIMEE"

While "Fighting Bob" Shuler was stirring up the "Okies" with his fiery sermons and cries for white supremacy, another evangelist was presenting a kinder, gentler message. She did so with flamboyant presentations that were right out of a Hollywood musical and, in fact, the regular appearance of movie stars at her services was one of her claims to fame. The evangelist's name was Aimee Semple McPherson and the Pentecostal church that she founded, the International Church of the Foursquare Gospel, still exists today. Like Bob Shuler, Aimee was a Methodist, but Shuler hated her ministry with a passion, so that was the only common ground between them.

"Sister Aimee," as her thousands of followers called her, was born Aimee Kennedy and was raised on a farm in Ontario, Canada. Growing up, she was introduced to an inclusive, positive theology, which as practiced by her grandfather, a Salvation Army captain. After a crisis of faith, she was converted to Pentecostalism by evangelist Robert

Sister Aimee Semple McPherson at the height of her popularity (Library of Congress)

Semple, whom she joined in preaching revivals and married in 1908. Two years later, while they were awaiting their papers to travel into China as missionaries, Semple died in Hong Kong. Aimee, now with an infant daughter, returned to the U.S. and began working for the Salvation Army in New York. She married a second time, in 1912, to a grocery salesman named Harold McPherson, and gave birth to a son. Aimee tried to settle down to the quiet life of a housewife, but she was unable to do it. She felt that she was destined for bigger things and was in her heart, an evangelist.

She divorced McPherson in 1918 and she, her children, and her mother, Minnie, with nothing more than $100 and a tambourine, drove to Los Angeles. It was a trip that Aimee later referred to a as spiritual quest that ended in a revelation. She believed that the "City of Angels" was the doorway to heaven and, for a time, it certainly seemed to be.

She began spreading her message in every way possible, even throwing tracts from an airplane as it flew over neighborhoods populated by recent arrivals to the area. She was soon packing standing-room-only crowds into the Philharmonic Auditorium, the largest venue in L.A. By 1923, she had her own Angelus Temple, which seated 5,300 people and cost more than $1.5 million to build. At her services, she entertained the curious and the faithful alike with bizarre stage sketches that featured a USC football player making a touchdown for Jesus and a LAPD motorcycle cop riding in to arrest sin. Everyone loved the show and soon her popularity would rival that accorded to some movie stars. To thousands, she was "God's Little Child."

Besides entertaining and

preaching, Aimee was also an avid organizer. She added some 250 affiliated churches, a rescue mission, a publications division, an orchestra, and a radio station, creating a massive organization that is only rivaled by today's mega-churches. She also composed 180 hymns and several musical pageants, all of which were very upbeat and offered redemption. In keeping with her Salvation Army background, she also designed uniforms for herself and her female bodyguards.

Not surprisingly, Aimee had a talent for raising money, which supported the church, her mansion near MGM Studios in Culver City, her expensive clothes, and fine automobile. At collection time, she would often tell her supporters from the stage, "Sister has a headache tonight. Only quiet money, please."

As the money rolled in, stories of miraculous cures began to spread. A "miracle room" in the Angelus Temple was filled with discarded crutches, wheelchairs, and even the leg braces of a 10-year-old polio victim. He was so confident when he came to visit Sister Aimee that he brought another pair of shoes with him to wear home. The stories claimed that he walked out of the Temple.

Then, in 1926, Aimee's glory days came to an end. A scandal captured the imagination of readers across America and titillated them for weeks afterward.

On the afternoon of May 18, 1926, Aimee was spotted swimming off Ocean Park Beach in Santa Monica – and then vanished without a trace. She was presumed to have drowned, but after a massive search effort (during which a church member and a professional diver drowned), no body was recovered. Then, on June 23, three days after a all-day memorial service attended by thousands of weeping, hysterical mourners, she turned up in the Mexican town of Agua Prieta, claiming that she had been kidnapped and held in a shack in the Sonoran desert. On her return to Los Angeles, a carpet of roses was spread when she disembarked from the train and more than 100,000 of her followers lined the streets and cheered as she drove by.

But all was not what it seemed to be. It was soon discovered that, despite Aimee's angry denials, she had actually spent the month at a cottage in Carmel, shacked up with Kenneth Ormiston, a married engineer on the staff of her radio station. For nearly six months, L.A. District Attorney Asa Keyes gathered evidence (which included a Carmel grocery store shopping list in her handwriting), planning to charge her with conspiracy to produce false testimony. "Fighting Bob" Shuler took the opportunity to enter the fray, denouncing Aimee, her Temple, and her ministry. Since he and Aimee alternated their broadcasts on the same radio wavelength, he had no trouble reaching her followers. Somehow, he tracked down Harold McPherson and had him on the air for four straight broadcasts, airing all of Aimee's dirty laundry. For her part, Aimee claimed the entire scandal was the "work of the Devil."

Aimee's fame saved her from prosecution. Inexplicably, the District Attorney decided that the case that he had built against her was too weak to bring against a person of her tremendous popularity. On the evening that D.A. Keyes made the announcement, the faithful mobbed Aimee and the newspapers spread the news in glaring headlines. But the damage was already done, for most of America, Aimee had become a dirty joke.

Aimee Semple McPherson carried on for 20 more years, preaching and defending herself against the old scandal. It never seemed to go away and in 1930, she suffered a nervous breakdown. She was prescribed seconal to deal with her anxieties and on September 27, 1944, she died in San Francisco from an accidental overdose. Some of her closest friends attributed the accident to a combination of a broken heart and exhaustion from her endless struggle to restore her name, popularity, and influence. At her funeral, held at the Angelus Temple, more than 40,000 mourners passed by her casket and bid their farewell to "God's Little Angel."

Strangely, a weird rumor followed Aimee to the grave. When she was buried at Forest Lawn Cemetery in a huge tomb with an iron gate, guarded by two kneeling marble angels, it was said that a direct telephone line to the Angelus Temple was buried with her. That way, when she returned (as her followers believed she would), she would be able to alert someone to come to the cemetery and let her out of the tomb.

As author David Wallace said, if the story isn't true, it should be.

SECTS, CULTS & "FAMILIES"

In spite of their pro-Ku Klux Klan support, claims of miraculous healings, and suspicious disappearances, the ministries of Bob Shuler and Aimee Semple McPherson were among the mainstream sects and churches that sprang up in L.A. in the early 1900s. They were far from alone. Starting at about the same time that the film industry discovered Hollywood and made its home among the palm trees, scores of "spookeries" and "fairy farms" began showing up, too.

What follows only scratches the surface, but they are among the weirdest of the cults to exist in the L.A. area, including some of the creepiest – and most deadly – of the strange sects.

LOVE CULTS

Decades before the hippie movement made "free love" an international phenomenon, love cults flourished all over Southern California. The first word of them spread in the middle 1920s and began making news a few years later, like one "nest of love" on Santee Street where women were forced to "speak in tongues," perform "devil dances," and engage in "soul mating" with "spiritual husbands."

In 1939, the High Priestess Regina Kuhl captured the attention of the authorities when she was caught indoctrinating male students at L.A. City College into her "Temple of Thelma." The temple was set up in the basement of one of the dorms and there, she would don robes, chant some suggestive passages from an Aleister Crowley book and "embrace the power of the lifted lance" – or more simply put, engage in sex with multiple partners.

In 1946, Henry "King Daddy" Newson was arrested for running his own sex camp called Ten Oaks. According to newspaper reports, he molested sixteen underage girls over the course of two years. In his defense, he claimed that he was teaching them the "beauty" of sexual intercourse. Several of the girls claimed that he controlled their minds through hypnosis.

THE BLACKBURN CULT

The religious group known as the Blackburn Cult, the Divine Order of the Royal Arms of the Great Eleven, or the Great Eleven Club, was started around 1925. The group's founder, May Otis Blackburn, claimed to receive revelations directly from God and believed that she had been charged by the archangel Gabriel to write books that revealed the mystery of heaven and earth, life and death. Apparently, Gabriel thought the goal of teaching the earth should be accomplished though strange rituals that involved animal sacrifice, copious amounts of sex between followers of the cult, and by stealing thousands of dollars from naïve believers.

The cult began to fall apart in 1929 after police officers made a gruesome discovery at the home of the Rhoads family on Vermont Avenue. Under the floor of one of the bedrooms was a specially built,

The horrible state of Willa Rhoads' body after it was found beneath her parent's house in 1929. (LAPD Crime Photo)

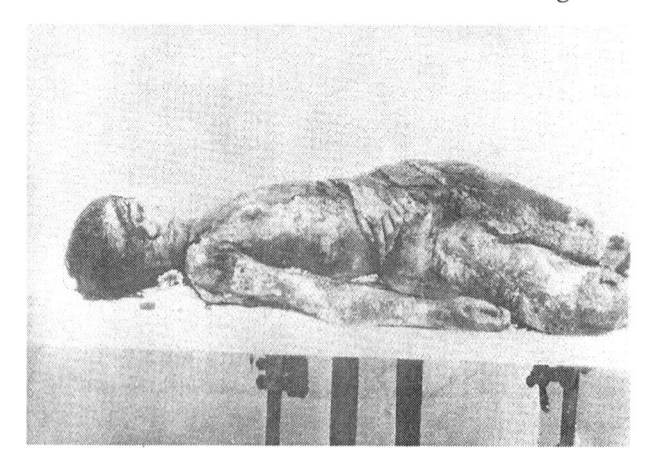

Dead Men Do Tell Tales: Bloody Hollywood - Page 38

refrigerated "sleeping chamber" that contained the corpse of their 16-year-old daughter, Willa. The girl's body was covered in spices and salt and was surrounded by seven dead dogs. The Rhoads later confessed that they had placed the girl in the tomb at the direction of May Otis Blackburn, who convinced them that she would be resurrected when the archangel Gabriel came to earth.

Group leaders were indicted later that year for theft and were also investigated in the disappearance of several members. The indictments made newspaper headlines when the strange rituals of the cult were revealed to the public. May Otis Blackburn was charged with 12 counts of grand theft and the cult collapsed after she was sent to prison for stealing $40,000 from group member Clifford Dabney.

MANKIND UNITED

Eerily foreshadowing the modern cult of Scientology (on which a religion is based on the writings of a science-fiction novelist) was the Mankind United sect, which was created by another science-fiction writer, Arthur Bell. During the height of the Great Depression, Bell penned a book called *Mankind United*, a turgid, repetitive text that was filled with bold type and large blocks of capitalized text. It told the story of a malevolent conspiracy that ran the world (the "Hidden Rulers" and "Money Changers") who were not only responsible for war, poverty and injustice – they were also aliens living on earth.

Opposing them was another group of aliens, the "Sponsors," who had arrived on earth in 1875. According to Bell, the benevolent Sponsors were shortly going to announce their presence and would put in place a world-wide utopia, based on universal employment and a financial system based on credits. The workday would be four hours a day, four days a week. Needless to say, all of this sounded pretty good to tired, worn-out people who were struggling to put food on their tables.

In order for the Sponsors to put their plan into place, they had to receive massive support from the people. The plan would be promoted by the "Pacific Coast Division of North America, International Registration Bureau" – which was, of course, run by Arthur Bell. He announced that when 200 million people accepted the Mankind United plan, the Sponsors would overthrow their rival alien groups and, within 30 days, the new utopia would begin.

Of course, there were no Sponsors, no evil aliens, and no "International Bureau." The whole thing had been concocted by Bell and it never numbered more than a few thousand followers, if that. The only true beneficiary of the group was Bell, who had several luxurious apartments and mansions, including a swanky place on the Sunset Strip that had an indoor pool, a pipe organ, and a cocktail bar. Bell was spotted in all of the most swinging nightclubs and spent cash freely. He received about $50,000 a year in tax-free income, which adjusted for inflation would be the equivalent of nearly $1 million today. His followers, on the other hand, worked in various cult businesses full-time, including hotels and shops. They were paid less than $40 a month, worked up to 16 hours a day, seven days a week – which was quite a bit more than the utopian work week they had been promised in Bell's book.

The cult gained the attention of the authorities during World War II. Bell incorporated as a church (the Church of the Golden Rule) to obtain tax exemption and began making even more bizarre claims, such as the idea that he could be beamed to several different places at once, that the Sponsors had advanced technology that allowed the dead to be resurrected on other planets, and more. None of these turned out to be quite enough to gain popular support and in 1951, Bell's group folded and the cult faded away completely. As some would later discover, though, he was simply a man ahead of his time. If he had started his church a few decades later, he might be able to count some of the biggest stars in Hollywood as his members!

HEAVEN'S GATE

Perhaps the strangest of the modern-day "alien" cults in Southern California was Heaven's Gate, a UFO religion that was based out of San Diego and led by Marshall Applewhite and Bonnie Nettles. At some point in the early 1970s,

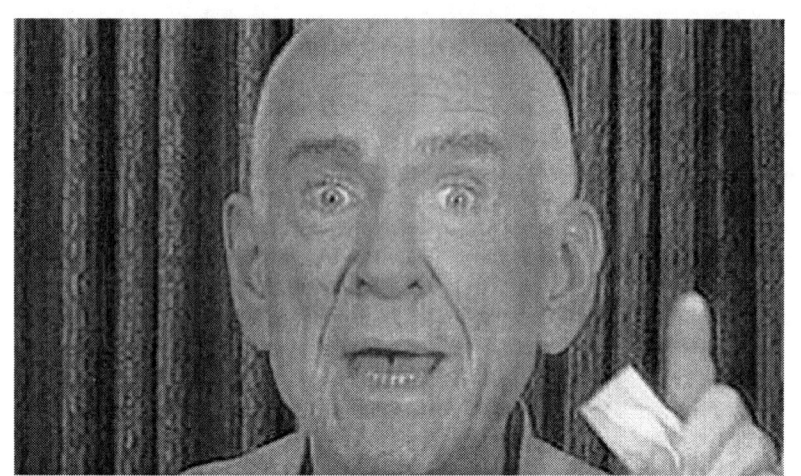

Marshall Applewhite, the dangerously insane leader of the Heaven's Gate cult, seen here in one of his bizarre video broadcasts

Applewhite became convinced that he was an alien who was transported to earth and reincarnated into the body of a man – named Marshal Applewhite. From that point on, he believed that it was his mission to teach everyone he came into contact with about the creed of transcendence. With the help of his partner, Bonnie Nettles, he gathered a number of followers and convinced them to give up everything that they owned (including their children) and to prepare themselves for the trip to the "Evolutionary Level Above Human." Applewhite's preparation included months of extreme psychological mind control experiments, starvation, and celibacy. Some cult members even went as far as to castrate themselves.

Although mostly unknown to the mainstream media, Heaven's Gate was known in UFO circles and had been the subject of criticism by respected UFO writer Jacques Vallee. In *Messengers of Deception*, he described an unusual public meeting organized by the group and expressed concerns about many UFO contactee groups' authoritarian political and religious outlooks, including the views of Heaven's Gate.

The group's end coincided with the appearance of Comet Hale-Bopp in 1997. Applewhite convinced 38 followers to commit suicide, which he claimed would allow their souls to board a spaceship that they believed was hiding behind the comet. The cult believed that the planet Earth was about to be "recycled," or wiped clean, and that the only chance they had to survive was to leave it immediately.

On March 26, 1997, 38 members of the cult, along with Marshall Applewhite, were found dead in a rented mansion in the upscale San Diego community of Rancho Santa Fe. As the Hale-Bopp comet approached the earth, the group members drank citrus juice to ritually cleanse their bodies of impurities. The suicides were then accomplished by ingesting phenobarbital, mixed with vodka, and by tying plastic bags around their heads to induce asphyxiation. The cult members were found lying neatly on their bunk beds, their faces and torsos covered by a square, purple cloth – and plastic bags secured over their heads. Each member carried a five dollar bill and three quarters in their pockets. All 39 were dressed in identical black shirts and sweat pants, brand new black-and-white Nike athletic shoes, and armband patches reading "Heaven's Gate Away Team."

FOUNTAIN OF THE WORLD

One of the most famous cults in Southern California was Krishna Venta's WKFL (for Wisdom, Knowledge, Faith and Love) and it began as a quiet monastery in Canoga Park in 1948.

The Fountain of the World, as the group became known, first got the attention of the press in the 1940s and 1950s for its members' habit of dressing in robes and going barefoot. Male members were required to grow beards and wear their hair long. The Fountain was marginally controversial because one of the requirements for membership was that one donate all his or her worldly assets to the group prior to joining. For most members, this was irrelevant, since few of them had much to begin with.

The group was responsible for a multitude of positives, including fighting wildfires, offering shelter to those in need, and feeding the homeless. The group gained national exposure in 1949 when the newswires picked up the story that Fountain members had been among the first on the scene to offer aid to the victims of Standard Airlines Flight 897R, which had crashed into the Simi Hills, killing 35 of 48 persons onboard. Krishna Venta also taught his followers to set up free food services for the poor, offer free room and board to the homeless, and help emergency relief groups in times of need.

But things at the commune were stranger than most people knew. In addition to promoting charitable works, Venta also claimed that smoking was healthy, that human beings were evolved from aliens, that he was 244,000 years old and would never die (he did), that he arrived on earth in 1932 on Mount Everest, and led a convoy of rockets here from the extinct planet Neophrates. He also claimed that he was none other than Jesus Christ himself. To prove it, he liked to show his detractors that he had been born without a belly button, proof that he was Jesus, an alien, or something.

Krishna Venta had been born Francis Herman Penovic in 1911. He was married in 1937 and divorced seven years later. He was arrested in 1941 after sending a threatening letter to President Roosevelt. Later, using the name Frank Jensen, he committed a series of crimes including burglary, larceny and kidnapping. He also spent a few months in a mental hospital. In 1948, he changed his name and founded his religion. He also got involved in the California legal system again when he was ordered to pay child support from 1945 to 1951. He claimed a religious exemption but the court ruled against him in 1955.

Venta died on December 10, 1958 in a suicide bombing instigated by two disgruntled former followers (Peter Kamenoff and Ralph Muller) who, although never offering any proof to support their claims, charged that Venta had both mishandled

Krisha Venta (a.k.a. Francis Penovic), founder of the Fountain of the World Cult

cult funds and been intimate with their wives. Krishna Venta is buried in Valhalla Memorial Park in Burbank. His grave is unmarked but near that of Oliver Hardy, of Laurel and Hardy fame. A monument to Venta still exists in the canyon in Canoga Park where the commune once stood.

A branch of the Fountain of the World cult was also established in Homer, Alaska, in the years prior to Venta's death. Cult members were referred to as the "barefooters" by locals. But Fountain membership at both sites declined rapidly following Venta's death, and the cult ceased to exist entirely by the middle 1970s.

THE PROCESS CHURCH OF THE FINAL JUDGMENT

The Process, or in full, The Process Church of the Final Judgment, began to flourish in the 1960s and 1970s. Its founders were an Englishman named Robert Moore (who later changed his name to Robert DeGrimston) and Mary Anne MacLean. It originally developed as a splinter cult group from Scientology, and Moore and MacLean were declared "suppressive persons" by L. Ron Hubbard in December 1965. In 1966 the members of the group moved to Xtul on Mexico's Yucatan Peninsula, where they developed their peculiar

(Left) Robert DeGrimston (a.k.a. Robert Moore) in the 1960s. (Right) DeGrimston presides over a marriage ceremony for members of the Process Church.

theology. They later returned and established a base of operations in the United States.

The Process Church combined community activism with the peculiar belief that Jehovah, Christ and Satan were not enemies, but all equal parts of Creation. The Process members were often viewed as satanic on the grounds that they worshipped both Christ and Satan. Their belief is that Satan will become reconciled with Christ, and together they will come at the end of the world to judge humanity: Christ to judge and Satan to execute judgment. Like many cults of the time, the church depended on the youthful enthusiasm of its members, instilling control by separating them from friends and family, and using general brainwashing techniques to keep them in line while "The Teacher" DeGrimiston and "The Oracle" MacLean waited for the end of the world.

The world didn't come to an end, but the 1960s did – with the Manson Family murders. Manson was originally associated with the Process by several writers most notably in *The Family: The Manson Group and Its Aftermath*, a book about Manson written by Ed Sanders. Vincent Bugliosi, the prosecutor at the Charles Manson Family trial, comments in his book *Helter Skelter* that there may be evidence Manson borrowed philosophically from the Process Church, and that representatives of the church visited him in jail after his arrest.

According to the representatives, the purpose of the visit was to interview Manson about whether he had ever had any contact with church members or ever received any literature about the church, but that was all. As a result of a lawsuit, Ed Sanders' publisher agreed to remove the chapter about the Process from the book in later printings.

By the early 1970s, the group was beginning to fall apart. DeGrimston began to show a predilection for the darker side of the cult's theology, wearing black robes, practicing animal sacrifices, and employing a swastika as his primary insignia. His increasing fascination with group sex and the importance of Satan in his writings alienated many members of the Process – and besides that, Satan made fundraising more than a little difficult.

DeGrimston was ousted from the church in 1974 and a new group rose from the ashes called the Foundation Faith of the Millennium. The Founders kept things going until the late 1970s, but by then, were little more than a newsletter. The David "Son of Sam" Berkowitz slayings of 1977 didn't help the splinter group, as both the Process and a supposed Satanic fringe group were implicated in the murders. This conspiracy theory was promoted by a book called *The Ultimate Evil* by Maury Terry, which was released at the height of the "Satanic Panic" movement in 1987. However, there is no hard evidence that The Process had anything to do with David Berkowitz or the Son of Sam murders, outside of Berkowitz's own confused and contradictory testimony. However, some believe that he might have been involved with a radical offshoot of the group (see next section) that went far beyond anything that Robert DeGrimston might have imagined.

After being removed from the Process, Robert DeGrimston attempted to restart the Process Church several times, but he could never replicate his original following. The Founders renounced DeGrimstons' doctrines and teachings but were never really able to succeed without him. The organization has since ceased to operate.

THE FOUR P MOVEMENT

In 1969, while gathering material for a book on the Charles Manson case, journalist Ed Sanders encountered reports of a sinister satanic cult alleged to practice human sacrifice in several parts of California. Calling itself the "Four Pi" or "Four P" Movement, the cult originally boasted 55 members. The leader of the group were said to be middle-aged and the rest were young men and women in their early 20s. The group's founder, who was dubbed the "Grand Chingon" or "Head Devil," was said to be a wealthy L.A. businessman and a former member of the Process Church (which might explain later confusion about the connections between the Process Church and various murders). The "Grand Chingon" compelled the younger members of the cult to act as his virtual slaves and ordered them to commit murders on command. The object of the cult? To promote the "total worship of evil."

Beginning in June 1968, the Four P Movement allegedly began holding secret gatherings that were based on a stellar timetable and included the ritual sacrifice of Doberman and German Shepherd dogs. Soon after, law enforcement officers began discovering the dogs' corpses, skinned and drained of blood. According to later accounts by cultists, members of the sect were drinking the blood of the dogs – and later of their human victims. If these accounts are to be believed, the cult members sacrificed their victims, consumed their blood, and then removed and ate the victims' hearts. The evidence of the murder was then burned in a portable crematorium that was mounted on the back of a truck. The victims were reported to be mainly hitchhikers, drifters, and runaways, with occasional volunteers from within the ranks of the cult.

In early 1969, the group fractured with one segment striving to de-emphasize satanic ritual and concentrate more on kinky sex, and the other clinging to the traditional blood and murder. According to author Maury Terry in the previously mentioned book, *The Ultimate Evil*, the group survived the schism and the traditional segment had expanded to 1,000 or more members across the country by 1979. Terry cited New York as one hotbed of activity, where 85 German Shepherds and Dobermans were found skinned between October 1976 and October 1977.

Along the way, the Four P Movement allegedly brushed shoulders with a number of notorious killers, including Stanley Dean Baker, a purported member of the cult. When Baker was arrested on a moving violation charge in 1970, police found a human finger in his pocket. Baker claimed that it belonged to a human sacrifice victim and then took police officers to a site where he claimed to have buried a number of people for his church.

Charles Manson and his family reportedly had contact with the Four P Movement, prior to making headlines in Los Angeles. Ed Sanders reports that some of Manson's followers referred to him -- in Sanders' presence -- as the "Grand Chingon," distinguished from the original article by his age and the fact that Manson was jailed while the real "Chingon" remains at large. Likewise, family killer Susan Atkins later described the sacrifice of dogs by Manson's group, and searchers digging for the remains of Manson victim Shorty Shea reportedly found large numbers of animal bones at the family's campsite, which was more than a little strange for a group reputedly comprised of vegetarians.

Convicted killer David Berkowitz, famous as the "Son of Sam" who terrorized New York in 1976 and '77 , also professed membership in the cult, revealing inside knowledge of a California homicide allegedly committed by the group. In 1979, Berkowitz smuggled a book on witchcraft out of his prison cell, with passages on Manson and the Four P movement underlined. One page bore a cryptic notation in the killer's handwriting: "Arlis Perry. Hunted, stalked, and slain. Followed to California."

Author Maury Terry researched the information and found that it led to an unsolved murder that was committed at Stanford University in October 1974. On October 11, a young woman named Arlis Perry was found in the campus chapel at Stanford, nude from the waist down, a candle protruding from her vagina. Her blouse had been ripped open, and another candle stood between her breasts. She had been beaten and choked and then an ice pick had been rammed into her skull behind her left ear. Berkowitz later claimed that Perry had been killed by Four P Movement members as a "favor" to cultists in her hometown Bismarck, N.D., whom she had apparently offended in some way.

Despite the testimony of several reputed Four P Movement members, authorities have yet to build a case against the movement – leading some to dismiss the "cult" as nothing more than scary stories created by sensationalistic writers and unhinged murderers, like David Berkowitz, looking for attention. Is the Four P Movement truth or fiction, or elements of both?

Hope that you never find out for sure.

THE MANSON FAMILY

Charles Miles Manson remains today one of the most sinister criminals in American history. His name is instantly recognizable and he is often held responsible for bringing an end to the era of love and peace in the 1960s. As the leader of the "Family," a quasi-commune and cult, he was found guilty of a series of murders that were carried out by cult members on his orders. He called the killings "Helter Skelter," a term that he took from the Beatles song of the same name and that he construed as the start to an apocalyptic race war that he planned for the murders to set into motion. This connection with rock music, and the fame of one of his victims, linked him to the culture of the 1960s, for which he became a dark symbol of murder, insanity, and the macabre.

Born Charles Maddox to unmarried, 16-year-old Kathleen Maddox in Cincinnati in 1934, Manson never knew his real father. For a time, after her son's birth, Kathleen Maddox was married to a laborer named William Manson and the boy was given his last name. Manson's mother, allegedly a heavy drinker, once sold him for a pitcher of beer to a childless waitress, from whom his uncle retrieved him a few days later. When his mother was sentenced to five years in prison for robbing a Charleston, W.Va., service

Charles Manson

station in 1939, Manson was placed in the home of an aunt and uncle. His mother was paroled in 1942 and he was returned to her, faced with a life of run-down hotel rooms and flophouses. Kathleen could only handle the boy for about five years and in 1947, she tried to have him placed in a foster home. With no spaces available, the court sent him to the Gibault School for Boys in Terre Haute, Ind. After 10 months there, he fled and returned to his mother, who wanted nothing to do with him.

Soon after, Manson had his first brush with crime and he spent the next few years in and out of reformatories and boy's homes, often escaping or being released to simply break the law and wind up incarcerated again. He was tested by psychiatrists and social workers who found Manson to have a high I.Q., but labeled him "aggressively antisocial." After being transferred from one institution after another, each more secure than the next, because of continued disciplinary problems, he finally became a model prisoner and was paroled from his last reformatory, in Ohio, in 1954.

After temporarily honoring a parole condition that he live with his aunt and uncle in West Virginia, Manson sought out his mother again. He moved in with her for a time and then in January 1955, he married Rosalie Jean Willis, 17, a waitress with whom, but his own account, he found genuine, but short-lived happiness. He supported them by working at a series of low-paying jobs that included parking lot attendant and bus boy – and by stealing cars. In October of that same year, Manson stole a car and moved his pregnant wife to Los Angeles. The unlucky Manson was caught again, and charged with interstate theft. After a psychiatric evaluation, he received five years' probation. His subsequent failure to appear at a Los Angeles hearing on an identical charge filed in Florida resulted in his March 1956 arrest. His probation was revoked and he was sentenced to three years' imprisonment at Terminal Island in San Pedro, Calif.

Charles Manson, Jr., Manson's son by Rosalie, was born while Manson was behind bars. During his first year at Terminal Island, Manson received visits from his wife and mother, who were now living together in Los Angeles. In March 1957, the visits ceased and Manson's mother informed him that Rosalie was now living with another man. Manson was caught trying to escape less than two weeks before a scheduled parole hearing and needless to say, his parole was denied.

Manson finally got out again in September 1958 to find himself divorced and once again, in trouble with the law. By November, he was pimping a 16-year-lold girl and was receiving additional money from another girl with wealthy parents. In September 1959, he entered a guilty plea to attempting to cash a forged U.S. Treasury check but received a 10-year suspended sentence after a young woman with a history of prostitution arrests tearfully told the court that she and Manson were in love and would get married if he were freed. The young woman, whose name was Leona, actually did marry Manson before the year was out and Manson took her and another woman from California to New Mexico to work as prostitutes. There, Manson was held and questioned for violation of the Mann Act, which prohibited taking women across state lines for the purposes of prostitution. Though he was released, Manson was convinced he was still being investigated and he disappeared. Now in violation of his probation, a bench warrant was issued and he was arrested in Laredo, Tex., when one of his girls was picked up for prostitution. Manson was returned to Los Angeles and for violating his probation for the check-cashing charge, he was ordered to serve his 10-year sentence.

Manson spent a year trying to appeal the revocation of his probation and ended up being transferred from the Los Angeles County Jail to the federal penitentiary at McNeil Island. In 1963, Leona was granted a divorce and during the proceedings, alleged that she and Manson had a son, Charles Luther.

In June 1966, Manson was sent to Terminal Island in preparation for an early release. By the time he got out, on March 21, 1967, he had spent more than half of his 32 years incarcerated in one institution or another. He later claimed that he requested to be allowed to stay at Terminal Island, as the prison had become his home.

After his release, Manson was allowed to move

to San Francisco, where, with the help of a prison friend, he obtained an apartment in Berkeley. It was here, during the famed "Summer of Love" that Manson began to develop the influence that he had over women, which had started to emerge a few years before. He would also begin the early formation of the Family. Manson was mostly panhandling in San Francisco, until he met Mary Brunner, an assistant librarian at UC Berkeley. They moved in together and in a short time, Manson overcame her resistance to bringing other women into bed with them. Before long, they were sharing Brunner's apartment with 18 other young women. Manson quickly established himself as a guru of sorts in San Francisco's Haight-Asbury. Using his age (he was normally several years older than his followers) and some of the Scientology techniques that he studied in prison, he soon had his first group of cult followers, most of them young and female.

Before the summer was over, Manson and a group of his followers piled into an old school bus that had been renovated in hippie style. The seats had been removed and colored rugs and pillows were placed on the floor. Hitting the road, they roamed through California, Mexico and the Southwest. When they returned to L.A., they continued to move from place to place, living in Topanga Canyon, Malibu, and Venice.

The events that would culminate in the murders were set in motion in the spring of 1968. According to accounts, Dennis Wilson of The Beach Boys picked up two hitchhiking Manson girls one night and brought them to his Pacific Palisades home. Returning home in the early hours of the morning following a late night recording session, Wilson was approached in his driveway by Manson, who had walked out of the house. Nervous, Wilson asked the bearded, shaggy-haired Manson if he intended to hurt him. Assuring the musician that this was not his intention, Manson dropped down and started kissing Wilson's feet. Inside the house, Wilson discovered 12 strangers, mostly girls.

At first, Wilson was likely flattered by the attention and happy to have as houseguests a group of pretty young women (whose belief in free love was enthusiastic), but those feelings undoubtedly changed when, over the next few months, their number doubled. Family members who crashed at Wilson's Sunset Boulevard home cost him at least $100,000. This included a large medical bill for the treatment of gonorrhea and $21,000 for the accidental destruction of a borrowed uninsured car.

Wilson paid for studio time to record songs written and performed by Manson, and he introduced him to friends in the entertainment business. They included songwriter Gregg Jakobson, record producer Terry Melcher, and Rudi Altobelli, who owned a house that he rented to director Roman Polanski and his wife, actress Sharon Tate.

By August 1968, Wilson had had enough. He got his manager to clear Manson and his Family out of his house and soon after, Manson established a home for the group at Spahn's Ranch, not far from Topanga Canyon. The ranch had once been a location for shooting Western films but by 1968, the old sets were deteriorating and largely

Beach Boy Dennis Wilson, who unknowingly befriended Manson and his followers in 1968.

The Spahn Movie Ranch, where Manson and his Family came to live after being kicked out of Dennis Wilson's house in August 1968.

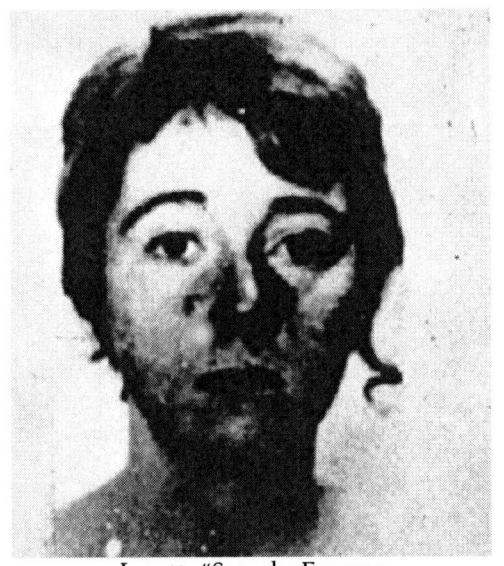

Lynette "Squeaky Fromme

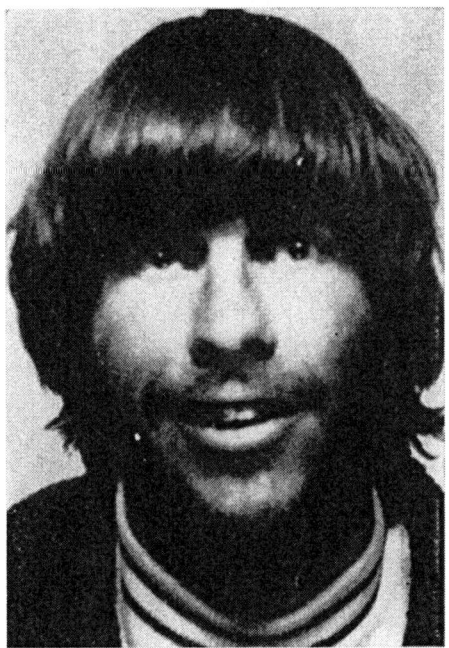

Charles "Tex" Watson

abandoned. It was primarily doing business offering horseback rides and Manson convinced the elderly, nearly blind owner, George Spahn, to allow the Family to live at the ranch in return for doing work around the place. It was not hard to convince Spahn. Manson had Lynette Fromme, one of his girls, act as Spahn's eyes and she, along with other girls, serviced the old man sexually. Because of the tiny squeal that Lynette would emit when Spahn pinched her thigh, she acquired the nickname "Squeaky."

The Family was joined at Spahn's Ranch by Charles Watson, a Texan who had met Manson while he was still living at Dennis Wilson's house. Watson had quit college and moved to California where he met Wilson when he gave the hitchhiking Beach Boy a lift after his car had broken down. Watson's southern drawl earned him the nickname "Tex" from George Spahn.

In early November 1968, Manson established the Family at alternative headquarters in Death Valley, where they occupied two old ranches, Myers and Barker. The former was owned by the grandmother of a new girl in the family and the latter was owned by an elderly local woman who believed that Manson was a musician in need of a place to work. She agreed to let them stay, as long as they fixed things up.

In December, Manson and Watson visited a friend who lived in Topanga Canyon and he played the Beatles' White Album for them, which had

(Left) Terry Melcher and his mother, actress Doris Day (Right) The house at 10050 Cielo Drive, which Manson believed was still the residence of Melcher. He was not aware that it had been rented to Sharon Tate and her husband, Roman Polanski.

recently been released. Manson was obsessed with the band and some of the songs on the album played right into some of the crazed rhetoric that he had been spouting for some time: that America was going to become embroiled in a race war between blacks and whites. He told the Family that the social turmoil he had been predicting was also foreseen by the Beatles. The White Album songs, he said, spoke to him in code. In fact, he said, the album had been intended for the Family, a carefully selected group that was being instructed to preserve the world from the coming disastrous events.

In early 1969, the Family positioned itself to monitor the tension that was allegedly coming to L.A. by moving into a bright yellow house in Canoga Park, not far from the Spahn Ranch. Manson believed that the house would allow the group to remain "submerged beneath the awareness of the outside world" and he called it the "Yellow Submarine," another Beatles reference. At this house, the Family prepared for the apocalypse, which Manson had termed "Helter Skelter" after the Beatles' song.

Within a couple of months, Manson's vision was complete. The Family would create an album with songs that would trigger the predicted chaos. Ghastly murders of white people by black attackers would be met with retaliation and a split between the racist and non-racist whites would bring about the white race's annihilation. The blacks would then turn to the Family to lead them after the storm had cleared. The Family would survive by riding out the conflict in a mysterious cave called the Devil's Hole in Wingate Pass, hidden away in Death Valley. Legend had it that an underground city was below the earth there, and the family planned to stay there until the war had ended.

As the yellow house, family members worked on vehicles and studied maps, preparing for their desert escape. They also worked on songs for their "world-changing album." When they were told Terry Melcher was coming to the house to hear the material, the girls cleaned up and prepared a huge meal, but Melcher never arrived.

On March 23, 1969, Manson entered, uninvited, property at 10050 Cielo Drive, which he had known as the residence of Terry Melcher. The house was actually owned by Rudy Altobelli and Melcher had once been a tenant but no longer lived there. The new tenants were Sharon Tate and Roman Polanski.

Manson was met by Shahrokh Hatami, a photographer and Tate friend, who was there to photograph Sharon before she left for Rome the next day. He saw Manson through a window as he approached the main house and went out onto the porch to ask him what he wanted. When Manson told Hatami he was looking for someone whose name Hatami did not recognize, Hatami informed him the place was the Polanski residence. Hatami advised him to try the guesthouse, beyond the main house. Manson made no effort to move and a moment later, Sharon Tate appeared in the doorway to ask who was calling. Hatami said that it was a man looking for someone and they watched as Manson, without a world, went back to the guesthouse, returned a minute or two later, then left.

That evening, Manson returned to the property and again went back to the guesthouse. He walked into the enclosed porch and spoke with Rudi Altobelli, who was just getting out of the shower. Although Manson didn't ask for Melcher, Altobelli got the impression that the man was looking for him. Through the screen door, he told Manson that Melcher had moved to Malibu but he lied and said that he did not know his new address. In response to a question from Manson, Altobelli said he himself was in the entertainment business, although, having met Manson the previous year, at Dennis Wilson's home, he was sure Manson already knew that. At the time, he had lukewarmly complimented Manson on some of his musical recordings.

Manson decided to try and get Altobelli to listen to the Family's new recordings but Altobelli told him that he was going out of the country the next day. When Manson said he'd like to speak with him upon his return; Altobelli lied and said he would be gone for more than a year. Altobelli also told him not to come back to the property because he didn't want his tenants disturbed.

Manson left. As Altobelli flew with Tate to Rome the next day, Sharon asked him whether "that creepy-looking guy" had gone back to the guesthouse the day before.

At some point, Manson had managed to track down Melcher, who visited the Spahn Ranch to hear a performance by Manson and the girls. Melcher came back again a short time later and brought a friend who owned a mobile recording unit. However, he himself never recorded the group.

By June, Manson was telling the Family that

Bobby Beausoleil

Susan Atkins (a.k.a. Sadie Mae Glutz)

they might have to show the blacks how to start "Helter Skelter" When Manson gave Tex Watson the job of getting money together to help the Family with the conflict to come, Watson ripped off a black drug dealer named Bernard "Lotsapoppa" Crowe. The dealer responded with a threat to wipe out everyone at the Spahn Ranch, but Manson got to Crowe first and shot him at his Hollywood apartment on July 1. Manson assumed that Crowe was dead and this mistake was seemingly confirmed by a news report that announced the discovery of the body of a Black Panther member in Los Angeles. Although Crowe

Sharon Tate in 1969

Jay Sebrig

Abigail Folger & Wojciech Frykowski

was not a member of the group, Manson concluded that he had been and expected retaliation from the radical group. He turned the Spahn Ranch into an armed camp, putting out night guards and passing weapons around. The Family was convinced that "Helter Skelter" was coming.

Still looking for money, Manson sent sometime Family member Bobby Beausoleil, along with Mary Brunner and Susan Atkins, to the house of acquaintance Gary Hinman on July 25, 1969. Manson had heard rumors that Hinman had recently inherited some money and Manson wanted it. The three Family members held an uncooperative Hinman hostage for two days, during which Manson showed up with a sword to slash his ear. After that, Beausoleil stabbed Hinman to death, acting on Manson's instructions. Before leaving the Topanga Canyon residence, Beausoleil, or one of the girls, used Hinman's blood to write "Political piggy" on the wall and to draw a panther paw, a Black Panther symbol.

Beausoleil was arrested on August 6, 1969, driving Hinman's car. The murder weapon was found in the tire well. Two days later, Manson told the Family members at Spahn Ranch, "Now is the time for Helter Skelter."

On the night of August 8, Manson directed Watson to take Susan Atkins, Linda Kasabian and Patricia Krenwinkel to "that house where Melcher used to live" and "destroy everyone... as gruesome as you can." The girls were instructed to do whatever Watson told them to do. When the four of them arrived at the entrance to the Cielo Drive property, Watson (who had been to the house before on Manson's orders) climbed a telephone pole and cut the telephone lines. It was now just after midnight on August 9, 1969.

They parked at the bottom of the hill and walked up to the gate. Assuming that it might be alarmed or electrified, they climbed up an embankment and dropped onto the grounds. Just then, headlights came their way from within the property and Watson ordered the girls to hide in the bushes. He stopped the approaching car and shot the driver, 18-year-old Steven Parent, to death. After cutting the screen of an open window of the main house, Watson told Kasabian to keep watch down by the gate. He removed the screen, entered through the window, and let Atkins and Krenwinkel in through the front door.

The first person to encounter the intruders was a friend of Polanski, Wojciech Frykowski, who was sleeping on the living room couch. When he awoke, Watson kicked him in the head. The man asked who he was and what he was doing there and Watson replied, "I'm the devil, and I'm here to do the devil's business."

Susan Atkins found the house's three other occupants and, with Krenwinkel's help, brought them into the living room. The three were Sharon Tate, who was eight and a half months pregnant; her friend, Jay Sebring, a noted hairstylist; and Frykowksi's girlfriend, Abigail Folger, heiress to the Folgers Coffee fortune. Roman Polanski was in London at the time, working on a film project.

Watson tied Tate and Sebring together by their necks with a rope that he'd brought along and he threw it up over a ceiling beam. When Sebring protested about his rough treatment of the pregnant Tate, Watson shot him. After Folger was taken back into the bedroom to get her purse, which held about $70, Watson stabbed the wounded Sebring seven times with a large knife.

Frykowski, whose hands had been tied together with a towel, managed to get free and he began struggling with Atkins, who stabbed him in the legs with a knife she was carrying. Frykowski got loose and began running for the front door, but Watson caught up with him on the porch and struck him several times with the gun (breaking the gun's right grip in the process), stabbed him repeatedly, and then shot him twice. Around this

Linda Kasabian

Patricia Krenwinkel

time, Linda Kasabian came up from the driveway after hearing "horrifying sounds." In a vain effort to halt the massacre, she lied to Atkins, telling her that someone was coming.

Inside the house, Abigail Folger escaped from Krenwinkel and ran out a bedroom door to the pool area. Krenwinkel pursued her and tackled her in

The front door to 10050 Cielo Drive, with the word "PIG" written on the door in blood.
(Below) The blood-spattered front doorway.

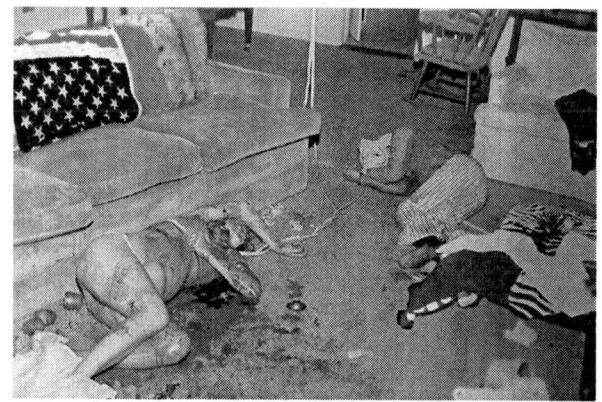

A horrific crime scene photograph of Sharon tate and Jay Sebrig, tied together and murdered in the living room of the 10050 Cielo Drive House.

Abigail Folger's bloody corpse was found on the lawn of the house. She had been stabbed 28 times.

the yard. Folger was stabbed several times by her captor and then Watson joined in with his own knife. Abigail Folger died after being stabbed 28 times. Frykowski had been stabbed 51 times. Atkins, Watson, or both of them, killed Sharon Tate, who was stabbed 16 times. She pleaded with her killers to let her live long enough to have her baby and she cried, "mother... mother..." until she finally died.

Earlier that night, as the four Family members had left Spahn Ranch, Manson told the girls to "leave a sign... something witchy," at the house. After the murders, Atkins wrote "pig" on the front door of the house in Sharon Tate's blood. Then they fled, changing out of their gore-soaked clothing and dumping the clothes, along with the weapons, in the hills.

The next night, six Family members, including the four from the previous night's murders plus Leslie Van Houten, and Steve "Clem" Grogan, were sent out with instructions from Manson. This time, Manson went along with them. He gave Kasabian directions to 3301 Waverly Drive, home of supermarket executive Pasqualino "Leno" LaBianca and his wife, Rosemary, who was co-owner of an upscale women's clothing store. Located in the Los Feliz section of L.A., the LaBianca home was next door to a house at which Manson and Family members had attended a party the year before.

Manson and Watson went into the house first and, according to Watson's later version of the events, Manson ordered him to bind Leno LaBianca's hands with a leather cord. Rosemary LaBianca was brought into the living room and Watson followed Manson's instructions to put pillowcases over the couple's heads. Manson then left, sending Krenwinkel and Leslie Van Houten into the house with instructions that the couple be killed.

Rosemary was sent back into the bedroom with the girls and Watson began stabbing Leno LaBianca with a bayonet, which had been given to him by Manson when Watson complained about the inadequate weapons that had been provided for the previous night's murders. Watson's first thrust went into LaBianca's throat. Suddenly, he heard noises in the bedroom and he went in to find Rosemary LaBianca was keeping the girls away from her by swinging a lamp that they had tied to her neck. Watson charged forward and stabbed the woman several times with the bayonet, sending her to the floor. He then went back into the living room and renewed his attack on Leno LaBianca, stabbing him a total of 12 times. He then carved the word "war" on the man's abdomen.

Returning to the bedroom, where Krenwinkel was attacking Rosemary LaBianca with a kitchen knife, Watson, who had been told by Manson that each of the girls needed to play a part in the murders, ordered Van Houten to stab her, too. She did so, jamming the knife into the

Leno & Rosemary La Bianca, the next victims of the Manson Family

woman's back and buttocks. Rosemary LaBianca died after being stabbed 41 times. While Watson cleaned off the bayonet and showered in the LaBianca's bathroom, Krenwinkel used the victims' blood to scrawl "Rise" and "Death to Pigs" on the walls and "Healter Skelter" on the refrigerator door (she was not sure how to spell it). She also stabbed Leno LaBianca 14 times with an ivory-handled, two-tined carving fork, which she left jutting out of his abdomen. She jammed a steak knife into his throat and left it there when she and her companions left the house.

Planning to carry out two murders on the same night, Manson sent Kasabian to the Venice home of an actor acquaintance of hers. Manson dropped off the second set of Family members at the man's

The La Bianca home in 1969

The words "Death to Pigs" were scrawled on the walls of the La Bianca house in blood. Manson had instructed his killers to try and incite a race war with the murders.

apartment building and then drove back to the Spahn Ranch, leaving all of them to hitchhike home. Kasabian deliberately thwarted this murder by knocking on the wrong apartment door and waking a stranger. As the group abandoned the murder plan and left, Susan Atkins defecated in the stairwell.

On August 10, as the bodies from the Tate murders were being autopsied and the LaBiancas' bodies were yet to be found, detectives from the L.A. County Sheriff's Department, which had jurisdiction in the Hinman case, informed LAPD detectives assigned to the Tate case of the bloody writing that had been found at the Hinman house. They even mentioned that their suspect, Beausoleil, hung out with a group of hippies led by "a guy named Charlie." The detectives on the Tate case, believing that the murders were connected to a drug deal gone bad, ignored the information.

Steven Parent, the young man who had been killed in the Tate driveway, had no connection to the other victims. He was an acquaintance of William Garretson, who had been hired by Rudi Altobelli to watch over the property while Altobelli was out of town. When the killers arrived, Parent had been leaving Cielo Drive, after visiting Garretson. Held for a short time as a possible murder suspect, Garretson told the police that he was living in the guesthouse but had neither seen nor heard anything on the night of the murders. He was released on August 11, after a polygraph exam showed that he was not involved in the crimes.

On August 12, the LAPD announced to the news media that it had ruled out any connection between the Tate and LaBianca murders. On August 16, sheriff's deputies raided the Spahn Ranch and arrested Manson and 25 others – but not for murder. They were picked up as suspects in an auto theft ring that had been stealing Volkswagens and converting them into dune buggies. Weapons were seized, but because the warrant had been misdated, the Family was released a few days later.

By the end of August, virtually all leads in both cases had gone nowhere. As it turned out, a report by LaBianca detectives (younger than those assigned to the Tate murders), noted a possible connection between the bloody writings at the LaBianca house and the latest album by "the singing group of the Beatles" but nothing further was done to follow up on this.

In mid-October, the LaBianca team, still working separately from the Tate team, checked with the sheriff's office about any possible similar crimes and learned of the Hinman murder, which had been ignored by the detectives on the Tate case. They also learned that Hinman detectives had spoken with Beausoliel's girlfriend, Kitty Lutesinger, who had been arrested a few days earlier with members of the Manson Family.

Those arrests had occurred at the desert ranches, to which the Family had moved while they searched for the Devil's Hole in Death Valley and access to the secret underground city. A joint force of National Park rangers and officers from the California Highway Patrol and the Inyo County Sheriff's Office had raided both the Myers and Barker ranches after following clues left behind when Family members burned an earthmover owned by Death Valley National Monument. The officers had found stolen dune buggies and other vehicles and had arrested two dozen persons, including Manson. A Highway Patrol officer found Manson hiding in a cabinet under a bathroom sink at the Barker Ranch.

LaBianca detectives spoke with Lutesinger and also made contact with members of a motorcycle gang that she'd told them Manson tried to hire as guards for the Spahn Ranch. While gang members were providing information that suggested a link between Manson and the murders, a cellmate of Susan Atkins informed the LAPD of the Family's involvement in the crimes. Atkins had been arrested at Barker Ranch and while at the Sybil Brand Institute, an L.A. detention center, she spoke to bunkmates Ronnie Howard and Virginia Graham about the crimes she had taken part in.

On December 1, 1969, acting on the information from these sources, the LAPD announced warrants for the arrest of Watson, Krenwinkel, and Kasabian in the Tate case. The suspects' involvement in the LaBianca murders was also noted. Manson and Atkins, already in custody, were not mentioned. At this point, it was not known that Leslie Van Houten, also arrested near Death Valley, had been involved in the LaBianca case. Watson and Krenwinkel had also been arrested. Both had fled from L.A. but authorities in McKinney, Tex., and Mobile, Ala., had picked them up after being notified by the LAPD. Informed that there was a warrant out for her arrest, Linda Kasabian voluntarily surrendered to authorities in Concord, N.H., on December 2.

Soon, physical evidence like Krenwinkel's and Watson's fingerprints, which had been found at Cielo Drive, was enhanced by evidence recovered by the public. On September 1, 1969, the distinctive .22-caliber Hi Standard Buntline Special revolver Watson used to shoot Parent, Sebring, and Frykowski had been found and given to the police by a 10-year-old who lived near the Tate home. In December, when the *Los Angeles Times* published an account of the crimes based on information from Susan Atkins, the boy's father made several telephone calls to the police and they finally connected the gun to the murders. Acting on the same article, a local ABC television crew quickly located the bloody clothing that had been discarded by the killers.

At the trial, which began on June 15, 1970, the prosecution's main witness was Linda Kasabian, who, along with Manson, Atkins, and Krenwinkel, was charged with seven counts of murder and one count of conspiracy. Since she did not take part in the actual killings (and even tried to stop some of them), she was granted immunity in exchange for testimony that detailed the events that occurred on the nights of the crimes.

Because of his conduct, including violations of a gag order and submission of "outlandish" and "nonsensical" pretrial motions, Manson's permission to act as his own attorney (which had been reluctantly granted in the first place) was withdrawn by the court before the trial ever started. His strange behavior continued once the trial actually began. On Friday, July 24, the first day of testimony, Manson appeared in court with an "X" carved into his forehead and issued a statement that stated that since he was considered to be

(Left) Manson at the time of his trial (Right) Prosecutor Vincent Bugliosi

Members of the Manson Family lurked outside of the courthouse during the trial. Eventually, the girls shaved their heads in support of their leader.

inadequate to represent himself, he had placed an "X" on his head to cross himself out of the "establishment's" world. That weekend, all of the female defendants duplicated the marks on their own foreheads and within a day or two, most of the other Family members did, too.

Prosecutor Vincent Bugliosi named Manson's interpretation of "Helter Skelter" as the main motive in the murders. The crime scenes' bloody White Album references were correlated with testimony about Manson's predictions that the murders that blacks committed at the outset of the race war would involve the writing of the word "pigs" in their victims' blood. Testimony that Manson said, "Now is the time for Helter Skelter" was backed up by Kasabian's testimony that, on the night of the LaBianca murders, Manson considered leaving Rosemary LaBianca's wallet lying on the street in a black neighborhood. His plan was for someone to pick up the wallet and use the credit cards inside it, making it seem that "some sort of organized group killed these people." Manson directed Kasabian to leave the wallet in the ladies room of a gas station near a black neighborhood. "I want to show blackie how to do it," Manson told Family members after the LaBianca murders.

During the trial, Family members lurked in the entrances and corridors of the courthouse. To keep them out of the courtroom itself, the prosecution subpoenaed them as prospective witnesses. That way, they were unable to enter the courtroom while others were testifying. The Family established a vigil on the sidewalk outside and each of them carried a large, sheathed hunting knife. Since it was carried in plain sight, it was legal. The knives, along with the "X" carved into his or her forehead, made Family members easily identifiable.

On August 4, despite precautions taken by the court, Manson flashed the jury a *Los Angeles Times* front page with a headline that read "Manson Guilty, Nixon Declares," a reference to a statement made the previous day when U.S. President Richard Nixon complained about what he saw as the media's glamorization of Manson. When questioned by the judge, the jury members stated that the headline did not influence them. The next day, the female defendants stood up and said in unison that, in light of Nixon's opinion, there was no point in going on with the trial.

And this was not the end of the disruptions. On October 5, after the court refused to allow the defense to question a prosecution witness that they had earlier declined to cross-examine, Manson jumped over the defense table and tried to attack the judge. He was wrestled to the floor by court bailiffs and was removed from the courtroom with the female defendants, who had risen to their feet after Manson's outburst and began chanting in

Dead Men Do Tell Tales: Bloody Hollywood

Latin.

On November 19, the prosecution rested its case – and so did the defense, without ever calling a witness. Lawyers for the women were unwilling to let their clients testify and assume all of the guilt, believing that Manson had instructed them to do this. The next day, Manson was permitted to testify, but because his statements would possibly violate a California statute by implicating his co-defendants, the jury was removed from the courtroom. Manson spoke for more than an hour, blaming everything on music, which was instructing young people to rise up against the establishment. He also stated that he didn't ever recall telling the girls to "get a knife and a change of clothes and go do what Tex says."

As the trial was concluding, attorney Ronald Hughes, who had been representing Leslie Van Houten, disappeared during a weekend trip. Hughes tried to separate the interests of his client from those of Manson, a move that angered Manson and may have cost Hughes his life. He hoped to show that Van Houten was not acting independently, but was completely controlled in her actions by Manson. Despite Hughes' disappearance, Judge Charles Older ordered the trial to proceed and appointed a new attorney, Maxwell Keith, for Van Houten. Keith was appointed to represent Van Houten during Hughes' absence but this caused a two-week delay as Keith familiarized himself with the case. The girls angrily demanded the firing of all their lawyers, and asked to reopen the defense. The judge denied the request and the trial resumed just before Christmas. However, disruptions caused by the defendants during the closing arguments forced the judge to ban them from the courtroom. Not long after this, Ronald Hughes' decomposed body was found wedged between two boulders in Ventura County. Due to the severe decomposition, he had to be identified by dental records and the cause and nature of his death was ruled as "undetermined."

On January 25, 1971, guilty verdicts were returned against Manson, Krenwinkel and Atkins on all counts. Van Houten was convicted on two counts of murder and one of conspiracy. During the trial's penalty phase, Manson shaved his head and

Linda Kasabian with Los Angeles authorities shortly after she surrendered to New Hampshire police. She was the leading witness against Manson and the others during the trials.

told the press that he was the devil. Once the jury retired to weigh the state's request for the death penalty, the female defendants shaved their heads, as well. On March 29, 1971, the jury returned verdicts of death against all four defendants. The judge agreed with their findings and on April 19, sentenced them to death.

The lengthy proceedings to extradite Charles Watson from Texas, where he had returned a month before he was arrested, resulted in his being tried separately for the murders. The trial began in August 1971 and by October, he had been found guilty on seven counts of murder and one of conspiracy. He was sentenced to death.

The death penalties were never carried out. In February 1972, the sentences of all five parties were automatically reduced to life in prison by California v. Anderson, a case in which the California Supreme Court abolished the death penalty in the state.

In a 1971 trial that was held after his convictions in the Tate and LaBianca murders, Manson was found guilty in the murders of Gary Hinman and Donald "Shorty" Shea and was given a life sentence for those crimes. Shea, a Spahn Ranch stuntman and horse wrangler, had been killed about 10 days after the August 16, 1969 sheriff's raid on the ranch. Manson, who suspected that Shea had helped set up the raid, believed that the stuntman was trying to get the Family removed from the ranch. In separate trials, Family members Bruce Davis and Steve "Clem" Grogan were also found guilty of Shea's murder.

With the murders solved and the defendants safely locked behind bars, it seemed the Family would fade away for good. But neither Manson, nor many members of the Family, could remain out of the spotlight. On September 5, 1975, the Family found national attention again when Lynette "Squeaky" Fromme attempted to assassinate U.S. President Gerald Ford. The attempt took place in Sacramento, where she and fellow Manson girl Sandra Good had moved to be near Manson while he was incarcerated at Folsom State Prison. A subsequent search of the apartment shared by Fromme, Good, and a Family recruit turned up evidence that, coupled with later actions on the part of Good, resulted in Good's conviction for conspiring to send death threats through the U.S. mail. The threats were against corporate executives and government officials for what she saw as their neglect of the environment.

Manson himself seemed to enjoy being seen as the "crazed cult leader" and made a number of notable television appearances in the 1980s. He appeared on all three major networks from the California Medical Facility and San Quentin and was interviewed by Tom Snyder, Charlie Rose, and Geraldo Rivera, who spoke with Manson as part of a prime-time special on Satanism.

On September 25, 1984, while imprisoned at the California Medical Facility, Manson was seriously burned by a fellow inmate who poured paint thinner on him and then set him on fire. The prisoner later stated that Manson had threatened him. Despite suffering second and third-degree burns on about 20 percent of his body, Manson recovered from his injuries.

Although it seems unlikely that he will ever be released, Charles Manson became eligible for parole after California v. Anderson nullified the death sentences in the state in 1972. This made Manson eligible to apply for parole after just seven years in prison. His first parole hearing was held in 1978 and on May 23, 2007, he was turned down for parole for the eleventh time. He will not be eligible for parole again until 2012.

He remains an inmate today in the Protective Housing Unit at California's Corcoran State Prison, relishing his continued notoriety and the attention that he receives on websites, in books, and within the underground culture of America.

A recent photo of Charles Manson, who remains safely behind bars today.

HOLLYWOOD CRIME BEAT: A ROGUE'S GALLERY OF KILLERS

Los Angeles has seen more than its share of crime over the years and has been the scenes of some of the most horrific murders – and murder sprees – in American history, including many that will be featured in later sections of the book. In this chapter, the reader will find a collection of other Hollywood and L.A. killers, all of whom have splashed their names in blood across the pages of Southern California history.

L.A.'S BLUEBEARD

The name of James P. Watson is largely unknown today to anyone other than the most avid crime buffs, but it's likely that he was the first serial killer to operate in Los Angeles. His story ranged throughout the early 1900s and he cut a bloody swath up and down the West Coast before he was finally captured and connected to several murders.

Watson is known to have married at least 40 women and killed 25 of them. The rest managed to escape with the loss of all their savings, which they gave him hoping he would propose marriage. Several of his wives followed him from one end of the country to the other and, even after he was imprisoned for murder, they remembered him fondly for the special attention that he showered on them. Strangely, Watson was not a handsome man, but his surviving wives always claimed there was something indefinable about him managed to capture, and keep, their attentions. All of these women were lucky that Watson had only grown tired of them before he moved on to another woman. Others had not been so lucky. He hid his victims so well that none of their bodies were ever recovered, except for one – whose whereabouts he confessed to the police.

James Watson was born Charles Gillam in Paris, Ark. He ran away at the age of 12 and soon adopted the name of J.P. Watson, varying the first name to whatever suited him at the time. He killed his first woman in 1893, a passionate young woman who had run away with him and then announced that she was pregnant. After she tried to get him to marry her, Watson poisoned her and quickly left town with her possessions. After that, he never murdered another woman without marrying her first. Years later, he said that he felt that his victims were entitled to a small measure of happiness before he took their lives.

By 1913, Watson had married 10 women and had killed four of them. To attract new victims, he began advertising in newspapers. One such advertisement read:

Gentleman: Neat appearance, courteous disposition, well connected in business, has quite a little property, also connected with several corporations and has a substantial bank account. Would be pleased to correspond with refined young lady or widow, object matrimony. This advertisement is in good faith, and all answers will be treated with respect.

Watson picked through hundreds of responses to find the most likely victims. Between 1915 and

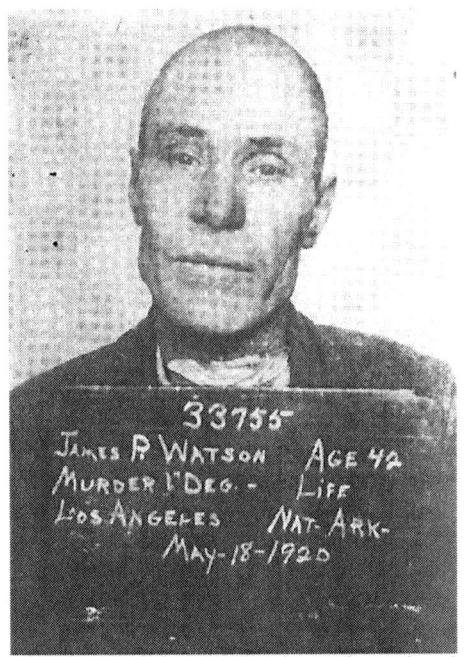

James Watson, who romanced -- and murdered -- scores of women before he was caught.

Items found in James Watson's possession that had been taken from his murdered wives.

1920, he operated along the West Coast, dumping and burying his victims in scenic locations in the mountains, in lakes, and along rivers. The bodies that he secreted remained hidden and to this day, have never been found.

Watson's downfall came about as a result of suspicions that had nothing to do with his murderous activities. In 1919, a dressmaker in Spokane, Wash., named Kathryn Wombacher decided to answer a personal ad in the local newspaper. She soon made a date with a man named Walter Andrew, a federal agent who had recently moved to the area while working on a special case. The two of them got along quite well and were soon married.

The honeymoon didn't last long, however. They fought often and as a result, Andrew often vanished for extended periods without telling his new wife where he was going – other than that he was "working on a case" and was "sworn to secrecy." Naturally, Kathryn became suspicious and assumed that he was seeing another woman. When he announced that he was going to L.A. for an extended period of time, she demanded that he take her with him. Andrew refused, stating that it was against bureau policy.

Kathryn managed to find Andrew's name on a hotel registry and showed up in Los Angeles with her suitcase in hand. Her husband was livid but eventually, he found her a small apartment in Hollywood. After a few days, he announced that he was about to be sent on another extended assignment, this time to Washington, and was not sure when he would be back. Frustrated and angry, Kathryn found the Nick Harris Detective Agency in downtown L.A. and hired them to follow her husband, who she believed was seeing another woman.

Detective J.B. Armstrong discovered that Kathryn's suspicions were correct. Andrew was seeing another woman, but this was only part of the bad news. The other woman was also his wife and they had been married in a civil service two weeks earlier. The news was shocking, but it was nothing compared to the revelations that followed. Her husband's name was not Walter Andrew but James Watson and Detective Armstrong had found a trunk that her husband kept in a private locker. The trunk was filled with marriage licenses, bankbooks, wedding rings, and photographs. From these mementoes, Armstrong came to believe that Watson had been married to at least 22 women in 10 years, women that he had met through personal ads. The worst news of all was that many of these women were missing, believed dead, or murdered.

Armstrong alerted the authorities and when the LAPD finally caught up with Watson, he was relaxing at a local café, romancing yet another prospective bride. He was taken into custody and relentlessly questioned. The detectives knew that they had a "master Bluebeard" on their hands, but they were unable to bring murder charges against him. Not a single body could be found.

Then, while Watson was in custody, a woman's remains turned up in Plum Station, Wash. Watson had hidden some of his victims' bodies nearby and he became worried that the woman who had been found might have been one of his victims. In a desperate move, he made a deal with the L.A. district attorney to reveal the hiding place of one of his victims, provided that the D.A. guarantee him nothing worse than a life sentence and to fight any extradition efforts to other states. Since there was no case without a body, the district attorney agreed to the deal. Watson led officers out into the desert and showed them where to find the remains of Nina Lee Deloney.

After that, Watson confessed to eight murders and hinted at many more. His confession stunned the country. Dozens of people wrote to him asking for information on missing loved ones, but Watson ignored them. He couldn't remember every woman that he had married, or what had become of them, he said.

Watson was convicted in 1920 and received a life sentence. He died in San Quentin in 1939 and was buried in the prison cemetery.

Ironically, his confession never needed to be made. It was later discovered that the body found in Plum Station was not one of his victims.

THE "GHOST IN THE GARRET"

One of the strangest tales of sexual obsession and murder in L.A.'s seamy history began in 1913 but would not be exposed to the public until many years later, after a murder plot began to unravel in 1922. The tale involved a woman named Walburga "Dolly" Oesterreich, a seemingly innocent housewife who was not innocent at all. Dolly was a woman who liked men – lots of men – and she almost always had several of them in her life. Her husband, Fred Oesterreich, was a wealthy manufacturer of women's clothing. The couple first lived in Milwaukee, and then moved to Los Angeles. But they didn't move to L.A. alone...

Dolly's secret lover, Otto Sanhuber, followed

Dolly Oesterreich and her "sex slave" Otto Sanhuber, a former sewing machine repairman who secretly lived in the attic of her home.

them to the West Coast. In 1913, Dolly had seduced Sanhuber, then 17, while he was working as a sewing machine repairman in her husband's factory. Dolly had started the affair by calling Fred at work and telling him that her sewing machine was broken. When Sanhuber arrived at her home, Dolly greeted him at the door wearing nothing but stockings and a silk robe.

The short, owlish-looking Sanhuber, who later described himself as Dolly's "sex slave," not only became obsessed with his mistress, but he moved into her house, silently retreating into the attic each night when Fred Oesterreich came home from work. And whenever the Oesterreichs moved, Sanhuber moved with them. During the day, Sanhuber made the beds, did housework and kitchen chores, and kept Dolly satisfied. He lived on scraps from the kitchen. At night, in the attic, he lived a solitary life, reading murder mysteries by candlelight and writing stories that he later sold to magazines. When the strange tale later became publicly known, the newspapers called him the "ghost in the garret."

The Oesterreichs frequently argued, but a particularly loud fight, along with the sounds of a struggle, finally brought Sanhuber out of the attic on the night of August 22, 1922. Fearing for his lover's safety, he grabbed two small pistols and came downstairs to confront Fred Oesterreich. The undoubtedly startled husband recognized Sanhuber as his former employee and the two men began to fight. They grappled with each other and in the struggle Oesterreich was shot three times, once in the back of the head.

The lovers decided to make it look like Oesterreich had been killed by burglars. Sanhuber locked Dolly in a bedroom closet, threw the key down the hallway, hid Fred's expensive diamond watch, and then retreated to his attic hiding place. Dolly began to scream Fred's name and she was found slumped on the floor of the closet when the police came, alerted by neighbors who had heard the sound of gunfire.

For almost a year, the story held up. Dolly moved to another house in the neighborhood, again installing Sanhuber secretly in the attic. She began an affair with the attorney who was settling her husband's estate, Herman S. Shapiro, and as a gift to her new lover, she presented him with Fred's diamond watch. When Shapiro recognized it as belonging to her late husband, Dolly explained that she had found it under a cushion on the couch, but didn't think she needed to tell the authorities about it.

Then, Dolly added a third lover, a businessman named Roy Klumb. She asked Klumb for a favor, convincing him to dispose of an old gun that was similar to the one that had killed her husband. Of course, it was not the same gun, she told him, but it would be embarrassing for her if the police ever found it. Klumb threw the gun into what turned out to be a shallow spot in the La Brea Tar Pits.

A crime scene photograph of Fred Oesterreich's murder
(LAPD Crime Scene Photograph)

She asked a friendly neighbor to do her a favor with the other gun and he buried it under a rose bush in his backyard.

Unknown to Dolly, detectives had always been suspicious of her story, especially when it was known that Fred Oesterreich had been killed with a .25-caliber gun, which seemed like a small weapon to be used by professional thieves. Looking into the case, a detective learned that Herman Shapiro had Fred's "stolen" diamond watch. And Klumb, after breaking things off with Dolly, told the police about disposing of the gun for her. They retrieved the weapon from the tar pits and when the story hit the newspaper, the neighbor brought in the gun that had been hidden under the rose bush. Dolly was quickly arrested for murder.

In jail, Dolly begged Shapiro to take food to Sanhuber, who was still hidden in her attic. When he did, the two men began talking and Shapiro learned of the other man's decade-long obsession with Dolly. He threw Sanhuber out of the house.

Meanwhile, in hearings that dragged on for months, the authorities searched for a motive and more evidence, as well as an explanation for how Dolly could have locked herself into the bedroom closet and still managed to dispose of the key in the hallway. Both guns were rusted and damaged, so it was impossible to prove that either of them had been the murder weapon. Still incarcerated, Dolly became so ill that it was reported that she was dying. Eventually, she was released on bail and then all charges against her were dropped for lack of evidence.

Shapiro, her remaining lover, moved into Dolly's house and they lived together for the next seven years. Finally, their tumultuous relationship ended in 1930 and when Shapiro moved out, he told the police about Sanhuber, the mysterious "ghost in the garret." Dolly and Sanhuber were both arrested this time – Dolly being charged with conspiracy and Sanhuber with murder. The jury found Sanhuber guilty of manslaughter, but since it was now a year beyond the statute of limitations for a manslaughter conviction, Sanhuber was set free. In a separate trial, Dolly was saved by a hung jury. Lacking any more evidence against her, the district attorney ended the case against her by declining to try her again.

After that, Sanhuber disappeared. Dolly apparently learned her lesson and became a one-man woman. She lived quietly with the same man for the next three decades, until her death in 1961.

THE "TIGER WOMAN"

In 1922, Clara Phillips, dubbed the "Tiger Woman" by newspapers, became something of a celebrity after she carried out the vicious murder of her husband's mistress. Clara, an attractive former dancer and showgirl, had a passionate, possessive streak, especially when it came to her new husband, Armour Phillips, a wealthy L.A. oil-stock broker. That passionate streak turned deadly when she learned – by angry comments from her husband and by listening in on his private telephone conversations – that he had been seeing a pretty bank clerk named Alberta Meadows. Clara even heard him say that he was in love with Meadows and considered running away with her.

"Tiger Woman" Clara Phillips

One afternoon, after spending part of the day drinking in a Long Beach speakeasy with her friend, Peggy Caffee, Clara took Peggy and went to the bank where Meadows worked. When Alberta came outside, they asked for a ride from her. Alberta, who didn't know Clara, drove as directed to Montecito Heights, a quiet, isolated area north of downtown Los Angeles.

When they arrived, Clara got Meadows out of the car and attacked her with a claw hammer. She hit her in the face and the head and then used the claw hammer's head to disembowel the young woman. She hit her again and again with such force that the hammer broke off in her skull. Unbelievably, Alberta was still not dead so Clara choked the last bit of life out of her body. Hardened detectives and newspaper reporters were so sickened by the sight of the corpse that they noted that it looked as though Meadows had been attacked by a tiger, hence the "Tiger Woman"

Clara Phillips in court (Los Angeles Public Library)

nickname that was given to her killer.

After the murder, Clara told her husband that she had killed Meadows. Her helped her to hide Alberta's car and then put her on a train headed for Mexico. But the next morning, Phillips had second thoughts. He had no desire to be charged as an accessory in the murder so he went to his attorney for advice. The attorney called well-known Undersheriff Eugene Warren Biscailuz, who would later serve as the L.A. County sheriff for two decades. Police officers in Arizona took Clara Phillips off the train at Tucson and returned her to Los Angeles to be tried for murder.

In court, Clara's attorney first tried to prove that her friend, Peggy Caffee, killed Alberta Meadows. When that didn't work, he tried for an insanity defense, claiming that the mutilation of Alberta's body could have only been done by someone who was insane. Both sides called psychiatrists, then called alienists, to make their cases. The doctors who testified for the prosecution fared far better with the jury. Clara was convicted on charges of second-degree murder, with a sentence of 10 years to life in prison.

But Clara Phillips had two things going for her, even in jail. She had always displayed charm, tenacity and a great resourcefulness, traits that she shared with her sister, Etta May Jackson. In addition to, or perhaps because of this, she also had a great many admirers, both men and women. Her jail cell was flooded with letters, flowers, and candy – and some offered more practical support. One of these was a man named Jesse Carson. To this day, it's unclear how he managed to do it, but Carson helped Clara to escape from the old Los Angeles County jail eight days after her conviction. She hid out for a few days and then she, her sister, and Carson made their way to Mexico and then on to Honduras.

Morris Lavine, a reporter for the *Los Angeles Examiner*, tracked Clara to the banana republic. Contacted through the Honduran consulate in L.A., officials in Honduras took Clara and her sister into custody to await extradition. Lavine, Undersheriff Biscailuz, and Biscailuz's wife went down to bring them back. But by then, Clara had become as popular among the Hondurans, including the city of Tegucigalpa's chief of police, as she had been in Los Angeles. Many influential Hondurans were reluctant to see Clara and Etta May leave and with the country near revolution, and no formal U.S. extradition request in hand, it looked as through Honduran officials were going to let the sisters go free. The police chief even had gunboats patrolling the harbor of Puerto Cortes to keep them in the country. When Lavine made contact with Clara, he argued with her that if she was truly innocent, she should come back to L.A. and prove it. He didn't mention that her lawyer had died when she was gone and that he had filed an appeal too late to be considered. In any event, Clara agreed to return and Biscailuz smuggled them out of the country on a banana boat that docked in New Orleans.

More than 2,000 Los Angelenos met the train from Louisiana that brought Clara back to the city in June 1923. Standing on the observation platform of a railroad car, she and her husband kissed and embraced for the benefit of the crowds and the press. However, with no appeal possible, the train continued north, taking her to San Quentin.

Clara remained popular during her stretch in prison. She played the saxophone and organized and conducted a seven-piece orchestra made up of female inmates. She wrote and performed in a theatrical production and learned to be a dental assistant. When she was moved to the new women's prison at Tehachapi, she remained the center of prison social life.

She never returned to the front pages of newspapers, though, even when she was paroled in 1935. She moved to La Mesa, near San Diego, living with her mother and three sisters. In 1938, she divorced Armour Phillips, who had vanished without a trace several years before. She announced that she planned to marry again, but her husband was never publicly identified. Clara worked as a dental assistant until 1961, when she moved to Texas and disappeared completely from the pages of history.

"FATE," "DEATH" & "THE FOX"

To a parent, there is no greater, or more heart-shattering, crime than the kidnapping – and death – of a child. This was exactly the horrifying event that faced Perry Parker, a prominent Los Angeles banker, on December 15, 1927 when his 12-year-old daughter, Marion, was abducted. The girl was taken from her junior high school. The kidnapper walked into the principal's office that afternoon, claiming that Perry Parker was ill, and that he wanted to see his daughter. The kidnapper didn't realize there were twin Parker daughters, and did not know either child's name, but the school administrator turned one of the girls over to him. The next day, the first of three ransom notes arrived at the Parker home, demanding $1,500 in $20 gold certificates.

Letters began to arrive in the mail for Perry Parker over the course of the next few days. All of the correspondence, which taunted him with threats against his daughter's life, was signed with names like "Fate," "Death," and "The Fox." The

The kidnapped girl, Marion Parker

negotiations with the kidnapper continued until the price was agreed upon and a meeting was set. Parker placed the ransom money, $1,500 in cash, in a black bag and drove off to meet "The Fox."

Parker, alone in his car, met the kidnapper, a shadowy young man, at an isolated spot on the outskirts of Los Angeles. As both men faced off from their separate automobiles, Parker asked the abductor if his daughter was alive. He could see Marion, wrapped in a blanket and apparently sleeping, slumped in the passenger's seat of the kidnapper's car. "Give me the money and I'll leave her down the road a way," the kidnapper softly told him.

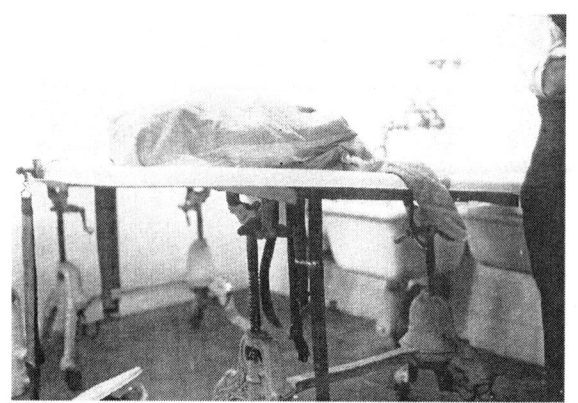

Parker threw the money from the window of his car into the young man's auto. The kidnapper sped away. Minutes later, following the road, Parker saw a blanket-wrapped bundle on the side of the road. He stopped and ran back to his daughter. Throwing back the blanket, he moaned in despair. Marion was dead. She had been choked so hard that her head had been severed. Her eyes had been wired open to make it appear that she was still alive. Her killer had insanely – and inexplicably – severed her legs. Her internal organs had been removed and later, were found strewn about the L.A. area.

The vicious killing shocked the country and set off one of the greatest manhunts in California history. The search involved over 20,000 police officers and huge cash rewards were offered to anyone who could provide information that led to the identification and capture of "The Fox." Suspicion quickly settled upon a former employee of Parker named William Edward Hickman. Several years before the abduction, Hickman was arrested on a complaint by Parker regarding stolen and forged checks. Hickman was convicted and did prison time, so investigators were able to compare his fingerprints on file with prints found on the ransom note. The fingerprints were a definite match. Hickman's photo was plastered all over the newspapers and sent to every police department on the West Coast.

Only a week after the murder, two police officers who recognized him from the wanted posters, found Hickman in Echo, Ore., where he took a vacation with the ransom money. Hickman was sent south on the first train to L.A. He was docile while in captivity, but tried twice to commit suicide in the train's washroom. They were feeble attempts, designed to convince his guards, and later

The shrouded torso of Marion Parker in the morgue. Detectives found her body parts scattered through Elysian Park (Los Angeles Public Library)

William Hickman in court (Los Angeles Public Library)

the jury in his trial, that he was insane.

Thousands of curious spectators gathered at stations along the route of the train, hoping to catch a glimpse of the murderer who had been featured some prominently in the previous week's headlines. Hickman idiotically waved and smiled at them. Some of them nervously waved back.

Hickman was grilled by investigators and was quick to admit his guilt. "This is going to get interesting before it's over," he told detectives. "Marion and I were good friends," he said, "and we really had a good time when we were together and I really liked her. I'm sorry that she was killed."

Hickman never said why he had killed the girl and cut off her legs. He was one of the earliest defendants to use California's new law that allowed pleas of not guilty by reason of insanity. The jury didn't buy it, though, and he was sentenced to death.

Hickman was hanged at San Quentin prison on February 4, 1928 – bringing in an end to one of the most tragic cases in Southern California history.

THE "RATTLESNAKE MURDERER"

Robert James made newspaper headlines in the 1930s as the "Rattlesnake Murderer", a case so unnerving that it inspired a crime-noir novel. James' love for women, kinky sex, and money electrified L.A. when he was put on trial for his wife's bizarre and gruesome murder.

James was born Major Raymond Lisenba in Alabama but changed his name after his first wife divorced him and then several pregnant women with whom he had affairs began pressuring him for money. After becoming Robert James, he headed west to California, where he found a wide-open field of lovely women that he could pursue. James loved women and he loved to lavish money on them, more money than he could earn as a barber. He also dressed impeccably and had a southern charm that served him well in L.A.

Soon after arriving in the city, he married two more times and in the process, discovered that there was money to be made by causing accidents to happen to people. When he killed his third wife, at a vacation cabin in the Canadian woods, he collected $14,000 from various insurance policies that he had taken out on her. The police treated the woman's death as an accidental drowning.

In 1934, James opened a barbershop in downtown Los Angeles. He was now driving an expensive Pierce-Arrow convertible and was escorted by his 17-year-old niece, Lois Wright, whom he had seduced and now introduced as his wife. While Lois worked as a manicurist in the barbershop, James went out looking for other women. Although he was making good money with his shop, his spending on his various affairs required more cash. He married another woman in 1934, but had the marriage annulled when he found out that his new bride didn't believe in life insurance.

Later that year, he became involved with Mary Busch, 25, a young woman that he had hired to be a manicurist. They married and moved into a new home and soon after, Mary became pregnant. In August, James brought two friends home for dinner and Mary was nowhere to be found. They searched the house and the yard and discovered Mary's lifeless body floating face down in the backyard fishpond. Her left leg was purple and swollen.

Investigators check out the backyard fishpond at the murder scene (Los Angeles Herald-Examiner)

Robert James in court. He showed little emotion as the verdict was read (Los Angeles Herald-Examiner)

The police investigated but the coroner ruled that Mary's death was an accidental drowning. He dismissed her swollen leg as the result of an insect bite. The insurance company paid James' claim, but a suspicious insurance investigator told Jack Southard, chief investigator for the L.A. district attorney's office, that the claim seemed questionable. The D.A.'s office started a full-time surveillance on James, including using listening devices and renting the house next door to where he lived. They learned that not only was he into violent, kinky sex, but that he had multiple women partners and was having incestuous sex with his niece, Lois.

Chief Deputy District Attorney Eugene Williams became convinced that James had murdered his wife and decided to see what would happen if he started looking for more information. Williams had James arrested one night while he was having sex with his niece and then he gave the story – including the rough sex and the suspicious deaths of his two wives – to the newspapers. The tactic worked and investigators managed to get a tip from a man named Charles Hope, a former sailor turned short-order cook, who lived in Hermosa Beach.

According to Hope, he had met James when he had come into his shop for a haircut. As James cut his hair, he brought up the subject of rattlesnakes and told Hope that he would pay him $100 if he could get two of them for him. Hope had a tough time with the assignment, but he eventually brought James two snakes, named Lethal and Lightning.

Hope then recounted that James had convinced his wife to have an abortion. Since the operation was illegal, he insisted that it be performed on their kitchen table with Hope playing the role of the doctor. James gave his wife whiskey to drink as an anesthetic and then taped her eyes and mouth shut, allegedly to protect the identity of the doctor doing the abortion. He also tied her down on the table so that she was unable to move. Hope brought the snakes into the house in a sliding box. James then shoved his wife's left leg into the box, where one of the agitated rattlesnakes bit her.

Hope took the snakes and left the house. He resold them to their original owner and then, that evening, came back to the James house. Mary was still alive, although she was in agony from the poisonous venom that was coursing through her body. James and Hope went into the garage and drank, waiting for her to die. Finally, James grew tired of waiting and convinced Hope to help him drown the nearly comatose woman in the bathtub. When she was dead, they placed her body in the fishpond.

Both men were tried for first-degree murder. The horrific story shocked the people of L.A. and the courtroom was filled with notables like Walter Winchell and James M. Cain, who was said to have been so inspired by the story that he used it as a basis for one of his books. Actor Peter Lorre came to the courtroom each day to study James in preparation for an upcoming role as a psychotic killer. The snakes were brought in as evidence, further adding to the titillating atmosphere of the shocking trial. However, a rather tense moment occurred when Lethal slithered out of his box and got free in the courtroom. No one was injured and the rattlesnake was quickly recaptured.

Hope was given life in prison and James'

attorney told him to brace himself when his own verdict was announced. "I can take it," James coolly replied. He was given the death sentence and on May 1, 1942, Robert James, the "Rattlesnake Murderer," became the last man to be hanged in the state of California.

DEATH OF THE "RED LIGHT BANDIT"

One of the most controversial and galvanizing cases in L.A. criminal history is that of Caryl Chessman, the so-called "Red Light Bandit," who was executed in the gas chamber at San Quentin on May 2, 1960. It was one of the strangest cases to ever work its way through the California legal system and even today, there are many who wonder if an innocent man died that day in the gas chamber.

Caryl Chessman was born in St. Joseph, Mich., and quickly got into trouble as a young man. He was a four-time loser (he entered his first reformatory at age 16) who spent most of his adult life behind bars. In January 1948, at age 27, he had been on parole for six weeks from California's Folsom Prison when he was arrested in Los Angeles and charged with being the notorious "Red Light Bandit." The "Bandit" would follow people in their cars to secluded areas and flash a red light that tricked them into thinking he was a police officer. When they opened their windows or exited their vehicles, he would rob and, in the case of several young women, rape them. Chessman confessed his role in the crimes to the police, but later claimed that the confession had been beaten out of him.

In July 1948, Chessman was convicted on 17 counts of robbery, kidnapping, and rape and condemned to death. Part of the controversy surrounding the Chessman case stems from how the death penalty was applied. At the time, under California's version of the "Little Lindbergh Law," (based on the kidnapping and murder of Charles Lindbergh's baby son), any crime that involved kidnapping with bodily harm could be considered a capital offense. Two of the counts against Chessman alleged that he dragged a woman a short distance from her car before raping her. Despite the short distance the woman was moved, the court considered it sufficient to qualify as kidnapping, thus making Chessman eligible for the death penalty.

Chessman was sent to Death Row at San Quentin, and his first execution date was set for March 28, 1952. Soon after began the famous drama of "Cell 2455, Death Row." That prison address became the title of a best-selling book for Chessman, which sold a half-million copies and was translated into a dozen languages.

Acting as his own attorney, Chessman vigorously asserted his innocence from the outset, arguing throughout the trial and the appeals process that he was alternately the victim of mistaken identity, or a much larger conspiracy seeking to frame him for a crime he did not commit. He claimed at other times to know who the real culprit was, but refused to name him. None of these ploys did much to create credibility for his claims and when all else failed, he fell back on his

Convicted "Red Light bandit" Caryl Chessman

assertion that this confession had been coerced by the police.

With the success of his book, Chessman retained a group of lawyers to help with his appeals. Over the course of the next 12 years, the attorneys filed dozens of appeals and Chessman successfully avoided eight execution deadlines, often by mere hours. The main focus of his appeal became that his original trial was improperly conducted and that subsequent appeals were seriously hampered by incomplete and incorrect transcripts of the original trial proceedings. These appeals were successful and the U.S. Supreme Court finally ordered the State of California to either conduct a full review of the transcripts or release Chessman. The review concluded that the transcripts were substantially accurate and Chessman was scheduled to die in February 1960.

Chessman's case had become one of the most intense anti-capital punishment campaigns in history. Protests against his execution came from all levels of society and millions of people in the United States, and around the world, signed petitions pleading for his life. The case focused attention on the politics of the death penalty in the United States at a time when most Western countries had already abandoned it, or were in the process of doing so. California Governor Edmund G. "Pat" Brown's office was flooded with appeals for clemency from noted authors, intellectuals, and public figures including Aldous Huxley, Ray Bradbury, Norman Mailer, Dwight MacDonald, and Robert Frost, Arthur Koestler, former First Lady Eleanor Roosevelt, and Christian evangelist Billy Graham.

Chessman's fight went on for 12 years. Ultimately, it failed, even with the repeal of California's "Little Lindbergh Law" and Governor Brown's outspoken opposition to the death penalty. Most of the inmates who had been convicted under the statutes of the law saw their sentences converted to life in prison. Some of them even earned parole years later, but not Chessman. His sentence was upheld and Governor Brown refused to grant clemency. Simply put, he believed that Chessman was guilty of the crimes.

Chessman's last appeals ran out in April 1960. Exhausting a last-minute attempt to file a writ of habeas corpus with the California Supreme Court, Chessman finally went to the gas chamber at San Quentin Prison on May 2, 1960.

During the execution, the emergency telephone rang just as the chamber was filling with gas. The caller was Judge Goodman's secretary, with a one-hour stay of execution. Ironically, as the prison's telephone number passed through several persons, a digit was omitted. The number had to be verified and re-dialed and by the time it was put through, it was simply too late – the execution had already begun. There was no way to stop the fumes, and no way to open the door and rescue the condemned man without taking the lives of others.

Inside the gas chamber, Chessman had turned to look at a female supporter who was there as a witness. His lips formed a final message to her, "Take it easy, it's all right and tell Rosalie [one of his attorneys] goodbye..." As the pellets dropped and the chamber began to fill with fumes, Chessman strained to see if the message had been understood. The woman, a reporter, nodded at him.

The gas chamber at San Quentin

Chessman half-smiled and then winked at her.

The next day, one news account of the execution – as inaccurate as the stories that had portrayed him as an innocent victim of circumstance – started out with "Sex terrorist Caryl Chessman ended his 12-year fight for life today with a wink and a smile."

THE "HILLSIDE STRANGLER"

In the late 1970s, the national and L.A. media had a field day with the crimes of the "Hillside Strangler," a media nickname that was given to two men, Kenneth Bianchi and Angelo Buono, cousins who were convicted of kidnapping, raping, torturing, and killing girls and women ranging in age from 12 to 28 during a four-month period from late 1977 to early 1978. They committed their crimes in the hills above Los Angeles – and sent a wave of fear throughout Southern California.

Devious and calculating, Kenneth Bianchi murdered for the sheer joy of killing. He and his cousin, Angela Buono, claimed their victims without the slightest trace of remorse. Bianchi had been raised in Rochester, N.Y., but in 1977, he moved to Los Angeles to live with Buono, an upholsterer who worked out of his home, repairing chairs and sofas in his garage. Drinking beer one night, the cousins began talking about killing people, particularly young women who would not be missed, like the ones who came to Hollywood every year, hoping to make it in the movies, but turning to prostitution to survive. They made plans to bring girls to Buono's house, where they would indulge their perversions before committing murder.

The first victim of the "Hillside Strangler" was a Hollywood prostitute identified as Yolanda Washington, whose body was found, posed lasciviously at Forest Lawn Cemetery on October 18. The corpse was cleaned and faint marks were visible around the neck, wrists, and ankles where a rope had been used. She had been viciously raped.

Police next found the naked body of Judith Lynn Miller, 16, on a Glendale hillside, close to the road. She had been wrapped in a tarp and, like the previous victim; marks were visible on her neck, ankles and wrists. Detectives concluded that she been raped, sodomized, and then strangled. Because her body had been found on the hill, the press dubbed her killer the "Hillside Strangler."

On November 6, 1977, the nude body of another woman was found near the Glendale Country Club. Similar to Judith Miller, she had been strangled with a ligature. The woman was identified as 21-year-old Elissa Kastin, a waitress, who was last seen leaving work the night before her body was discovered.

On November 13, 1977, two young girls, Dolores Cepeda, 12, and Sonja Johnson, 14, boarded a bus and headed home after school. They were last seen getting off a bus and approaching a car that reportedly had two men inside. On November 20, a young boy who was cleaning up trash on a hillside near Dodger Stadium found the bodies of the two girls. Both of them had been raped and strangled.

Later that same day, hikers found the nude, sexually assaulted body of Kristina Weckler, 20, on a hillside near Glendale. Unlike previous victims,

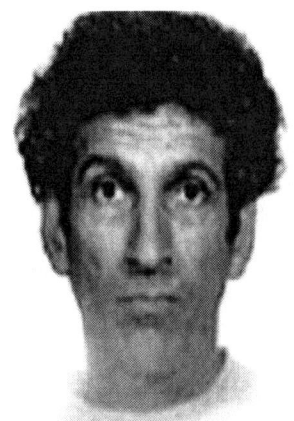

(Left) Kenneth Bianchi and (Right) Angelo Buono

there were signs of torture, indicated by oozing injection marks on her arms and body.

On November 23, the decomposed body of Jane King, 28, was found near an off-ramp of the Golden State Freeway. She had vanished on November 9 and investigators believed that she had been killed soon after. At this point, a task force was formed to catch the so-called "Hillside Strangler."

On November 29, the authorities discovered the body of Lauren Wagner, 18. She had also been strangled with rope and burn marks on her hands indicated that she had been tortured. By this time, the task force, which consisted of members from the LAPD, the Los Angeles County Sherriff's Department, and the Glendale Police Department, had come to believe that more than one person was responsible for the killings, although the media continued to use the moniker of the "Hillside Strangler."

On December 13, police found the body of a prostitute, Kimberly Martin, 17, on a hillside. After that, the slaying stopped until after the first of the year, when the last Los Angeles murder occurred. That final victim was discovered on February 16, 1978, when a helicopter spotted an orange Datsun abandoned off a cliff in the Angeles Crest area. Police responded to the sighting and found the naked body of the car's owner, Cindy Hudspeth, 20, locked in the trunk.

On a map that was displayed in the task force's office, detectives had placed pins at all of the points where the Strangler's victims had been found. The pins formed a circle and detectives theorized that the killer lived somewhere inside that circle. And they were right – all of the victims had been killed in Buono's home and then taken out to various points from the house to be dumped and placed on public display. In spite of this theory, leads in the case failed to produce a suspect. The police routinely reported that they had several suspects and expected things to break wide open at any time, but eventually, every lead dwindled away.

Strangely, after the February murder, the killings ceased. Detectives were baffled and as time wore on, most of the men assigned to the case were back working their regular duties. No one could understand why the murders had stopped and detectives wondered if perhaps their investigations had gotten too close, sending the killers into hiding. However, this was not the case. They had stopped because of the relationship between Bianchi and Buono. The cousins had grown to dislike one another and they constantly argued. Buono was said to be especially upset with his cousin's filthy habits, leaving garbage around the house and not bathing for days at a time. Finally, Bianchi moved out of the house and left the area, likely thinking that the "Hillside Strangler" murders would never be solved.

Bianchi moved to Bellingham, Wash., and there, he had the nerve to apply for a position with the Bellingham Police Department. He stated on his application that he had applied for a job with the LAPD, but had not gotten the position. Ironically, this was true. While he and Buono were killing women in Los Angeles, Bianchi not only tried to become a police officer, but he also went with officers on police ride-alongs – sometimes even with officers investigating the "Hillside Strangler" murders!

Bianchi didn't make it onto the Bellingham police force, but he did find a job as a security guard. Even though far away from L.A., Bianchi couldn't help killing again. He set up a fake house sitting job and lured two college girls, Diane Wilder and Karen Mandic, to his home, where he raped and murdered them. He locked the bodies in the trunk of Mandic's car, but this time, he left evidence behind. Detectives worked hard on the case and soon had witnesses to identify Bianchi as the man last seen with the girls before their deaths.

Bianchi was arrested and immediately claimed to be insane. He had been planning this all along, in case he was ever captured. He had spent years reading psychiatric studies and books about multiple personalities. He claimed that one of his multiple personalities committed the murders while he was in an altered, unconscious state. Court psychologists, notably Dr. Martin Orne, observed Bianchi and found that he was faking the illness, so Bianchi agreed to plead guilty and testify against Buono in exchange for leniency. He stated that Buono was the real "Hillside Strangler."

Authorities agreed to his terms, but on the

condition that Bianchi plead guilty to the Washington crimes. He was given a life sentence and then shipped back to Los Angeles, where he implicated Buono in the "Hillside Strangler" murders. He related how he and Buono had drive around in Buono's car, stopping young girls and flashing fake police badges. The victims were ordered into the car and were driven to Buono's house, where the pair brutally raped them. They were tortured and strangled and then the bodies were thoroughly washed to eliminate any evidence. The bodies were then driven to local hillsides, where they were displayed to the horror of the public.

Buono was arrested in 1979, shortly after Bianchi's Washington trial. His trial began in 1981 and did not conclude until November 14, 1983. Buono's prolonged trial was an expensive, media-crazed extravaganza with more than 400 witnesses and 55,000 pages of trial transcript pages. Throughout the whole thing, Buono insisted that he was innocent. He defied the authorities to find anything in his home that could connect him to the murders. Buono's home, indeed, was spotless. Anticipating arrest, he had cleaned and scrubbed the place from top to bottom, eliminating every trace of the victims – and of himself. The authorities did not find even a single fingerprint that belonged to Buono in the house. But they did find other things. Incredibly, a forensics team found a single eyelash belonging to one of the victims and was able to match fibers from a chair in Buono's house to fibers found on the bodies of some of the victims.

Finally, Buono was convicted. At the trial's conclusion, presiding Judge Ronald M. George said he would impose the death penalty without a second thought if the jury had allowed it. Bianchi is serving a life sentence in Washington. Buono died of a heart attack on September 21, 2002, in Calipatria State Prison where he was serving a life sentence.

THE SUNSET SLAYER

In 1980, a famous L.A. roadway became the haunt of an unlikely pair of serial killers that the press dubbed the "Sunset Slayer," believing at first that it was one killer acting alone. The "Slayer" was actually two killers, Douglas Daniel Clark and Carol Mary Bundy, and together, they prowled the Sunset Strip, which was legendary for its Hollywood nightlife.

The pair made a very odd couple. The 32-year-old Clark was a good-looking womanizer who had been born in 1948, the son of a retired U.S. Navy admiral turned engineer. Clark had lived in 37 countries by the time he settled in Southern California. Clark's sexual conquests usually involved dowdy, middle-aged matrons with money, which helped to support his lifestyle, but he also relished his kinky liaisons with under-aged girls and young women. He fantasized about rape and murder, mutilation and necrophilia, hoping someday to make those dark dreams come true.

He finally got his chance when he met Carol Mary Bundy, who was typical of the type of woman that Clark attached himself to. At age 37, Bundy was an overweight and depressed vocational nurse with two children. She had left her abusive husband in January 1979 and quickly fell in love with the manager of the apartment building that

Dowdy, unattractive and practically blind Carol Mary Bundy fell under the spell of a serial killer and became a murderer herself.

she moved into. The manager, John Murray, who also sang part-time in a country-western bar, was kind and paid attention to her, which was all the incentive that Bundy needed to pursue him.

Knowing that Bundy suffered from severe cataracts, Murray took her to the Social Security office and helped to get her declared legally blind, bringing in $620 each month for Carol and her sons. Next, he took her to an optometrist, where she was fitted for glasses, substantially improving her vision. Bundy was enraptured with him and began deliberately clogging toilets and drains in her apartment so that he would have to pay attention to her. She eventually wore Murray down and soon they were lovers. The problem was that Murray was married and he refused to give up his family for her. In October, Carol approached his wife and offered her $1,500 to leave her husband and disappear. The effort backfired and Murray blew up at her, suggesting that she find another place to live.

Three months later, Carol was in a bar one night when she met Douglas Clark. He immediately swept her off her feet. Clark moved into her home on the same night they met, working by day in the boiler room of a soap factory in Burbank and devoting his nights to satisfying Carol in ways that made her his virtual slave. He had such control over her that she didn't hesitate when he brought younger women into their home for sex. Carol also never complained when kinky sex turned to pedophilia and Clark brought home an 11-year-old that he met when she was roller-skating in the park.

His constant talk of death and mutilation soon led to the real thing. On June 11, 1980, half-sisters Gina Narano, 15, and Cynthia Chandler, 16, vanished from Huntington Beach. They had been on their way to meet some friends and never arrived. The next morning, their bodies were discovered along the Ventura Highway, near Griffith Park. Each of them had been shot in the head with a small-caliber pistol. At home, Clark gleefully confessed the murders to Bundy, shocking her with details of what he had some to each of the girls. But she was not shocked enough by his account to stop from going along with him a few weeks later. Soon, their nighttime escapades became a regular routine.

Using an unregistered car, they cruised Sunset Boulevard, looking for prostitutes, usually with Clark in the driver's seat and Bundy sitting in the back. When they found one that they liked, they pretended to be husband and wife with Bundy asking if she could buy her husband "something special" for his birthday. Then, once the hooker was in the passenger seat, they would drive to a remote area to consummate the act. As Clark unzipped and the prostitute got down to business, Bundy would hand him his gun just moments before he reached orgasm. The idea, which they apparently succeeded in doing on several occasions, was to shoot the women in the head at the moment of ejaculation.

In the early morning hours of June 24, Karen Jones, a 24-year-old prostitute, was found dumped behind a Burbank steakhouse. She had been shot in the head at close range. Later that same morning, the police were summoned to Studio City, where another female victim --- this one with no head – was found by horrified pedestrians. Even without her head, she was identified as Exxie Wilson, 20, another hooker. Wilson's head was taken home by Clark and Bundy as a souvenir, which they hid in the freezer until Bundy's sons left to go and stay with relatives. Clark then placed it on the counter and ordered Bundy to make up the face with cosmetics. She later recalled, "We had a lot of fun with her. I was making her up like a Barbie with makeup." When he got tired of this, Clark took his trophy to the bathroom, for a shower and a bout of oral necrophilia.

Newspapers had already started reporting the crimes of the new "Sunset Slayer" by June 27, when Exxie Wilson's head was found in a Hollywood alley, stuffed in an ornate wooden box. The authorities noted that it had been cleaned and scrubbed before being discarded by the killer.

Three days later, some snake hunters near Sylmar, in the San Fernando Valley, discovered a woman's mummified corpse, which was identified as a runaway named Marnette Comer. She had been last seen on June 1 and like the other victims, was a prostitute who had worked Sunset Boulevard.

The murders continued. On July 25, a young,

unidentified woman was found on Sunset Boulevard, shot once in the head. Two weeks later, hikers near Malibu turned up another unidentified corpse. It had been dismembered by predators but a small-caliber bullet hole was still visible in the head.

Despite her involvement with Clark, Carol Bundy was still hanging around John Murray, mostly at the country-western bar where he performed in the evening. She did not hold her liquor well and, after dropping a few hints about her lover's criminal activities, she panicked one night when Murray said that he might report Clark to the police. On August 5, she arranged a midnight rendezvous with Murray in his van, which was parked about two blocks away from the bar, but instead of sex, she murdered him. Found four days later, Murray had been stabbed nine times and slashed across the buttocks. His head had been severed and was not found at the crime scene.

But Murray's murder was a breaking point for Bundy. Two days after the singer's body was found, she broke down at work and sobbed to a fellow nurse about some of the things that she had done. Her friend tipped off the police and they showed up at Bundy's home, retrieving three pairs of panties that had been taken from victims as trophies, along with photographs of Clark and his 11-year-old victim. Clark was arrested at his job in Burbank and four days later, investigators found a pistol that he had hidden in the boiler room. Ballistics tests linked the gun to the bullets that were recovered from five of the known "Sunset Slayer" victims.

At his trial, serving briefly as his own attorney, Clark blamed Carol Bundy and John Murray for the slayings, claiming that he knew nothing about them. Jurors were not convinced and Clark was convicted on six counts of first-degree murder with "special circumstances," plus one count each of attempted murder, mayhem, and mutilating human remains. Tragically, investigators believed that it was more likely that he had killed as many as 50 women, but those were the only murders they could prove.

Clark represented himself during the penalty phase of the case and inexplicably declared, "We have to vote for the death penalty in this case. The

Douglas Daniel Clark in court. This smiling portrait was taken as his verdict was being passed down from the jury. He was sentenced to death.

evidence cries out for it." The jury agreed with him and he was sentenced to death on February 15.

At her own trial, Bundy, who was charged with murdering Murray and one of the unidentified females, first entered a plea of insanity, then reversed herself and admitted the murders. According to her statement, John Murray was shot in the head, and then decapitated to remove any ballistic evidence. She also admitted handing the gun to Clark when he killed one of the unnamed prostitutes. How many more she helped to kill will never be known. Bundy was convicted on the basis of her own confession and received consecutive terms of 27 years to life on one count, plus 25 years to life on the other.

THE "NIGHT STALKER"

From June 1984 to August 1985, Richard Ramirez, a vagrant from El Paso, Tex., terrorized the people of Los Angeles. He entered homes in the middle of the night (the media dubbed him the "Night Stalker" after an AC/DC song) and shot or strangled the men present so that he could rape and murder the females and children in the house. The year of terror that he brought to Southern California in the 1980s was unlike anything ever experienced in the region before.

Ricardo Munoz Ramirez was born in El Paso, the youngest of five children to working-class Mexican immigrants Julian Ramirez and Mercedes Munoz. Those who knew him always referred to him as a loner, even as a childhood. Ramirez received early inspiration for his later crimes from his cousin, Mike, a Vietnam veteran who enthralled Ramirez with photographs of Vietnamese women that he tortured and killed during the war. The two spent a lot of time together, often driving around and smoking pot, and Ramirez later claimed that Mike showed him the best ways to cut and kill people. Ramirez was only a boy when Mike murdered his wife, further enhancing his fascination with blood and death.

In the years that followed, Ramirez began getting into trouble. He started skipping school, smoking marijuana and sniffing glue. He attended Thomas Jefferson High School in El Paso, but dropped out in the ninth grade after being arrested twice for drug possession. He continued to use drugs and was arrested several times for possession and minor incidents of theft. He eventually ended up in California, where he was arrested two more times for auto theft in 1981 and 1984. During this time, Ramirez also began cultivating a "demonic personality," inspired by his drug use, interest in rock music and the pseudo-Satanism that became a part of the heavy metal culture of the late 1970s and 1980s. He often etched five-pointed pentagrams on his body, a symbol that when turned upside-down is associated with Satanism, and years later, at his trial, he would shout "Hail Satan!" in open court. Ramirez also stated that the AC/DC song "Night Prowler" became an inspiration for his "Night Stalker" persona.

At some point in 1984, Ramirez began to put all of his passions for death, murder, blood and chaos into practice and his murder spree began.

On June 28, 1984, Ramirez removed a window screen and crept into the home of a 79-year-old woman named Jennie Vincow of Glassell Park in Los Angeles. Her body was discovered by her son, Jack, the next morning. She had been sexually assaulted, stabbed repeatedly and her throat slashed so savagely that she was nearly decapitated.

Ramirez also ransacked the place and made off with any valuables that he could find.

Ramirez stayed quiet for the next ten months and then on March 17, 1985, Maria Hernandez, 22, was attacked as she got out of her car in the garage of the condominium that she shared with a roommate, Dayle Ozazaki, 34. Hernandez described the man who assaulted her as tall and dressed entirely in black, with a baseball cap pulled down low on his head. He came at her with a gun in his hand and shot at her face as she raised her hands in self-defense. The bullet hit her in the hand and was deflected by her car keys, which she still gripped in her fist. As Maria fell to the ground, Ramirez pushed his way into the condominium. She lay there without moving for some time and then went out the garage door and around to the front door. She hid when she saw Ramirez leaving, but he spotted her and raised the gun to shoot her again. She asked him not to kill her and he lowered the gun and ran away.

Moments later, Hernandez entered the house though the open front door. She found Okazaki lying dead on the kitchen floor. She had been shot in the head at close range and her blouse had been pulled up to expose her breasts. Maria called the police and on the ground outside, investigators found a baseball cap with AC/DC on the front of it.

Four days after the attack on Maria Hernandez and murder of Dayle Okazaki, near Monterey Park, a car driven by Tsia-Lian Yu was forced to a stop by a car driven by a man later identified as Ramirez. Ramirez jumped out pulled Yu out of her car. Joseph Duenas stepped out onto the balcony of his nearby apartment after hearing a woman screaming for help. When he saw what was happening, he ran inside and called the police, then stepped back onto the balcony. Duenas saw the man push Yu away, get into her car and drive away. As Ramirez drove, he passed a car containing Jorge Gallegos and his girlfriend. Gallegos saw the driver's profile and noted the number of the license plate of the car. Both men later testified at Ramirez's trial. Meanwhile, Yu crawled a short distance and then collapsed on the ground. When the police arrived, she was still alive, but barely. She stopped breathing moments later and officers offered assistance until an ambulance arrived – but it was too late. She died before she could be taken to the hospital. An autopsy revealed that she had been shot twice in the chest at close range. The .22-caliber bullet recovered from Yu's body was fired by the same gun as the one that killed Dayle Okazaki.

Ramirez's next victims were found a few days later, on the morning of March 27. Vincent Zazzara, 64, was a retired investment banker who had opened his own pizza place. His son, Peter, came to visit that morning and after ringing the bell several times with no answer, he let himself into the house. His father's body was found on a couch in the den. He had been shot in the head. Vincent Zazzara's wife, Maxine, 44, was found naked on the bed. Her eyes had been torn out and she had been stabbed repeatedly in the face, neck, stomach, and groin. She had also been shot in the head. Mercifully, the coroner believed that she was already dead when Ramirez began stabbing and mutilating her. The house had been ransacked and burglarized.

On April 15, Ramirez returned to Monterey Park and broke into the home of William and Lillian Doi, entering their bedroom while they slept. Ramirez first shot William Doi in the face, the bullet passing through his tongue and becoming lodged in his throat. Then Ramirez beat him into unconsciousness. Lillian Doi was slapped into submission and then Ramirez bound her hands behind her back as he searched the house. Before he left, he returned to the bedroom and raped her. However, he had not killed her husband, who managed to crawl from his bed and dial the police. He was unable to tell the dispatcher what had happened, but the call was traced and an ambulance and patrol car were dispatched to the Doi's address. William Doi died in the ambulance on the way to the hospital. Lillian Doi was treated for her injuries and was able to give the police a description of the couple's attacker.

As the attacks continued, Los Angeles was plunged into a state of panic. One police official referred to the murderous rapist as the "Valley Intruder," while newspapers initially referred to him as the "Midnight Stalker." Meanwhile, Ramirez

Richard Ramirez

was just getting started with his bloody spree.

On May 29, police officers found Malvia Keller, 83, and her invalid sister, Blanche Wolfe, 80, in their Monrovia home. Both women had been beaten severely with a hammer and Wolfe had a puncture wound above one ear. An inverted pentagram had been drawn in lipstick on Keller's inner thigh. A second pentagram was found on the bedroom wall over Wolfe's body. Ramirez had raped Keller, the older sister. Forensics showed that the sisters had been attacked about two days before they were found. Doctors were able to revive Wolfe, but Keller died soon afterwards.

On May 30, Ramirez entered the Burbank home of Ruth Wilson, 41, and awakened her by shining a flashlight in her face. He ordered her out of bed at gunpoint and marched her to the bedroom of her 12-year-old son. Ramirez put the gun to the child's head, warning Wilson not to make a sound. He then handcuffed the boy and locked him in a closet. Assuming that he was only a burglar, Ruth tried to cooperate but Ramirez tied her up with pantyhose and raped her on her bed. Bravely, she told Ramirez that he must have had a "very unhappy life" to have done this to her. He reportedly told her that she looked "pretty good" for her age and said he was going to let her live although he had killed many others. She complained that the pantyhose that he tied her up with was cutting off the circulation in her arms and Ramirez loosened them, and then brought her a robe before releasing her son from the closet. He handcuffed them side-by-side and departed. The boy was able to get to the phone and call 911.

On July 2, the body of Mary Louise Cannon, 75, was found in her Arcadia home. She had been beaten and her throat slit. The house had been ransacked.

On July 5, Ramirez returned to Arcadia and savagely beat Whitney Bennett, 16, a junior at La Cañada High School, with a tire iron. Whitney required 478 stitches after the attack, but she survived. Two days later, on July 7, the body of Joyce Lucille Nelson was found in her home in Monterey Park. She had been beaten to death with a blunt object.

Later that same night in Monterey Park, Sophie Dickman, 63, was awakened at around 3:30 a.m. by a "tall, skinny man dressed in black." The man ordered her out of bed at gunpoint and locked her in the bathroom. After he ransacked the house, he returned and pushed her back onto the bed. He attempted to rape and sodomize her but could not maintain an erection. Frustrated and humiliated, he screamed at her furiously, and then gathered up her valuables and left. Sophie was amazed that she had survived the encounter.

On July 20, Ramirez showed up in Glendale. He entered the home of Max and Lela Kneiding, both 66, who had been following the crimes in the news. Although all of the windows and doors of the home were locked, Ramirez cut through a screen on a sliding door and unlocked it. He entered the bedroom, turned on the lights and began to scream. With a machete, he hacked at Max's neck and then swung at Lela, but missed. He pulled his .22-caliber pistol from his pocket and pulled the trigger, but the gun jammed. As his victims begged for their lives, Ramirez cleared the gun and shot them to death. Then, he horrifically cut them apart and mutilated them with the machete. He robbed the house and this time, Ramirez had a police scanner with him and fled when a report of shots being fired came over the radio.

On August 6, Ramirez targeted another couple, Christopher and Virginia Petersen, ages 38 and 27. He entered again through a sliding door and slipped into the house. Just before he entered the bedroom, he cocked a .25 automatic pistol. Virginia, a light sleeper, awoke to the sound. As Ramirez walked toward her, she screamed and he shot her in the face. The bullet went through the roof of her mouth and down her throat; exiting out the back of her neck. Christopher Petersen awoke to the commotion and Ramirez shot him in the temple. However, the ammunition in the gun was old and had lost its potency. The bullet only glanced off Petersen's skull. He jumped up and attacked Ramirez, who shot at him two more times. Both shots missed and as they fought, Petersen was thrown onto the floor. Ramirez fled the house through the open sliding door. The Petersens both survived the attack.

Two nights later, Ramirez attacked again. He broke into the home of Elyas and Sakina Abowath, 35 and 29. He immediately shot Elyas in the head and killed him, and then attacked Sakina. He raped and sodomized her and forced her to perform oral sex on him. He left the house after robbing it, leaving Sakina battered but alive.

Los Angeles County was terrorized by the brutal attacks and murders. The "Night Stalker" crimes were becoming more and more frequent and each attack seemed bloodier than the last. Detectives had no doubt that he would strike again – and soon. But as it turned out, Ramirez decided to abandon familiar territory and after the attack on the Abowaths, he headed north to San Francisco.

On August 18, Peter and Barbara Pan were found in their blood-soaked bed in a housing development in San Francisco. Both had been shot in the head. Peter, 66, was pronounced dead at the scene but Barbara, 64, survived, although she was an invalid for the rest of her life. Ramirez had scrawled another inverted pentagram on the wall, along with the words "Jack the Knife," which was from a song called "The Ripper" by heavy metal band Judas Priest. Fearing that the "Night Stalker" had traveled north, San Francisco detectives sent a bullet removed from Peter Pan to a forensic team in L.A. The bullet matched those recovered from earlier Los Angeles crime scenes.

"Night Stalker" panic had now spread to San Francisco. Hoping to allay the fears of the public, Mayor Dianne Feinstein spoke publicly about the hunt for the killer, angering detectives who felt that she gave out too much information about the crimes, impeding the investigation. But the San Francisco police caught a break when the manager of the Bristol Hotel, a cheap dive in the Tenderloin District, came forward with information about a young man who fit the "Night Stalker's" description and who had stayed in the place several times over the past year. Detectives searched the room he had last stayed in (he had checked out on August 17) and found a pentagram drawn on the bathroom door. Investigators then located a man who said that he had purchased some jewelry – a diamond ring and a pair of cufflinks – from a man who fit the killer's description. The items had belonged to Peter Pan.

On August 24, while San Francisco cops were scrambling to find the mysterious tenant of the Bristol Hotel, Ramirez was targeting new victims in Mission Viejo, about 50 miles south of Los Angeles.

Bill Carns and his 29-year-old fiancée had just fallen asleep when they were suddenly shocked into consciousness by the sound of gunshots in their bedroom. Instinctively, the young woman reached for her fiancée, but he had already been seriously wounded. Before she could react, the intruder grabbed her by the hair and dragged her into another bedroom, where he tied her wrists and ankles. He rummaged through the house, looking for small items to steal, but found little that was portable. Angry, Ramirez returned to the bedroom and raped the young woman two times.

Afraid of what he might do to her next, she tried to get him to take some money that Carns had in a dresser drawer. Ramirez forced her to "swear to Satan" that she was telling the truth about the money. She did as he asked and Ramirez found the money. He then demanded that she swear her love for Satan. Terrified, she mumbled, "I love Satan." He ordered her to say it again and again. He yanked her by the hair, made her kneel and then forced her to perform oral sex on him. When finished, Ramirez pushed her back on the floor and left her there. As soon as she could free herself from her bindings, she immediately called the police.

Ramirez didn't know it yet, but his days of chaos were numbered.

Earlier that night, a teenager who had been working on his motorcycle in his parent's garage had noticed an unfamiliar orange Toyota driving around the neighborhood. He noticed it again later on. Something about the car and the driver made him suspicious, so he wrote down the license plate number. The next morning, he called the police and it was discovered that the 1976 Toyota had been stolen in L.A.'s Chinatown while the owner was having dinner. An alert was put out for the car and, two days later, it was located in the Rampart section of Los Angeles. The police kept the car under surveillance in hopes that the "Night Stalker" would return for it, but he didn't. A forensics teams scoured the car and came up with a fingerprint that was matched a few hours later. The print belonged to Ricardo "Richard" Ramirez and it matched a print that had been lifted from the windowsill of the Pan's home in San Francisco. The police finally had an identity for the dreaded "Night Stalker" – now they needed to find him before he killed again.

While all of this was going on, Ramirez had gone to Arizona to visit his brother. He returned to L.A. on August 31, arriving at the Greyhound bus station. As he was leaving the station, he noticed that the area was flooded with cops but managed to slip away unnoticed. He had no idea that he had been identified as the "Night Stalker." However, as he walked into a corner store, the owners recognized him and shouted in alarm. Ramirez turned to run and saw a newspaper rack that had his face on several covers. He grabbed one of them and ran.

Ramirez ran for the next two miles, heading east from downtown. He hopped fences and ended up in the yard of Faustino Pinon. Spotting a Ford Mustang in the driveway, with the keys in the ignition, he jumped in and started the engine. But he didn't notice that the car's owner was underneath it, working on the transmission. As soon as Pinon heard the car start up, he rolled out from under it. Angry, he reached through the window and grabbed Ramirez by the neck. Ramirez cried out that he had a gun, but Pinon ignored him. Ramirez put the Mustang into gear and tried to drive away, but Pinon refused to let go of him. The car crashed into a fence, then into the garage.

Pinon got the door open, pulled Ramirez out, and threw him onto the ground. Ramirez crawled away and then scrambled to his feet. He fled out into the street just as a young woman named Angelina de la Torres was getting into her Ford Granada. Ramirez ran to the car and stuck his head into the driver's window, demanding that she give him the keys, stating that he would kill her if she didn't. Angelina screamed for help and her husband, Manuel, came running from the backyard. He grabbed a piece of metal fence post as he passed through the gate next to the house.

At the same time, Jose Burgoin, who had heard the struggle in Faustino Pinon's driveway, had called the police. He ran outside to help Pinon, and when he heard Angelina's scream, he called to his sons, Jaime and Julio, for assistance. As the brothers ran to help Angelina, they saw the stranger climbing across the front seat of her car. Jaime recognized him from photographs on television and yelled that this was the killer, and the men made a mad dash to catch him. Ramirez ran, but Manuel de la Torres caught up with him and hit him across the neck with the metal post he was still carrying. Ramirez tried to keep running but Manuel hit him again and again. Jaime Burgoin caught up with Ramirez and punched him. Ramirez stumbled and fell, but quickly got up and continued running with Manuel and the two Burgoin boys right behind him. Finally, one of Manuel's swings struck him in the head and the "Night Stalker" collapsed on the ground. Jaime and Jose kept him there until the police arrived. Ramirez turned out to be no match for these stubborn and determined men.

One day after Ramirez's face was presented to the public, the "Night Stalker" was behind bars. When he was arrested, Ramirez was charged with 14 murders and 31 other felonies related to his 1985 crime spree. He was also charged with a 15th murder in San Francisco and rape and attempted murder charges in Orange County.

Ramirez was brought to trial on July 22, 1988 and on September 20, 1989, he was found guilty on 13 counts of murder, 5 attempted murders, 11 sexual assaults, and 14 burglaries. During the penalty phase of the trial on November 7, 1989, he was sentenced to death in California's gas chamber. The trial was one of the most difficult and longest criminal trials in American history. Nearly 1,600 prospective jurors were interviewed and more than 100 witnesses testified. Ramirez performed for the press throughout the proceedings, playing up the "Satanic" angle of his crime spree. He flashed the palm of his hand, where he had etched a pentagram, and on other occasions, as he sat listening to the prosecutors, he placed two upturned fingers on either side of his head to indicated horns and chanted, "evil... evil... evil."

By the time of his trail, Ramirez had twisted fans who were writing him letters and paying him visits. A freelance magazine editor named Doreen Lioy wrote him more than 75 letters after his 1985 incarceration. In 1988, he proposed to her and on October 3, 1996, they were married at San Quentin. Lioy has stated that she plans to commit suicide when Ramirez is executed – which might finally occur sooner, rather than later. In 2006, the California State Supreme Court ended his first round of appeals by upholding his convictions and death sentence.

He remains on Death Row today, awaiting what will hopefully be the inevitable.

2. HAUNTED HOLLYWOOD HOTSPOTS WHERE THE STARS STILL LINGER

No chronicle of the hauntings of Hollywood's scandals, murders, and unsolved mysteries would be complete without a short look at some of the places that played an important role in the lives of those whose spirits still linger in Tinseltown today. The movie studios, the theaters, the hotels, and notorious nightspots are a large part of what caused Hollywood to capture the imagination of the American public in a way that no other place ever has.

HOLLYWOOD'S HAUNTED MOVIE STUDIOS

For nearly a century, the movie studios of Hollywood have entranced, mystified, and entertained us with their visions of life. Sometimes real, sometimes tragic, and always spectacular, American motion pictures have enthralled generations of moviegoers. Some of the most popular films to be released have been those dealing with the dark side -- ghosts, monsters and the supernatural. Not surprisingly, many of the movie studios where such films have been made have their own tales of ghost and hauntings.

Most believe ghosts to be the spirits of the dead who are unable to find their way to the next plane of existence. Or perhaps these spirits refused to cross over so that they can complete some piece of business left undone in this world. They may want to pass along vital information to someone or perhaps their life ended so abruptly they don't feel as though they got a chance to complete everything that needed to be finished.

In Hollywood, the need to continue a life that was cut short seems to be a common theme for ghosts. The local spirits seem to give meaning to the classic "theater ghost," a former actor or director who never was able to complete that final "big show" during their lifetime and for this reason remains behind to haunt the place where they knew the most happiness. In other cases, the lingering spirits are those who may have been killed in an accident while working on a film and simply never departed from this world to the next.

Working during the night at some of Hollywood's older movie studios can be an interesting experience. According to reports from security guards and technicians, it can also be a hair-raising one. In the words of one long-time employee, "I've seen some things here that I

Nestor Studio, Hollywood's first movie studio

wouldn't want to try and explain to anyone!"

The first Hollywood movie studios can all be traced back to a spot called Gower's Gulch. In 1869, a farmer named John T. Gower came to California and bought a 160-acre tract of land in what is now Hollywood. Today, the intersection of Sunset Boulevard and the street named in Gower's honor is bracketed by movie industry restaurants and hangouts. But when Hollywood was just getting started, the corner of Sunset Boulevard and Gower Street was the start of everything that would eventually grow into the single most important influence on popular culture as we know it: America's film and television industry.

The first Hollywood stage set was built exactly on this spot, at the northwest corner of what was then a dusty, unpaved intersection. In 1911, the first movie that was made here was "The Law of the Range" by producers William and David Horseley. It was called Nestor Studio and the owners paid $30 a month for the property, which included a barn used for props, a corral for horses, and several smaller buildings, including a bungalow that was turned into offices. Nestor quickly established a method of film production that would be used in the industry for years: crank 'em out fast. Two or more one-reelers were shot at the same time using a single stage that had a different background at each end. Most of the scripts were written the night before the shoot.

Nestor Studios may have filmed the first movie in a Hollywood studio, but it was not the first picture to be filmed in Hollywood. In 1910, D.W. Griffith had shot "In Old California," a melodrama that was set in Mexican California in the 1800s. The company stayed in Hollywood for a few months and made several films before returning to New York.

Regardless, the establishment of Nestor Studios, as well as the Biograph films shot by Griffith, began attracting film companies and performers to the California sunshine. Within a few months, the intersection of Gower and Sunset became the center of working Hollywood. So many small and struggling film companies started along Gower that it was dubbed "Poverty Row," or, perhaps more politely, "Gower Gulch." During the 'teens and early 1920s, dozens of these small studios like Sterling,

Monogram Pictures on "Poverty Row"

Dead Men Do Tell Tales: Bloody Hollywood - Page 82

Waldorf, Quality, and Goodwill Studios barely existed there, always on the edge of bankruptcy, churning out one and two-reel films. "Poverty Row" was also home to studios like Republic and Monogram, which became popular for their low-budget films in the 1930s and 1940s.

The origin of the name "Gower Gulch" has been the subject of a lot of speculation over the years. Some believe that the high walls of the sound stages along Gower, south of Sunset, prompted the name. Others say that it's because so many westerns were made in the areas or because of a nearby ditch that once carried runoff from the Hollywood hills. Whatever the origin of the nickname, Gower Gulch's accessibility to all sorts of locations certainly enhanced its popularity among early filmmakers.

In 1920, Harry Cohn and his brother, Jack, located their fledging CBS Studio at the intersection and quickly changed the name to Columbia Pictures, fearing that CBC might seem like an acronym for "corned beef and cabbage." The soundstages remain there today, but are now leased as indoor sports facilities. On the Gower side of these soundstages, huge billboards once advertised the studio's latest productions, but they vanished into history when the studio moved its operations to Burbank.

Down Gower at Melrose were the soundstages of RKO Pictures, which released classic films like "King Kong," "Citizen Kane," the Fred Astaire-Ginger Rogers films of the 1930s, and scores of others. In its later years, RKO was taken over by maverick industrialist Howard Hughes and finally by the General Tire and Rubber Company. The original RKO Pictures ceased production in 1957 and was effectively dissolved two years later. RKO moved into the television age when Lucille Ball and Desi Arnaz used part of the studio for their DesiLu Productions. Their former building is now part of Paramount Studios.

A mile or so west of Gower on Santa Monica Boulevard was one of the most famous of Hollywood's early studios. It was erected in 1922 on the site of the Jesse B. Hampton Studio by America's most famous couple, Douglas Fairbanks and Mary Pickford. It was later expanded and became United Artists, a company founded by Fairbanks and Pickford, along with Charlie Chaplin and D.W. Griffith, to control distribution of their films. Later, it became Samuel Goldwyn Studios and now, it's a branch of Warner Brothers, which is itself headquartered in Burbank. In 1919, Charlie Chaplin built his own studio near the intersection of Sunset and La Brea and it still stands today as the home of Jim Henson Productions.

Just to the east of the intersection of Gower and Sunset is the headquarters of Los Angeles' independent television station, KTLA. Once belonging to Warner Brothers, this is where the "The Jazz Singer," the first successful sound picture, was made in 1927. The huge studio of 20th Century Fox was once located a little farther east, at the intersection of Sunset Boulevard and Western Avenue. In the middle 1930s, Fox moved everything to its back lot in West Los Angeles, most of which has subsequently been developed as the shopping and office community known as Century City. The original site was turned into an equally huge discount food market.

There is no question that this area was the heart of the Hollywood film industry for many years. All around "Gower Gulch" were countless satellite industries, among them costumers, film laboratories, camera rental companies, and prop houses, as well as the offices for the media that covered the industry like *Variety* and the *Hollywood Reporter*. Like some of the studios and production companies, many of them remain today.

UNIVERSAL STUDIOS

The founder of Universal was Carl Laemmle, a German Jewish immigrant who settled in Oshkosh, Wisc., where he managed a clothing store. On a 1905 buying trip to Chicago he was struck by the popularity of nickelodeons. Within weeks of his Chicago trip, he gave up dry goods to buy the first of several nickelodeons. For Laemmle and other such entrepreneurs, the creation in 1908 of the Edison-backed Motion Picture Trust meant that exhibitors were expected to pay fees for any Trust-produced film they showed. The trust also managed to collect fees for any films shown using equipment

(Left) Universal Studios entrance (Right) Carl Laemmle and Carl Laemmle, Jr.

that Edison had a patent for, which effectively created a monopoly on distribution.

Soon Laemmle and other disgruntled nickelodeon owners decided to avoid paying Edison by producing their own pictures. In June 1909, Laemmle started the Yankee Film Company with partners Abe and Julius Stern. That company quickly evolved into the Independent Moving Picture Company, or IMP. Edison never believed in giving credit to the actors in the films, but Laemmle changed that. By naming his stars, he was able to attract some of the leading performers of the day. In 1910, he promoted Florence Lawrence, then known as the "Biograph Girl," and this may have been the first instance of a studio using a film star in its marketing.

In June 1912, Laemmle merged IMP with eight smaller companies to form the Universal Film Manufacturing Company. Laemmle was the primary figure in the partnership and eventually, he bought out everyone else. The new Universal studio was not only a movie production company, but handled distribution, as well. The company was incorporated as Universal Pictures Company, Inc. in 1925.

By 1912, Universal had moved to Hollywood and in 1915, Laemmle opened the world's largest motion picture production facility, Universal City Studios, on a 230-acre farm just over the Cahuenga Pass from Hollywood. Unlike other movie moguls, Laemmle opened his studio to tourists. Universal became the biggest studio in Hollywood, and remained so for a decade.

Unlike many other studio heads of the time, Laemmle chose not to develop a theater chain. He also financed all of his own films, refusing to take on debt. This policy nearly bankrupted the studio several times when directors insisted on excessive and over-the-top productions, but Universal managed to get most of its money back by launching sensational ad campaigns that brought huge crowds into the theaters.

In 1928, Laemmle made his son, Carl, Jr., head of Universal Pictures as a 21st birthday present. Universal already had a reputation for nepotism; at one time, 70 of Laemmle's relatives were on the company payroll. To his credit, though, the younger Laemmle persuaded his father to bring Universal up to date. He bought and built theaters, converted the studio to sound production, and made several forays into high-quality production. His early efforts included the 1929 part-talkie version of "Show Boat," the lavish musical, which included Technicolor sequences and "All Quiet on the Western Front," winner of the Best Picture Academy Award for 1930. Laemmle, Jr. also created a successful niche for the studio, beginning a long-running series of monster movies, affectionately dubbed "Universal Horror." Among them were "Frankenstein," "Dracula," and "The Mummy."

Ironically, Universal's updates nearly broke the company. Taking on the task of modernizing and upgrading a film company in the depths of the Depression was risky, and for a time Universal slipped into receivership. The theater chain was scrapped, but Carl, Jr. held fast to distribution, studio and production operations. Soon, though, the Laemmles would lose control of the company. Forced by the company shareholders into taking out a loan to re-make "Showboat," Universal couldn't make the payments when the loan was called in by the Standard Capital Corporation. Standard foreclosed and seized control of the studio in April 1936. "Show Boat" was released later that same year and is widely considered to be one of the greatest film musicals of all time. However, it was not enough to save the Laemmles, who were kicked out of the company they had created.

The new studio heads instituted severe cuts in production budgets. By the start of World War II, the company was concentrating on smaller-budget productions: westerns, melodramas, serials, and sequels to the studio's horror classics. Since Universal couldn't afford its own stable of stars, the company often borrowed talent from other studios, or hired freelance actors. James Stewart, Marlene Dietrich, and Bing Crosby were some of the major names who made pictures for Universal during this period. Some stars came from radio, including W. C. Fields, Edgar Bergen, and the comedy team of Abbott and Costello (Bud Abbott and Lou Costello.) The comedy team's military film "Buck Privates" (1941) was a huge success and made them two of the biggest movie stars in America, finally improving Universal's bottom line.

During the war years Universal focused on low-budget films that were geared toward the neighborhood theaters of America. The general public was pleased with comedies, musicals, adventures, westerns, and serials. The studio also fostered a number of series: The "Dead End Kids" and "Little Tough Guys" action features and serials, the comic adventures of infant Baby Sandy, Hugh Herbert comedies, horror thrillers bringing back Frankenstein, Dracula, The Wolfman, The Invisible Man, and The Mummy, Basil Rathbone and Nigel Bruce in Sherlock Holmes mysteries (1942-46), teenage musicals with Gloria Jean, Donald O'Connor, and Peggy Ryan (1942-43), and screen adaptations of radio's "Inner Sanctum" Mysteries. Since Universal made mostly low-budget films for many years, it was one of the last major studios to begin using full Technicolor in the middle and late 1940s.

In 1945, Universal was re-organized again and its new heads tried to bring prestige to the company by stopping the studio's low-budget productions, including "B" musicals, comedies, and westerns and serials, and curtailing Universal's famous monster films and series. The company became responsible for the distribution of a number of British productions, including such screen classics as David Lean's "Great Expectations" and Laurence Olivier's "Hamlet."

Production at Universal struggled. While there were a few hits like "The Egg & I," "The Killers," and "The Naked City," the new theatrical films often met with a disappointing response at the box office. By the late 1940s, the studio reverted to the low-budget fare it knew best. The inexpensive "Francis the Talking Mule" and "Ma and Pa Kettle" series became mainstays of the new company. Once again, the films of Abbott and Costello were among the studio's top-grossing productions.

By the late 1950s, the motion picture business was in trouble. The rise of television saw a large part of the audience drift away from theaters. After a period of complete shutdown, Universal agreed to sell its studio lot to MCA in 1958, for $11 million. Although MCA owned the studio lot, but not

Universal Pictures, it was increasingly influential on Universal's product. The studio lot was upgraded and modernized, while MCA clients like Doris Day, Lana Turner, and Cary Grant were signed to Universal Pictures contracts.

The actual, long-awaited takeover of Universal Pictures by MCA, Inc. finally took place in mid-1962. With MCA now in charge, Universal became what it had never really been: a full-blown, first-class movie studio with leading actors and directors under contract, offering slick, commercial films; and a studio tour subsidiary that it started in 1964. But it was too late, since the audience was no longer there, and by 1968, the film-production unit began to downsize. Television was now dominating the studio. Universal was all over the American networks, especially NBC, and for several seasons, provided more than half of the prime-time shows.

Though Universal's film unit did produce occasional hits, among them "Airport," "The Sting," "American Graffiti," "Earthquake," and the first real summer blockbuster, "Jaws," Universal in the 1970s was primarily a television studio. There would be other film hits like "E.T: The Extra-Terrestrial," "Back to the Future," and "Jurassic Park," but overall the film business was still questionable for the company.

In the years that followed, control of Universal changed several times, being bought out by companies as diverse as Matsushita Electronics and the Canadian liquor distributor, Seagram. In June 2000, Seagram itself was sold to French water utility and media company Vivendi, which owns StudioCanal. Universal then acquired the rights to several of StudioCanal's films, such as "Mulholland Drive" and "Brotherhood of the Wolf."

Loaded down by debt, Vivendi sold 80 percent of Universal to General Electric, the parent company of NBC, in 2004. The resulting conglomerate remains NBC Universal today. Over the years, Universal has made deals to distribute and co-finance films with various small companies, such as Imagine Entertainment, Amblin Entertainment, Morgan Creek Productions, Working Title Films, StudioCanal, and many others. Thanks to this, Universal remains a powerful and integral part of Hollywood, carrying on a legacy that dates all of the way back to the beginnings of the film colony.

The hauntings that have been reported at Universal Studios have their roots in the early days of the company. Universal, located in Burbank, has brought movie audiences some of the greatest horror films of all times. In the 1930s, such screen fare as "Dracula," "Frankenstein" and "The Mummy" thrilled and terrified the public and all of these films are considered classics today. These films created stars of men like Bela Lugosi, Boris Karloff and Lon Chaney, who ushered in Universal's heyday in the 1920s with such films as "The Phantom of the Opera."

Chaney was dubbed "The Man of a Thousand Faces" and he became one of the most versatile and powerful screen actors of the silent era. The actor was so respected that, when he died on August 26, 1930, every studio in Hollywood observed two minutes of silence.

Lon Chaney was born on April 1, 1883, in Colorado Springs, Colo. Both of Chaney's parents

Lon Chaney, "Man of a Thousand Faces"

were deaf, so as a child, Lon became adept at pantomime, a skill that would serve him well in the early film industry. He started his stage career in 1902, traveling on the vaudeville circuit of the day. In 1905, he met and married a singer named Cleva Creighton and a year later, their first child and only son, Creighton Chaney (a.k.a. Lon Chaney, Jr.) was born. The Chaney family continued touring with vaudeville shows but, in 1910, they settled in Southern California.

Unfortunately, marital troubles developed between the Chaneys and in April 1913, Cleva went to the Majestic Theater in downtown L.A., where Lon was managing the Kolb & Dill Show, and tried to commit suicide by swallowing mercury dichloride. The suicide attempt failed and it ruined Cleva's singing career. Divorce and scandal followed, forcing Chaney out of the theater and into the fledgling film business.

Until about 1917, Chaney worked for Universal Studios, doing bit and character parts. His outstanding skill with makeup gained the attention of directors and led to many roles that he might not have gotten otherwise. While working at Universal, he became friends with the husband-wife director team of Joe De Grasse and Ida May Parke, who offered him substantial roles in their films and encouraged him to play macabre characters.

During this time, Chaney married Hazel Hastings, a chorus girl from the Kolb & Dill touring company. While little is known about Hazel, their marriage was a happy one and the new couple soon gained custody of Chaney's 10-year-old son, Creighton, who had been living in various homes and boarding schools since his parents' divorce.

Chaney continued to make small gains in his quest to be recognized as a prominent actor. He was featured in a substantial role in the William S. Hart picture "Riddle Gawne" in 1918 but his real breakthrough came in 1919 when he played a character called "The Frog" in George Loane Tucker's "The Miracle Man." The film not only showed off Chaney's acting ability, but his talent as a master of makeup. The critical praise and commercial success of the film elevated Chaney to the status of America's foremost character actor.

Chaney is chiefly remembered as a pioneer in such silent horror films as "The Hunchback of Notre Dame" and many others. His ability to transform himself using self-invented makeup techniques earned him the nickname of "The Man of a Thousand Faces.", He exhibited this ability with makeup in a number of films, including "The Penalty" where he played an amputee gangster. He appeared in a total of 10 films for director Tod Browning, often playing bizarre or mutilated characters, including carnival knife thrower Alonzo the Armless in "The Unknown," with Joan Crawford. In 1927, Chaney starred in the now-lost Tod Browning horror film "London After Midnight," which is quite possibly the most famous lost film ever. His last film was a talkie remake of his silent classic, "The Unholy Three." This was the only film in which he also displayed his versatile voice. In fact, Chaney signed a sworn statement declaring that five of the key voices in the film (the ventriloquist, old woman, parrot, dummy and girl) were in fact his own.

Chaney was a beloved figure in early Hollywood. He and Hazel led a discreet private life, distant from the Hollywood social scene, although he was quick to make friends and was respected by other actors and crewmembers alike. He earned the respect and admiration of up and coming actors by helping them out, showing them the ropes, and by always being willing to talk to the cast and crew about his experiences between takes. Chaney's role as a tough Marine drill instructor in "Tell it to the Marines," one of his favorite films, earned him the affection of the U.S. Marine Corps, who made him the first honorary member of the corps from the motion picture industry.

During the filming of "Thunder" in the winter of 1929, Chaney developed pneumonia and a short time later, he was diagnosed with bronchial lung cancer. Despite aggressive treatment, his condition gradually worsened, and seven weeks after the release of the remake of "The Unholy Three," Chaney died. His death was deeply mourned by his family, the film industry and by his fans. The U.S. Marine Corps provided a chaplain and an honor guard for his funeral. He was interred at Forest Lawn Cemetery and fellow actor Wallace Beery

Lon Chaney in his most famous role as Erik, the "Phantom of the Opera"

flew his plane over the funeral and dropped floral wreaths. It was a sad and tragic ending for an actor of such immense talent.

But have we heard the last from "The Man of a Thousand Faces?"

Chaney worked under contract for Universal Studios from 1912 to 1917, doing small character roles. He returned to the company in 1924 to create the role that he is perhaps best known for, "The Phantom of the Opera." Released in 1925, this film became Chaney's masterpiece and a special stage was constructed, Stage 28, for the filming of the movie. The massive set of the opera house was so gigantic that construction began on Stage 28 in 1923, two years before the film's release and it has gone on to become a permanent fixture on the Universal lot. Some believe that Lon Chaney has become a permanent fixture, as well.

Visitors to Stage 28, along with employees who have worked there, have long maintained that it is haunted. For years, there have been sightings by electricians, designers, carpenters, art directors, and security guards of a man in a black cape who seems to come and go without warning. Those who have gotten more than just a glimpse of him say that the cloaked man is Lon Chaney himself.

In addition to studio employees, many visitors who do not know the history of Stage 28 have reported the man in the black cape. He is often seen running on the catwalks overhead. Even security guards who have laughed off the idea of a resident ghost, admit to being "spooked" by lights that turn on and off by themselves and by doors that open and close on the empty stage at night.

It's possible that Chaney still continues to make his presence known at Stage 28, the scene of his greatest screen triumph, perhaps unable to let go of the life that he once knew and that was taken away from him far too soon.

CULVER STUDIOS

Culver Studios remains one of Hollywood's most historic studios. Located in Culver City, it was the site of filming for "Gone With the Wind," "Citizen Kane" and other classics. Over the years, the film lot has been home to such names as RKO, Howard Hughes, and DesiLu Studios. In addition to film classics, Culver Studios was also the birthplace to favorite television shows like "The Andy Griffith Show," "Lassie," "Hogan's Heroes," and "Batman." Previous owners of the studios have included Cecil B. DeMille and eccentric billionaire Howard Hughes.

Culver Studios was started in 1918 by pioneer Hollywood filmmaker Thomas Ince, a man considered to be the "Father of the Western" and the man who introduced the world to Mary Pickford by making her "America's Sweetheart." Ince rose from a $15 a week actor to become the head of a studio and to this day, still has a street named after him in Culver City: Ince Boulevard.

In 1915, Ince partnered with D.W. Griffith and Mack Sennett to create the Triangle Motion Picture Company in Culver City. Somewhere along the way, the deal went sour and Ince sold out and entered into a lease with Harry Culver for a new 14-acre studio fronting on Washington Boulevard. It

(Left) Pioneering film maker Thomas Ince (Right) Culver Studios

took two years to build the Thomas H. Ince Studio, and in December 1918, a Los Angeles newspaper called it "a motion picture plant that looks like a beautiful southern estate." Ince, a visionary in the industry, promoted the glamour of moviemaking and he entertained the King and Queen of Belgium and President Woodrow Wilson at the studios. The administration building became a well-known landmark and Ince was rapidly expanding his successful facility.

Unfortunately, it was not meant to last – and neither was Ince's revered status. Sadly, Ince is remembered much more today for his scandalous death than for his contribution to the art of movie making. Ince died in November 1924 while celebrating his birthday on board a yacht owned by newspaper magnate William Randolph Hearst. The real story of how Ince died will never be known -- but Hollywood rumors tell a strange and twisted tale.

Ince's mysterious death will forever be linked to Marion Davies and William Randolph Hearst, the greatest newspaper baron and one of the most powerful men in American history. By the 1920s, Hearst had also become a major film financier, as well. He had first become interested in film through newsreels in 1911, but soon his hobby turned to a quest for profit. It was not long before his zeal for the movies was enhanced due to his passion for furthering the film career of sweet, but untalented, film actress Marion Davies, with whom Hearst had been carrying on a notorious affair. Hearst bought stock in MGM and created Cosmopolitan Productions, a company that specifically produced Marion's films. His newspapers and magazines proclaimed her to be a "miracle of the movies" and he did everything he could to entrench her into the Hollywood film colony.

Parties thrown at Marion's beach house were the most extravagant in town and people grabbed at the chance of an invitation to a Hearst affair. In addition, being able to relax at Hearst's vast mansion in San Simeon, with millions of dollars worth of imported furnishings, tapestries, paintings, and 35 automobiles in the garage, was a must for anyone lucky enough to get an invitation for the weekend. Marion also earned high marks as a hostess, even if privately the party attendees made fun at her attempts at acting on the screen.

Another popular party spot was Hearst's 280-foot yacht, the *Oneida*. Invitations to the boat were even more highly coveted than those for the beach

William Randolph Hearst & Marion Davies

house parties. On the night of Saturday, November 15, 1924, the yacht left San Pedro Harbor for a weekend cruise to San Diego. The cream of Hollywood's charmed circle received invitations to a party on board the Oneida that weekend. There were a number of guests on board, but the only names that became available after the party were Hearst, Mario Davies, actress Seena Owen and author Elinor Glynn. That weekend marked the 43rd birthday of Thomas Ince, who was in the midst of negotiations with Hearst concerning the use of his Culver City studios as a base for Cosmopolitan Productions. It had been planned to throw Ince a birthday party on board the yacht. Mrs. Ince, who had also been invited, decided not to go along on the trip because she was not feeling well.

Ince, the guest of honor, missed the boat when it sailed from San Pedro because of his attendance at the premiere of "The Mirage," his latest film. It is believed that he took the last train to San Diego, where he met the *Oneida*, and joined the party for the return trip. The celebration on board was said to be a wonderful occasion, but then things got murky.

In the early morning hours of the following Wednesday, Thomas Ince died at his Benedict Canyon home. His death was attributed to "heart failure."

When the news reached the press, all sorts of ugly rumors began to circulate, as well as a hash of conflicting stories. Things became so heated that Chester Kemply, the District Attorney in San Diego, where the yacht had been anchored for the weekend, was forced to open an investigation. The principals were all strangely absent at the hearings that followed. Hearst could not be reached for a statement. Marion, Elinor Glynn, and Seena Owen – the only names known for certain to have been on board – were not called by the D.A. to give testimony. The only person present at the hearing in San Diego was a doctor named Goodman, an employee of Hearst. His official version of events, which was printed in Hearst newspapers, stated that, after eating and drinking too much at the party, Ince died of "acute indigestion." He was taken from the yacht and rushed home, where he later died.

After the hearing, the case was closed. Originally, D.A. Kemply had insisted that he planned to call every single person who had been on board the yacht to give their version of events, but not only did he not call any of them, he suddenly, after just the one session, called off all further inquiry altogether. He was satisfied that Ince's death had been explained – but others were not.

In Long Beach, a columnist named C.F.

Adelsperger wrote, "At the risk of losing something of a reputation as a prophet, the writer will predict that some day one of the scandal-scented mysteries in filmdom will be cleared up. Motion picture circles have suffered alike from scandals and rumors of scandal. Deaths from violence or mysterious sources have been hinted at but never proved. If there is any foundation for suspicioning that Thomas Ince's death was from other than natural causes an investigation should be made in justice to the public as well as to those concerned. If there was liquor aboard a millionaire's yacht in San Diego Harbor, where Ince was taken ill, it should be investigated. A District Attorney who passes up the matter because he sees 'no reason' to investigate is the best agent the Bolshevists could employ in this country."

One of the strangest facts about the cruise was that no accurate list of the guests on board the ship that weekend has ever been revealed. There were obviously many more people on board than has ever been reported. Several well-known personalities of the film world have been mentioned as Heart's guests that weekend, but none of them ever publicly admitted to being on board the yacht. Of course, there were many rumors about who was there, just what actually occurred – and what really happened to cause the death of Thomas Ince.

Perhaps the most exciting rumor to make the rounds in Hollywood involved the presence of Ince's friend, Charlie Chaplin, on board the *Oneida* for the party. Rumor had it, however, that Chaplin had not been invited just because he was Ince's pal. Hearst was insanely jealous of other men's attention to Marion Davies and his detectives had recently informed him that Marion and Chaplin had been seen together during a period of time when he was out of town. Hearst allegedly invited the comedic actor on board the yacht for the weekend cruise so that he could observe for himself how Chaplin and Marion behaved around one another.

It is believed that Hearst saw Marion and Chaplin slip off together during the party and that he discovered them together on the lower deck. A loud altercation followed and Hearst ran for his cabin to retrieve a diamond-studded revolver that he kept on board. (Heart was rumored to be an expert shot and often amused his guests on the boat by shooting down seagulls with a single bullet.) In the confusion that followed, it was rumored a shot was fired but it was Thomas Ince, and not Chaplin, who ended up with a bullet in the head!

Ince's funeral was held on November 21, attended by his family, Marion Davies, Chaplin, Mary Pickford, Douglas Fairbanks, and Harold Lloyd. Hearst was noticeably absent. The body was immediately cremated and an official inquest was never held.

Despite the fact that the evidence was now in ashes, Hearst knew he could be in trouble with the Hollywood rumor mill. Everyone on board the *Oneida* was sworn to secrecy (and it wouldn't be wise to cross Hearst) but, in spite of this, persistent rumors linked Hearst to Ince's death. No one could resist talking about the way the hearings into Ince's death had been called off, the lack of an official inquest, or the damning story that Charlie Chaplin's secretary had seen Ince carried off the yacht bleeding from a bullet wound to the head.

Some thought it no coincidence that famed gossip columnist Louella Parsons was awarded a lifetime contract with Hearst soon after the incident since it was rumored that she had seen everything that had happened. Louella also felt the need to do a little covering up of her own and insisted that she had been in New York at the time of Ince's death. The only problem with this story was that Vera Burnett, Marion's stand-in, clearly recalled seeing Louella with Marion and Davies at the studio, ready for departure on the yacht. Vera valued her job, though, and decided not to make a big deal out of it.

Marion and Hearst managed to ride out the scandal unscathed, but as DW Griffith remarked in later years, "All you have to do to make Hearst turn white as a ghost is mention Ince's name. There's plenty wrong there, but Hearst is too big to touch." It was widely known in Hollywood that, if you ever wanted to attend another party at Marion's beach house or the San Simeon castle, you didn't mention Ince's name anyplace where Hearst might hear you.

In the years that followed, Hearst discreetly

provided Ince's widow, Nell, with a trust fund that was later wiped out by the Depression. Broke and penniless, Nell finished out her days as a taxi driver. As for Hearst, the entire affair was eventually reduced to a sardonic joke in Hollywood as the Oneida became known as "William Randolph's Hearse."

Strangely, though, death did not bring an end to sightings of Thomas Ince and his mysterious death also started rumors about Culver Studios being haunted. Ince built the studios, but they changed hands several times after his death. Cecil B. De Mille, Howard Hughes, David Selznick, Desi Arnaz and Lucille Ball made significant contributions to film and television history on this lot.

The rumors of the haunting have persisted for years. Employees have reported ghostly figures roaming the lot at night while others recount being frightened by the apparition of a woman who appears on the third floor from time to time. She always disappears quickly, leaving a cold spot of chilling wind behind.

Most famous, however, are the sightings of Thomas Ince himself. Witnesses have reported seeing the ghost of a man climbing the stairs in the main administration building, heading for the executive screening room. This had been Ince's private projection room during his tenure at the studio. Remodeling seemed to bring out the worst in Ince's ghost in 1988 when he began to reveal his displeasure over some major renovations.

The first to encounter him were two workmen who looked up to see a man in an odd, bowler-type hat watching them from the catwalks above Stage 1-2-3. When they spoke to him, he frowned and then turned and walked into the second floor wall. Later that summer, special-effects man Eugene Hilchey spoke to another worker who had also seen a man wearing an odd hat, this time on Stage 2-3-4. Hilchey was convinced the man's description matched that of Ince. The workers' statement was enough to cement his belief. The ghost had reportedly turned to the workmen and said, "I don't like what you're doing to my studio." Then he vanished into the wall.

Even after the renovations, much of Ince's original studio remains as it was and the sense of history here is very strong. Today, Culver Studios remains one of the busiest lots in town. Hopefully, Thomas Ince's spirit can find a little peace in that!

PARAMOUNT STUDIOS

Perhaps the most haunted of all of the Hollywood Studios is Paramount. Over the years, the ghostly sightings and strange reports have become as much a part of the legend of the place as the movies themselves. Being the last major studio to be actually located in Hollywood, Paramount makes the perfect setting for ghostly activity. It is located right next door to the Hollywood Forever Cemetery (formerly Hollywood Memorial Park,) which is no stranger to ghost stories itself, serving as the final resting place for stars like Rudolph Valentino, Douglas Fairbanks, and scores of others.

In fact, many of the stars who worked for Paramount are buried in the cemetery and the stories say that some of their spirits are still seen walking through the studio gates – or simply passing directly through the walls from one lot to the next. Apparently, when you love something as much as these former actors loved their work, it is hard to separate yourself from it. Even death is not powerful enough to keep them away.

Paramount Pictures can trace its beginning to the creation of the Famous Players Film Company in May 1912. Founder Hungarian-born Adolph Zukor, who had been an early investor in nickelodeons, put together a company that planned to offer feature films that were aimed at the middle class, starring the leading theatrical players of the day. The company's slogan was "famous players in famous plays." By the middle of 1913, Famous Players had completed five films and Zukor was on his way to a successful career.

That same year, another aspiring producer, Jesse L. Lasky, opened the Lasky Feature Play Company with money that he borrowed from his brother-in-law, Samuel Goldfish (who later became known as Samuel Goldwyn.) The first employee hired by the Lasky Company was an inexperienced stage director who knew nothing about film named Cecil B. DeMille. He was given the task of finding a suitable location site in Hollywood, near Los Angeles, for the company's first film.

Beginning in 1914, both Lasky and Famous Players released their films through a start-up company, Paramount Pictures Corporation, which had been organized early that year by a Utah theater owner named W.W. Hodkinson. By buying out and merging several smaller firms, Paramount became the first successful national distributor.

The ambitious Zukor soon began working deals with Hodkinson and Lasky. In 1916, Zukor managed a three-way merger of his Famous Players, the Lasky Company, and Paramount Pictures. The new company, Famous Players-Lasky Corporation, grew quickly with Lasky and his partners, Goldfish and DeMille, running the production side, Hiram Abrams in charge of distribution, and Zukor making big plans. With the only other competition being First National, Famous Players-Lasky and its "Paramount Pictures" soon dominated the movie business.

From the very beginning, Zukor believed that having famous actors in his films was the key to success. With this in mind, he signed and developed many of the leading early stars, among them Mary Pickford, Douglas Fairbanks, Gloria Swanson, Rudolph Valentino, and Wallace Reid. With so many important players, Paramount was able to introduce "block booking," which meant that an exhibitor who wanted a particular star's films had to buy a year's worth of other Paramount productions. This questionable business practice gave Paramount a leading position in the 1920s and 1930s, but it also led to the government pursuing the studio for anti-trust violations for more than two decades.

There was no question that the driving force behind Paramount's rise was Adolph Zukor.

The main gates at Paramount Studios

Adolph Zukor

Throughout the 1910s and 1920s, he built a theater chain of nearly 2,000 screens, ran two production studios, and became an early investor in radio, holding a 50 percent interest in CBS by 1928. By acquiring the successful Balaban & Katz chain in 1926, he gained the services of both Barney Balaban, who became Paramount's president, and Sam Katz, who began running the Paramount-Publix theatre chain. In 1927, Famous Players-Lasky took on the name Paramount-Famous Lasky Corporation. Three years later, because of the importance of the Publix theater chain, it was later known as Paramount-Publix Corporation.

Eventually, Zukor bought out most of his early partners. Lasky hung on until 1932 when, blamed for the near-collapse of Paramount during the Depression years, he was driven out. Zukor's overexpansion and use of overvalued Paramount stock for purchases led the company into receivership in 1933. The company was re-organized by the banks and the company was kept intact, with Zukor still in charge. In 1935, Paramount Publix went bankrupt. in 1936, Barney Balaban became president, and Zukor was bumped up to chairman of the board. In this role, Zukor reorganized the company as Paramount Pictures, Inc. and was able to successfully bring the studio out of bankruptcy.

As always, Paramount continued to place importance on its stars. By the 1930s, talking pictures introduced a wide range of powerful new actors like Marlene Dietrich, Mae West, Gary Cooper, Claudette Colbert, the Marx Brothers, Dorothy Lamour, Carole Lombard, Bing Crosby, and others. During this period, Paramount was literally a "movie factory," churning out 60 to 70 pictures a year. In 1933, Mae West would also add greatly to Paramount's success with her movies "She Done Him Wrong" and "I'm No Angel." However, West's sex appeal in these movies would also lead to the enforcement of the Production Code, as the newly formed organization the Catholic Legion of Decency threatened a boycott if it wasn't obeyed.

In 1940, Paramount agreed to a government-instituted decree that prohibited block booking and "pre-selling," the practice of collecting up-front money for films not yet in production. Paramount almost immediately cut back on production to a more modest 20 films annually during the war years. Still, with more new stars like Bob Hope, Alan Ladd, Veronica Lake, Paulette Goddard, and Betty Hutton, and wartime theater attendance at record numbers, the studio-theater combinations made more money than ever. With all of this money flowing in, the Federal Trade Commission and the Justice Department decided to reopen their case against five studios that also owned theater chains. This led to the Supreme Court decision United States v. Paramount Pictures, Inc. (1948) holding that movie studios could not also own movie theater chains. This decision broke up Adolph Zukor's amazing creation and effectively brought an end to the classic Hollywood studio system.

The 1950s through the 1970s were often rough times for Paramount, although the studio saw great success during a period when Robert Evans, who was then a virtually unknown producer, was installed as head of production. He restored Paramount's reputation for commercial success with films like "Love Story," "Chinatown," "Rosemary's Baby," and "The Godfather." Films like "Saturday Night Fever" and "Grease" carried the studio into the 1980s, when it saw successful productions like "Footloose," "Fatal Attraction," the "Friday the 13th" series, "Raiders of the Lost Ark," and the "Star Trek" series on film and on television.

The most successful period for Paramount in recent times was from the middle 1990s to the middle 2000s, when Jonathan Dolgen was the chairman and Sherry Lansing was president. Under their leadership, Paramount had an almost decade-long, unbroken track record of success, including six of the company's highest grossing films, including "Titanic" and "Braveheart." Meanwhile, Paramount Television developed and produced the record-breaking "Frasier," a spin-off of their earlier '80s hit, "Cheers."

In the years that followed Paramount's film and television divisions worked with Viacom, CBS, and DreamWorks, LLC to produce a wide variety of quality, and often award-winning, films and television shows. The studio continues a grand tradition in Hollywood today as America's longest-

CENSORED HOLLYWOOD!

Hollywood's Production Code (also known as the Hays Code) was a set of industry censorship guidelines that were imposed on American films in 1930. The Motion Picture Association of America (MPAA), adopted the code in 1930 and spelled out what was morally acceptable and morally unacceptable content for motion pictures produced for a public audience in America. The Production Code had three general principles:
- No picture shall be produced that will lower the moral standards of those who see it.
- Correct standards of life, subject only to the requirements of drama and entertainment, shall be presented.
- Law, natural or human, shall not be ridiculed, nor shall sympathy be created for its violation.

There were also lots of other things that you couldn't do in the movies. Nudity and "suggestive dances" were prohibited. Religion could not be ridiculed. Illegal drugs were forbidden and alcohol could only be featured when required by plot. Certain types of crime (like arson or safe-cracking) could not be shown. No reference could be made to sexual perversion (i.e. homosexuality) and childbirth could not be depicted. The language section banned various offensive words and phrases and adultery and illicit sex, although recognized as sometimes necessary to the plot, could not be explicit or justified and were not supposed to be presented as an attractive option. And the list went on...

Hollywood was on the hot seat after the scandalous days of the 1920s and after the deaths of a number of stars by murder, drug overdose, and suicide. Such scandals resulted in persistent calls for censorship and the "cleaning up" of Hollywood. The stories were often sensationalized and made headlines across the country, confirming that Hollywood was just what the preachers and politicians claimed that it was, "sin city." Public outcry over "immorality" in Hollywood and in the movies led to the creation of the Motion Pictures Producers and Distributors Association (which became the MPAA 1945), an industry trade and lobby organization. The association was headed by Will H. Hays, a well-connected Republican lawyer who had previously been United States Postmaster General and the 1920 campaign manager for President Warren G. Harding.

In 1927, Hays compiled a list of subject, which he felt Hollywood studios would be wise to avoid. In 1930, Hays created the Studio Relations Committee (SRC) to implement his censorship code, but the SRC lacked any real enforcement capability. The advent of talking pictures in 1927 signaled the need for further enforcement. Martin J. Quigley, the publisher of a Chicago-based motion picture trade newspaper, began lobbying for a more extensive code that not only listed what should be banned from movies, but also contained a moral system that movies should help to promote – a system specifically based on Catholic theology. He recruited Father Daniel Lord, a Jesuit priest and instructor at the Catholic St. Louis University, to write such a code and on March 31, 1930, Hays' committee adopted it formally. It has become known to posterity as the Hays Code.

For a few years, though, Hollywood got away with ignoring the code. The studios continued to produce racier fare than the code, with no aggressive enforcement body, was able to do anything about. This brief time of Hollywood filmmaking has become known as the "pre-code era."

But it was not meant to last. In response to movies like "Baby Face" with Barbara Stanwyck and just about anything with Mae West, Martin Quigley and Joseph I. Breen, Will Hays's Los Angeles–based assistant, conspired to use the Catholic Church to exert pressure on the Hollywood studios. They helped spearhead the creation of the Catholic Legion of Decency, as well as boycotts and blacklists of the movies throughout the country.

In 1934, an amendment to the code was passed that forced all films to obtain a certificate of approval before they could be released. The studios were forced into playing along, which they did for more than 30 years. Hollywood worked within the confines of the Production Code until the late 1950s, by which time the "Golden Age of Hollywood" had ended. The studios soon faced threats from television (within an ever-stricter code) and foreign films, which could not be enforced. Hollywood began to push the envelope with new productions and after studios were forced to give up ownership of theaters due to violations of the anti-trust laws, independent art houses began to appear that would play films that did not have certificates of approval. Finally, a boycott from the Legion of Decency no longer guaranteed a commercial failure, and thus the code prohibitions began to vanish when Hollywood producers ignored the code and were still able to earn profits.

The MPAA struggled with the codes for years but by the late 1960s, enforcement had become impossible and the Production Code was abandoned entirely. The MPAA began working on a rating code that, while changed several times over the years, remains in use today.

A photo from Hollywood Forever Cemetery and the Paramount Studios water tower in the background

Former Hollywood Forever Cemetery owner, Jules Roth (known as Hollywood Memorial Park at the time)

running movie studio.

In spite of the wide range of actors who have worked at Paramount over the decades, many believe that the source of the hauntings at the studio is connected to the cemetery that lies just outside of Paramount's borders.

Hollywood Forever Cemetery has been around even longer than Paramount Studios. It was founded as Hollywood Memorial Park in 1899 by local residents I.N. Van Nuys and Colonel Isaac Lankershim in the heart of the small community. Some of the most famous personalities in Hollywood history, including Rudolph Valentino, Douglas Fairbanks, Peter Lorre, Tyrone Power, Clifton Webb, Mel Blanc, "Little Rascals" stars Darla Hood and Carl "Alfalfa" Switzer, Paul Muni, Benjamin "Bugsy" Siegel, William Desmond Taylor, Marion Davies, Cecil B. DeMille, John Huston, Fay Wray, Don Adams, Darren McGavin, and many others, have been laid to rest there.

By the late 1900s, the cemetery had fallen into a state of disrepair and was on the verge of being closed down, thanks to the mishandling of funds by the owner. Jules Roth, a convicted felon who had served five years in San Quentin for grand theft and securities fraud, purchased the cemetery in the late 1930s and, over the years, pocketed millions of dollars of the burial ground's revenues. During his ownership, Roth sold off 40 acres of the original 100 and purchased a yacht to be used for "burials at sea," although it was actually used for lavish parties. He also hung a large painting of Hell in the lobby of the cemetery's main building. Roth's workforce dwindled, the lawn became overgrown, and the graveyard became a haven for gangs and the homeless. Roth actually began making more money from disinterments than burials, as families began moving their loved ones to better cemeteries. State officials finally began asking questions in the 1980s and the property was seized in 1995. Roth was under investigation by the state's attorney when he died in 1998.

The cemetery was scheduled for closure when Tyler Cassity, from a family in the cemetery business in St. Louis, purchased Hollywood Memorial Park at auction. He spent more than $7 million renovating the property, changed the name, and updated the services offered to include live internet broadcasts of funeral services for family members who could not be present and computer kiosks around the property that contain biographies of those interred on the grounds.

The connection between the Hollywood Forever Cemetery and Paramount Studios begins with a common wall that separates the two properties. It continues with hauntings carried out by many former Paramount actors who are now resting uneasily in the graveyard next door.

The cemetery is located closest to stages 29 through 32. The reports of spirits seen entering the studio lot describe them as wearing clothing from the 1930s and 1940s. Out of all of the sound stages in that area, Stages 31 and 32 seem to have the most activity. Footsteps are often heard tapping through stages that have been secured for the night and it is not uncommon for equipment to turn on and off and to operate by itself.

It is well known that the stage doors here make a very loud sound when they are opened or shut. There is simply no way to muffle a door that closes on these stages. When someone enters or leaves, it is plainly heard. There is a story that tells of three guards who secured Stage 32 for the night. One of the men had gone outside and he closed and locked the door behind him. The remaining two guards looked around the place, making sure that everything was in order, and then heard someone walking behind one of the stage flats. They walked over and looked behind the partition, but no one was there. Moments later, they heard the stage door being opened. Puzzled, but convinced that it was the third guard, they secured the rest of the stage and left to find the third member of the team sitting outside. He had not entered the sound stage at all.

Another guard had a more frightening experience on this same stage. He was working by himself to secure Stage 32 for the night. Shortly after finishing his rounds, he turned the lights out and then left to go check in and make a telephone call to his girlfriend. Just as he was leaving, he heard someone walking across the stage. He wondered how they could see anything since the stage was very dark and was filled with props and scenery for the next day's filming. He knew that it was difficult to move around even when the lights were on. Somehow, though, the footsteps continued, crossing the darkened stage unobstructed. The startled guard turned on his flashlight and checked out the sound, but he saw no one. The door had never opened, but there was no one in the building. After that, he never closed down that stage by himself again.

Paramount Studios has many entrances and some of them are walk-in gates, like the one at Lemon Grove, located a few feet from the cemetery. It is there where many of the ghosts from the graveyard are also said to enter the studio lot. Some of them, according to guards posted here, actually appear as heads that poke through the cemetery wall and then disappear. Others actually walk through the gate itself, like the ghost of silent film heartthrob Rudolph Valentino. While his ghost many be one of the most-traveled spirits in Hollywood (see next chapter for more about Valentino,) many insist that he haunts Paramount Studios, as well.

Valentino died in 1926 at the age of 31 and was buried in Hollywood Memorial Park. He was a driving force at Paramount in his day and rumor has it that he was buried in his white costume from the film, "The Sheik," for which he is best remembered. It is in this costume that his ghost is sometimes reported.

One of the most mysteriously romantic stories of Hollywood Forever Cemetery involves the crypt of Valentino and the "Lady in Black" who returns there each year on the anniversary of his death. She began appearing there at the time of his internment, walking through the cemetery to the main mausoleum and placing a bouquet of red roses in the holder of his crypt. She then brushed her gloved hand over the metal plaque that bears his name, making sure that it was free of dust, and then knelt to pray before she silently departed.

Rumors have surrounded the first "Lady in Black" for years, but it's believed that the original mourner was Ditra Flame. As a child, she was once very sick and ended up in the hospital. Valentino, who was a friend of her mother's, came to visit her and brought the child a red rose. Legend has it that

Valentino's grave plaque at the Hollywood Forever Cemetery mausoleum

(Right) A staged photo of the famous "Lady in Black", who placed roses at the grave site for many years. The tradition still continues today.

he told her, "If I die before you do, please come and stay by me because I don't want to be alone. You come and talk to me."

Ditra recovered, but Valentino went to an early grave. He died on August 23, 1926 and Ditra brought a bouquet of red roses to his crypt on that date every year until 1955. Others took over for her after her death and the tradition still continues today. Karie Bible, who offers a tour at Hollywood Forever Cemetery, confesses that she keeps up the tradition today, donning a vintage black dress and a veil every August 23.

In addition to Valentino, other ghosts from the cemetery sometimes appear at the Paramount gates, a fact that does not please security guards, especially those who work the night shift at the Lemon Grove gate. The gate is located at the northeast corner of the studio lot facing Lemon Grove Avenue and a wall is all that separates it from the cemetery. It is here where most of the uninvited visitors are usually seen, but these sightings are mostly harmless, leaving the officers confused over where the "trespasser" disappeared to. Other times, these sightings can leave a few rattled nerves.

One night, a veteran security guard was working the late night shift. Most of the guards know everyone who comes in and out of the gates because they see them every day. On this evening, the guard noticed an unfamiliar person lurking about. He followed the man to a corner of the wall by the cemetery and, thinking he had him trapped, he waited for the suspicious visitor to come out. After a minute or two, he looked around the corner -- just in time to see the man vanish into the cemetery wall! From that time on, he refused to work the Lemon Grove gate at night.

Of all of the hauntings at Paramount, however, the most active one has nothing to do with the cemetery. The Hart Building is considered to be the most haunted site on the studio lot. It is one of the oldest buildings there and was once part of the DesiLu Studios, owned by Desi Arnaz and Lucille Ball. They say that the spirit of a woman haunts the upper floors and one of the things that witnesses notice about her is that she gives off the strong smell of an old, flowery-like perfume. She tends to be seen mostly by men and stories have circulated that she often takes things from desks and private places and throws them onto the floor.

One story has also circulated about a security guard who was working in the Hart building one night. He was checking the place to be sure that all of the windows and doors were locked when suddenly, one of the doors slammed shut on its own. Strangely, the door is on a suspension hinge that only allows it to shut very slowly. Instead, it had slammed shut, as though someone were violently pushing against it.

There have also been stories about windows and doors that have unlocked on their own, lights turning on and off, and claims of people being touched or tapped on the shoulder. Another well-known tale (and one allegedly in the security record) involves an actress who decided to set up her production offices on the third floor of the Hart Building. The story goes that an executive of the company went into the bathroom and was washing his hands at the sink. He looked up into the mirror and saw that his eyes were glowing red! Frightened, he ran into his office and told his secretary to look at his eyes. She sat him down in chair and peered into his face. She also saw the red color and began screaming as she ran for the door. The executive tried to get up from his chair, but claimed to feel hands pressing down on his shoulders. Finally, he managed to escape. Not surprisingly, the production company moved out of those offices the following day.

The Hart Building at Paramount Studios

There are other hauntings on the Paramount lot, as well.

On December 30, 1993, another strange occurrence was entered into the security record. A skeleton security crew was assigned for the holidays since this is typically a slow production time. One person was always assigned to the main gate and about four others were always on duty to patrol the lot. Each officer was given a particular area to cover. A trainee was present on December 30, along with a seasoned veteran officer. Together, the two men were assigned to cover an area between the Chevalier and Ball buildings. As they walked along the path between the buildings, the trainee noticed someone looking down at them from the second floor of the Ball Building. Moments later, the person was gone. He told his partner and they went to investigate. However, neither man had the keys to get into the second floor, so they called a supervisor over to the scene.

While they waited for the supervisor, another guard arrived on the scene and while they were filling him in on what had happened, they saw a light come on in the Chevalier Building across the way. The older guard and the third officer went to investigate because no one was supposed to be in the building. They searched the building, but turned up nothing. Finally, the supervisor arrived on the scene and left the veteran officer outside. He then sent the trainee and the third man around the bottom floor to check things out, while he went up to the second floor to search for the intruder. He checked every room himself and made sure that each door and window was locked. No one could have entered the building without a key and no could have left without the security guards seeing them. That night, however, they found the place empty and deserted.

This would not be the last strange incident to take place in the Ball Building either. As this is a small building, most of the staff members know the other employees by sight and see them on an almost daily basis. Late one night, a man and a woman were leaving their office on the second floor. The building was empty and quiet and they were sure of being the last ones in it that evening. However, on their way out, they passed an old woman who was walking toward them. Neither of the staff members

A vintage view of Grauman's (later Mann's) Chinese Theater

recognized her and they thought that perhaps she was lost. Moments after she passed by them, one of them turned to ask the lady if she needed some help. In those few seconds, she had vanished!

FLICKERING IMAGES: HOLLYWOOD'S HAUNTED MOVIE THEATERS

There is an adage that states, "every good theater has a ghost." While such a saying likely came about thanks to the spirits who lurk in the old stage theaters of yesterday, it should come as no surprise to find that movie theaters have their ghosts, too. What is about a theater that seems to attract a ghost? Could it be the range of emotions expressed by the actors, from joy to sorrow to fear? Perhaps these expressions of emotion attract spirits who need such energy to exist. In some cases, tumultuous events that occur in the buildings also leave an impression behind. Such impressions are often regarded as hauntings.

Theaters also demand a great love and devotion from the staff members who work there and in many cases, these same staff members return to their favorite theaters after death. Many of them remember the theater as the place where they found their greatest happiness, while others return because of some unfinished event that was never completed in life.

Regardless, theaters all over America play host to a great number of ghosts that range from the frightening to the playful to the tragic --- and Hollywood is no exception.

GRAUMAN'S CHINESE THEATER

One of Hollywood's haunted theaters, Mann's Chinese Theater, is one of the most easily recognized landmarks in the world. There are two different ghosts connected to the building, one of which only came to his Hollywood Boulevard haunt in recent times and one that has been here much longer.

The building was originally known as

Grauman's Chinese Theater. It was one of Hollywood's original movie palaces and was built by Sid Grauman to follow up on his success with the Egyptian Theater, located nearby. Grauman financed the Oriental-style building, along with his partners, Mary Pickford and Douglas Fairbanks. Of course, one of the most unique features of the theater is the concrete sidewalk in front, which is marked with the names, hand- and footprints, and unique signatures of Hollywood's biggest stars. Legend has it that the sidewalk of fame got started by accident. The story goes that screen star Norma Talmadge made a misstep one night that became Hollywood history. Apparently, Talmadge was unaware that cement had been freshly poured outside the theater's lobby and accidentally stepped into it. Her shoes left a permanent impression in the concrete and a tradition was born.

However, Sid Grauman told a different story. In an interview at the end of a 1937 Lux Radio Theatre program, Grauman told Cecil B. DeMille that the idea of putting hand- and footprints in the cement was, "pure accident. I walked right into it. While we were building the theatre, I accidentally happened to step in some soft concrete. And there it was. So, I went to Mary Pickford immediately. Mary put her foot into it." The theatre's third partner, Douglas Fairbanks, was the next celebrity to be immortalized in the cement.

Regardless of how it all got started, scores of celebrities have left their hand- and footprints outside of the theater since those early years and this stretch of sidewalk has become one of Hollywood's most popular tourist attractions.

However, the film fans that flock to this spot most likely have no idea that this piece of the sidewalk is believed to be haunted by actor Victor Kilian, who was killed nearby in 1979. Kilian started out as a vaudeville actor but came to Hollywood and achieved a modest amount of success as a character actor. Frequently cast as a villain, Kilian suffered the loss of an eye while staging a fight scene with John Wayne in 1942. During the McCarthy era of the 1950s, Kilian was blacklisted for his political beliefs, but because the Actors' Equity Association refused to go along with

Character actor Victor Kilian

the ban, Kilian was able to earn a living by returning to perform on stage. After Hollywood's blacklisting ended, he began doing guest roles on television series during the 1970s. He is best known for his role as "Grandpa" in the "Mary Hartman, Mary Hartman" series.

Killian's wife, Daisy Johnson, to whom he had been married for 46 years, died in 1961. The actor lived alone in an apartment that was about a block away from the Chinese Theater. On March 11, 1979, the 88-year-old actor went for a drink in a local bar. Police later speculated that he struck up a conversation with a stranger and that the two of them must have left the bar and gone to Kilian's apartment. The actor's badly beaten body was found the following day. His apartment had been ransacked and burglarized. Kilian's murderer has never been captured, but apparently, Kilian has never given up his pursuit of the man who killed him. Local lore has it that his ghost still walks the route from the Chinese Theater to his apartment, perhaps hoping that his murderer will return to the scene.

THE WARNER PACIFIC THEATER

While the old Warner Pacific Theater on Hollywood Boulevard has quieted somewhat in recent years, the stories about Sam Warner's ghost haunting the place make it the perfect haunted Hollywood theater.

In the late 1920s, after a number of failures, the four Warner brothers, Harry, Albert, Sam and Jack, risked everything they had on the production of a new movie called "The Jazz Singer." This risky venture would be the first talking film and would hopefully be instrumental in the development of sound in theaters. In addition to this uncertain project, the Warner Brothers were hurrying to complete their new theater, the largest in Hollywood. It was supposed to be finished before the release of "The Jazz Singer" and it would be at this new venue that the film would premiere. While the movie was being filmed, Sam Warner personally supervised the installation of the sound system, all the while worrying over the rumors that were going around town about talking pictures being nothing more than a fad. Between construction delays at the theater and the production of the film, Sam barely had time to eat and sleep. It was said that when he realized that the theater was not going to be ready for the opening, he stood in the lobby and cursed the place.

"The Jazz Singer" opened in New York on October 6, 1927 to excited crowds and wonderful reviews. Unfortunately, though, none of the Warner brothers were able to attend. Just 24 hours before the premiere, Sam Warner suffered a cerebral hemorrhage and died in Los Angeles. His brothers hurried home from New York before the film ever opened.

The Warner Pacific Theatre opened six months later with a forgotten film called "The Glorious Betsy" with Conrad Nagel. In spite of this, Al Jolson emceed the night and a ceremony was held for Sam during which a plaque was placed in the lobby in his honor. It has been said that while Sam Warner was not physically present that night -- he was undoubtedly there in spirit. A man like Sam Warner would never leave this world with his work unfinished!

Since that night in April 1928, random sightings of Sam Warner have taken place at the theater and in the administration offices above. People who live nearby report seeing him in the lobby, walking back and forth and looking frustrated and tired. Late one night in the 1970s, two men on a

(Left) The Warner Pacific Theater

(Above) Sam Warner

Dead Men Do Tell Tales: Bloody Hollywood - Page 102

cleaning crew saw Warner walk across the lobby and enter the elevator. He stepped onto it, pushed the button, and then the door closed and the elevator went up. When a security guard made his rounds through the lobby, the startled men told him what they had seen and then quit on the spot! The guard, however, was not bothered by the story. He only wondered why a ghost would use an elevator.

While Sam has not been seen in recent years, the security company that watches over the theater when it is closed is quite familiar with his comings and goings. When things are quiet, they often hear him in the offices upstairs, moving chairs around, scratching on doors or tapping on things to get attention. The elevator continued to operate by itself for many years, until it was damaged in the Northridge Earthquake of 1994.

Some believe that perhaps Sam Warner is not seen as often as he once was because his work here is finally completed. However, strange things do continue to occur. According to Paul Miller, the director of the USC Entertainment Technology Center Digital Cinema Lab, which now uses the old theater doing research for the future of the movie business -- replacing old prints with digital projection -- Sam Warner's ghost is still very much in evidence here.

"While the elevator is no longer operational things still do move around suspiciously," Mr. Miller wrote to me. "It seems Sam may have a propensity for high technology items. Cellular phones, PDAs, and digital cameras frequently turn up missing in the theatre, never to be seen again. He also has an affinity for sharp objects and hand tools that mysteriously disappear and only occasionally show up again later in another location. In fact, two pairs of scissors went missing some months back only to be replaced later by another pair of scissors, not one of the missing pairs."

The Pantages Theater

Howard Hughes

PANTAGES THEATER

The Pantages Theater is the last of the glorious Hollywood movie palaces. It is considered an Art Deco masterpiece and most would call it one of the most beautiful theaters in the world. In 1949, eccentric billionaire Howard Hughes purchased the Pantages as part of his national theater chain when he bought RKO Pictures. Hughes was truly an enigma as far as American personalities go. In his time, he was a daredevil aviator, a moviemaker, an inventor, a playboy and in the end, a sad and possibly insane recluse. It has been said that his days in Hollywood were the happiest of Hughes' life. This may explain why he has purportedly returned to haunt the Pantages Theater.

Howard Robard Hughes, Jr. was born in Texas in 1905, heir to the lucrative Hughes Tool Company empire, which had patented a bit for the drilling of oil. In addition to a vast fortune, Hughes also inherited an interest in all things mechanical. As a boy, he invented a motorized bicycle from parts taken from his father's steam engine. Although an indifferent student, the brilliant young man showed a strong aptitude for aviation and mathematics. After his parents died, Hughes, then 19, took over the family business and became one of the wealthiest young men in the world.

Hughes dropped out of Rice University shortly after his father's death and moved to Los Angeles, hoping to make a name for himself in the movie business. Hughes was first dismissed as a rich man's son trying to edge into the movies but when his first two films, "Everybody's Acting" and "Two Arabian Nights," were financial successes, people began to take notice. His next films, "The Racket" and "The Front Page" were nominated for Academy Awards. Following this, Hughes spent what was then an unbelievable amount of his own money ($3.8 million) to make "Hell's Angels," an epic flying adventure that became a huge hit after overcoming many obstacles. He produced another hit, "Scarface," in 1932. One of his best-known films was "The Outlaw," which turned Jane Russell into a movie star. Hughes designed a special bra for Russell to wear in the film, highlighting her ample breasts, which infuriated censors.

Hughes signed an unknown actor named Davis Bacon to play Billy the Kid in "The Outlaw," and then later replaced him with Jack Buetel. Homosexual rumors arose after Bacon was murdered in 1943. Bacon's widow, Greta Keller, later claimed that Bacon and Hughes had a sexual relationship and that when Bacon wanted out of his movie contract, Hughes refused. Bacon then claimed that he was prepared to reveal details about their affair in a manuscript in order to secure a release from the studio. He was killed soon afterward and the manuscript vanished. Greta Keller blamed Hughes. All rumors aside, though, no real evidence has ever emerged to suggest that Hughes was gay, or even bi-sexual. None of the hundreds of depositions from Hughes' friends and associates, including his lifelong friend and business partner, Noah Dietrich, have ever hinted that Hughes was involved in any homosexual relationships. Dietrich, whose many "duties" for Hughes included cleaning up the numerous wrecks created by Hughes' womanizing, states in his own biography that he heard the rumors and knew that they were false. In addition, the FBI, which thoroughly investigated Hughes, could find nothing to suggest that he was gay.

Hughes was a notorious ladies' man who spent time with many famous women, including Billie Dove, Bette Davis, Ava Gardner, Olivia de Havilland, Katharine Hepburn and Gene Tierney. Jean Harlow accompanied him to the premiere of "Hell's Angels," but Noah Dietrich wrote many years later that the relationship was strictly professional—Hughes personally disliked Harlow. Dietrich also wrote that Hughes genuinely liked and respected Jane Russell, but never sought romantic involvement with her. According to Russell's autobiography, however, Hughes once tried to bed her after a party. Russell refused him and Hughes promised it would never happen again. The two maintained a friendship for many years. Hughes also remained good friends with Gene Tierney. When Tierney's daughter, Daria, was born deaf, blind and severely retarded due to Tierney being exposed to the German measles during her pregnancy, he saw to it that she received the best medical care and paid all expenses.

Hughes had been married when he first came to Hollywood, but his wife's loneliness led to her going back to Texas and filing for divorce. In 1957, Hughes married actress Jean Peters but this marriage was also troubled. Peters filed for divorce from Hughes in 1971 and the two had not lived together for many years. She accepted a lifetime alimony payment of $70,000 a year and waived all claims to the Hughes estate. Hughes never spoke ill of Jean and did not insist upon a confidentiality agreement as a condition of their divorce. Regardless, she refused to discuss her life with

Hughes and declined several lucrative offers from big-name publishers and biographers. Peters would state only that she had not seen Hughes for several years before their divorce, because his psychological problems forced him to stay in a separate room, talking with her only by phone.

In 1948, Hughes gained control of RKO, a struggling major Hollywood studio. During his tenure, RKO suffered as a result of his rather bizarre management style. Just weeks after he took over the studio, he fired three-fourths of the staff and shut the place down for six months while he investigated the politics of the remaining employees. Completed pictures would be sent back for reshooting if he felt his star (especially female) was not properly presented, or if a film's anti-communist politics were not sufficiently clear.

Hughes let go of the RKO theaters in 1953 as settlement of the United States v. Paramount Pictures, Inc. antitrust case. With the sale of the profitable theater chain, the film studio suffered even further. Hughes was sued several times by RKO's minority stockholders for financial misconduct and mismanagement and the lawsuits became an increasing nuisance. Eager to be rid of the distraction, Hughes offered to buy out all other stockholders at a cost of more than $24 million. By the end of 1954, he had near total control of RKO. Six months later, Hughes sold the studio to the General Tire and Rubber Company for $25 million. This marked the end of his 25-year involvement in motion pictures and although he nearly destroyed a major Hollywood studio, he walked away from Hollywood with a huge personal profit.

After his run in the movie business, Hughes returned to his real love of aviation. Even during his Hollywood years, Hughes developed and flew a variety of aircraft, including the Boeing Stratoliner, the Lockheed L-049 Constellation, and the XF-11 prototype plane, which nearly killed Hughes in July 1946.

Hughes was piloting the experimental Army reconnaissance plane over L.A. when an oil leak caused one of the counter-rotating propellers to

Hughes in the cockpit of the H-4 Hercules, which became known as the "Spruce Goose"

reverse pitch. Hughes tried to save the craft by landing it on the Los Angeles Country Club golf course, but seconds before he could reach it, the XF-11 fell from the sky and crashed in the Beverly Hills neighborhood surrounding the country club. After hitting three houses, the fuel tanks exploded, setting fire to the aircraft and a nearby home. Hughes lay seriously injured beside the burning XF-11 until he was rescued by Marine Master Sergeant William L. Durkin, who happened to be in the area visiting friends. Hughes sustained significant injuries in the crash; including a crushed collarbone, 24 broken ribs and numerous third-degree burns.

Hughes' most controversial aircraft was the H-4 Hercules, nicknamed the "Spruce Goose." The aircraft was originally contracted by the U.S. government for use in World War II, as a way to transport troops and equipment across the Atlantic that steered clear of German U-Boats. In 1947, it was the largest aircraft ever built, weighing 190 tons, but it was not completed until just after the end of World War II. The Hercules flew only once for one mile, with Hughes at the controls, on November 2, 1947.

Hughes was also involved in a controversy over Trans-World Airlines (TWA). In 1939, at the urging of Jack Frye, president of TWA, Hughes quietly purchased a majority share of TWA stock and took control of the airline. After World War II, Hughes found himself under investigation by the U.S. Senate because he had failed to deliver the H-4 Hercules as promised. However, he believed that his ownership and plans for TWA were what were really behind the investigation. Pan American World Airways chief Juan Trippe sought to monopolize international air travel and had influenced powerful Maine Senator Owen Brewster to propose legislation securing Pan Am as the sole American airline allowed to fly overseas at a time when Hughes planned TWA service to Europe. Hughes turned the hearings into an attack on Brewster and exposed his questionable business dealings with Pan Am. He also later helped defeat his re-election bid by pouring considerable funds into the campaign of Brewster's opponent, Frederick Payne.

In 1960, Hughes was forced out of TWA, although he still owned 78 percent of the company and battled to regain control. In 1966, he was forced by a federal court to sell his shares in TWA. The court cited a conflict of interest due to his ownership of both TWA and his Hughes Aircraft company. The sale netted him almost $547 million.

Unfortunately, most of Hughes' pioneering efforts in the film business and in aviation have been forgotten by those who only remember him for his eccentric behavior and bizarre reclusive life. Hughes was likely a victim of obsessive-compulsive disorder (OCD) and an addiction to prescription drugs. His mother may have also suffered from OCD and she first provided him with a means of escaping social situations and pressures with illness as an excuse. As a young boy, he wanted to attend summer camp at a time when the public feared the spread of polio. His mother wanted assurances that he would be protected, but when the assurances never came, she kept him home. After finally attending camp one summer, Hughes avoided a second year by complaining about headaches and bad dreams. At one point in his childhood, he stayed out of school for most of a year after he developed a form of paralysis that was never diagnosed and which disappeared on its own a few months later.

Hughes was once one of the most visible men in America, but he eventually vanished from public view, although tabloids and magazines continued to follow rumors of his behavior and his whereabouts. He was usually reported to be terminally ill, mentally unstable, or even dead.

In the 1930s, friends later reported that Hughes was obsessed with peas, one of his favorite foods, and he used a special fork to sort them by size. While working on "The Outlaw," Hughes became obsessed with a flaw in one of Jane Russell's costume blouses, claiming that the fabric bunched along a seam and made it look as though she had two nipples on each breast. He was so worried about this matter that he wrote a detailed, multi-page memo to the crew about how to fix the problem. His fixation on trivial details and odd mood swings led many film crews to wonder if the movies they were working on would ever be completed.

In a bout of business obsession, Hughes decided to purchase all of the restaurant chains and luxury hotels that had been founded within the borders of his home state of Texas. He bought scores of them and ownership was placed in trust and then resold a short time later.

Thanks to injuries that he sustained during aviation mishaps, especially after the XF-11 crash, Hughes spent much of his life in pain. He eventually became addicted to painkillers, including codeine and several other prescription drugs. The addiction compounded the symptoms of Hughes' OCD and brought on new ones, like insisting on using tissues to pick up objects so that he could protect himself from germs. He would go through dozens of boxes of tissues each week. On one occasion, he watched the 1968 film "Ice Station Zebra" over 150 times.

In later years, Hughes always had a barber on call, but only had his hair cut and his nails trimmed about once a year. He also had several doctors available to him at all times, but he rarely saw them and never followed their advice. Toward the end, his inner circle was largely comprised of Mormons (they were referred to as the "Mormon Mafia") because he considered them absolutely trustworthy, even though Hughes was not a member of the church.

Hughes was also obsessed with using every trick conceivable to avoid paying taxes to the government. In the early years of Hughes Aircraft, he attempted to move the company from Southern California to Nevada to take advantage of Nevada's low tax rates. He later donated all of his stock in Hughes Aircraft to a medical charity that he established, Howard Hughes Medical Institute, thus turning the military contractor into a tax-exempt charity. He was also able to keep his managers working for him for many years by promising them large sums of money at the end of their careers. In order to give them money without taxation, he arranged with them to publicly criticize them at the time of their retirement. Then, the manager would sue Hughes in court for public defamation. A settlement in court was not subject to taxes and he arranged this for many of his best employees.

After living in California for many years, he came up with the idea of living in hotels so that he would not have to legally declare a residency in any state, thus avoiding the payment of personal income taxes. Shortly after he devised this plan, though, legislation was passed requiring payment of income taxes by any living in a certain state for 180 days or longer. After that, Hughes would live in a hotel for 180 days and then move to another one, staying on the move every six months or so. His creative efforts were so successful that even after his death, the states of California and Texas were unable to collect inheritance taxes from his estate since it could not be proven that he was a legal resident of either state.

Hughes stayed on the move for the last 10 years of his life, living in penthouse suites of hotels in Beverly Hills, Boston, Las Vegas, the Bahamas, Vancouver, London, Nicaragua, Acapulco, and many other locations. In November 1966, he arrived in Las Vegas by railroad and moved into the Desert Inn. Refusing to leave the hotel, he bought the Desert Inn in early 1967. The hotel's eighth floor became the headquarters for his empire and the ninth-floor penthouse became Hughes' personal residence. Between 1966 and 1968, Hughes bought several other hotels and casinos which had previously been Mafia-owned. He also bought several local televisions stations because, as a chronic insomniac, he always wanted to have something to watch during the early morning hours. Hughes had spent nearly $300 million on his many properties during his Las Vegas buying spree.

As the owner of several major businesses in Las Vegas, Hughes wielded enormous political and economic power in Nevada and was able to influence elections in that state and beyond. In the 1960s and early 1970s, Hughes became obsessed with the underground nuclear testing that was then taking place in Nevada. He was terrified of the risks posed by residual nuclear radiation from the tests and he worked hard to try and halt the testing. When the testing began, despite Hughes' efforts, the detonations were powerful enough to cause the Desert Inn to sway on its foundation. In two separate, last-ditch efforts, Hughes instructed his representatives to offer $1 million bribes to presidents Lyndon B. Johnson and Richard M. Nixon, begging them to stop the tests. His aides never offered the bribes. They simply told Hughes they had been turned down. Following the tests, Hughes made it clear in his personal correspondence that the nuclear detonations led directly to his self-imposed exile from the United States, which ended only with his death. Hughes lived in Nicaragua and then in the penthouse of the Xanadu Princess Resort on Grand Bahama Island, which he purchased, for the last four years of his life.

Hughes died on April 5, 1976 while on an aircraft that was traveling from his penthouse in the Bahamas to the Methodist Hospital in Houston, Tex. His seclusion, drug use, and physical condition made him almost unrecognizable from the tall, robust figure that was well known in newspapers and magazines of the past. His hair, beard, and fingernails had grown grotesquely long and he weighed only 90 pounds. The FBI had to resort to fingerprints to identify his body. A subsequent autopsy showed that kidney failure was his cause of death, but he was in terrible condition. X-rays revealed that broken hypodermic needles were embedded in his arms and he suffered from severe malnutrition. Hughes was buried in Glenwood Cemetery in Houston, next to his parents.

But the strangeness surrounding Howard Hughes did not end with his death.

About three weeks after Hughes died, a handwritten will was found on the desk of an official of the Mormon Church (Church of Jesus Christ of the latter-Day Saints, or LDS) in Salt Lake City. The so-called "Mormon Will" gave $1.56 billion to various charities; nearly $470 million to the upper-management of Hughes' companies and his aides; $156 million to his first cousin, William Lummis; $156 million split equally between his two ex-wives; and $156 million to a gas station owner named Melvin Dummar.

Initially, Dummar claimed to have no knowledge about the will, but changed his story when his fingerprints were found on the envelope. He soon had a peculiar story to tell. He claimed that late on evening in December 1967, he found a dirty and disheveled old man lying along U.S. Highway 95, about 150 miles north of Las Vegas. The man asked for a ride and Dummar dropped him off at the Sands Hotel. As he was getting out of the car, he told Melvin that his name was Howard Hughes. Dummar then claimed that a few days after Hughes' death, a "mysterious man" showed up at his gas station and gave him an envelope that contained the hand-written will. Not sure what to do with it, or even if it was genuine, he delivered it to the LDS office. After a trial that lasted for seven months, the "Mormon Will" was rejected by the Nevada courts as a forgery. In June 1978, it was declared that Hughes had died without a valid will.

In 1983, Hughes' $2.5 billion estate was split among 22 cousins and Melvin Dummar was discounted by the public as a phony and an opportunist, despite his claims about what really happened on the Nevada highway that night.

After Howard Hughes acquired the Pantages Theater, he set up two offices on the second floor, where theater-circuit mogul Alexander Pantages and his sons had once had their own offices. Hughes ensconced himself in these offices whenever he was in Hollywood, but abandoned them in 1953 when he was forced to sell off the theater chain. In spite of this, many believe that he has never completely cut his ties with the theater.

In 1967, Pacific Theaters bought the Pantages and later, in conjunction with the Nederlander Corporation, restored the place to its original splendor. Staff members who have since worked in the second floor offices often report feeling a presence, especially in the conference room, which had once been Howard Hughes' office. Karla Rubin, an executive assistant at the theater, noted that, "there's something about the temperature of this room -- a coldness. I often feel a wind go past me where there's no air-conditioning on." She and other employees frequently heard bumping and banging sounds that had no explanation, as well as the clicking of brass handles like those on desk drawers. Every once in awhile, a cold wind would blow through the executive suites and when it did, it brought with it the faint aroma of cigars.

Rubin also stated that she twice caught sight of an apparition, a tall man that she believed to be Howard Hughes. Dressed in modest business clothes, he was seen rounding a corner in the remodeled suite where his original office door was once located.

And if Hughes does walk at the Pantages, he doesn't walk there alone. There are also the tales of a singing woman that dates back to around 1932. That year, a female patron died in the mezzanine during a film. Ever since then, when the auditorium is dark and quiet, the voice of a woman can sometimes be heard singing in the silence. The voice comes in the daytime and at night and, a few years ago, was picked up on a microphone during the stage setting for a live performance.

Perhaps the most eerie encounter at the Pantages occurred when a wardrobe woman was the last to leave the theater. As she walked toward the side exit in the auditorium, the emergency lights in the aisles went out. Left to stumble around in the darkness, she became confused and was unable to find her way out. Then, from out of the blackness around her, a firm hand gripped her by the elbow and led her to the door. She opened it, letting in some light, and turned to thank her rescuer for his assistance.

There was no one there.

CHECKING IN, BUT NEVER CHECKING OUT AGAIN:
HOLLYWOOD'S HAUNTED HOTELS

Many of Hollywood's older hotels are much like Hollywood itself. They are aging and slightly faded, still trying to hang onto the shimmer of glamour that they enjoyed in the days gone by. In times past, before you could find hookers on Hollywood Boulevard, the hotels of Hollywood were luxurious pleasure palaces where the stars of the silver screen went to dine, dance and rendezvous with secret lovers. Like some parts of Hollywood, a few of the hotels have seen face-lifts in recent years, which have stirred up memories and "spirits" of the past. Not all of the ghostly stories, and wicked scandals, are products of recent times, however, many of them have been around for years.

The first hotel in Hollywood was the famous Hotel Hollywood (or the Hollywood Hotel; the names were interchangeable over the years), which was opened by H.J. Whitley in 1902. It was located on the west side of Highland Avenue and it fronted a dusty, unpaved road that would eventually become Hollywood Boulevard. In less than three years, Whitley was compelled to add an additional wing onto the place and it expanded almost as soon as it was opened. Eventually, it covered the entire block and Whitley installed a wide lobby, a chapel, music room, ballroom, and 125 guest rooms.

The Hotel Hollywood soon became the most

prestigious lodging house in the region and when the movie colony began to grow, it attracted luminaries like Louis B. Mayer, Irving Thalberg, Jack Warner, Wallace Reid, Gloria Swanson, Greta Garbo, Pola Negri, Rudolph Valentino, and many others. In fact, for many years between 1903 and 1956, when the hotel was razed, it was the social center of Hollywood.

There was a continuous stream of movie stars that arrived at the hotel daily. Many of the great silent movie actors made their homes in the Hollywood Hotel and attended the dances held every Thursday night in the ballroom. It was considered "the" place to be seen. To identify where certain people regularly sat and dined, the hotel had stars with the names of celebrities painted on the ceiling above their tables. Those who didn't live in the hotel lived nearby and the close-knit community made the place their second home.

Soon after the Hotel Hollywood was opened, an eccentric millionaire spinster from Iowa, Mira Parker Hershey, who was then staying at a hotel in Los Angeles, rode out to see the new hotel in Hollywood that was being advertised in local newspapers. She then became a guest; lured, the legend goes, by the cuisine, particularly the apple pie. She fell in love with the hotel and bought shares, eventually becoming sole owner of the place.

In 1909, Carrie Jacobs Bond wrote her then-famous song, "The End of a Perfect Day" at the Hotel Hollywood, which had inspired the tune. Five years later, opera star Geraldine Farrar was welcomed to Hollywood with the town's first white-tie-and-tails party in the hotel's famous ballroom. The Hearst newspapers' famous gossip columnist Louella Parsons made the hotel's name synonymous with glamour when she broadcast live over the radio from the lobby during the height of her popularity.

By the 1920s, the hotel was so connected to the film colony's high living that it became a target for the tabloids and scandal rags of the era. The film magazines were correct in assuming that a lot of "hanky-panky" was going on at the hotel and the antics of the stars always made for good gossip. Nevertheless, the Hotel Hollywood attempted to maintain at least a bit of respectability. When John Barrymore climbed into the room of a female companion from the garden, the management ordered cactus to be planted under the windows of all ground floor room to dissuade others from trying the same thing. When that proved ineffective, all of the ground floor windows were nailed shut.

In 1919, a desk clerk demanded that Valentino produce a marriage license before he could go upstairs with his new wife, Jean Acker, on their wedding night. As it turned out, he needn't have bothered. That night, after he led his bride to her room, Acker, a lesbian, slammed the door in Valentino's face, locked it, and wept that she had made a terrible mistake. That was the end of their marriage, although they were not divorced for three years – three years during which Valentino would become one of the most famous screen lovers in history.

Mira Hershey died in 1930. In the early 1940s, developers acquired the historic hotel, planning to tear the place down and redevelop the block. They were only halted because of World War II, having to wait until the release of building materials. By the 1950s, the hotel was run down and faded, only a relic of its former glory. The developers were adamant that renovating and restoring the property was out of the question. Many of the remaining residents of the hotel had been there for years, even decades. Just before the building was torn down, writer Ezra Goodman interviewed many of them. One old woman, who had lived in the hotel for 35 years, was depressed at the idea of leaving a place that she loved so near to the end of her life. "I don't want to go to heaven," she said. "I just want to stay here."

The Hotel Hollywood was finally razed in August 1956, destroying a piece of history from Hollywood's early days. But if the old hotel had ghosts of film stars from days gone by, those stars would be smiling if they learned what replaced their beloved hotel. In 2001, the Hollywood and Highland entertainment complex, which includes the Kodak Theatre, the "official" home of the Academy Awards, opened on the site of the former Hotel Hollywood.

KNICKERBOCKER HOTEL

The Knickerbocker Hotel was built was in 1925 and throughout the tumultuous decade of the 1920s, it played a key role at the heart of Hollywood. It first opened as a luxury apartment building and became a hotel later on in its history. One of the attractions of the place was the Renaissance Revival bar, which played host to the cream of the Hollywood crop. One frequent guest was Rudolph Valentino, who reportedly loved to dance the tango to the live music performed in the saloon. The hotel served many guests, and was home to many scandals over the years.

The hotel lobby features a huge crystal chandelier, which cost over $120,000 in 1925, and it was under this chandelier that epic film director D.W. Griffith died of a stroke in 1948. At the time of his death, Griffith, who was a pioneer in the Hollywood film industry, had been largely forgotten by his peers. He eked out a painful and lonely existence at the Knickerbocker, spending most of his time in the hotel bar, talking to anyone who was willing to listen to him. His dismissal by Hollywood was as great a tragedy as his death and it would not be until years later that he would be regarded as the genius that he undoubtedly was.

Another Knickerbocker tragedy was actress Frances Farmer, whose all-too-brief career electrified Hollywood in the 1930s. She made her film debut in 1936 in "Too Many Parents" and over the next six years, she appeared in 18 films, three Broadway plays, thirty major radio shows and seven stock company productions. She was only 27 years old, but her star was soon to fade – and then plummet from the sky in a haze of alcohol and mental illness.

Frances was born in Seattle, Wash., in 1931 and as a young woman was involved in writing and drama, for which she won several awards. She studied drama at the University of Washington and during the 1930s, its drama department productions were considered citywide cultural events and were widely attended. In late 1934, she starred in the school's production of "Alien Corn," speaking foreign languages, playing the piano and receiving rave reviews in what was then the longest-running play in the department's history.

In 1935, Frances was in New York, hoping to launch a legitimate theatrical career. Instead, she was referred to a Paramount Pictures talent scout, Oscar Serlin, who arranged for a screen test and then offered her seven-year contract with the studio. Frances soon found herself in Hollywood, with top billing in two well-received, low budget pictures. She wed actor Leif Erickson in February 1936 while shooting the first of the movies. Later that year, Frances was cast opposite Bing Crosby in her first major release, "Rhythm on the Range." During the summer of 1936, she was loaned to Samuel Goldwyn to appear in "Come and Get It," based on the novel by Edna Ferber. Both films were sizable hits, and she was praised by the public and critics, with several reviews greeting Farmer as a new-found star.

But Frances was not happy with her career. She felt stifled by Paramount's tendency to cast her in films that depended more on her looks than her talent. Her outspoken style made her seem

Frances Farmer

uncooperative and contemptuous and in an era when the studios dictated every facet of a star's life, she rebelled against the studio's control and resisted every attempt they made to glamorize her private life. She refused to attend Hollywood parties or to date other stars for the gossip columns.

Finally, hoping to enhance her reputation as a serious actress, she left Hollywood in 1937 to do summer stock theater on the East Coast. There, she attracted the attention of director Harold Clurman and playwright Clifford Odets. They invited her to appear in the Group Theatre production of Odets' play "Golden Boy." Her performance at first received mixed reviews, but Frances' box office appeal made it the company's biggest hit. In 1938, the production went on a national tour and critics began giving her rave reviews. But these days of happiness were not mean to last.

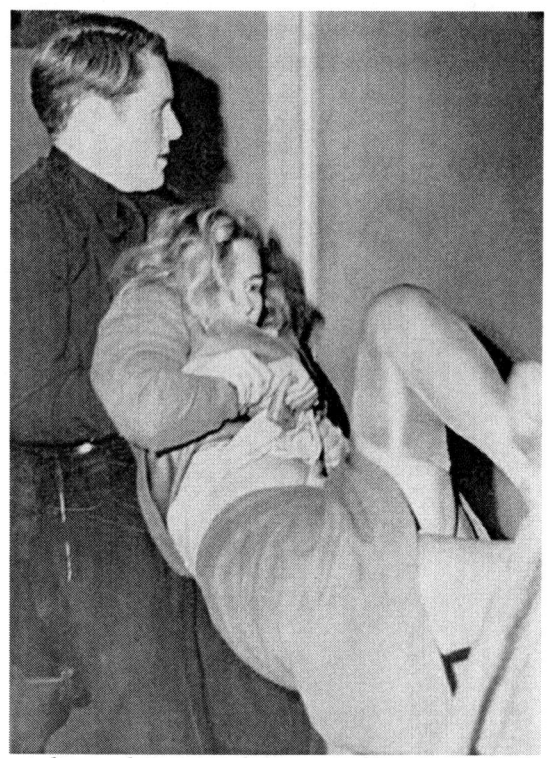

A distraught Frances during one of her tussles with police officers in 1943.

Frances had an affair with Clifford Odets, but he was married to actress Luise Rainer and refused to commit to her. Feeling betrayed, Frances quickly ended the relationship. Soon after, the Globe Group chose another actress for the London run and she began to believe that they had been using her to further the success of the play. She returned to Hollywood and went back to work. Even though she returned to Broadway for several short runs, she largely worked in the movies, being loaned out to other studios for starring roles and taking co-starring parts for Paramount, which she found unchallenging.

Frances began drinking heavily after her break-up with Odets and her temperamental work habits and burgeoning alcoholism began to damage her reputation. In 1940, after abruptly quitting a Broadway production of a play by Ernest Hemingway, she starred in two major films, both loan-outs to other studios. A year later, however, she was again relegated to co-starring roles. In 1942, Paramount canceled her contract, reportedly because of her alcoholism and increasingly erratic behavior during pre-production of "Take A Letter, Darling.". Meanwhile, her marriage to Erickson had fallen apart.

On October 19, 1942, Frances was stopped by the police in Santa Monica for driving with her bright headlights on during the wartime blackout zone that affected most of the West Coast. Reports later claimed that she was unable to produce a driver's license and was verbally abusive to the officers who stopped her. The police suspected her of being drunk and she was jailed overnight. Frances was fined $500 and given a 180-day suspended sentence. She immediately paid $250 and was put on probation.

In January 1943, a bench warrant was issued for her arrest after she failed to pay the rest of the fine from her traffic stop. At almost the same time, a studio hairdresser filed an assault charge against her, alleging that Frances had dislocated her jaw on the set of the film "No Escape." These charges came on the heels of claims that she had recently lost her sweater in a drunken nightclub brawl and had streaked topless through traffic down the Sunset Strip. The police found Frances at the

Knickerbocker Hotel and after getting no answer at her door, opened the room with a passkey. Frances immediately ran into the bathroom and locked the door. The police broke the door open and, after a wild struggle, she was taken from her room and dragged half-naked through the hotel lobby.

At her hearing the next morning, she behaved even more erratically. She claimed the police had violated her civil rights, demanded an attorney, and threw an inkwell at the judge. He immediately sentenced her to 180 days in jail. Frances put up an immediate fight, which led to a policeman being knocked down and another one injured. She managed to get into a telephone booth, where she tried to call her attorney, but was subdued by the police. Thanks to the efforts of her sister-in-law, a deputy sheriff in Los Angeles County, Frances was transferred to the psychiatric ward of Los Angeles General Hospital. She was placed under the care of a psychiatrist who stated that she was suffering from manic-depressive psychosis.

Within days, having been sent to the Kimball Sanitarium in La Crescenta, Farmer was diagnosed with paranoid schizophrenia. She was given insulin shock therapy, a treatment then accepted as standard psychiatric procedure but later discredited, and for the next several years, she became trapped in the world of psychiatric treatment and alleged abuse. She believed that the insulin treatments were giving her brain damage and that she would never be able to learn lines and act again. Convinced that she would be destroyed if she remained in the hospital, Frances walked away from the minimum-security facility one afternoon and walked to her half-sister Rita's house, which was over 20 miles away. The pair called their mother in Seattle to complain about the insulin treatments, which the family had never consented to.

Frances' mother, Lillian, traveled to California and began a lengthy legal battle to have guardianship of her daughter transferred from the state of California to her. Although several psychiatrists testified that Farmer needed further treatment, her mother prevailed. The two of them left Los Angeles by train on September 13, 1943. Frances moved in with her parents, but she and her mother fought bitterly. It should be noted that when Frances was first arrested, her mother told reporters that there was nothing wrong with her and that her daughter's problems were merely a publicity stunt designed to give her some real experience in jail for an upcoming role. Within six months, Frances physically attacked her mother and she was committed to Western Washington State Hospital, where she endured electroshock treatments and ice water baths. Three months later, during the summer of 1944, she was pronounced completely cured and released.

While traveling with her father to visit at an aunt's ranch in Reno, Nev., Frances disappeared. Wandering and hitchhiking, she spent time with a family she met on the road (they had no idea who she was), but was eventually arrested for vagrancy in Antioch, Calif.. Her arrest received wide publicity. Offers for help came in from across the country, but Farmer ignored them all. After a long stay with her aunt in Nevada, Farmer went back to her parents. In May 1945, she was committed again to Western Washington State Hospital and remained there for almost five years.

According to accounts, conditions in the hospital were worse than barbaric. Criminals, patients and mentally retarded people were housed together and their meals were thrown on the floor for them to fight over. Frances was again subjected to regular electroshock "treatments" and in addition, she was allegedly prostituted to soldiers from the local military base and repeatedly raped and abused by hospital orderlies. On March 23, 1950, at her parents' request, Farmer was paroled back into her mother's care – but she was never the same again.

The once-popular movie star took a job sorting laundry at the Olympic Hotel in Seattle. This was the same hotel where Farmer had stayed in 1936 at the world premiere of her film "Come and Get It." Fearing that her mother could have her institutionalized again, Frances petitioned the courts in 1953, 10 years after her arrest at the Knickerbocker Hotel, to have her competency and full civil rights restored. Over the course of the next year, Frances was married briefly to a utility worker named Alfred H. Lobley and then moved to

Eureka, Calif., where she worked anonymously as a secretary and bookkeeper for almost three years in a photo studio.

But not everyone had forgotten about Frances Farmer. In 1957, Frances met Leland C. Mikesell, an independent broadcast promoter from Indianapolis who helped her move to San Francisco. He got her work as a receptionist in a hotel and arranged for a reporter to "recognize" her and write an article. This led to renewed interest from the entertainment world. She made two appearances on the "Ed Sullivan Show" and also appeared on "This is Your Life." When asked about her alcoholism and mental illness, she maintained that she had never been mentally ill. She claimed, "If a person is treated like a patient, they are apt to act like one."

During the spring of 1958, Farmer appeared in several live television dramas, and that same year, she made her last film, "The Party Crashers," produced by Paramount. During this period, she divorced Lobley and married Mikesell. She soon accepted an offer to host afternoon movies on a local television station in Indianapolis. In March 1959, newspapers reported that she was separated from Mikesell and he was suing her for breach of contract. Their divorce was finalized in 1963.

Frances' television show, "France Farmer Presents," ran from 1958 to 1964. It was number one in its time slot for the entire duration of its run. She was also in demand as a public speaker. During the early 1960s, Farmer was actress-in-residence at Purdue University and appeared in some campus productions.

By 1964, however, her behavior had turned erratic again. Frances was fired, re-hired and fired from her television program. She seemed to break down after an appearance on NBC's "The Today Show" which had been meant to garner her some good publicity. Instead, speaking about her years of mental illness on national television was too much for her. Frances' last acting role was in "The Visit" at Loeb Playhouse on the Purdue University campus, which ran from October 22 to October 30, 1965. During this engagement, she was arrested for drunken driving.

After that, Frances attempted to start two small businesses with her friend, Jean Ratcliffe, but both of them failed. She was arrested again for drunken driving and her license was suspended for a year.

In 1959, Frances became a Catholic and was baptized at the St. Joan of Arc Church in Indianapolis. She lived quietly until her death in 1970 from esophageal cancer at the age of 56. At the time of her death, the once beautiful and headstrong star was penniless, broken, and alone. It was a tragic end to what had been a promising life.

Tragedy and legends continued to be born at the Knickerbocker as time went by. The stories say that author William Faulkner and Meta Carpenter, a script girl from the Fox studios, began their lengthy affair at the Knickerbocker. Marilyn Monroe and Joe DiMaggio honeymooned there in 1954. Elvis Presley often stayed at the Knickerbocker and in 1956, when he was filming "Love Me Tender," he posed for "Heartbreak Hotel" photos in one of the rooms. Other stars who lived or stayed at the Knickerbocker included rocker Jerry Lee Lewis, Mae West, Lana Turner, Cecil B. DeMille, Frank Sinatra, Laurel and Hardy and many others.

Character actor William Frawley, who played Fred Mertz on the "I Love Lucy" show, lived at the hotel for decades. In March of 1966, he was walking into the Knickerbocker when he dropped dead of a heart attack on the sidewalk outside. His nurse carried him into the lobby and attempted to revive him, but it was too late.

Perhaps the strangest tragedy took place in November 1962 with the suicide of Irene Gibbons, an actress and costume designer at MGM. She designed costumes for a number of famous actresses including Marlene Dietrich, Elizabeth Taylor, Claudette Colbert, Hedy LaMarr, Judy Garland, Lana Turner, Ingrid Bergman, and many others.

Gibbons, whose real name was Irene Lentz, started out as an actress under her birth name, appearing in secondary roles in silent films beginning with Keystone Studios in 1921. The director of her first film was F. Richard Jones and the two of them became involved in a relationship

(Above) The extended roof over the lobby where Irene's body was found

(Left) Irene Gibbons

that led to a marriage that lasted until his premature death in 1930. Irene decided to get out of acting after her husband's death and, with skill as a seamstress and a flair for style, she opened a small dress shop. The success of her original designs in her shop eventually led to an offer from the Bullocks Wilshire luxury department store to design for their Ladies Custom Salon, which catered to Hollywood's wealthiest women, including a number of film stars.

Irene's designs at Bullocks garnered her attention from the film community and she was contracted by independent production companies to design wardrobes for some of their films. Billing herself simply as "Irene," her first screen work appeared in 1933 for the film "Goldie Gets Along," worn by star Lily Damita. Her big break came when she was hired to create gowns for Ginger Rogers in a 1937 outing with Fred Astaire called "Shall We Dance." This was followed by more designs for Ginger Rogers, as well as work for Walter Wanger Productions, Hal Roach Studios, and major companies like RKO, Paramount and Columbia. During the 1930s, Irene worked with most of the major female stars in Hollywood.

Through her work, Irene met and married short story author and screenwriter Eliot Gibbons, the brother of multi-Academy Award winning Cedric Gibbons, head of art direction at MGM Studios. Cedric Gibbons has been generally regarded as the most important and influential production designer in the history of American films and he hired Irene when gown designer Adrian left MGM to join Universal Studios. By 1943, she was a leading costume supervisor at MGM and earned international recognition for her designers. She is best remembered for Lana Turner's avant-garde wardrobe in "The Postman Always Rings Twice" and in 1948, was nominated for an Academy Award for Best Costume Design for "B.F.'s Daughter."

Despite her success, working under the powerful and arrogant Cedric Gibbons, while being married to his brother, was not easy. In 1950, Irene left MGM to open her own fashion house. She was out of the film industry for nearly 10 years when her friend Doris Day requested her talents for a Universal Studios production, "Midnight Lace." Irene earned her second Oscar nomination for her work for Doris Day in this film. The following year, she did another costume design for Doris Day and during 1962, worked on her last production, "A Gathering of Eagles."

While working with Irene on designs for the 1962 film, Day noticed that her friend seemed upset and nervous. Irene finally confided in her that she was in love with actor Gary Cooper and that he was the only man that she had ever truly loved.

Hollywood's Knickerbocker Hotel

Sadly, Cooper had passed away a short time before. Irene seemed unable to get over the loss.

On November 15, Irene took a room at the Knickerbocker Hotel, checking in under an assumed name. She cut her wrists but when this did not prove to be immediately fatal, she jumped to her death from her bathroom window on the 14th floor, landing on the extended roof of the lobby, where she was discovered later that same night (not two days later, as is often reported). She had left caring notes for friends and family, for her ailing husband, and for the hotel residents, apologizing for any inconvenience her death might cause.

Undoubtedly, the first thing of a supernatural nature to occur at the Knickerbocker was the anniversary séance to contact the spirit of magician Harry Houdini. During his life, Houdini had been an opponent of the Spiritualist movement, but made a pact with his wife and friends that should contact be possible from the other side, he would attempt it. For 10 years after his death, his wife, Bess Houdini, continued to hold séances in hopes of communicating with her late husband. The last "official" Houdini séance was held on Halloween night of 1936 – on the roof of the Knickerbocker Hotel.

Houdini was perhaps America's greatest magician and escape artist during the 1910s and early 1920s. He was also a born showman and when the film industry gained popularity, it was a natural fit for him to try his hand at Hollywood. While playing at the Hippodrome in New York in 1918, Houdini signed a contract with B.F. Rolfe of Octagon Films to star in a movie serial called "The Master Mystery." Houdini would play Quentin Locke, an undercover agent for the Justice Department, who used his expertise as an escape artist to thwart the efforts of the villain of the serial. In different scenes, Houdini's character was buried alive in a gravel pit, tied in the bottom of an elevator shaft as the car was lowered to crush him, suspended upside down over boiling acid, and even strapped into an electric chair. Somehow, he always survived. Houdini broke three bones in his left wrist while filming one of the early scenes but production continued. He had to wear a leather wrist support when he returned to perform at the Hippodrome in

Harry Houdini

The ruins of Houdini's mansion in Laurel Canyon

(Right) Poster from Houdini's film, "The Grim Game"

August. In spite of this, he managed all of his escapes and illusions without a hitch.

Houdini made his first Hollywood feature film, "The Grim Game," for Paramount Pictures in the spring of 1919. His left wrist was fractured again when he fell during a jail escape scene. His second film, "Terror Island," was made soon after and confident that he could write and produce movies, as well as star in them, he formed the Houdini Picture Corporation. "The Man from Beyond" and "Haldane of the Secret Service" followed the pattern of his earlier films with Houdini playing a hero who managed to escape from his adversaries' diabolical traps and tortures. The films enjoyed a modest success and, thanks to the amount of time that he was spending in Hollywood, Houdini purchased a house in Laurel Canyon. The house was a looming mansion that had come from the estate of a local furniture magnate and he soon moved in. The mansion certainly fit his theatrical personality with its parapets, battlements and spooky towers. The foundation of the mansion was honeycombed with tunnels, secret passages and chambers. One tunnel even ran beneath what is now Laurel Canyon Road. In one of the castle's lower chambers was a deep pool in which Houdini practiced his underwater escapes. For years, it was even rumored that in these subterranean passages was a hidden chest containing Houdini's greatest secrets. If it was there, it has never been found.

Throughout the last years of his life, Houdini spoke out against fraudulent Spiritualists who were taking advantage of the gullible. A portion of each of his stage shows exposed how the fake mediums did their tricks and Houdini became the sworn enemy of practicing Spiritualists all over the world. Throughout all of this, however, Houdini claimed to have an open mind and a willingness to believe in the supernatural even though he had never experienced contact with the spirit world himself. To show that he was willing to accept proof if it came along, he made a pact with his wife and a number of other magicians that if it was possible for him to communicate from beyond the grave, he would certainly do so.

Houdini's pact was almost a foreshadowing of things to come. His final season began in the fall of 1926 and during this tour, the show began to be plagued with problems and mishaps and soon, the curtain would fall on the great magician for all time.

In Providence, R.I., Houdini's wife, Bess, became ill with ptomaine poisoning. Houdini called a doctor immediately and arranged for a nurse to come to New York and travel with her. He was less worried about his own health. On the night of October 11, a chain slipped during Houdini's famous Chinese Water Torture Cell escape and fractured his ankle. A doctor in the audience advised him to end the show and go to the hospital, but he refused. In fact, he finished the entire performance painfully hopping on one foot. Afterwards, he stopped at Memorial Hospital in Albany, N.Y., for treatment and x-rays. He was ordered to stay off his feet for at least one week, but he continued his shows anyway. He fashioned a leg support for himself and went on to Schenectady and Montreal.

On the afternoon of October 22, two McGill University students, who had heard Houdini give a lecture the week before, stopped by the magician's dressing room at the Princess Theater. One of the young men was drawing a portrait of Houdini when a third student, J. Gordon Whitehead, came in and began talking to the magician. Houdini was very courteous to the young men, but was also occupied with his mail. He wasn't paying close attention when Whitehead asked if it was true that Houdini could withstand powerful blows to the stomach. He absently replied that he could as long as he had time to brace himself in anticipation of the punch. The boy, thinking that Houdini had given permission for just such a demonstration, suddenly leaned forward and struck him four times in the abdomen with a clenched fist. When Houdini looked startled, the boy quickly backed away, explaining in a panic that he thought that Houdini had given him permission to hit him. The artist and his friend thought Whitehead had gone mad and grabbed for the boy to pull him away. Houdini stopped them with a pained wave. Whitehead felt terrible seeing the performer so clearly in pain, but the magician soon recovered enough to reassure the young man and then step onto the stage for his show.

Throughout the evening, Houdini was seen wincing in pain and late that night, he admitting to crippling pains that continued to get worse. He was unable to sleep when he returned to his hotel room and Bess, believing that he had a stomach cramp or a strained muscle, massaged him in an effort to make him more comfortable.

His performances over the next two days consisted of hours of agony, save for brief intermissions when he fell into a restless sleep. After his final Saturday show, he finally told his wife about what had happened in the dressing room. By then, it was too late to get a doctor. An assistant wired the show's advance man in Detroit and told him to have a physician ready that could see Houdini when they arrived. The train arrived late and Houdini went straight to the Garrick Theater rather than to the Statler Hotel, where Dr. Leo Dretzka was waiting in the lobby. When the doctor finally got to the theater, he found Houdini busy helping his assistants with props for the evening show. There was no cot in the dressing room where Dr. Dretzka could examine the magician, so Houdini stretched out on the floor. He was diagnosed as having acute appendicitis. He had a fever of 102 degrees, but refused to go to the hospital for the emergency surgery that he needed. He was scheduled to perform at a sold-out show that night and was determined to be there.

By the time he took the stage, Houdini's fever had gone up to 104. He was tired, feverish and tormented by abdominal pains. He somehow managed to perform the entire show, though, although his terrified assistants were constantly forced to complete some motion that Houdini couldn't manage. Between the first and second acts, he was taken to his dressing room and ice packs were placed on him to try and cool his fever. This was repeated between acts two and three, as well. Toward the end of the evening, he began doing what he called "little magic" with silks and coins, card sleights and accepting questions and challenges from the audience. He remained on the stage throughout the evening but just before the third act, he turned to his chief assistant and said "Drop the curtain, Collins, I can't go any further." When the curtain closed, he literally collapsed where he had been standing. Houdini was helped back to his dressing room and he changed his clothes but still refused to go back to the hospital.

He went to his hotel, still convinced that his pain and illness would subside. It was not until the early morning hours that the hotel physician was summoned. He contacted a surgeon and Houdini was rushed to the hospital, of course, against his will. An operation was performed immediately, but the surgeons agreed that there was little hope for him to pull through. His appendix had ruptured and despite the efforts of medical experts, it was suggested that Bess contact family members.

Despite the seriousness of his condition, Houdini managed to hang on until the early afternoon of October 31. In the darkness, he turned to Bess and his brother, Theo, who he affectionately called "Dash," and spoke quietly to them: "Dash, I'm getting tired and I can't fight anymore".

A moment later, Houdini stepped through the curtain between this world and the next.

Not long after Houdini's death, the famous "Houdini Séances" began and not surprisingly, they continue today, although the official sanction of the Houdini estate ended years ago. While Bess planned to honor her husband's request about attempting contact with him after death, this may not have been what prompted her to seek the secret code that he promised to send her from beyond the grave, if possible. Bess was at a loss as to what to do with her life with Houdini gone. They had been together since Bess had been a young woman and she had been living inside of his closed world, filling the role as his wife and assistant for decades. She had been his partner in a very real sense and he always stated that Bess was his "beloved wife... and the only one who had ever helped me in my work." Although their life had not been perfect, it had never been dull and as huge as Houdini's ego had been, he never made it a secret that he depended on her totally. With him gone, Bess seemed to be drifting. It's no surprise that she wanted desperately to speak with him again.

But her life moved shakily on. While she was not rich, Houdini had left a trust fund for her and substantial amounts of life insurance had been carried on him. Unfortunately, her life became lost in a haze of alcohol and misery. She tried opening a tearoom and thought of taking a vaudeville act on the road, but none of these projects really got off the ground. She soon began to spend her time attempting to contact her departed husband. Every Sunday at the hour of his death, she would shut herself in a room with his photograph and wait for a sign. She spread the word that she was waiting for a secret message from her husband and word spread far and wide that Bess had offered $10,000 to any medium who could deliver a true message from Houdini.

Almost weekly, a new medium came forward claiming to have broken the code, but none of them did until 1928, when famed medium Arthur Ford announced that he had a message for Bess. He told her that the message had come from Houdini's mother and consisted of a single word, which was "forgive." With this, Bess had a startling announcement to make --- claiming that Ford's message was the first that she had received which "had any appearance of the truth."

In November, another message came to Ford, this time from Houdini himself. In a trance, the medium relayed an entire coded message: "Rosabelle, answer, tell, pray, answer, look, tell, answer, answer, tell."

After this information was relayed to Bess, she invited Ford to her home and he asked her if the words were correct. She said they were and Ford asked her to remove her wedding ring and tell everyone present what "Rosabelle" meant. This was the word that made the message authentic, a secret known only to Bess and Harry themselves. It was the title of a song that had been popular at Coney Island when they first met. The rest of the message was a series of code words that spelled out the word "believe." The code was one that the Houdinis had used during the "mind-reading act" they perfected in their early days touring with the circus.

This seemed to make the message authentic and appeared to be the final clue that Houdini had promised to relay from the next world. But did Houdini actually communicate from the other side?

Not surprisingly, there were soon accusations of fraud leveled against Arthur Ford. Even though Bess claimed the message was correct, many claimed that Ford had gotten the code from a book about Houdini published in 1927. The press, the skeptics and Houdini's friends refused to accept that Ford had broken the code and Bess, on their advice, withdrew her reward offer.

So, did he really break the "impossible" code? Arthur Ford certainly maintained that he had, going to his grave in 1974 with the firm belief that he had actually received a message from Houdini. In 1928, Ford had been the pastor of the First Spiritualist Church of Manhattan and was a respected member of the psychic community. He had also recently distinguished himself by challenging the magician Howard Thurston to a debate at Carnegie Hall, which Ford won. Thurston, who had been carrying on Houdini's tradition of exposing fraudulent mediums, was stymied by being unable to explain some of the effects that Ford produced. After he came forward with the code, jealous colleagues turned on Ford and newspaper reporters and debunkers began to charge him with perpetrating a hoax, along with Bess, despite both of their claims of innocence. Shortly afterwards, Arthur Ford was expelled from the United Spiritualist League of New York but was later reinstated on the grounds of insufficient evidence.

But was he a fraud? Many people believe so and state that he actually found the "secret" code on page 105 of a book that was published the year before. Incidentally, the code was not one that was specially prepared by Houdini and Bess. It was very old and had been used in their act even though it had been around for years. Despite all of this however, it should be noted that while Ford could have easily found the code somewhere --- there has never been an adequate explanation (outside of a fraud perpetrated with Mrs. Houdini, which was denied by both parties) as to where he got the message that he gave to Bess.

Could it have come from the other side?

Bess Houdini continued to hold séances in hopes of communicating with her late husband but as the years went by, she began to lose hope that she would ever hear from him. The last "official" Houdini séance was held on Halloween night of 1936, 10 years after Houdini had died. A group of friends, fellow magicians, occultists, scientists, and Bess Houdini herself gathered in Hollywood, on the roof of the Knickerbocker Hotel. Eddy Saint, a former carnival and vaudeville showman who had also worked as a magician, had arranged the gathering. He had been recommended to Bess a few years before in New York to act as her manager, although concerned friends had actually hired him to watch over her and to protect her from being taken advantage of. A genuine affection developed between then and eventually they began sharing a bungalow together in Hollywood, a place where Bess had enjoyed living during her husband's brief movie career.

Coverage for the Final Houdini Séance was provided by radio and it was broadcast all over the world. Eddy Saint took charge of the proceedings and started things off with the playing of "Pomp and Circumstance," a tune that had been used by Houdini to start his act in the later years. He noted for radio audiences: "Every facility has been provided tonight that might aid in opening the pathway to the spirit world. Here in the inner circle reposes a "medium's trumpet," a pair of slates with chalk, a writing tablet and pencil, a small bell and in the center reposes a huge pair of silver handcuffs on a silk cushion."

Saint continued coverage of the event, finally crying out to make contact with the late magician: "Houdini! Are you here? Are you here, Houdini? Please manifest yourself in any way possible... We have waited, Houdini, oh so long! Never have you been able to present the evidence you promised. And now, this, the night of nights... the world is listening, Harry... Levitate the table! Move it! Lift the table! Move it or rap it! Spell out a code, Harry... please! Ring a bell! Let its tinkle be heard around the world!"

Saint and the rest of Bess' inner circle attempted to contact the elusive magician for over an hour before finally giving up. Saint finally turned to Bess: "Mrs. Houdini, the zero hour has passed. The 10 years are up. Have you reached a decision?"

The mournful voice of Bess Houdini then echoed through radio receivers around the world. "Yes, Houdini did not come through," she replied. "My last hope is gone. I do not believe that Houdini can come back to me --- or to anyone. The Houdini shrine has burned for 10 years. I now, reverently...

A photograph from the 1936 Houdini Séance at the Knickerbocker Hotel. Bess is seen standing in the center, With Eddy Saint directly to the left.

turn out the light. It is finished. Good night, Harry!"

The séance came to an end, but at the moment it did, a tremendously violent thunderstorm broke out, drenching the séance participants and terrifying them with the horrific lightning and thunder. They would later learn that this mysterious storm did not occur anywhere else in Hollywood --- only above the Knickerbocker Hotel! Some speculated that perhaps Houdini did come through after all, as the flamboyant performer just might have made his presence known by the spectacular effects of the thunderstorm.

Although Houdini's ghost has never been reported to make an appearance at the Knickerbocker, the place has long been considered to be haunted. The most "spirited" spot was always thought to be the hotel bar, so not surprisingly, when the Knickerbocker closed in 1971 and became a senior citizen's retirement building, the old bar was sealed off. The rooms remained closed and unused for nearly 25 years until the early 1990s, when it was re-opened as a nostalgic coffee shop called "The All-Star Theatre Café & Speakeasy." The Art Deco cafe' opens at 7 p.m. and stays hopping until the early morning hours. Star spotters will be intrigued to know that it frequently attracts studio wrap parties and film shoots, playing host to a number of today's celebrities.

However, these are not the only stars that have been spotted here. Many believe that celebrities from the past often put in appearances here as well. The ghost of Valentino (once again, Hollywood's most traveled ghost!) has occasionally been reported, along with that of Marilyn Monroe, who has been seen in the women's restroom. Other anonymous spirits sometimes show up as well and staff members are quick to recall instances of lights turning on and off and things moving about on their own. Even after all of these years, the Knickerbocker remains a glamorous, and often mysterious, place.

ALEXANDRIA HOTEL

The Alexandria Hotel opened in Hollywood in 1906 and for many years served the restaurant and theater crowds of the surrounding district. It became a meeting place for the burgeoning film industry and by 1910, the dining room had become the lunch location of choice for studio heads, famous actors, and those of Hollywood power. During its heyday, it played host to people like Winston Churchill, Enrico Caruso, King Edward VIII, (later known as the Duke of Windsor) and American presidents like Taft, Wilson and Theodore Roosevelt. It would be at the Alexandria that D.W. Griffith, Charlie Chaplin, Mary Pickford and Douglas Fairbanks would make movie history by announcing the formation of their independent company, United Artists.

But Hollywood would not remain so kind to the Alexandria. As Los Angeles began to develop in a westerly direction, the stars abandoned the hotel for the more modern Biltmore and Ambassador. The Alexandria became just a memory and it fell into silence and disrepair. Then, in the early 1970s, the hotel was given a multi-million dollar facelift and the past began to come alive at the hotel -- in more ways than one!

Nancy Malone and Lisa Mitchell were hired to bring back the flavor of old Hollywood to the hotel. They named rooms for famous former residents and decorated the hallways with portraits of stars and photographs of Hollywood in its early days. Is it possible that this connection to the past helped to awaken the ghosts of the old hotel?

Author Laurie Jacobson interviewed Nancy Malone, who vividly recalled her first sighting of the hotel's famed "lady in black." Malone was hanging pictures on the wall in a hallway in the early morning hours when she spotted a woman dressed entirely in black and wearing a large black hat. She was standing at the other end of the hall and began walking away. Nancy remarked that she could not see through the woman, but that "she wasn't solid either." The woman walked a short distance and then vanished.

Since that time, she continues to be seen, but who is she? Lori Jacobson believes that she might be a former resident of the hotel who died while in mourning for some loved one. "Stricken with grief," the author writes, "she barely noticed her own passing and continued to grieve for more than seventy years."

Alexandria Hotel

HOLLYWOOD ROOSEVELT HOTEL

The most famous haunted hotel in Hollywood is, without a doubt, the Hollywood Roosevelt. Today, the hotel has been refurbished and remodeled to capture the spirit of its early days but the new furnishings and decor don't stop the stories of the old spirits from being told.

The Hollywood Roosevelt opened in 1927 and was, from the beginning, designed to serve the new movie industry as a luxury hotel. The most famous movie stars of the day, Douglas Fairbanks and Mary Pickford, helped bring the hotel to life and the grand opening hosted the biggest celebrities of the day like Gloria Swanson, Greta Garbo, Will Rogers, and Clara Bow, among others. The hotel remained popular for many years and then in 1984, underwent a restoration. Since that time, the ghosts, they say, have been putting in frequent appearances.

The first strange event took place in December 1985, about two weeks before the grand re-opening. Alan Russell, personal assistant to the general manager, was in the Blossom Room, where the first Academy Awards banquet was held in 1929. He was sweeping the floor when he noticed an extremely cold spot in one part of the room. He and the other employees who were present were perplexed to find there were no drafts or air conditioners to explain away the chill. Psychics who have investigated the hotel believe there is a man in black clothing who haunts this room, although who he may be, no one knows.

On that same day, another employee named Suzanne Leonard was dusting a mirror in the manager's office. She looked into the glass and saw the reflection of a blond woman. She turned quickly around but there was no one behind her, although the reflection remained for some time before fading away. So, who was this mysterious

Hollywood Roosevelt Hotel

figure? It was later learned that the mirror once hung in Suite 1200 of the hotel, a suite that was frequently used by Marilyn Monroe. Could she still be lingering behind at the Roosevelt? Based on the many lingering questions about Marilyn's tragic death (see Chapter 4), it certainly seems possible that her spirit might be a restless one.

As guests began to arrive at the refurbished hotel, the staff was told of other encounters. They frequently heard complaints about loud talking in nearby rooms and of voices in hallways -- rooms and corridors that would prove to be empty. Phones were lifted from receivers in empty suites; lights were turned on in empty, locked rooms; a maid was inexplicably pushed into a supply closet; a typewriter began typing in the middle of the night in an empty, locked office; a man in a white suit (who was seen by three different people on two different days) walked through a door and vanished; extra bedspreads that were hung on a rod in the basement began moving on their own; a little girl was seen playing in the lobby and then

Dead Men Do Tell Tales: Bloody Hollywood - Page 123

vanished before the eyes of a startled staff member and much more.

Some employees also reported strange shadows on the ninth floor, prompting many of them to refuse to work on that level. Strange things were especially connected to Room 928. There, housekeepers reported cold spots that brushed by them and other felt a strong presence watching them or walking beside them. One night in 1992, a female guest reported that a man's hand patted her on the shoulder while she was reading. She turned, thinking that it was her husband, only to find him sound asleep.

Room 928 has been most prominently connected with actor Montgomery Clift, who lived in the room for three months in 1952 while filming "From Here to Eternity." Clift was said to restlessly pace his room and the corridor outside, rehearsing his lines and practicing the bugle. Some say that he still does...

On screen, Montgomery Clift exuded an aura of vulnerable masculinity that appealed to both men and women alike; however, his real life was filled with insecurities that were often too much for him to bear. His gradual deterioration was once described as "the slowest suicide in show business."

Clift was born in Omaha, Neb., in 1920. He grew up the privileged son of a Wall Street stockbroker and traveled all over the world with his family and private tutors. When Wall Street crashed in 1929, the Clifts changed their lifestyle and moved to a small home in Sarasota, Fla. There, Clift would try acting for the first time at the age of 13. He joined a local youth theatrical group and his mother, realizing his natural talents, pushed him toward an acting career. After the family moved to Massachusetts, Clift was able to audition for a part on Broadway. He won the role and his new career was started at the age of 17.

Over the next three years, Clift played a number of leading roles on Broadway, while members of the film industry tried to lure him to Hollywood. He rejected every offer until he finally was able to get the studios to agree to hire him on his terms. Almost immediately, United Artists agreed to what he wanted and he was cast alongside John Wayne and Walter Brennan in what became one of the most famous westerns of all time, "Red River."

After that, Clift began to work in other roles and became friends with actress Elizabeth Taylor, who he appeared with in "A Place in the Sun." He would later appear with Taylor in two other films, "Raintree County" and "Suddenly Last Summer." He accepted both roles without even looking at a script. He just wanted to act with Taylor. After a two-year hiatus following "A Place in the Sun," Clift returned to the movie screen with "From Here to Eternity," with Burt Lancaster and Frank Sinatra. The film would be nominated for eight Academy Awards and Clift would be nominated for Best Actor. After that, he starred in the Alfred Hitchcock film, "I Confess," and in "Indiscretion of an American Housewife." He would not be seen on the stage or screen again for more than three years.

About this time, Clift's personal life began to

Montgomery Clift

be plagued by his own inner demons. Despite his talents, he was utterly insecure. His mother controlled his life until he was in his 20s and he constantly tried to hide the fact that he was a homosexual, which was a "career-killer" in the Hollywood of the 1950s. His emotional difficulties were enhanced by his rise to stardom and he became an alcoholic and habitual drug user. Soon, the booze and pills began to interfere with his work and during the making of "From Here to Eternity," the cast and crew began commenting about his drunken behavior on the set.

One night in May 1957, Clift attended a dinner party at the home of Elizabeth Taylor during the shooting of "Raintree County." As he was driving home, he veered off the road and his car collided with a telephone pole. Taylor arrived at the crash scene and discovered that Clift was having trouble breathing. She forced her hand down his throat and pulled out two of his broken teeth, which were blocking his airway. The accident left Clift with a broken jaw and nose, a crushed sinus cavity, two missing teeth, and severe facial lacerations that required plastic surgery. Somehow, he recovered and returned home from the hospital after just eight weeks. He was able to complete filming on "Raintree County".

Clift had other problems apart from his self-destructive personality. He suffered from various illnesses including colitis and a thyroid condition, the symptoms of which were almost indistinguishable from the effects of alcohol and drugs. When Clift co-starred in "The Misfits" – both Clark Gable and Marilyn Monroe's final movie – Marilyn said of Clift, "He's the only person I know who is in worse shape than I am."

In 1962, Clift was hired for the title role in John Huston's "Freud" and Universal sued him because he was incapable of remembering his lines. Studios were now in the habit of insuring their productions and Clift's shaky track record made him a liability. He didn't act for three years after that, until Elizabeth Taylor got him a part in the 1967 production, "Reflections in a Golden Eye." Clift was also offered a part in "The Defector," which he felt was an inferior film, but he was so desperate to prove that he was worthy of "Reflections in a Golden Eye" that he signed on. He did all of his own stunts in "The Defector," just to show the studio that he was able to work.

On Friday night, July 22, 1966, Clift went to sleep and never woke up again. When a friend entered his bedroom and found Clift naked except for his glasses, he planned to cover him up and leave him alone. He was used top Clift's drunken stupors, but this time was different. Clift did not seem drunk, but dead. Unable to find a pulse, he called a doctor, who pronounced that Clift had died in his sleep. Although many assumed that he succumbed to alcohol or a drug overdose, Clift actually died from a heart attack.

All of Clift's friends from his long career on stage and screen had encountered him once or twice before his inevitable demise and each had a heart-breaking story to tell about the once-intelligent and gifted actor who was destroyed by drink, drugs, and poor health. Clift's life was ruined, but his film work remains the product of a one of the greatest actors of all time. That's how he is remembered today – along with being one of the continued guests at the Hollywood Roosevelt Hotel.

3. SEX, SIN & SUICIDE
HOLLYWOOD SCANDALS & THE RESTLESS SPIRITS LEFT BEHIND

The Hollywood movie colony came into existence thanks to a group of East Coast filmmakers and businessmen who saw a good thing in the nickelodeons that were springing up all over America. They were lured to the West Coast by the promise of that fabled Southern California sunshine (which was said to appear 355 days a year), by low-cost land and by the opportunity to elude the process servers of Thomas Edison (who filed lawsuits against anyone who copied his design for the early movie cameras). They settled into the city of Los Angeles and began building open-air stages and makeshift studios. In Los Angeles, and nearby Hollywood, the early moviemakers began cranking out primitive one- and two-reelers, which captivated the hearts and imaginations of the American public.

Soon, word trickled back to Hollywood that audiences across the country were flocking to see their favorite performers and at this point, the actors (who prior to this were seen as little more than anonymous hired help) suddenly gained importance as a sure way to sell tickets. The rapidly becoming famous faces took on new names and soon earned salaries to match their new status. Almost overnight, the once-obscure and disreputable performers suddenly found fame and fortune, becoming America's royalty. Some of them managed to cope with this quite well -- while others did not.

Throughout the early 1900s, Hollywood re-invented itself almost daily as the movies began to emerge as a new art form. Money began to roll into studio coffers and then into the pockets of the stars. Cocaine, or "joy powder" as it was called in those days, became the drug of choice. It has been rumored that some of the manic silent film comedies actually came about with more than a little help from the drug and became known as the Triangle-Keystone "cokey comedies." In 1916, British drug afficionado and occultist Aleister Crowley journeyed to Hollywood and noted the locals as being the "cinema crowd of cocaine-crazed sexual lunatics." And that's quite a statement coming from Crowley, who created a reputation for himself as "the wickedest man on Earth".

In addition to drugs, sex was always plentiful in Hollywood and gossipmongers in the movie colony always had much to talk about. Was it true that famed director D. W. Griffith had an obsession, onscreen and off, with young girls? Could it be true that Lillian and Dorothy Gish, up and coming young sisters, were also lovers? Were the tales of Mack Sennett's "casting couch" actually true -- and were some of Sennett's Sunshine Girls, like Gloria Swanson and Carole Lombard, really part of his handpicked harem? And what about Hollywood's sex goddess, Theda Bara, who was allegedly a French-Arab demon of depravity born beneath the Sphinx -- was it true that she was actually Theodosia Goodman, a Jewish tailor's daughter from Ohio? And such tales, whispers, and rumors were only the beginning.

Within a few years of its founding, Hollywood would be the most maligned place to ever be spoken of from church pulpits across America. Preachers and evangelists would brand Hollywood as a place of legendary depravity and would call for boycotts of films and protests against theaters that would dare to show anything made in such a place. But the general public all but ignored the outcry and they continued to spend their hard-earned money at the movies.

The 1920s have been referred to as Hollywood's Golden Age and they were, in terms of both the numbers of movies made and in the amount of cash these films raked in. Unfortunately, though, sometimes the golden ones fall just like the rest of us and when they do fall, they fall very hard.

OLIVE THOMAS: THE FIRST HOLLYWOOD SCANDAL

The shocking news was first heard on the radio, on the night of September 10, 1920, and it would later make newspaper headlines: Olive Thomas, Ziegfeld Follies star, Selznick Pictures actress and wife of Jack Pickford, was dead from poison in Paris. She was found on the floor of her hotel suite, nude and lying on a sable opera cape. In her hand was a blue glass bottle containing mercury bichloride. The nude woman was Mrs. Jack Pickford, known to millions of fans as Olive Thomas – one of America's original movie stars.

Thomas was born as Olivia Duffy (most who her knew her called her "Ollie") and she grew up in a working class family in the Pittsburgh area town of Charleroi, Pa. Her father died when she was

Olive Thomas, All-American Girl

young and Olive was forced to leave school to help support her mother and two younger brothers. In April 1911, at the age of 16, she married Bernard Krugh Thomas in McKee's Rocks, another small Pennsylvania mill town. During the two-year marriage, she reportedly worked as a clerk in Kaufman's department store in Pittsburgh. After her divorce, she went to stay with an aunt in New York City where she found work in a Harlem department store.

In 1914, after answering a newspaper ad, she won the title of "The Most Beautiful Girl in New York City" in a contest sponsored by the celebrated commercial artist, Howard Chandler Christy. She then modeled for artist Harrison Fisher and eventually landed on the cover of the Saturday Evening Post.

A letter of recommendation to Florenz Ziegfeld resulted in Olive being hired by the Ziegfeld Follies. She subsequently performed in the much more risqué Midnight Frolic, a show staged after hours in the roof garden of the New Amsterdam Theatre. Unlike in the Follies, the women in the Midnight Frolic maintained a strict decorum on stage no matter how skimpy the costumes. The performers were clad only in balloons, allowing the virtually all male audience the opportunity to burst the balloons with their cigars.

Midnight Frolic was primarily a show for famous male patrons with plenty of money to bestow on the young and beautiful female performers. Before long, the attractive Thomas was the center of attention of the in-crowd associated with Condé Nast. She soon found herself being pursued by a number of very wealthy and powerful men. She received expensive gifts from her admirers, with rumors that the German Ambassador had given her a $10,000 string of pearls. She also posed nude for famed Peruvian artist Alberto Vargas.

It came as no surprise that Olive's newfound fame led to her departing for Hollywood. She signed with International Film Company as the leading lady in the Harry Fox movies. She went on to appear in more than 20 Hollywood films over the next four years, including "A Girl Like That," "Betty Takes a Hand," "Prudence on Broadway," and "The Follies Girl." In 1917, Olive moved to Triangle Pictures, where she worked with Thomas Ince. Shortly after, news broke of her engagement to Jack Pickford, whom she had actually married the year before. Olive did not want anyone to think that she was only succeeding because of the Pickford name, which was already reaching legendary status in early Hollywood. During her time with the company, Olive was nicknamed the "Triangle Star."

In December 1918, Olive was persuaded by Myron Selznick to sign with Selznick Pictures Company. She hoped for more serious roles than the madcap comedies that she had been cast in and, believing that with her husband signed to the same company, she would have more influence. She soon became the first Selznick star and created the image of the "baby vamp."

In 1920, she was a huge hit in a film called "The Flapper." She was the first actress to be described by the term "flapper," preceding stars like Clara Bow, Louise Brooks, and Joan Crawford. She would go on to play the "flapper" role in her final films, including "A Youthful Folly" and her last movie, "Everybody's Sweetheart." The formula proved successful and by the time of her death, Thomas was making $3,000 a week.

The fact that Olive was found dead, and had possibly committed suicide, just months after her greatest success made headlines around the world and became the subject of much controversy. She was only 26 when she died, had wealth, beauty, fame and the adoration of millions of fans. Newspapers referred to her and her husband as the "perfect couple." So, what went wrong?

Selznick Studios was deluged with letters from around the country and both the American Embassy and the French authorities promised full investigations. Unfortunately, the revelations of these investigations did not match the public image of "Everybody's Sweetheart" Olive Thomas.

Unknown to the American public, Olive had a reputation for partying, heavy drinking, and wild ways, which increased after she married Jack Pickford. Alcohol fueled most of the drama in her marriage and possibly led to several automobile accidents. She was involved in three car crashes in two years, one seriously injuring a 9-year-old child. She eventually hired a driver for herself.

Olive met actor Jack Pickford, brother of Mary Pickford, one of the most powerful silent stars, at a beach cafe on the Santa Monica Pier. Pickford also was known for his wild partying and together the pair was trouble. She eloped with Pickford in October 1916 and married him in New Jersey. By most accounts, Olive was the love of Pickford's life, even though the marriage was stormy and filled with violent conflict, which was always followed by lavish making-up and the exchange of expensive gifts. Pickford's family never really approved of Olive, although they liked her. Mary Pickford later said that she knew Olive and Jack were madly in love, "but I always thought of them as a couple of children playing together..."

Olive Thomas & Jack Pickford

For several years, Olive and Jack had planned to vacation together but with both of them always working and traveling separately, their plans were constantly postponed. In August 1920, they finally arranged to take a second honeymoon and traveled to Paris, hoping to combine a vacation with some film preparation.

On the night of September 9, Jack and Olive went for a night of entertainment and partying at one of the famous bistros in the Montparnasse Quarter of Paris. Returning to their room in the Hotel Ritz around 3 a.m., Pickford either fell asleep or, according to some sources, had left the room to

> Although her ghost has never been spotted in Hollywood, Olive Thomas is believed to haunt the New Amsterdam Theatre in New York City, where she appeared in the Ziegfeld Follies and the racy Midnight Frolic in the New Amsterdam's roof garden theater.

look for drugs. It was rumored that he and Olive were using cocaine and heroin that night but it has never been proven.

Olive was found by her husband a short time later. It was believed that the intoxicated actress had accidentally ingested a large dose of mercury bichloride, which had been prescribed for her husband's chronic syphilis. Since the label on the bottle was in French, she may have thought that it was a sleeping medicine. Pickford summoned help but it was too late, she had already swallowed a lethal dose. Olive was taken to the American Hospital in the Paris suburb of Neuilly, where Pickford remained at her side until she succumbed to the poison a few days later. Soon after her death, rumors began that she tried to commit suicide or had been murdered. The police believed that her death was accidental – but rumors and suspicions ran rampant.

Most of the rumors involved the cocaine and wild parties that the Pickfords had been involved in, both in Hollywood and in Paris. The stories also claimed that the couple had been seen in a number of clubs in Paris, often in the company of members of Paris' underworld. One story that circulated claimed that Jack had left the hotel suite that night to look for heroin because he was a hopeless addict. Olive, unable to cope with the erratic behavior caused by the addiction, committed suicide. When this story appeared in the press, Jack was undergoing treatment for a nervous collapse that he suffered after Olive's death and he was unable to refute the claims. However, Mary Pickford issued a statement that denied the "sickening aspersions" on her brother's good name.

Jack brought Olive's body back to the United States and several accounts state that he tried to commit suicide while en route, but was talked out of it. On September 29, 1920, a funeral service was held for Olive at St. Thomas Episcopal Church in New York. According to newspaper accounts, a police escort was needed and the entire church was jammed. Several women fainted at the ceremony and several men had their hats crushed in the rush to view the coffin. She was buried in the Woodlawn Cemetery in the Bronx, N.Y.

Sadly, though, the investigations in Olive's death revealed much more about the beautiful actress than most of her adoring fans wanted to know. She was no longer the "ideal American girl" but "Olive Thomas, dope fiend," and watch societies began to speak out against this new menace to American maidenhood. In the 1920s, the film colony lured young would-be stars from across the land and many warned these hopefuls about the dark allure of drugs and fast living. Olive's death provided good newspaper copy for almost a year after her demise, forever destroying the legacy of a young woman who worked hard to leave small town America and make it big in the bright lights of Hollywood.

THE FALL OF THE "FUNNY FAT MAN"
THE FATTY ARBUCKLE SCANDAL

In 1921, the death of a young movie actress named Virginia Rappe would make newspaper headlines around the world. The scandal that followed her death had nothing to do with the fame, or lack of it, of the pretty actress – it was her link to the man who was known as "America's Funnyman" Roscoe "Fatty" Arbuckle. Virginia's death destroyed the career of the man who was then America's best-known comedic actor and created one of Hollywood's first lingering ghosts.

Roscoe Arbuckle was Hollywood's original loser. Few actors have even been as badly treated as Arbuckle was in the 1920s. The rotund comedian, nicknamed "Fatty" by his fans because of his 300-pound girth, achieved his original success in the 1910s. He was more popular than even Charlie Chaplin and at the time of his downfall in 1921, he was earning over $1 million a year, a tremendous sum in those days. But it was not meant to last and some would say that Fatty's success was what stacked the deck against him. It was one thing to fall from grace and almost go to prison, because of one's own mistakes and the scandal that followed them. It was another thing entirely to be falsely accused of a crime that was never committed, used by an ambitious district attorney for his own political gains, and savaged by the Hearst newspapers, which sensationalized Fatty's plight and made a bundle in circulation sales. Making things even worse, Arbuckle's own studio led the behind-the-scenes intrigue that sabotaged his career, some say as revenge against a star who had become too big to control.

Roscoe Arbuckle was born (weighing in at a whopping 16 pounds) on a small farm in Smith Center, Kans., on March 24, 1887. The following year, his family relocated to Santa Ana, Calif., and opened a small hotel. In the summer of 1895, Roscoe made his stage debut, playing in blackface with a traveling theater troupe. The shy and overweight youngster immediately felt at home on the stage. Four years later, his mother died and the boy was sent to live with his father, who was then residing in Watsonville, Calif. When his father vanished a short time later, a local hotel owner took Roscoe in. When not working at odd jobs, he was tutored by a teacher who lived in the hotel. However, he preferred appearing on amateur night at the town's vaudeville theater to reading and writing. In 1902, he was reunited with his remarried father in Santa Clara, Calif. and when not attending school, he waited tables in his father's restaurant.

Roscoe got into show business a few years later, working in vaudeville and burlesque shows in California and the Pacific Northwest. During a 1908 summer stock engagement in Long Beach, Calif., he met a singer and dancer named Armanta "Minta" Durfee. The two of them were married and toured the Southern California vaudeville circuit. After being unable to find stage work for a time, Roscoe decided to try his luck in the fledging movie industry.

Roscoe "Fatty" Arbuckle

Legend had it that Arbuckle was an overweight plumber when Mack Sennett discovered him. The story goes that he had come to unclog the film producer's drain, but Sennett had other plans for him. He took one look at Roscoe's hefty frame and offered him a job. Arbuckle's large frame and bouncing agility made him the perfect target for Sennett's brand of film comedy, which included mayhem, pratfalls, and pies in the face. Of course, this story is more legend than truth. Regardless of how it happened, though, Arbuckle became a member of Mack Sennett's Keystone Film Company in April 1913. He was soon making dozens of two-reelers as a film buffoon and audiences loved him. He made one film after another, all of them wildly successful. He also made a rather substantial fortune.

In the summer of 1916, Arbuckle joined the East Coast-based Comique Film Corporation as a star and director with an annual income of more

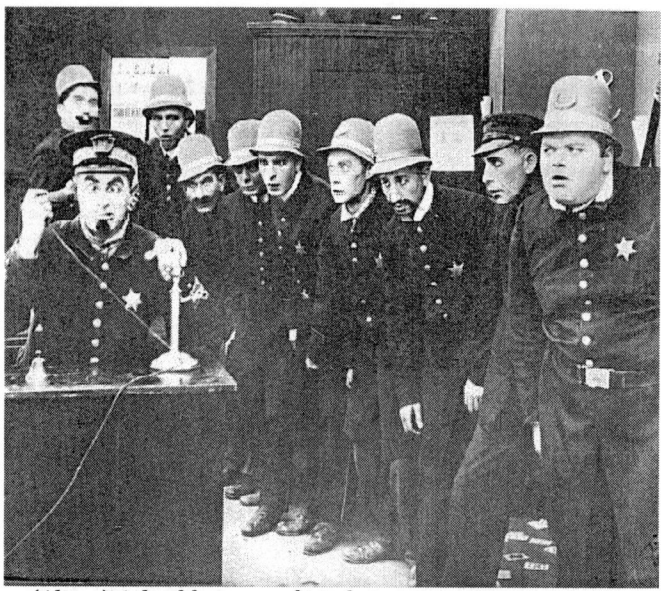

(Above) Arbuckle as one of Mack Sennett's "Keystone Cops" (Fatty on the far right) in his early comedies.

(Below) Arbuckle in a starring role in "Brewster's Millions"

than $1 million. The following March, he attended a banquet in Boston hosted by his studio for regional theater exhibitors and this became Fatty's first brush with scandal. After the dinner, Arbuckle retired to his hotel room, however company executives (including founder Adolph Zukor) and others continued partying at Brownie Kennedy's Roadhouse, a tavern and brothel in nearby Woburn, Mass. Almost immediately, news circulated in Boston about the orgy, and the gossip claimed that Arbuckle had been present. In fact, some stories had him dancing on tables with prostitutes in the roadhouse's backroom. Because of the publicity, the city's mayor raided the brothel. After paying a fine, the madam was released. However, the stories about what went on that night were too racy to simply fade away. Zukor was informed that unless money changed hands, the bawdy activities were sure to make national news. Zukor paid $100,00 to keep the matter quiet and in the process, did nothing to clarify that Arbuckle had not been present that night.

In October 1917, Arbuckle transferred his filmmaking to Hollywood. By now, his marriage to Minta had fallen apart and she remained in New York to pursue her acting career. Although separated, their divorce was not finalized until 1925.

With 1920's "The Round Up," Arbuckle began making full-length movies. In January 1921, he signed a lucrative new contract with Paramount Pictures, which led to Adolph Zukor pushing him into an exhausting schedule that ended with him filming three movies at the same time in the summer of 1921. By Labor Day weekend, Fatty was worn out and planned to go to San Francisco to relax over the holiday. Zukor asked him to remain in town to take part in an exhibitors' convention that weekend and when Roscoe refused, Zukor was enraged. Arbuckle didn't let this bother him and he went on the trip anyway.

Fatty was joined on his trip up the coast by actor friend Lowell Sherman. Then, director Fred Fischbach, whom Arbuckle had known for years, invited himself along. The three men set out on early Saturday morning, September 3, and arrived in San Francisco later that evening. Fatty was driving his flashy new Pierce-Arrow automobile and took his friends to the luxurious St. Francis Hotel. Fatty took three adjoining suites on the 12th floor.

On Sunday, the trio did some sightseeing and visited friends and on Monday, Labor Day, the party got under way. Fischbach got in touch with a bootlegger connection and soon, the guests and the liquor began to arrive. Among the guests was Fred's friend, film talent manager Al Semnacher, who was in San Francisco for the weekend trying to concoct evidence for his pending divorce. He had brought along Bambina Maude Delmont, a woman with an extensive police record involving blackmail, prostitution, and swindling, to help him out. A friend of Bambina's also came along: a minor actress named Virginia Rappe.

Virginia came to Hollywood in 1919. She was a lovely brunette whose unfortunate reputation preceded her. It was no secret in Hollywood that she was a girl with loose morals. She had had several abortions before the age of 16, when she had an illegitimate baby that she gave away. She caught the eye of Mack Sennett and wrangled some movie roles on the Keystone lot, where she met Arbuckle. It was rumored that Virginia had worked her way through the cast and crew of the company and at one point, she passed around a rather sensitive infestation of body lice that was so severe that Sennett had to close the studio and have it fumigated. In spite of her drunken escapades and reports of unprovoked nudity, she did earn some film roles, including "Fantasy," "Paradise Garden," and "Joey Loses A Sweetheart," in which she appeared with Arbuckle. Virginia was noticed by William Fox, shortly after winning an award for the "Best-Dressed Girl in Pictures," and he took her under contract. There was talk of her starring in a new Fox feature and Virginia certainly seemed to be on her way to the top.

In 1920, Virginia began dating director Jack White. When he left Hollywood for New York, she was left with an unwanted pregnancy to deal with. Her manager, Al Semnacher, suggested that she have an abortion in San Francisco, where there was

Actress Virginia Rappe

less chance of the Hollywood gossips finding out about it. Since she was going up north and Semnacher had plans with Bambina Delmont that weekend, he arranged for her to drive there with him on September 3.

Salesman Ira Fortlois arrived at Roscoe's suite at noon on Monday to find the party already in full swing. Arbuckle was reportedly not happy to discover that Fred Fischbach had invited Semnacher, Delmont, and Rappe to the party, thanks to their questionable reputations, but he was enjoying himself too much to press the issue. At one point during the party, Fischbach suddenly left, claiming that he had business elsewhere. The crowd grew to a couple of dozen people. The young women were downing gin-laced Orange Blossoms, some of the guests had shed their tops to do the "shimmy," guests were vanishing into the back bedrooms for sweaty love sessions, and the empty bottles of booze were piling up.

Meanwhile, Delmont, who was well liquored, disappeared into Lowell Sherman's suite with him and locked the door. Virginia, roaring drunk, began tearing off her clothes and screaming hysterically. Because Delmont and Sherman were locked in room 1221, and room 1220 had no bathroom, Virginia was rushed into room 1219, Fatty's suite, to use the facilities there. Soon, unaware of what was happening, Roscoe tried to enter his bathroom, only to find Virginia vomiting into the toilet. He helped her up and got her to lie down and rest on his bed. Next, he went in search of some ice. He hoped that the ice would quiet the woman down as well as determine, by holding a piece of ice against her thigh to see if she reacted to the chill, whether she was suffering from hysterics.

By now, Fischbach had returned. As Roscoe applied the ice to the wailing woman's leg, Maude Delmont walked into the room. Rappe yelled that she was dying – words heard by several other female party guests. Next, the bathtub in room 1219 was filled with cold water to cool of the distraught young woman. But Virginia suddenly awoke and began screaming at Arbuckle. "Stay away from me!" she cried and then turned to Delmont, "What did he do to me, Maudie?" Virginia was bodily placed in the cold water tub and she seemed to settle down. A short time later, she was taken to another room down the hall where Delmont could take care of her.

Later, a doctor brought to the hotel decided that Virginia was merely drunk. The party continued, with Arbuckle leaving the hotel for a time to arrange to have his car shipped back to Los Angeles because he planned to return by boat. By the time Fatty returned, another doctor was administering morphine to the ailing woman. When the physician asked Delmont what had transpired, she calculatedly created a fabricated tale that she later told the police – but never swore to in court.

According to her version of events, Fatty, wearing only pajamas and a bathrobe, had steered a drunken Virginia into his suite at around 3 p.m. on Monday afternoon. Delmont stated that the festivities in the adjoining suites came to a halt when screams were heard in the bedroom. She also said that weird moans were heard from behind the door. A short time later, Fatty emerged with ripped pajamas and he told the girls to "Go in and get her dressed. She makes too much noise." When Virginia continued to scream, he yelled for her to shut up, or "I'll throw you out the window." Delmont and another showgirl, Alice Blake, found Virginia nearly nude and lying on the unmade made. She was moaning and told them that she was dying. Bambina later reported that they tried to dress her, but found that all of her clothing, including her stockings and undergarments were so ripped and torn, "that one could hardly recognize what garments they were."

Arbuckle knew nothing of the story that Delmont was spreading and on Tuesday, September 6, he checked out of the St. Francis, generously paying for everyone's expenses. By now, Virginia, at Delmont's direction, was being treated by another doctor, this one associated with the private

Witness against Fatty -- Maude Delmont

Wakefield Sanitarium. Having been assured that Virginia was in no danger, Arbuckle and his friends returned by ferry to Los Angeles.

On September 8, the still-stricken Virginia was transferred from the hotel to the Wakefield Sanitarium, where she died the next afternoon. An illegal postmortem exam was conducted on her body and her ruptured bladder and other organs were placed in specimen jars, which would prevent a proper autopsy by the legal authorities. Convinced that she could turn the entire incident into something she could profit from, Delmont swore out a complaint against Arbuckle with the police. Back in Hollywood, Roscoe's new film, "Gasoline Gus," had just opened successfully and at the same time, he learned of Virginia's death. Shocked, he volunteered to return to San Francisco. Paramount, meanwhile, panicked at the possible repercussions of the weekend, hired attorneys to represent their high-priced star.

From the start, the newspapers were filled with lurid headlines ("Fatty Arbuckle Sought in Orgy Death") and graphic, false details supplied by Delmont. Newspapers around the country were revealing shocking "truths" about the alleged events in the death of the virtuous Virginia Rappe at the hands of the lust-crazed Fatty Arbuckle. Everything from Arbuckle's past was raked up, including the false story that he had been party of the 1917 orgy in Massachusetts and new stories claimed that he had killed Virginia because she had rebuffed his advances. They also claimed that he had killed her because his immense weight pressed down on her too hard during sex. And it was no longer just sex, the newspapers told a nation of stunned fans, but "strange and unnatural sex." According to reports, Arbuckle became enraged over the fact that his drunkenness had led to impotence, so he ravaged Virginia with a everything from a Coca-Cola Bottle, to a champagne bottle, to an over-sized piece of ice. Other stories claimed that Fatty was so well endowed that he had injured the girl, while others stated that the injury had come when Fatty had landed on the slight actress during a sexual frolic.

Soon, churches and women's groups were crusading against the "lustful" Arbuckle. In Hartford, Conn., a group of angry women ripped down a screen in a theater showing an Arbuckle comedy, while in Wyoming, a group of men opened fire in a movie house where another Arbuckle short was being shown. Thanks to the newspapers, Arbuckle had been found guilty in the public's eyes before charges have ever been filed against him. Angry, and increasingly boisterous, voices were calling for Hollywood to clean up its act. Finally, Arbuckle's films were pulled from general release. Arbuckle had been placed on suspension by Paramount, invoking the morals clause in his contract.

San Francisco District Attorney Matthew Brady hoped the Arbuckle case would be his ticket to the governor's office. The coroner's inquest met on September 12 with Brady demanding that Arbuckle be charged with murder. By then, he knew that most of what had been printed in the newspapers were lies by since his vow to prosecute the movie star to the fullest extent of the

Fatty Arbuckle's mug-shot

law had already been featured in the press, he proceeded with the case. Over the next few days, with Arbuckle jailed without bail, a special grand jury voted to indict the actor on a manslaughter charge. It was their belief, based on the evidence, that Arbuckle had used "some force" that led to Virginia's death. On September 28, a judge ruled that the defendant could be charged with manslaughter, but the rape charge was dismissed. Arbuckle was released on his own recognizance and returned to Los Angeles. He was accompanied by his estranged wife, Minta, who had arrived to offer moral support.

The trial began on November 14, 1921 with Roscoe taking the stand and denying any wrongdoing. The defense introduced evidence of Virginia's past medical problems (including chronic cystitis) and her recurrent bouts of abdominal pain that often led to her yanking off her clothing. The key witness, Maude Delmont, never took the stand to continue her fanciful claims against Arbuckle – something that the defense pointed out several times to the jury. After much conflicting testimony, the jury remained deadlocked after 43 hours of deliberation. One juror was adamant that Fatty was guilty "until hell freezes over." The judge declared a mistrial.

Fellow comedian Buster Keaton never wavered in his support for Arbuckle and did everything he could to help him after he was banned in Hollywood

Unwilling to give up, D.A. Brady pushed for another trial. One of the tactical errors this time around was made by the defense. Overly confident that Arbuckle would be acquitted, they did not have him testify again and simply read his prior testimony into the record. This made Arbuckle look cold and uncaring about the young woman's death and made the wrong impression on the jury. In addition, his attorney, assured of victory, never bothered to make a closing statement. After many more hours of deliberating, the jury was deadlocked again, although this time they had voted almost in favor of conviction. Fatty had not been convicted, but he was paying for his "crime." He had been forced to sell his home in Los Angeles, along with his luxury automobiles, to pay lawyer's fees that the studio was no longer footing the bill for.

Unbelievably, Brady took Arbuckle to trial a third time. This time, Fatty took the stand and patiently answered questions about the fateful party for three hours. The defense introduced evidence about Virginia's questionable past, the prosecution's intimidation of witnesses, as well as the fact that the prosecution still had never produced Maude Delmont to testify. This time, the jury adjourned for only five minutes and returned with a vote of acquittal and a written apology:

"Acquittal is not enough for Roscoe Arbuckle. We feel a grave injustice has been done him and there was not the slightest proof to connect him in any way with the commission of any crime. We wish him success, and hope that the American people will take the judgment of fourteen men and women that Roscoe Arbuckle is entirely innocent and free of all blame."

Fatty may have been free, and cleared by a well-meaning jury, but he was hardly forgiven by Hollywood. Paramount canceled his $3 million contract and his unreleased films were scrapped, costing the studio over $1 million. Fatty's career was finished after he was banned from the movies by Will Hays and his Hollywood Production Code. Hays wanted to show that he meant business when it came to cleaning up the movies and decided to make Arbuckle an example. Strangely, Hays acted at the urging of Adolph Zukor and Paramount Pictures. Years later, it was also discovered that Zukor had made a mysterious payment to D.A. Matthew Brady on November 14, 1921. It was assumed to be a possible bribe to control the case's outcome – although not in Arbuckle's favor. Some have also theorized that Zukor, eager to regain control over Arbuckle, had masterminded the St. Francis Hotel party through Fred Fischbach (who mysteriously vanished for a time), but that the situation, which was simply to make Arbuckle look bad, got wildly out of control.

By Christmas, Hays had rescinded his ban on Arbuckle in Hollywood productions, but civic groups and the press remained opposed to his return to film. Because of this, the studios just couldn't afford to have his name connected to their pictures. Only a few friends, like Buster Keaton, remained by his side. In fact, it was Keaton who suggested that Arbuckle change his name to "Will B. Good." Actually, Arbuckle did adopt the name William Goodrich in later years and he was able to gain employment as a gag man and as a comedy director. Friends helped him as best they could, but the next few years were difficult ones. He tried stage and vaudeville work and opened a club and a hotel, which closed down during the Depression. He married and divorced a second time, and then found happiness with his third wife, actress Addie McPhail. In 1931, Roscoe appeared in a fan magazine article, begging to be allowed to return to the screen. Hal Roach offered him a contract, but pressure from several women's groups caused the deal to fall through.

After again turning to vaudeville, Arbuckle was given a contract by New York's Vitaphone Studios head, Sam Sax, to star in a 1932 film short. The "comeback" Vitaphone two-reeler was so successful that Sax gave Fatty a contract to make five more, in preparation for a feature film with Warner Brothers. Unfortunately, Arbuckle died on the night following the completion of his last Vitaphone short "Tomalio" on June 29, 1934.

Even in death, Fatty Arbuckle could not find peace. The slanderous stories about him still exist today and despite evidence presented to the contrary, he continues to be perceived as the "lustful rapist" portrayed in newspapers of the day. Was Fatty Arbuckle guilty of anything that he was accused of? In the state of mind called Hollywood. It's never really mattered. The Arbuckle case managed to change the image of Hollywood from one that was linked to dreams – to an image that was forever tarnished by scandal.

And the remembrance of this scandal returns us to Hollywood Forever Cemetery and the rumored ghost of Virginia Rappe. Little explanation needs to be offered as to why Virginia's ghost might be a restless one. She lost not only her life over the course of the Labor Day Weekend of 1921, but she lost a promising career and her tattered reputation, as well. Was it a fate that she brought on herself? Perhaps, but the press was nearly as savage to the sickly and misguides young actress as it was to Fatty Arbuckle.

While most newspapers painted Virginia as an "innocent" victim of Arbuckle's lust-crazed advances, the Hearst newspapers were especially cruel to the actress and managed to turn the affair into a national scandal. While Heart's papers were always known for their yellow journalism and lurid headlines, the Arbuckle case received even more coverage than normal. As it happened, Heart's affair with a starlet named Marion Davies became big news at the same time that details began to emerge about Fatty Arbuckle and Virginia Rappe. Marion Davies' career began to suffer and rumor had it that Hearst gave the go-ahead to his papers to exploit every Hollywood scandal of the time, including Fatty's, to take the focus off of himself and Davies. This made the unlucky Virginia Rappe an easy

> If there was ever a candidate for a ghost to linger behind in this world because of unfinished business, it's certainly that of Roscoe "Fatty" Arbuckle. Although he has never been reported to haunt any locations in Hollywood, Arbuckle has been reported roaming the old Brooklyn Vitaphone Studios in New York, where soap operas are produced today. Fatty's substantial spirit has allegedly been seen by several members of one television show, wandering the stages where he began his brief comeback attempt in 1932.
> Thanks to his death occurring just as he was on the verge of making a new feature film, Arbuckle was clearly not ready to depart from this world just yet.

target.

For this reason, it's not surprising to hear reports that her spirit still lingers behind. Visitors who come to Hollywood Forever Cemetery have reported hearing a ghostly voice that weeps and cries out near Virginia's simple grave. It is believed by many to be her ghost, still attached to this world, and still in anguish over her promising career, which was, like her life, cut short before it could really begin.

HAUNTS OF THE SHIEK
REMNANTS OF VALENTINO, HOLLYWOOD'S MOST FAMOUS LOVER

On August 23, 1926, some of the most heartbreaking news of the silent era reached the general public. New York's Polyclinic Hospital announced that Hollywood's "Great Lover," Rudolph Valentino, was dead. His official cause of death was stated to be peritonitis, following an operation for an inflamed appendix. However, in true romantic fashion, other rumors of the star's demise began to circulate, as well. Tales attributed his death to an "arsenic revenge" carried out by a well-known New York society woman, whom Valentino had dropped after a short affair while he was in town promoting his latest film, "Son of the Sheik." Other rumors said that he had been shot by an irate husband, or that he had contracted syphilis and had died when the disease struck his brain.

During the last years of his life, Valentino had been the dream lover of millions of women and one of the most popular stars of the silver screen. His death was met by chaos as thousands of weeping women filled the streets, mobbed the funeral parlor where his body lay in state and generally wreaked havoc on the city of New York.

Valentino was at the height of his enormous movie fame when he died suddenly at the age of only 31. The mass hysteria that followed his demise seems puzzling to many today, as he is barely remembered as one of the screen's greatest lovers and has been relegated to a bygone era of silent films and movie vehicles of questionable quality. Over the years, though, many biographies have raked up the notorious and unsavory aspects of Valentino's colorful life and made all sorts of claims about his sexual activities. Ironically, such stories and rumors have managed to keep what should have been a forgotten screen star in the public eye.

Are such tales, usually related to his scandals and escapades, what manages to keep his spirit so restless? There is no question that Valentino is the most prevalent phantom in Hollywood and between the "psychic chasm" torn open by his adoring fans at the time of his death, and the continued fascination with his life, Valentino seems to be lingering behind today.

Valentino was born in Castellaneta, Italy, in May 1895 as Rodolpho Alfonzo Rafaelo Pierre Filibert Guglielmi di Valentina d'Antonguolla. He was the bi-lingual and brilliant son of a military officer turned veterinarian and the daughter of a French surgeon. His life was middle-class and comfortable and when the boy was nine, the family relocated to the seaside city of Taranto. In 1906, Valentino's father died and soon after, his remaining childhood was marked with minor incidents of mischief. Hoping to instill in him some

Rudolph Valentino

much-needed discipline, the family sent him to a boarding school north of Rome. By age 15, the young man had relocated to Venice, hoping to gain admission to a naval technical school. He passed his entrance exams, but was rejected from the institution because his chest measurements did not meet the school's standards. This humiliation, which he interpreted as a slight on his manliness, haunted him for the rest of his life.

Rodolpho was next enrolled in an agriculture school in the mountain village of Nevri. However, an infatuation with the daughter of the school's cook distracted him from his work. He managed to graduate and finding no suitable work at home, he traveled to Paris in 1912. He lived a shiftless existence in the City of Lights. A broken romance with a music hall dancer left him depressed and penniless. When his mother sent him more money, he went to Monte Carlo and lost it all on the gambling tables. He returned home in disgrace and his relatives, anxious to be rid of him, booked passage for him to New York in late 1913.

Unlike many immigrants of the time, Rodolpho could speak passable English and had relative financial security, thanks to his family. The good-looking young man quickly made many friends and contacts during his Atlantic voyage and took advantage of them when he arrived in America. He was drawn to the glittering lights of New York's theater district and its fashionable shops and restaurants. Using his fluency in French, and enhancing his background, he made friends with a group of aristocratic European playboys. Fascinated by the high life, he used his good looks, flair for dancing, and sophisticated style to insinuate himself in the New York social crowd.

After a brief stint as a gardener's assistant on Long Island, Rodolpho discovered the lure of show business. No matter how good-looking he was, though, jobs were not easy to find and he quickly ran out of money. Finding himself sleeping in Central Park, he was too proud to write his mother and ask for money. Instead, he sent her occasional messages, assuring her that he was doing well. He worked a series of odd jobs and performed as an extra in a locally shot feature film.

Relying on his agility as a dancer, he gained employment as a dance partner for hire – a gigolo – at the fashionable Maxim's in midtown Manhattan. Rodolpho was now available to unescorted women of all ages on the dance floor of the upscale establishment. Part of the job description included private dance lessons upstairs for wealthy female patrons. Frequently, these "lessons" led to paid sex, a part of the job that Valentino would be highly sensitive about when the subject came up in later years.

Rodolpho made decent money as a gigolo at Maxim's, but he continued to be drawn to the movie business. He often appeared onscreen as a ballroom dancer or in fancy party scenes. His grace on the dance floor helped him to make connections in other places besides Maxim's, and with those who would be able to help his burgeoning film career. One of those was Mae Murray, a beautiful Broadway personality who was featured in the Ziegfeld Follies. Later, when she was a rising movie star, Murray helped him to break into Hollywood moviemaking. He also met entertainer Bonnie Glass, who hired him to partner with her in exhibition dancing for vaudeville and cabaret shows. He also teamed in the same way with Joan Sawyer, another prominent performer.

Rodolpho became a well-liked member of the Manhattan social set and developed a growing attachment to Blanca de Saulles, a Chilean who was among the city's wealthiest socialites. She was then married to an American businessman named John de Saulles and had a son with him. Her husband at the time was involved in a series of not-so-secret affairs, leaving his wife to spend her time in the Manhattan club scene. When she divorced her philandering spouse in 1916, Rodolpho testified on her behalf in court. She won her suit and gained custody of her son.

Whether it was a coincidence, or whether it was, as some suggested, revenge engineered by John de Saulles, Rodolpho was arrested a few weeks later at the apartment of Georgie Thym, the alleged owner of a brothel. The notorious incident was widely reported by New York newspapers and while no official charges were ever lodged against Rodolpho and Thym, they were held in jail as material witnesses against a corrupt public official who was supposedly tied to several brothels. Two days later, they both raised bail and were released.

Rodolpho's reputation was badly stained by the incident and because of it he was unable to find work. Things turned even worse in the summer of 1917 when Blanca de Saulles fatally shot her husband during a dispute over custody of their son. Afraid that he might be called as a witness in court, which would damage his fragile reputation even further, Rodolpho quickly left town. He joined the cast of a stage musical that was heading west and worked as a bond salesman and club dancer in San Francisco for a time. Around this time, he encountered a New York actor friend named Norman Kerry, who was in town making a film. Norman suggested that Rodolpho come to Los Angeles and try his luck in the Hollywood movie business.

Valentino's first Hollywood film appearance was as a dress extra in a ballroom scene in the film "Alimony." Over the course of the next few years, he had a number of minor roles where he was usually cast as the villain, thanks to his swarthy, Italian looks. Although he was cast in the lead role in the 1918 film "A Society Sensation," it would be his part as the "heavy" in 1919's "Eyes of Youth" that would be a turning point in his career. It would be from this role that June Mathis, a popular screenwriter, would urge that he be cast as "Julio" in Rex Ingram's epic "The Four Horsemen of the Apocalypse" in 1921.

First appearing in a barroom scene, Valentino hypnotized the audience and danced the tango to instant celebrity. As a professional dancer in New York, he had learned to move with grace and finesse in ways that were unknown to many silent films actors of the time. In those days, the actors were almost caricatures of themselves, moving and gesturing with great exaggeration. Valentino managed to make his movements subtle and in so doing, won many admirers.

Even before his big break, when still being cast in small roles, he gained admirers in the film community. Among them was Dorothy Gish, the popular screen star, who persuaded D.W. Griffith to cast Valentino in the 1919 film, "Out of Luck." Later that same year, in fall 1919, Rodolpho Valentino (who was soon to be known as Rudolph Valentino and simply Rudy to his friends) met Jean Acker, a 26-year-old actress. Jean was then a protégé of exotic stage and film star Alla Nazimova, who was well known in the film set as a lesbian. Whatever Jean's sexual orientation, Valentino was intrigued by her and knew that she had many acquaintances in the film business that could help his career. He was drawn to her and after only a two-month acquaintance, a persistent Valentino convinced Jean to marry him. After a modest ceremony in November 1919, the couple returned to the Hollywood Hotel, where Jean was living at the time. After dancing in the salon, Jean retired to her room. When Rudy came upstairs, she slammed the door in his face and locked him out of her bedroom. The deeply humiliated actor went back to his own apartment in disgrace.

Over the next several months, Valentino pursued his wife, but eventually tired of the draining, embarrassing situation. The pair divorced in January 1922 in a court hearing that brought forth the mortifying details of their

Valentino's first wife, Jean Acker

unconsummated wedding night.

But things soon changed for Valentino. Thanks to his promotion by Jean Mathis, he landed the starring role in the big-budgeted "Four Horsemen of the Apocalypse." In the film, he played a South American gaucho who becomes a tango expert in Paris in 1914 and then serves on the front lines during World War I. Valentino was so electrifying in this role of a Latin lover that he became a major star, seemingly overnight.

After the release of "Four Horseman of the Apocalypse," Valentino came to be hailed as a new type of leading man, one with an exotic appearance and unconventional mannerisms for the time. He brought a sex appeal and sensitivity to the screen and he attracted millions of women to theaters. Thanks to the newfound sexual freedoms of the 1920s, women were coming to the movies like never before and they were literally swooning over the new Latin heartthrob.

It would be the 1921 film "The Sheik" that would firmly establish Valentino's reputation as a great lover and his final film, "Son of the Sheik," that would ensure that volumes of fan mail would pour in and continue to do so even after his death. Despite his adoration by the female public, Valentino got more than his share of abuse by the newspapers and magazine columnists of the time. Many hinted that the "sensitive" actor was a homosexual and often questioned his virility. Such writings usually found their origins with Valentino himself. His eccentric tastes and extravagances made him the target of many such writers, along with his famous "slave bracelet," without which he was never seen in public, his gold jewelry, his preference for heavy perfumes, mink coats, and other accoutrements that seemed odd for a man of the day.

In 1921, Valentino co-starred with Alla Nazimova in her expensive screen adaptation of the stage show "Camille." On this production, he met beautiful Natasha Rambova, who designed the art deco sets for the show. The striking heiress, like Jean Acker, had become attached to Nazimova, but

Valentino's role as "The Sheik" made him an object of desire for women all over America.

the extent of their relationship remains unknown. Rudy again didn't let this bother him and he became infatuated with the wealthy, dominating young woman. Soon, Rudy and Natasha were sharing a bungalow with Valentino's friend and sometimes roommate, photographer Paul Ivano. As Valentino became more widely known to the public and the media, Natasha officially began residing at a nearby address for the sake of appearances.

Meanwhile, unhappy with the quality of the roles he was getting, Valentino signed with Famous Players-Lasky (forerunner of Paramount) and starred in "The Sheik" in 1921. As mentioned, this role made him even more popular with the movie-going public.

In 1922, after he completed "Blood and Sand," in which he played a Spanish bullfighter, Rudy and Natasha decided to end the illusion of their separate residences by officially getting married. Rather than waiting until his divorce from Jean Acker was to become final in March 1923, the couple got married in Mexico, thinking that their foreign nuptials would be allowed under California law. Unfortunately, though, a Los Angeles superior court judge labeled Valentino a bigamist a few days later. This situation, following on the heels of other recent Hollywood scandals, was enough to permanently destroy the young actor's growing career.

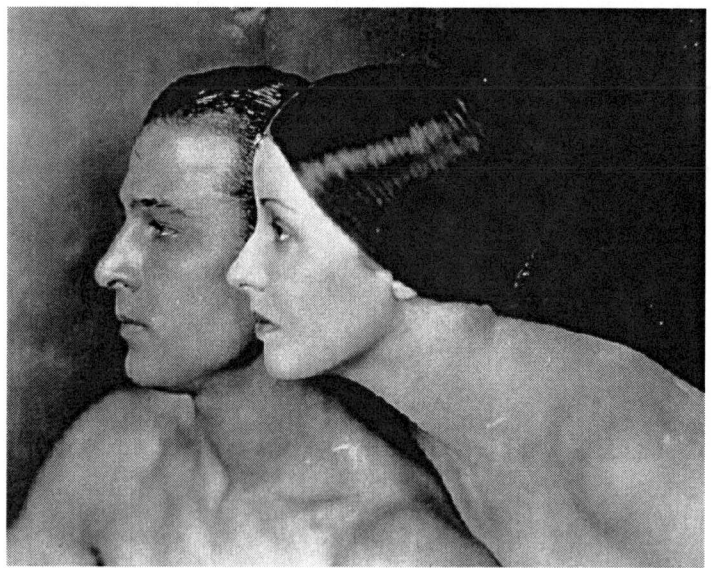

Valentino and his second wife, Natasha Rambova

(Right) One of the embarrassing photographs that Natasha arranged, which helped to create a less than manly image for the actor. Eventually, the studios would only work with him if Natasha was banned from the sets and kept out of his contract decisions.

Acting on advice from studio attorneys, Natasha fled to the East Coast, while a shaken Valentino turned himself in to authorities, claiming ignorance of the law. No help was forthcoming from the studio, which didn't want to be tainted by this new scandal, so it fell upon Rudy's friends to arrange his bail. As it turned out, Jean Acker refused to cooperate with the district attorney in the case and the charges against Valentino were dropped. Rudy and Natasha were eventually legally married in 1923. By then, Natasha had convinced Rudy to walk out on his lucrative studio contract, which prevented him from appearing in any other company's pictures. To support their lifestyle, the couple embarked on a national exhibition dance tour. They were married in Indiana in March 1923.

Eventually, Valentino temporarily patched up his differences with Paramount. However, 1924's "Monsieur Beaucaire," in which Natasha served as both art and costume designer and constantly interfered with the making of the film, presented Rudy as being far too prissy and alienated the public that was used to him played a dashing screen hero and lover. Many friends believed that Natasha was ruining his career and as an example of the hold that she had over him, they pointed to the "slave bracelet" that she insisted he wear. He also yielded to her demands that he pose for arty publicity photos, like the near-naked one in which he was dressed as a Native American. Such things did little to endear him to his straight, male audience and further fanned the gossip flames about his homosexuality.

Once his Paramount tenure expired, United Artists signed Valentino to a contract, convinced they could restore him to the top of the box office again. However, a term of the lucrative deal was that his wife could have no part in his moviemaking. When Valentino agreed to this term, it brought an end to his marriage with Natasha. She moved away and later divorced him in Paris in 1926. Having two wives abandon him eroded Rudolph's air of manliness with the public. His virility was questioned once again, especially when rumor had it that both of his wives were lesbians, or had at least been involved with one (Alla Nazimova) in some way. The story of Valentino's failure to consummate his marriage with Jean Acker was circulated again and rumors spread that his marriage to Natasha may never have been consummated either. Apparently, the "Great Lover" was not so adept at romance after all.

To mask his loneliness and perhaps cover his recent marital embarrassments, Valentino became involved in a well-staged and highly publicized relationship with Pola Negri, the Polish-born film star was also, not surprisingly, rumored to be a lesbian, or at least bi-sexual.

In 1926, Rudy went to New York to promote the opening of "The Son of the Sheik." During a stopover in Chicago, he read an editorial in the *Chicago Tribune* entitled "Pink Powder Puffs." As he read the piece, he became infuriated. The piece was a tirade against the pink powder vending machines that had recently been installed in the men's restroom at the local Aragon Ballroom. The anonymous writer blamed this embarrassment, along with the demand for "masculine cosmetics, sheiks, floppy pants, and slave bracelets" on an allegedly effete Valentino. The writer asked, "Why didn't someone quietly drown Rudolph Valentino years ago?"

Needless to say, Valentino was violently angry over this unwarranted print attack. In response, he used another Chicago newspaper to issue a challenge to the unnamed writer, daring him to step into the boxing ring with him. The challenge went unanswered. Still steamed, Rudy had his friend Jack Dempsey, the world heavyweight champion, arrange a demonstration bout between Valentino and a Manhattan sports writer. The event, filmed by newsreel cameras, showed the muscular movie star easily trouncing his taller, heavier opponent.

The controversy surrounding Valentino's questioned manhood helped to sell scores of tickets to "The Son of the Sheik," but the stress took a heavy toll on the star. Within days, he was hospitalized in Manhattan and was operated on for a perforated ulcer and appendicitis. His surgery wounds became infected and he died on August 23, 1926.

At the news of Valentino's death, two women attempted suicide in front of the hospital. In London, a girl took poison before his inscribed photograph. An elevator boy at the Ritz in Paris was discovered dead on his bed, which was covered with photos of Valentino. While the actor was lying in state at Campbell's Funeral Home in New York, the streets outside took on the air of a macabre carnival as a mob over 100,000 women (and many men) fought for a last glimpse of Valentino.

Among those who were permitted into the candle-lit viewing room of the funeral home were his ex-wife, Jean Acker, whose display of wild grief beside her former husband's casket may have been less extreme if she had known then that Valentino had only left her a solitary dollar in his will, and film star Pola Negri, who upstaged everyone with her designer mourning clothes. She sobbed and fainted before the coffin and, of course, before the photographers. Between her bursts of weeping, she claimed that she and Valentino had planned to be married. Another claim of eminent nuptials was produced in the newspapers a short time later by

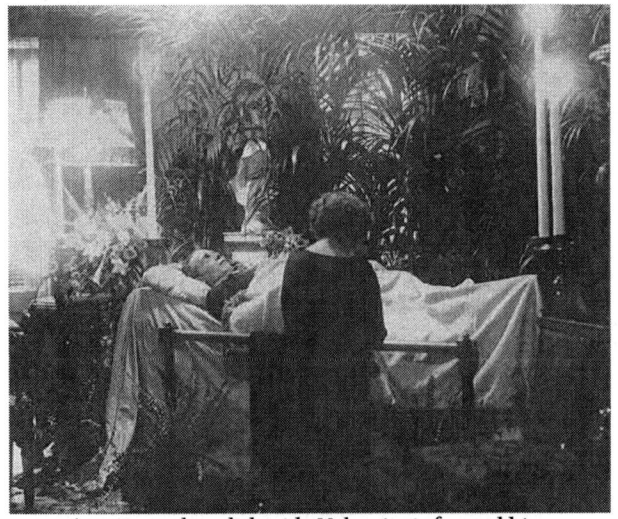

A mourner kneels beside Valentino's funeral bier (Library of Congress)

VALENTINO'S CURSED RING?

One of the strangest supernatural tales of Valentino involved a cursed ring that some believe may have led to Valentino's early death. According to the story, he bought the ring in 1920 in a San Francisco jewelry store, even though the owner told him that it had brought bad luck to everyone who had owned it. Valentino shrugged off the tale and bought the ring anyway. He wore it in his next film, "The Young Rajah," which turned out to be the biggest flop of his career. Wondering if the story of bad luck might have been true, he put the ring away and did not wear it again until his trip to New York after making "Son of the Sheik." It was while wearing the ring that he suffered an acute attack of appendicitis and died a few days later.

After his death, Pola Negri was asked to choose a memento from among Valentino's things and not knowing the strange tales behind it, chose the silver ring. Almost immediately, her health failed and an unknown ailment almost ended her career. A year later, while still recuperating from the odd sickness, she met a man named Russ Colombo, who was almost a double for Rudy Valentino. When Pola Negri was introduced to him, she was so struck by the resemblance between Colombo, a struggling singer, and the late actor, that she presented him with Valentino's ring. "From one Valentino to another," she said. Within a few days of receiving the ring, Colombo was killed in a mysterious shooting accident.

His cousin then gave the ring to Russ's best friend, Joe Casino, an entertainer. Taking no chances with the ring, Casino placed it in a glass case and refused to remove it, even when a request came to donate it to museum of Valentino relics. Eventually, though, Casino began to disregard the stories behind the ring and he decided to wear it. A week later, still wearing the ring, he was run over by a truck and killed.

Joe's brother, Del, then came into possession of the ring but he laughed at the idea of a curse and vowed that he would not be intimidated by old wives' tales. For quite some time, he wore the ring and suffered no ill effects from it. He also loaned it to a Valentino collector, who also had no problems. Many speculated that the story of a curse may have been nothing more than a series of coincidences. Then, one night, Del Casino's home was robbed. The burglar, a man named James Willis, was seen by the police running from the scene. A policeman fired at him (a warning shot, he later claimed) and Willis was killed. Among the stolen loot was the dreaded Valentino ring.

Around this same time, a producer named Edward Small decided to make a film about Valentino. Jack Dunn, a skater, was asked to film a test for the part and he dressed in one of Valentino's old costumes. He also wore the ring. Only 21 at the time of the screen test, Dunn died 10 days later from a rare blood disease. The ring was then placed out of sight and never worn by anyone.

A year after Dunn's death, a daring robbery took place at a Los Angeles bank and the thieves got away with more than $200,000 in cash. In the police ambush that followed, two members of the gang were caught and three onlookers were injured. The leader of the bank robbers, Alfred Hahn, was later convicted and sent to prison for life. At his trial, Hahn stated, "If I had known what was in that bank vault, apart from the money, I'd have picked myself another bank." What Hahn hadn't known was that in the safe deposit vault of the bank was the Valentino ring.

The executors of Del Casino, who took over ownership of the ring after his death, continued to store it under lock and key. For many years, it remained inside the bank vault, where over a five-year period a $50,000 bank robbery, a fire, and a three-week cashier strike occurred.

Can an inanimate object exert such a malign influence those who come in contact with it? Those who fell under the curse of the Valentino ring certainly believed that it could!

Ziegfeld girl Marion Kay Brenda, who stated that Valentino had proposed to her in Texas Guinan's nightclub the evening before he was felled by his illness.

To add to the carnival-like atmosphere, a commemorative song began to be played on radios across America at the same time that Valentino's body was being shipped west to what was then Hollywood Memorial Park Cemetery. The song, crooned by Rudy Vallee, was called "There's a New Star in Heaven Tonight - Rudy Valentino".

It was around Valentino's cemetery crypt that one of the most enduring legends of his death took root, that of the famous "Lady in Black," which was described in the previous chapter. In addition to this strange story, there is also the possibility that Valentino may be the most prominent, and best-traveled, ghost in Hollywood. There are a number of sites where his ghostly presence has been reported.

One location is the house known as Falcon's Lair, Valentino's home in Beverly Hills for one year until his death in 1926. According to the stories, and to Natasha Rambova (who claimed to be in contact with the actor's spirit for many years after he died), Valentino refused to accept the idea that he was dead. This is allegedly the reason why his ghost remains behind in the mansion.

Actor Harry Carey was one of the subsequent owners of the house who encountered Valentino's ghost there, but he would not be the only one. In fact, Millicent Rogers spent only one night in the place before being "chased away" by Valentino.

His life-like apparition appeared in dark corridors, in his former bedroom and in the old stables, where his beloved horse was kept. One stable worker reportedly walked out the front gate and never returned to the place after seeing the former master of the house petting one of the horses. Another account tells of a caretaker who ran screaming down the canyon in the middle of the night after meeting Valentino face-to-face. Passersby have allegedly seen a shadowy figure looking out of a window on the second floor of the house. When they remark that the figure looked a lot like Valentino, they are shocked to learn that the mansion was his home!

Not long after Rudy's death, a friend of the caretaker at Falcon's Lair was staying in the house while visiting Los Angeles from Seattle. She stated that she was up late one night, writing letters, when she heard footsteps in the hallway and actually witnessed doors opening and closing under their own power. Her only companions in the house at the time were Rudy and Brownie, Valentino's two Great Dane watchdogs. The animals had been trained by Valentino to bark and snap at any who entered the house -- except for Valentino himself. The witness remembered that the dogs were strangely quiet that night, as if in the presence of someone they knew well.

Valentino's magnificent Falcon's Lair in 1926

Valentino's ghost continues to be sighted, not only at Falcon's Lair (which is now a private residence) but in other locations, as well. One site is Valentino Place, an old apartment building that used to be an elegant speakeasy back during the days of Prohibition in the 1920s. Legend has it that Valentino often used to frequent the place for parties and romantic interludes and that his ghost still makes an occasional appearance.

In April 1989, a young actress who was living in the Hollywood apartment building said that she encountered the rather amorous apparition of Valentino in her bed. According to her story, she was drifting off to sleep one night when she felt a heavy weight press down onto the side of the bed. It sagged as though someone were sitting on the edge of it while she was lying there, too frightened to even move. The weight on the bed became the solid figure of a man and it shifted beside her, moving beneath the thin sheet. The form then slid closer to her, and pressed against her so that she could feel the bulge of the man's erection. As heavy breathing washed over her, she finally dared to open her eyes.

She claimed that she lifted the sheet and saw the handsome face of Rudolph Valentino. Handsome or not, though, she was so terrified that she literally fainted. When she awakened, the figure was gone, but the bed sheets and pillows were left in a complete disarray and strewn about the room.

Other sightings of Valentino's ghost have reportedly occurred at his former beach house in Oxnard, Calif. The house is now a private residence but, over the years, many witnesses have reported a dark figure pacing back and forth on the home's veranda. Valentino stayed at the house while filming "The Sheik," in 1921. Many believe that he has left an indelible mark on the location.

Another Valentino haunting is said to occur at the Santa Maria Inn in Santa Maria, Calif., about 30 miles south of San Luis Obispo. It is said that Valentino returns to his former suite there and that guests who stay in Room 210 feel a heavy presence on the bed and hear eerie knocking sounds from inside the wall. The inn was a favorite getaway spot for the actor and perhaps he is still getting away from his busy days haunting Hollywood after all of these years.

DRUGS & DEATH
THE TRAGEDY OF ALMA RUBENS

In the fast-paced world of Hollywood, an addiction to drugs such as sleeping pills, barbiturates, alcohol, cocaine, and heroin can not only endanger your career – it can end your life. Many actors and actresses have turned to drugs to help them overcome performance anxiety or depression, to get them through the rigorous days and nights of filming, or simply to get high – only to be abandoned by the studios when the addiction begins to take a toll on the star's acting abilities or looks.

The death of Olive Thomas may have been the first Hollywood scandal linked to drugs like heroin and cocaine, but it would certainly not be the last. Today's headlines are often filled with stories of celebrities and movie stars overdosing, being arrested, or checking into rehab. But drugs in Hollywood are a long-standing tradition that goes all of the way back to the early days of the film colony. The 1920s and 1930s saw the deaths of stars like Wallace Reid, the quiet adventurous actor from such films as "Birth of a Nation" and "The Valley of the Giants;" Marie Prevost, one of the loveliest actresses of the silent film era; Barbara La Marr, who was known as "The Girl Who is Too Beautiful," and many others.

One of the most tragic of the young, promising actresses to fall prey to a heroin addiction was Alma Rubens, a raven-haired star who devoted her energies, and a great part of her fortune, to securing the drugs that destroyed her.

Beautiful Alma Rubens

In the early afternoon of January 26, 1929, passersby at the intersection of Wilton Place and Hollywood Boulevard were startled to see a dark-haired woman rounding the corner and running at dizzying speed down the street. She screamed at the top of her lungs as she ran, "I'm being kidnapped! I'm being kidnapped!" As she ran, she tossed aside her hat, her gloves and finally, threw her purse into the gutter. At that time, this stretch of Hollywood Boulevard was a quiet section of apartments, boarding houses, and small stores.

The woman's cries seemed to be accurate, at first glance. Two men, one middle-aged and the other younger, were chasing after her. They were also shouting – imploring that someone stop the woman who was running away from them.

The woman ran, breathless and frazzled, into a service station on the corner. The startled attendant saw the wild-eyed woman stop next to one of the pumps and turn to face the two men who had caught up with her. Suddenly, she pulled a knife from a pocket in her dress. As the younger of the two men grabbed for her, she slashed him with the knife, cutting deep into his shoulder. The gas station attendant entered the fray, holding the woman from behind as the older man seized her arms and took away the knife. The weapon clattered to the pavement and the woman started to cry. She was led away down the street, to a house on Wilton Place. There, she was put into an ambulance and the two men drove away with her.

Of the few people who witnessed the incident, probably none of them recognized the distraught woman. But had they known her identity at the time – and they would certainly learn it later – the incident would have garnered more attention than it did. The woman was one of the greatest silent film stars of her day, Alma Rubens. The two men were her physician, Dr. E.W. Meyer, and an ambulance attendant named Harry Barnett. They had come to take her to a private hospital for drug addiction.

Alma Rubens was born in San Francisco in 1897. Born to a Jewish father and a Catholic mother, she was raised in a comfortable, happy home and was educated at the Sacred Heart Convent in San Francisco. The stage called to Alma early in life and she left home and went to New York in hopes of breaking into show business. She found success almost immediately, appeared in a number of plays, then toured the United States with a musical production that featured Franklyn Farnum as the leading man. Soon the stock company came to Los Angeles. After a short time, Rubens left the troupe on the advice of Franklyn Farnum. He was given a motion picture role and persuaded Rubens to follow him into movies. Farnum had other motives for keeping Alma in Hollywood and convinced her to marry him. The marriage lasted only a month and Alma filed for divorce on the grounds that the actor, who was 20 years older than she was, administered a beating to her on their wedding night and repeated it on other occasions.

But her broken marriage did not stop Alma from chasing after a movie career. She appeared in several small roles, but her breakthrough performance was in "Reggie Mixes In." She followed that with six more films. In 1917, she starred in "The Firefly of Tough Luck," a performance that caught the eye of Douglas Fairbanks. She played opposite Fairbanks in "The Half Breed," which earned her great notoriety. Alma also appeared in "The World and His Wife," "The Price She Paid," both of which earned her great reviews.

Alma also appeared in the part-talkie version of "Show Boat," based on the Edna Ferber film. It would turn out to be her next-to-last film. Her career, as fast as it had started, practically ended overnight.

In August 1923, Alma married for the second time to Dr. Daniel Goodman, who was then head of Consolidated Pictures. However, just 13 months later, she filed for divorce, claiming once again that her husband physically abused her. Alma declared that Goodman had beaten her while they were on holiday at Schroon Lake, N.Y., had hit her over the head at the Plaza Hotel, and finally, that he had struck her with an automobile outside of a friend's home on Christmas Day. Dr. Goodman seemed confused by the charges but while he denied the allegations, he allowed Alma to go through with the divorce.

While Alma's career was still rising in the late

Alma Rubens, her life and beauty destroyed by drugs, shortly before her death.

1920s, she met handsome leading man Ricardo Cortez, who she married on January 30, 1926, just two days after her final divorce decree from Dr. Goodman. This marriage was also doomed. Alma and Cortez separated after less than two years and soon, Hollywood began to realize the reason for the marital disasters of the famous star. A short time later, the news spread that Alma had been checked into a sanitarium by her doctor. Alma Rubens was a drug addict.

After she was checked into the sanitarium in Alhambra, Calif., she was released after a few weeks of treatment and allowed to return home with a nurse in attendance. But her recovery was short-lived. In April 1929, she attacked her nurse with a knife and was sent to California's State Hospital for the Insane at Patton.

Once again, Alma was "cured" after six months. She left the institution with great publicity. She told reporters that she felt wonderful and that she planned to return to New York to do some acting on stage. After that, she hoped to return to Hollywood. Alma traveled to New York in December 1930 and made an appearance on stage with her husband while she was there. She filed for divorce from Cortez and then returned to California at the end of the year. She made her final stage appearance in January 1930, a role in a play at the Writer's Club in Hollywood.

She had been back in California for less than two weeks when she was arrested at the U.S. Grant Hotel in San Diego, close to the Mexican border. On January 6, 1931, she was charged with the possession of 40 cubes of morphine. The authorities had been tipped off by a young actress named Ruth Palmer, whom Alma Rubens had met in New York and brought to Hollywood to help her make it in the movies. She told the police that she had become suspicious after the pair had returned to their hotel after a trip across the border to Mexico. She said that she saw Alma mixing something with a spoon and later, Alma got violent with her and struck her in the face. When the police entered the hotel room, Alma became abusive and claimed she was a victim of a frame-up. The officers found the drugs concealed in the hem of a dress that was hanging in the closet and hidden in her purse.

She was bound over to federal district court and released on bail. She appeared for a preliminary hearing the second week of January 1931 and was allowed to return home under the constant care of her mother, a nurse, and her physician. Her doctor stated that she was suffering from the ravages of the drugs that she had taken over the years, from lack of nutrition, and a weakened physical and mental condition. By this time, she was a ghost of her former self. Her beauty was gone, her fortune squandered, and her career beyond salvaging.

Rubens died of pneumonia the following week. She contracted a cold that worsened and turned into pneumonia because of her fragile state. She slipped into a coma and never recovered. She was only 33 years old when she died – a victim of the darkest side of Hollywood.

THE HAUNTED HOLLYWOOD SIGN
THE GHOST OF PEG ENTWHISTLE

Hollywood is no stranger to suicide. The rapid demise of a celebrity's once sparking career, resulting in a fall from the public's good graces, regularly leads to mental collapse and sometimes, suicide. Sometimes the aftermath of such a macabre event temporarily restores the fallen star to his or her limelight, but this usually results in the suicide upstaging any other talents that the dead star might have ever possessed. As a result, they are not remembered for their performances, or even their beauty, but for the fact that they took their own lives when Hollywood became too much.

Other Hollywood suicides simply never made it at all. Thousands came to the new "Film Capital of the World" in the early 1900s, hoping to make it big in the moving picture business. When failure came instead of success, many of them chose not to go on, to continue dreaming of wealth and celebrity that would never come. Unfortunately, many of these failed actors and would-be starlets found the fame in death they never achieved in life.

One such actress was Peg Entwhistle, who set a new standard for suicide in Hollywood. Not only would she use a Hollywood landmark as a novel way for ending her life, but she would also become a symbol of Hollywood failure and tragedy. And according to some Peg Entwhistle is no mere symbol. She maintains a powerful presence in the vicinity of the Hollywood sign, a presence that is still being felt today.

The Hollywood sign is perhaps the most famous sign in the world. Resting on Mount Lee in Griffith Park, it looms over the city of Hollywood as a constant reminder of the past. The original sign was built in 1923 as a publicity ploy to encourage the sales of homes in the Hollywoodland subdivision, which was located along Beachwood Canyon. Hollywood was in its infancy in those days and was being deluged by people from the East. They came looking for the fabled orange groves and sunshine and when they got there, they needed a place to live. Promoter and moviemaker Mack Sennett wanted the Hollywoodland subdivision to provide that place, but like almost everything else in Tinseltown, the sign was merely a facade. The

Peg Entwhistle's last walk from the back of the famous Hollywood sign

(Left) Peg Entwhistle, who could have gone on to become one of the bright stars of Hollywood -- if she had waited just a little while longer.

cheap construction was only designed to last for a year and a half.

It cost $21,000 to build and each of the letters was 30 feet wide and 50 feet high. The entire name was studded with low wattage light bulbs and could be seen for miles. In time, the sign fell into disrepair and the light bulbs burned out, were broken, or were stolen by vandals. Maintenance of the sign was discontinued in 1939. Then, late in 1944, the H. Sherman Company, who became the developers of the old Hollywoodland housing district, quit claimed to the city of Los Angeles about 455 acres of land adjoining Griffith Park. This property included the Hollywoodland sign.

The weather-beaten sign was untouched for the next five years, falling further into ruin. Then, in 1949, the Hollywood Chamber of Commerce made plans to repair and rebuild the sign. They also removed "land" from the line of letters so that it merely read "Hollywood." The cost to renovate the sign was around $4,000, but the light bulbs were not replaced. In spite of the work that was done, the sign continued to deteriorate until the late 1970s, when a fund-raising campaign was begun to replace the letters. Donors were asked to contribute $27,700 each to buy a replacement letter.

In August 1978, the Pacific Outdoor Advertising Company, along with Hughes Helicopters and the Heath Sign Company, demolished the remains of the original sign and installed new, all-steel letters in its place. The sign now stretches 450 feet along the side of Mount Lee and remains 50 feet tall.

Like the Chinese Theater, whether it's called Grauman's or Mann's, the Hollywood sign is one of the definitive symbols of Hollywood and perhaps the film industry itself. For those who are film buffs, no journey to southern California can be complete without a trip to view the sign. There is nothing quite like it in the world.

The Hollywood sign got its first taste of death on a dark night in September 1932. It was on this night that Lillian Millicent "Peg" Entwhistle climbed up the slopes of Mount Lee with the glowing sign as her final destination. When she arrived, she scaled the heights of the giant letter "H" -- and she jumped. Her body plunged down the side of the hill and broke on the ground below. As she had planned, the fall killed her, leaving her body battered and bloody on the unforgiving earth. Peg Entwhistle, Hollywood actress, was only 24 years old.

Peg had been born in London, England in

1908. She grew up in an acting family, although little is known about her early life, save for the fact that her mother died when Peg was quite young. She left Peg's father alone to raise a daughter and two sons, Robert and Milton. A short time later, Peg's father packed up and moved the family to New York, where he started working in local theater. Unfortunately, tragedy struck again and Peg's father was run over by a truck on Park Avenue, ending his life. Robert and Milton were sent to Los Angeles to live with Harold Entwhistle, their uncle, and Peg turned to the stage for solace.

She made her acting debut in Hamlet when she was just 17 years old. To everyone's surprise, she quickly became a bonafide star, loved by audiences, critics, and directors alike. There was no question about it, Peg was a knockout and possessed a gentle quality that won the hearts of just about everyone she ever worked with. She quickly became a Broadway star and a member of the New York Theater Guild.

While working on Broadway, Peg met a fellow actor named Robert Keith who was 10 years her senior. He was also a popular star and the two soon fell in love and got married. But the marriage soured quickly. During a visit to her mother-in-law's house, Peg noticed a photograph of a young boy on the mantel. She asked who he was and was informed that he was Robert's son from his first marriage – a son and a marriage that she knew nothing about. Incidentally, that surprise stepson was future actor Brian Keith, star of the television show "Family Affair" and dozens of movies.

Just weeks later, during a dinner party at their home, a police officer came to the door and demanded nearly $1,000 in back child support that Robert owed. Peg got the money together, but when she asked Robert about it, he became violent. The bad debts, lies and fights ended the marriage and they were soon divorced.

Peg went back to the Broadway stage, but this part of her life was also coming to an end. The Great Depression had arrived and the majority of the public could no longer afford the expensive theater tickets. Thanks to this, Peg's last seven New York plays bombed. But all wasn't lost. While Broadway may have been suffering, Hollywood was still in its boom era. During Peg's initial fame in New York, Hollywood was making the transition from silent films to talkies. Unfortunately, many of the silent film stars were just not cut out for talking roles and Hollywood producers looked to the stars of the New York stage to fill the acting rosters. Many other stage actors were making it big in Hollywood, so Peg packed up and took the train to California, sure that greater fame and fortune waited for her on the West Coast. When she arrived, Peg moved into a Beachwood Canyon bungalow with her brothers and Uncle Harold. The house was located in the Hollywoodland subdivision, just under the towering sign where Peg would later take her life.

Not long after she arrived in Hollywood, Peg found work in small theater. The first production she did was a play called "Mad Hopes," starring Billie Burke, who would go on to play Glenda the good witch in "The Wizard of Oz." Another performer in the show was a Hollywood newcomer named Humphrey Bogart. The play opened to decent reviews, but only lasted a week and a half. When the curtain fell, Peg saw it as another personal failure. She began to wonder if her New York jinx had followed her to Tinseltown. She went on to appear with Billie Burke in a few more small productions, although Bogart returned to New York. His days of fame and fortune were still to come.

Thanks to her good looks and her popularity on Broadway, Peg landed a short-term contract with RKO Studios and landed a part in the film "Thirteen Women." She knew that even though it was a small part, it would lead to other offers. It was only her first movie role, she realized, but little did she know that it would turn out to be her last.

During filming, Peg discovered the part was actually a supporting role, but a good one. Her hopes began to rise. The movie was released only to be savaged by the critics. RKO quickly shelved it. It was released quietly a short time later, but substantial cuts had been made to the 73-minute running time. Peg's part, despite her good showing, had been reduced to little more than a cameo appearance.

Once more, she was bitterly disappointed, but

vowed to not let it get to her. She began answering ads for small parts and going to auditions and casting calls. However, Peg soon found that she was just another pretty face in a town filled with beautiful women. All of them had come to Hollywood for the same reason, to make it into show business.

And things went from bad to worse. Her option with RKO ran out and they declined to renew it. She was cut loose and on her own, was unable to even find work in small theater. Soon, promises of future work quickly vanished. As her career fell apart, her new friends made themselves scarce, not daring to be seen with a "nobody" in Hollywood. Peg Entwhistle, the gorgeous young woman who had shot to fame on Broadway, had now fallen to the bottom of the Hollywood barrel. Her depression worsened when she was unable to even scrape together the train fare to go back to New York. She would never act again.

So, on that terrible night in September 1932, Peg announced to her Uncle Harold that she was going to take a walk. She was last seen alive heading down Beachwood Canyon toward Mount Lee. Apparently, Peg scratched her way up the slope to the Hollywood sign where she took off her coat and folded it neatly. She placed it, along with her purse, at the base of the maintenance ladder that led up the letter "H." She climbed to the top and then plunged to her death.

The next day, a woman hiker in Griffith Park discovered the purse and coat near the ladder. She opened the purse and discovered a suicide note inside. It read simply "I am afraid I am a coward. I am sorry for everything. If I had done this a long time ago it would have saved a lot of pain..... P.E." The hiker replaced the note and then, in the early morning hours, placed the purse and coat on the doorstep of the Hollywood police station. Two days later, authorities discovered the body of Peg Entwhistle in the brush at the bottom of Mount Lee.

Unsure of her identity, the police ran a description of the woman, along with the contents of the suicide note, in the newspaper. They were quickly contacted by Entwhistle's Uncle Harold, who had been frantically searching for his niece, who had been missing since she had left for her walk several evenings before. He feared the worst when he saw the initials attached to the end of the note. Not long after, he identified the body as that of Peg Entwhistle.

Soon after, an ironic event occurred – the kind of event that usually only seems to happen in the movies.

Two days later, Uncle Harold was sifting through the afternoon mail and he discovered a letter that had been mailed to Peg the day before she jumped to her death. The letter was from the Beverly Hills Playhouse and it had been written to offer her the lead role in their next production. The part they wanted her to play was that of a beautiful young woman who commits suicide.

But death was not the last act for Peg Entwhistle.

In the years following her suicide, hikers and park rangers in Griffith Park have told of strange happenings in the vicinity of the Hollywood sign. Many have reported sightings of a woman dressed in 1930s-era clothing who abruptly vanishes when approached. She has been described as a very attractive, blond woman, who seems very sad. Could this be Peg's ghost, still making her presence known? Could she also be linked to the pungent smell of gardenia perfume that has been known to overwhelm sightseers in the park? Perhaps it is, as the gardenia scent was known to be Peg's trademark perfume.

In 1990, a North Hollywood man and his girlfriend were walking on a Beachwood Canyon trail near the Hollywood sign with their dog when the animal suddenly began to act very strange. Instead of running around on the trail and through the brush as he normally did, he began to whine and hang back near the couple. They had never seen him act that way before and could find no cause until they spotted a woman walking nearby. One thing they noticed about her was that she was wearing clothing from the 1930s. However, thinking that you could see just about anything in Hollywood, they didn't pay much attention. The lady however, seemed to be walking in a daze. Thinking that perhaps she was drunk or on drugs, they started to steer clear of her when she suddenly just faded away before their eyes. At that time, they had no idea who Peg Entwhistle was, nor that she had committed suicide nearby, or even that her ghost reportedly haunted the area. They were shocked when they later heard the story.

Another eyewitness to this haunting was a Griffith Park ranger named John Arbogast. In an interview, he revealed his own encounters with the ghost of Peg Entwhistle. He stated that she normally made her presence known very late at night, especially when it was foggy, and always in the vicinity of the Hollywood sign. He also claimed to have encountered the scent of gardenias in the area as well.

Arbogast's duties as a ranger often involved the Hollywood sign itself. He explained that in recent years, alarms systems have been installed near the sign to keep people away. There is always a danger of vandals, and, of course, of suicides wanting to go out the same way that Peg did. The alarm systems incorporate the use of motion detectors and lights to keep intruders away.

Arbogast recalled a number of times when the alarm system indicated that someone was close to the sign, even though a check by the ranger revealed no one was there. "There have been times when I have been at the sign," he said, "and the motion detectors say that someone is standing five feet away from me -- only there's nobody there."

So, what could have made Peg Entwhistle choose to end her life in such a dramatic and violent way? No one knows, but we have to wonder. The Hollywood slogan states that the sign exists as a symbol of hope, so that those who answer the siren call of Hollywood will know that anything in the city is possible. But did Peg glimpse that sign one evening, after spending the day going from one pointless casting call to another, and see it not as a symbol of hope, but one of despair? Did she feel that the sign was mocking her, laughing that so many others had made it in the movies, so why couldn't she? Did its glowing lights remind her of why she had come to Hollywood, chasing the bright lights she would never catch up to? Or perhaps she just wanted to go out in a way that people would remember?

If this was the case, she was right. Most would have never heard of Peg Entwhistle if not for the fact that she took that fatal plunge from the very symbol of Hollywood itself? It is certain that Peg gained much more fame in death than she ever did in life.

THE LONELY DEATH OF LUPE VELEZ

Lupe Velez, known as the "Mexican Spitfire" was one of the least inhibited, wildest stars of the Golden Age of Hollywood. Her customary greeting was a kiss, not a handshake. Regulars at Hollywood parties in those days repeated many times how Lupe proved the boasts about her charms by lifting her dress up around her neck. And since she refused to wear any underwear, this was a very effective way of demonstrating those charms and eliminating any doubts about them.

Hollywood loved Lupe. She was warm-hearted, generous, without malice toward anyone or anything, and just generally fun to be around. The Mexican-born actress, who came across the

Lupe Velez

border to take Hollywood by storm, lived life to the fullest, but eventually, it all became just a little too much for her to take. She died a death that no one, especially someone as beloved as she was, ever deserved.

Lupe was born María Guadalupe Villalobos Vélez in the city of San Luis Potosí in Mexico, on July 20, 1909. Her father was an army officer and her mother was an opera singer. Her Catholic school education ended at the age of 14 and she began working as a shop girl in Mexico City. Lupe studied dancing at the Teatro Principal and appeared as the lead in a musical that was produced by the dance school. A producer saw her on stage, believed that she had the makings of a dramatic actress, and gave her a part in a Mexico City show. While it was running, an American actor named Richard Bennett saw her on stage and told her that she would do well in motion pictures. In 1924, Lupe moved to Hollywood.

Her first film work was in a Hal Roach comedy and her first feature-length film was in Douglas Fairbanks' "The Gaucho" for United Artists in 1927. The following year, she was named one of Hollywood's "Baby Stars," the young starlets deemed to be most promising for movie stardom. Most of her early films cast her in exotic or ethnic roles but within a few years, Lupe found her niche in comedies. She specialized in playing beautiful but volatile foils to comedy stars. Her slapstick battle with Laurel and Hardy in "Hollywood Party" and her wild presence opposite Jimmy Durante in "Palooka" are typical of the kind of performances that she became known for.

But Lupe was nearing 30 and hadn't yet become a major star. She decided to leave Hollywood and head for Broadway. In New York, she landed a role in "You Never Know," a short-lived Cole Porter musical. After that, she came back to Hollywood and snared the lead in a new comedy for RKO, "The Girl from Mexico." She had such a rapport with co-star Leon Errol that RKO made a quick sequel, "Mexican Spitfire," which became a very popular series. Lupe perfected her comic character, indulging in broken-English flubs, troublemaking ideas, and sudden fits of temper that had her unleashing torrents of Spanish. She occasionally sang in these films, and displayed a talent for hectic, visual comedy. She obviously enjoyed performing and can be seen openly breaking up at Leon Errol's comic ad-libs.

The "Mexican Spitfire" films rejuvenated Lupe's career, and for the next few years she starred in musical and comedy features for RKO, Universal, and Columbia, in addition to her continuing series. In one of her last films, Columbia's "Redhead from Manhattan," she played a dual role: one in her exaggerated comic dialect, and the other in her actual speaking voice, which surprisingly had only traces of a Mexican accent.

Emotionally generous, passionate, and high-spirited, Vélez had a number of highly publicized affairs, including a particularly emotionally draining one with Gary Cooper, before marrying Olympic athlete Johnny Weissmuller (of "Tarzan" fame) in 1933. The fraught marriage lasted five years; they repeatedly split and finally divorced in 1938.

Following her divorce from Weissmuller, the men came more frequently, but the relationships lasted for a shorter time. Perhaps the best known of these was Arturo de Cordova (a star in the Mexican film industry who came to Hollywood to follow in the wake of "Latin Lover" stars like Fernando Lamas and Ricardo Montalban), but most were forgettable actors and hangers-on from the Hollywood fringe. Often, Lupe would show up at one of the local nightspots with six or seven men in tow. No one knew who her favorite of the evening was. Perhaps it was all of them.

Eventually, Lupe's "Mexican Spitfire" series came to an end and it looked as though her star was beginning to fade. In 1938, she tried Broadway with Libby Holman and Clifton Webb and in 1943, she returned to Mexico and starred in an adaptation of Emile Zola's "Nana." It was not well received and she subsequently returned to Hollywood.

In 1944, Lupe told friends at a party, "I know I'm not worth anything. I can't sing well, I can't dance well. I've never done anything like that. It comes from my heart, or I wouldn't say these things."

When she was asked what she wanted to do with the rest of her life, she replied simply, "I just want to have fun."

But the beautiful actress was merely putting up a brave front. She knew that life was closing in on her and that her career was beginning to wind down. But no one wants to be seen with a "has-been" in Hollywood and she knew that she had to do whatever it took to keep smiling and making appearances on the Tinseltown party scene.

In the summer of 1944, Lupe met a young actor named Harald Maresch, who had changed his name to Harald Ramond to try and break into the movies. The young man, who came to Hollywood from Austria, was darkly handsome and told adventurous stories of his past, claiming to have fought the Nazis in Vienna and Prague and that he was captured and sent to Dachau, only to escape to France. In wartime Hollywood, it made for compelling conversations at cocktail parties. It's not surprisingly that Lupe fell madly in love with him, which was convenient for the struggling actor. Lupe took him everywhere and introduced him to all of her contacts. This gained him a couple of small, uncredited roles in "Hotel Berlin" and "Song of the Open Road," and finally, the part of Edmond in "Frenchman's Creek."

Unfortunately, like all of the Lupe's relationships, her romance with Ramond was a stormy one. After a time, even Lupe began to have mixed emotions about the situation, which made her discovery in late 1944 even more unnerving – she was pregnant with Ramond's child. She went straight from the doctor's office to her home on Rodeo Drive in Beverly Hills, where a birthday party was being held for her brother-in-law. She took her sister aside and made plans with her to give up the baby. Lupe would not consider the idea of an abortion, but she did not want to raise a child.

Lupe Velez's home in Beverly Hills

Her sister later reported that Lupe planned to have the baby in Mexico, then for her sister to adopt the child a few months later. They were going to talk things over again in a month, she said, but that was the last conversation they ever had about it.

Lupe then called her business manager, Bo Roos, and told him of the situation. Roos then called Ramond and asked him what he planned to do about the pregnancy. Roos later stated that Ramond wanted to think things over, then called him back and proposed a mock wedding ceremony for the press. He didn't really want to be married, but understood that Lupe being an unwed mother in Hollywood of the 1940s would be the death of her career. Ramond called again a little while later and this time agreed to marry Lupe, but only if she would sign a document saying that she knew he was only marrying her to give her baby a name. He wanted nothing to do the child.

Lupe reacted angrily to Ramond's terms and immediately cut off all contact with him. She managed to keep her pregnancy secret for the next three months but she knew by December 1944 that she needed to deal with it, and quickly. She called Roos again and said that she was either going to have to take a six or seven month long trip to Mexico, or she was going to have to make an

> Hollywood legend has it that Lupe Velez once visited a fortune teller, who told her that she would eventually die by her own hand. Although the fun-loving actress claimed to not put any stock in the prediction, friends say that it haunted her for the rest of her life. They were shocked when she actually committed suicide in December 1944.

appointment with a doctor. As far as Roos could tell, no decision had yet been made.

On December 13, Roos called to check on her. During their conversation, Lupe had mentioned suicide as a possible way out of her predicament, which worried her manager all day. He pleaded with her over the telephone not to take such a drastic measure. Her last words to him were that she would do nothing without speaking to him again the next day – a promise that she didn't keep.

Around daybreak, the police later estimated, she wrote a note to Harald Ramond: "To Harald, may God forgive you and forgive me too but I prefer to take my life away and our baby's before I bring him with shame or killing him, Lupe."

After that, Lupe put on her favorite blue silk pajamas, brushed her hair, climbed into bed, and arranged herself comfortably. She then swallowed an overdose of sleeping pills, closed her eyes, and drifted away. She was discovered a few hours later by her secretary and companion of 10 years, Beulah Kinder. Or at least that's how the official version of her death has been recorded.

Although there is no evidence to prove it, a popular Hollywood version of her death has it that Lupe actually died with her face in a toilet. The stories say that soon after swallowing the 75 seconal tablets that eventually killed her, Lupe had become sick and started to throw up. Her body was discovered, not on the bed, but by following a trail of vomit into the bathroom. Violently sick, she had allegedly stumbled on the bathroom tiles and fell headfirst into the toilet. She cracked her head on the porcelain and drowned in the water in the bowl. The story goes on to say that this embarrassing death was hushed up by the gossip columnists, who didn't want this to be the last thing people remembered about this beloved actress.

No matter how it happened, Lupe Velez died a lonely Hollywood death that she didn't deserve. The fact that she might have died in the bathroom, rather than in bed, makes it even worse. And not because it was more embarrassing, but because the fact that she ran for the bathroom seems to say that perhaps she had second thought about taking her own life in the end. The fact that she died anyway makes the story of Lupe Velez all the more tragic.

"IN LIKE FLYNN"
THE SCANDALS OF ERROL FLYNN & HIS LINGERING SPIRIT

It's always been a popular misconception with the general public that Hollywood stars could do whatever they pleased, regardless of laws and the moral standards of the country. With such a slanted view of the film colony – which normally came from press stories, jealousy, and the idea that studio heads could bend the truth and buy off public officials whenever they pleased – public

Dashing Errol Flynn

sentiment regarding a suspect celebrity was usually biased long before all of the facts were known. The case of Roscoe "Fatty" Arbuckle was a perfect example of this. When he was implicated in the death of a minor actress, the local district attorney and the tabloid newspapers turned everyone against the movie star. After three trials, Arbuckle was proved to be innocent, but his career was ruined.

On the other hand, in early 1943, when handsome, swashbuckling star Errol Flynn was put on trial for statutory rape, public sentiment was solidly on his side. Even so, in those moral, wartime days, the charge that the star was accused of was certainly not sanctioned by the general population. The normally footloose Flynn had much to be concerned about if the jury verdict went against him. Deep down, though, he probably wondered if such a thing could really happen. There was no question that Errol Flynn seemed to lead a charmed life.

He was born Errol Leslie Thomson Flynn on June 20, 1909 in Hobart, the seaside capital of Tasmania. His father, Theodor Thomson Flynn, was a well-known marine biologist and professor, and his mother, Mary Lily "Marelle" Young, was reportedly a pushy, self-focused woman who spent most of her time with assorted male friends. While there was always bitterness between mother and son, Flynn always got along well with his father. When he was 11, his sister, Rosemary, was born and the family moved to Sydney, Australia. The move had been made at Mrs. Flynn's prodding, as she hoped to find more sophisticated pursuits than were offered in Hobart. Soon after, she abandoned the family and moved to France.

By Flynn's own admission, he was always fascinated by the opposite sex. However, he had no interest in academics and by the age of 16, he had been kicked out of several schools for bad behavior. He fared no better in the employment field. He even lost a clerical post that his father obtained for him after he used the office's petty cash to bet at the racetrack. Soon after, he learned about a gold strike in Australian New Guinea and decided to make a clean start and go there. He never found gold, but during his four years in New Guinea, he held a score of jobs, including bird trapper, pearl diver, newspaper correspondent, charter boat captain, and diamond smuggler. In 1932, an Australian filmmaker happened to see Flynn's handsome face in a newspaper photograph and cast him in a film, "In the Wake of The Bounty."

But Flynn chose not to pursue his fledgling Australian movie career. Deeply in debt, he decided to move on. About this same time, he met the mysterious Dr. Hermann Erben, who had also been in New Guinea looking for gold. The two men sailed for Hong Kong in the spring of 1933 then moved on to Saigon, India, and eventually, Marseilles. There, they parted company, with Flynn traveling on to London. It later developed that Erben worked for German Intelligence and a few sources have alleged – but have never proven – that during World War II, Erben convinced Flynn to act as a spy for Hitler. It should be noted, however, that Flynn was much more interested in partying and womanizing than he was in politics, which makes these claims questionable, at best.

Flynn soon found himself broke in England. He began acting with a repertory company in Northampton, but was later fired. Moving back to London, he came to the attention of the British division of Warner Brothers and was hired for the lead role in the low-budget film "Murder at Monte Carlo." His screen presence quickly got him transferred to the Warner studios in California.

While en route to Hollywood, Flynn met French-born screen actress Lili Damita, a former model, dancer, and music hall performer who had appeared in movies in France, Germany, and America. The two embarked on a tempestuous romance and the volatile Lili cajoled Flynn into marriage in June 1935. In Hollywood, they settled into the famous Garden of Allah Hotel but Lili was unable to control her husband's persistent womanizing. Before long, the couple chose to live apart, but agreed to share a bed when the mood suited them.

After a few more minor roles, Warner Brothers cast Flynn in the title role of "Captain Blood," which was released in 1935. The film made him a major star and set the stage for other swashbuckling assignments, like the immensely

GARDEN OF ALLAH HOTEL

The Garden of Allah was Hollywood's most famous – or perhaps infamous – hotel during the 1930s and 1940s. Near the end of her career, silent film actress Alla Nazimova was advised by her manager to convert her mansion at the corner of Sunset Boulevard and Crescent Heights into a revenue-generating property to provide for her retirement. By the time she had completed remodeling the house and adding the bungalow complex in 1928, she was bankrupt and forced to sell out. Eventually she was reduced to renting a flat in one corner of her former home.

The Garden of Allah became a magnet for artistic visitors when they stayed in Hollywood. The facilities included the hotel, restaurant, bar, swimming pool, and a series of bungalows for the more "bohemian" guests.

Some of the celebrities who stayed at The Garden of Allah were in town for films they were working on and some lived there long-term. Some were between marriages or homes; some were there for the parties going on from sunset until dawn. But whatever the reason for visiting, the Garden of Allah provided an escape from reality. The furnishings were rather plain. The walls were thin enough for everyone to hear the goings on everywhere. And the food in the restaurant was terrible, but no one really cared.

It is said that Humphrey Bogart and Lauren Bacall began their romance there while making "To Have and Have Not" in 1944. Charles Laughton and wife Elsa Lanchester stayed there when they moved to California in the early '30s before settling in Santa Monica. Frank Sinatra stayed there while he was performing at the Ambassador Hotel's legendary Cocoanut Grove club in 1941. Tallulah Bankhead reportedly swam – nude – in the pool. Douglas Fairbanks, Mary Pickford, Tom Mix, Charlie Chaplin, John Barrymore, Marlene Dietrich, Ginger Rogers, Greta Garbo, Errol Flynn, and the Marx Brothers all visited at one time or another.

It was also a sanctuary for the literary celebrities who gravitated to Hollywood in the 1930s, including Robert Benchley, Dorothy Parker, F. Scott Fitzgerald, and Ernest Hemingway.

Unfortunately, the hotel never made any real profit over the years, even after several ownership changes. By the late 1950s, it was rundown and populated by transients and prostitutes. It closed in August of 1959 – but not before one last huge party. Over 1,000 people showed up, many dressed as the hotel's previous celebrity guests. Alla Nazimova's 1923 film "Salome" was screened for the partygoers.

The fabled hotel was replaced by a strip mall, a McDonald's and a bank: structures not worthy to take the place of this landmark of Hollywood's past.

popular "The Adventures of Robin Hood" in 1938. Other films in his career included "The Dawn Patrol" with his close friend, David Niven, "Dodge City," "The Sea Hawk," and "The Adventures of Don Juan."

Flynn played opposite Olivia de Havilland in eight films and while he acknowledged his attraction to her, they were never romantically involved, despite some claims to the contrary. She maintained that their relationship was always platonic and they got along well. The same could not be said about Flynn and some of his other female co-stars. During the filming of "The Private Lives of Elizabeth and Essex," Flynn and Bette Davis engaged in some legendary off-screen fights, with Davis striking him much harder than necessary during the filming of one scene. Their relationship was always strained, but Warner Brothers teamed them together twice, which later led to reconciliation. At one point, a contract was presented to lend them out as Rhett Butler and Scarlett O'Hara in "Gone with the Wind," but it failed to happen.

Flynn played an adventurer on-screen, but when it came to war, he was criticized for not doing his part. When America entered World War II, many complained about his failure to enlist in the way that other stars had done. In fact, Flynn actually attempted to join every branch of the service, but was rejected for health reasons. The studio remained silent about this because they didn't want the public to know about the state of the actor's health. Not only did Flynn have an enlarged heart, which had already resulted in several heart attacks, but he also had a bad back, and suffered from recurrent bouts of malaria that he had contracted in New Guinea.

But poor health didn't keep Flynn from romancing a long string of Hollywood beauties. By the late 1930s, his marriage had become one long quarrel, interspersed with attempts to try one more time. During one of the Flynns' infrequent reconciliations in 1940, Lili became pregnant. She gave birth to a son, Sean, in 1941. By then, the marriage was over for good, ending in a bitter

Flynn with Oliva de Haviland in "The Adventures of Robin Hood", one of my favorite Flynn roles -- and one of the biggest of his career.

divorce in March 1942.

Flynn moved into a customized mansion, Mulholland House, in Beverly Hills. Rumors state that the house contained peepholes and listening devices that allowed the voyeuristic Flynn to spy on his guest's sexual activities. He also purchased a yacht, the *Sirocco*, where he held wild seagoing parties and hosted orgies as he sailed between Los Angeles and Catalina.

Among Flynn's group of friends were character actor Guinn "Big Boy" Williams, leading man Bruce Cabot (who had saved Fay Wray from "Kling Kong"), stuntman Buster Wiles, and club owner Johnny Meyer, whose purported underworld connections were frequently used for finding girls for Flynn and the others.

In 1942, Cabot, along with wealthy British sportsman Freddie MacAvoy and actor Stephen Raphael, was sharing a Spanish-style mansion that once belonged to silent film actress Colleen Moore in Bel-Air. On September 27, the trio, along with Flynn, hosted one of their wild parties at the house.

Among those attending was 17-year-old Betty Hansen, a drugstore waitress who crashed the party with several friends, two of whom were employees at Warner Brothers. Betty came to the party with the idea that she might meet someone important who could help her get a job on the studio lot. During the afternoon, the young girl watched Flynn and others play tennis. Later, she chatted with Flynn, even sitting on his chair and later, his lap. By late in the day, she became so drunk that she threw up and Flynn took her into the house and helped her get cleaned up. Allegedly, he then took her somewhere quiet and raped her.

Days later, Hansen was picked up by police at the seedy Santa Monica hotel where she was staying and was arrested on vagrancy charges. Because she was still underage, she was sent to juvenile hall, where an officer, while examining her personal effects, found several telephone numbers, including those of Errol Flynn and Bruce Cabot. Hansen claimed that Flynn had had sex with her twice. Her claims brought L.A. officers to Mulholland House in early October and they took Flynn in for questioning in regard to a charge of statutory rape. If convicted of having sex with the 17-year-old, whether consensual or not, he could be sent to prison for 10 years. When asked about Betty Hansen, he vaguely recalled her as a "frowsy little blond" and then misspoke, saying, "I hardly touched her." That was enough for the cops and Flynn was taken into custody.

Flynn and his lawyer, Robert Ford, went to juvenile hall where, as a legal necessity for the prosecution to proceed, Hansen's police custodian confronted Flynn and explained the allegations that had been made about him. During subsequent interrogation, when asked by Flynn's attorney if she had put up any resistance to the alleged seduction, the girl replied, "No. Why should I?" The case eventually went to a grand jury and Warner Brothers retained the services of high-priced defense attorney, Jerry Giesler. The grand jury threw out the case, which would usually have brought an end to the matter.

In this case, though, L.A. District Attorney "Honest" John Duckweiller chose not to let things go. Observers thought that he was grandstanding to show Hollywood that he meant business, while others thought he was merely reacting to Warner Brothers' dismissal of the situation by stating that he and other city officials needed to find more important things to do. This made Flynn's reprieve from his legal problems a short-lived one. A few days after the grand jury threw out the case, the actor was arrested again.

This time, the charges not only involved Betty Hansen, on whose case the district attorney acted without a bill from the grand jury, but included a claim that on the weekend of August 2-3, 1941, Flynn had induced 15-year-old Peggy Satterlee to join his party about the *Sirocco* for a cruise to Catalina. Allegedly, he had sex with her two times while on board the yacht. When Peggy's mother learned of the alleged sexual activity, she attempted to press charges against Flynn. At the time, the police concluded there was insufficient evidence to pursue the case and convinced the Satterlees to drop the matter because pursuing it further would be embarrassing for the teenager. Later, there would be allegations that the family had initially sought to make Flynn buy their silence, including using an anonymous telephone caller who said, "Tell Jack I want $10,000" and hung up. The "Jack" in question was said to be Jack Warner, who could make the whole thing vanish for a pay-off that never came.

After the Betty Hansen matter, D.A. Duckweiller thought he could use the Satterlee affair to his advantage and beat Flynn. On October 16, 1942, the actor was arrested, booked, fingerprinted, and formally charged. He was released on $1,000 bail and told reporters how confused and bewildered he was by the entire situation.

For the usually devil-may-care Flynn, the pending prosecution seemed a hopeless situation. He said, "Even if I win, I lose. If the jury thinks I screwed her then I'm screwed." If the prosecution team of Thomas W. Cochran and John Hopkins could prove in court that he had engaged in sex with two underage girls, willing or not, he could end up behind bars for years. Rumor had it that Flynn had an airplane standing by to take him to Mexico, then Venezuela, just in case things went badly during the trial.

Even during the war years, the case grabbed headlines around the world. People everywhere took sides and placed bets over whether or not Flynn would be found guilty. During this time, he received the worst publicity from those who believed he was nothing more than a draft dodger who got out of serving his country because he was a movie star. Flynn kept his mouth shut about his 4-F status, vainly refusing to acknowledge the health problems that had kept him out of the war. Instead, he put on a brave face and continued working while many of his friends and co-stars, like Ida Lupino and Ann Sheridan, showed their support. Flynn was encouraged by this, but he also knew that many others were keeping their distance, afraid of being tainted by defending the accused. Meanwhile, the studio, with its huge investment in the actor, worked overtime to present Flynn in the best possible light.

When the trial opened, hundreds of fans were on hand to cheer Flynn as he made his way into the courtroom. In a very short time, defense attorney Giesler made it clear that he had been well worth his hefty fee. As he put together his case, he managed to uncover much more than the prosecution had – or at least what they would admit to.

Betty Hansen turned out to be a disaster on the stand for the prosecution. She came across as stupid and crude and with her prominent3 overbite, she didn't win any fans among the jury members, nine of them women and nearly all of them smitten by the handsome Flynn. During the trial, two of the female jury members were actually removed from duty for being blatantly biased in the defendant's favor.

The supposedly inexperienced victim testified on the stand that she had not resisted Flynn when he undressed her because she had no idea what was to follow. She said that their sexual activity lasted for an impressive 50 minutes and that she took a willing part in the performance of the act. She also slipped up and admitted that her ulterior motive was to gain material rewards from her liaison with Flynn, whom she didn't like as an actor or a person. Giesler managed to stain Hansen's "pure" image by getting her to admit that she was far more sexually experienced that she let on. In fact, it was learned that she had performed oral sex on her boyfriend, a messenger at Warner Brothers, an act that was then considered not only perverted, but illegal. The couple was facing a possible felony charge for this activity, which could lead to a four-year jail sentence. Giesler presented this to the jury as a motive for her alleged seduction fabrication. He also got several young men who went with her to the party to admit that she had had sex with them, as well.

Betty Hansen may have invented most of what happened between herself and the movie star, but Peggy Satterlee was another matter. She was 17 at the time of the trial, but there was no one in Hollywood who could have mistaken her for a blushing virgin. She was well known around town and was a dancer at Hollywood's Florentine Garden. She had first caught Flynn's eye when she was an extra on his western, "They Died with Their Boots On" in 1941. Flynn later said that Peggy had "sensational upholstery" and could have passed for anywhere between 20 and 25. However, when she showed up in court, she was decked out in pigtails, a young girl's dress, and flat shoes. She spoke in a child-like, timid whisper, hoping to make an impression on the jury. The defense sarcastically pointed out that this demure outfit was not her usual form of clothing choice.

During the weekend cruise in question, Peggy insisted that the first of her two seductions by Flynn occurred in her cabin on the *Sirocco*. She claimed that she had gotten into bed, taken off her clothing including her bra and then put her slip back on to use as a nightgown. However, she was forced to admit that she usually slept in the nude. When asked whether she resisted Flynn's advances, she said that she had, then confessed that she didn't mind when it happened, but felt ashamed afterwards. She couldn't say why she had not screamed for help from the crew or other passengers. She also had no explanation for why she stayed on the yacht for the entire weekend and seemed content and happy when photographed. As for her allegations that Flynn had sex with her again on board the yacht, she claimed that she had been lured to his stateroom because he told her that it had a wonderful view of the moon. However, Giesler was able to prove that the moon could not even be seen from that side of the boat on that night.

Peggy's credibility was in shambles by the time she left the stand and the defense had also discovered that she had once had an abortion, an illegal act for which she could be prosecuted. He suggested that, like Hansen, she had been coerced by the prosecution to go forward with her claims. It also came out that Peggy and her sister shared an apartment that was paid for by a 43-year-old Royal Canadian Air Force pilot. She and the pilot, apparently, had once run around a mortuary yanking the sheets off of corpses and had even pressed their faces against the naked bodies. How Giesler found out about this is anyone's guess, but his investigative skills did the trick, stunning and outraging the jury.

Flynn on board his new yacht, the *Zaca*

When Flynn took the stand, he denied everything and claimed that he had never had "an act of sexual intercourse" with either Betty Hansen or Peggy Satterlee. They jury apparently believed him. They deliberated for two days and then acquitted Flynn on all counts. The verdict was greeted by cheers from fans who had packed the courtroom. Flynn enthusiastically shook the hands of each jury member and told the press, "This just goes to show there is justice in the United States." One of the female jurors told a reporter, "We knew Flynn was not guilty all the time, but we didn't want to come out too soon because we wondered what the public would think if we did."

Over the course of the lengthy, notorious trail, a reporter had come up with a new saying, "in like Flynn," to suggest the status of a man getting his way with a woman. The expression became popular, especially among the G.I.s who were fighting in the war. Flynn seemed more amused than irritated with the expression. He was well aware that he would also be connected to the rape case and an attraction to young women but he didn't seem to mind. In fact, the only thing that he was thinking about after the trial was another young woman, an 18-year-old redhead named Nora Eddington. The pretty teenager was the daughter of the sheriff of Los Angeles County and at the time, she worked behind the cigar counter at the L.A. County Hall of Justice. Each day as the famous defendant passed by, she flashed him a bright smile. The two of them became much better acquainted after the trial and they married in Acapulco, Mexico, in August 1943. The couple had two children, Deidre and Rory.

After the trial, Flynn made several dozen more films and was divorced again. By the 1950s, he had almost become a parody of himself. Heavy drinking and abuse of painkillers for his chronic back pain had left him prematurely aged and bloated. In spite of this, he won acclaim as a drunken ne'er-do-well in "The Sun Also Rises," and as his idol John Barrymore in "Too Much Too Soon." His autobiography, *My Wicked, Wicked Ways*, was published just months after his death in 1959 and contains humorous anecdotes about

Hollywood. Flynn wanted to call the book *In Like Me*, but the publisher refused.

In the years that followed Flynn's death, it was widely rumored that his ghost was still around; haunting a unique property that once belonged to the actor, his yacht. After his scandalous trial, Flynn sold the Sirocco and replaced it with a 118-foot, two-masted schooner called the *Zaca*, which is Samoan for "peace." Just as the *Sirocco* was known for Flynn's drunken parties, the *Zaca* soon gained a similar reputation. Many of Flynn's friends, including Alan Hale, David Niven, Gary Cooper, and others, were guests aboard the new vessel. Flynn and Nora Eddington spent their happiest moments aboard the schooner – until Nora discovered just how many other women were spending their happiest moments on the boat, too.

Flynn's guests were often entertained by fights between him and various members of the crew. On one occasion, after a crewman got mixed up in a fight with Flynn, the actor picked up the unlucky sailor and threw him overboard.

Flynn spent the last peaceful times aboard the boat with 16-year-old Beverly Aadland, whom he had met at the Hollywood Professional School. She was the last of his many loves and she claimed that Flynn told her that he planned to marry her and move her to his home in Jamaica. Unfortunately, he never got the chance. Toward the end of his life, Flynn was ill, in constant pain, and having financial difficulties. He decided to move the *Zaca* up the coast from Los Angeles to Vancouver to prevent it from being impounded by the Internal Revenue Service.

Once he arrived there, he decided to sell the beloved vessel. He was badly in need of money and wanted to return to Jamaica. On October 14, 1959, a Vancouver couple who were in the process of buying the boat invited Flynn and Beverly to a party. It was early in the evening when Flynn said, "I think I'll lie down. I shall return." In a hallway that led to the host's master bedroom, Flynn collapsed from a massive heart attack and was dead before he reached the hospital.

His body was shipped back to Hollywood by train and just before the funeral, a well-known film director and close friend of Flynn's slipped six bottles of the star's favorite whiskey into his coffin. Friends agreed that he would have appreciated the gesture.

Flynn's death preceded a run of bad luck that seemed to affect those who were closest to him.

Beverly Aadland never became the movie star that Flynn promised her she would be. She appeared in just a handful of films; roles that Flynn helped obtain for her. A short time after Flynn's death, a man was found shot to death in her bedroom. The coroner ruled it a suicide.

Flynn's parents, both residing in England at the time of his death, died shortly after. His father

Flynn's *Zaca*, docked in Jamaica

had a stroke and his mother was killed in a car accident.

Sean Flynn, the actor's son, became a well-known news photographer, living out the adventurous life that his father had played on the silver screen. He went to Vietnam as a correspondent and vanished while covering an assignment. He was listed as missing and no trace of him has ever been found.

The *Zaca* was sold and the new owner sailed it to Europe. During the passage, Flynn's personal flag – a symbolic question mark against a plain background – was flown from the mast as a tribute to the fallen star. Before the return cruise began, the flag was taken down and the *Zaca* inexplicably broke down and had to be towed to a shipyard in France. It was left there to deteriorate for years.

But those years of decay were not years of silence and inactivity on board the ship. A number of witnesses reported seeing the eerie apparition of Errol Flynn pacing the decks of the vessel. Most often, his ghost was seen during the short period between sunset and darkness and often had a disconcerting effect on those who witnessed it. One watchman who saw the ghost jumped overboard and was in a state of shock when he was pulled from the water.

A captain whose own vessel was moored near the late actor's ship also witnessed some strange goings-on aboard the *Zaca*. He reported, "One night there was music coming from the *Zaca*. You could hear girl's voices and laughter, and the lights on board were going off and on. It was as though a wild party was going on. But there couldn't have been a party, because there was no one on board. There wasn't even any electricity on her. Something strange was going on."

In the late 1970s, the owners of the shipyard where the *Zaca* was moored decided to restore the vessel. There seemed to be only one problem with the plan: Flynn's ghost. The owners decided that they would hold an exorcism to banish the restless spirit. A 30-inch-long model of the *Zaca* to be used for the exorcism was taken to a church in Monte Carlo on December 18, 1978. It was carried by a painter who had seen the apparition while working on the boat. Others who had seen the ghost were also present and the exorcism was carried out by an Anglican archdeacon and a Catholic priest.

As the ritual began, the archdeacon removed salt from a glass container and spoke, "I exorcize thee, O creature of salt, by our living God. Let the spirit of pestilence abide here no more, nor the breath of moral perversion. Let every unclean spirit fly hence." As the archdeacon's words echoed in the church, the painter who had carried the model of the boat let out a moan and slumped forward in his pew, unconscious. He revived a few minutes later, unaware of what had happened to him.

The archdeacon continued the ritual, "Send thy holy angels from heaven above to protect and cherish all those who go aboard this ship. Let the *Zaca* be hallowed. Let cheer, joy, and health be given to all aboard *Zaca*. Deliver this vessel and all who board her from evil."

The entire ritual took about 20 minutes to complete and when it was finished, the priest stated that he was positive that the spirit had departed from the ship. "I prayed from my heart for Errol Flynn," he said, "for I remember his face. I hope that he may enter the Kingdom of God, where he may find eternal peace."

Everyone who took part in the ceremony felt that it was a success and apparently, it was. There were no further reports of a ghost aboard the *Zaca* and no more sightings of Errol Flynn. Apparently, the freewheeling actor, best known for his drinking, womanizing, and brawling, had finally found some peace from his wicked ways after all.

JAMES DEAN: TOO FAST TO LIVE

There are few Hollywood performers who have ever made the kind of impact on the American public – and never in so short a time – as James Dean. The charismatic, boyishly handsome actor left an indelible mark on popular culture and with only three films during his brief, spectacular career. In both life and death, he became the rebellious symbol of his era and remains a legend today, perhaps more popular in death then he ever was in life.

Dean lived fast, in more ways than one. As a passionate auto racing fan, he had an incredible need for speed and it was behind the wheel of his lightning-fast Porsche Spyder that he eventually died. Many of Dean's friends felt the car and driver had a fateful rendezvous with destiny, and they were right. The spectacular automobile accident that claimed the young actor's life created a legend – and a dark mystery – that has never been truly explained.

James Dean was born to Winton Dean and Mildred Wilson Dean at the Seven Gables apartment house in Marion, Ind., on February 8, 1931. The family moved to Santa Monica, Calif., when Dean was young and spent a few years there. He was 9 years old when his mother died and he returned to Indiana to live with his aunt and uncle, Hortense and Marcus Winslow, in Fairmount.

In high school, Dean's overall performance was lackluster, but he played well for the baseball and basketball teams and studied drama. His drama teacher, Adeline Nall, talked him into entering a public speaking contest, and he ended up winning the state trophy. After graduating from Fairmount High School in 1949, Dean moved back to California with his beagle, Max, to live with his father and stepmother. He enrolled in Santa Monica College and, going along with his father's wishes, majored in pre-law. He soon transferred to UCLA, where he changed his major to drama, which resulted in an estrangement from his father. While at UCLA, he beat out 350 other actors to land the role of Malcolm in "Macbeth." His roommate, actor William Bast, got him a job as an extra in a television commercial for Pepsi Cola. Next, Dead worked as an NBC network page, and then as a movie extra. In January 1951, he dropped out of college to pursue a career as an actor.

One of Dean's first roles after leaving college was as the disciple John the Beloved in "Hill Number One," an Easter television special. He also got walk-on roles in the movies "Fixed Bayonets," "Sailor Beware," and "Has Anybody Seen my Gal?" His only speaking role was in "Sailor Beware," a Paramount comedy with Dean Martin and Jerry Lewis. Dean played a boxing trainer in the film.

James Dean

While struggling to get jobs in Hollywood, he also worked as a parking lot attendant at CBS Studios.

At the suggestion of actor James Whitmore, Dean moved to New York in the fall of 1951 to look for work. Always a loner, he became even more so in Manhattan. However, he knew instinctively how to find opportunities and, through friends, he managed to find a string of jobs. He worked as a stunt tester for the game show "Beat the Clock" and appeared in episodes of several CBS television series including "The Web," "Studio One," and "Lux Video Theater." As his career picked up, he also found roles in early 1950s television shows like "Kraft Television Theater," "Robert Montgomery Presents," "Danger," and "General Electric Theater." While in New York, Dean also studied at the famed Actor's Studio, where director Eli Kazan hired him for an upcoming movie called "East of Eden."

As Cal Trask, one of Raymond Massey's tormented sons in the adaptation of John

Steinbeck's novel, Dean struck a chord with teenage moviegoers everywhere and became their new screen hero. Steinbeck's book dealt with the story of the Trask and Hamilton families over the course of three generations, focusing especially on the lives of the latter generations in Salinas Valley, Calif., from the middle 1800s through the 1910s. However, the film centered around Dean's character, Cal Trask, the rebellious son of a pious and constantly disapproving father, played by Raymond Massey. In March 1954, Dean left New York City and headed for Los Angeles to begin shooting. His performance in the film foreshadowed his role in "Rebel Without a Cause." Both characters were loners and misunderstood outcasts, desperately craving acceptance from a father figure.

Much of Dean's performance in the film was unscripted, such as his dance in the bean field and his curling up and pulling his arms inside of his shirt on top of the train during his ride home from meeting his mother. The most famous improvisation during the film was when Cal's father rejects his gift of $5,000. Instead of running away from his father as the script called for, Dean instinctively turned to Massey and, crying, embraced him. This cut and Massey's shocked reaction were kept in the film by Kazan. At the 1955 Academy Awards, Dean received a posthumous Best Actor in a Leading Role Academy Award nomination for this role, the first official posthumous acting nomination in Academy Awards history.

While shooting "East of Eden," Dean reportedly fell in love with Italian actress Pier Angeli, who was then a rising star at MGM. She was as moody as he was and just as much of a loner. Her emotional nature, along with outside pressure, led her to break off their intense engagement. In November 1954, when she married singer Vic Damone, Dean was spotted brooding across the street from the church.

But how genuine was their relationship? Many Hollywood insiders believed that it was arranged, as were most of Dean's romantic affairs, by the studios to present him as attractive to his female fans. Today, Dean is often considered an icon because of his "experimental" take on life, which included his ambivalent sexuality. There have been several accounts of Dean's sexual relationships with both men and women and it's no secret that the gay community accepts him as one of their own. A number of written accounts have stated that Dean was a homosexual, or at least bisexual.

Dean's relationships with women were (naturally, this was the 1950s) a big part of his Hollywood image. After he signed a contract with Warner Brothers, the studio's public relations department began generating stories about his liaisons with a number of young actresses who were mostly drawn from the clientele of Dean's agent, Dick Clayton. Studio press releases also grouped Dean together with actors like Rock Hudson, identifying them both as "eligible bachelors" who had not yet found time to commit to a single woman because "their film rehearsals are in conflict with marriage rehearsals."

The romance between Dean and Pier Angeli was also part of the studio charade, some writers believe. For a time, the affair was even promoted by Dean himself, who fed stories to various gossip columnists and his co-star, Julie Harris, who in

Dean with actress Pier Angeli

interviews reported that Dean told her about being madly in love with Angeli. When Angeli married Vic Damone in November 1954, gossip columnists reported that Dean, or someone dressed like him, watched the wedding from across the road on a motorcycle. Asked about this later, Dean denied that he, personally, would have done anything so "dumb." This caused many to believe that the "wedding sighting," like the entire affair, was little more than a publicity stunt.

Actress Liz Sheridan claimed that's he and Dean had a short affair in New York. In her memoir, she noted that he was also involved with a man who was a friend and who had helped him with his career. She had a negative response to this news. Others have noted that, contrary to popular opinions, the casting of Natalie Wood in "Rebel Without a Cause" did not lead to a romance with Dean. The young actress admitted to being fascinated with his charm and magnetic personality, but that was all. They got on well, she later said, and liked each other a lot. However, there was no affair and no sexual relationship.

The question for many people remains – was James Dean gay? While many have turned this into the biggest scandal of Dean's short life, the real question remains: Does it really matter?

Dean quickly followed up his role in "East of Eden" with a starring role in "Rebel Without a Cause," a film that proved to be immensely popular and would have taken Dean to even great heights if he had lived long enough to see it released. Nicholas Ray, who directed Dean in the film, said, "My feelings were that he surpassed any actor alive." The film co-starred Natalie Wood and Sal Mineo and is still revered today as a classic and the first authentic representation of teenage angst to appear on the silver screen.

James Dean in his Porsche Spyder

Dean was next hired by director George Stevens for his big-budget, Texas epic "Giant," in which Dean's character, Jett Rink, goes from a young, poor farmhand to a millionaire, middle-aged oilman. The movie was adapted from the book by Edna Ferber and also starred Elizabeth Taylor, Rock Hudson, Carroll Baker, Dennis Hopper, and Sal Mineo. This was the last of Dean's three film roles and his second and last Academy Award nomination. Dean was dead before the film was completely finished – dying behind the wheel of his beloved car.

As Dean's acting career took off, so did his taste for fast cars. He had grown up with motorbikes and motorcycles and his first true sports car was a red MG-TD. His favorite pastime with the car, he told friends, was to lower the top, fold the windshield forward and race along back roads at night "chasing the moon." Soon after, he began to become obsessed with racing. He entered his first race in April 1955, driving a newly purchased Porsche Speedster at Palm Springs. In that initial race, he won first place in the amateur division and took third in the professional class. Less than a month later, he entered the Bakersfield

National Sports car Races and drove to a first place position in his class. At Santa Barbara four weeks later, he was again a winner.

After that race, Dean spent most of the summer in west Texas, near the town of Marfa, for the filming of "Giant." Warner Brothers refused to allow their star to race during the film's production. Director George Stevens had rented a Chevrolet convertible for Dean to driving during the shoot, but when he saw how the actor was racing around the countryside in it, the filmmaker returned the car to the rental agency.

After Dean finished his part of the filming, he returned to Los Angeles. A small import sports car company had a new 1955 Porsche Spyder on the lot and offered it for $6,900. The Spyder was one of the hottest vehicles on the racing sports car circuits and Dean badly wanted one. He sold his Speedster and bought the Spyder, after driving it once around the block. Dean put a condition on the purchase, however. He would buy the car, but only if one of the company's mechanics, Rolf Wueterich, would personally prepare the Spyder and accompany him to his races as his mechanic. Wueterich, considered one of the best Porsche mechanics on the West Coast, agreed and Dean bought the car.

The Spyder, with its tartan plaid seats and two red stripes at the rear of its wheel well, was given the nickname "Little Bastard" by Bill Hickman, Dean's language coach for "Giant." Dean had the nickname painted on the car. Dean brought the car to George Barris (who later designed the "Batmobile") to have a racing stripe painted on it before he took the car to a race in Salinas, where "East of Eden" took place. Barris later recalled, "There was something strange about the car. It gave me an eerie feeling whenever I got near it. I've driven and customized thousands of cars but never did I encounter one that gave off such a weird feeling of impending doom. I had known Jimmy since I met him on the set of 'Rebel Without a Cause.' I worked on his other cars, including the Speedster, but none gave me the feeling like something's going to happen."

And Barris was not the only one of Dean's friends to have bad feelings about the Spyder. Ursula Andress was also uneasy about the Porsche.

"Jimmy dropped by my house with the car right after he bought it. He was really proud of it. He bought it as a present for himself after finishing his third picture. I told him that the car gave me a bad feeling. Laughing, he promised to be careful and said good-bye. I knew that I would never see him again," she said.

Alec Guiness called the car "sinister" and told Dean that if he were smart, he would get rid of it. He told his friend, "If you get in that car, you will be found dead in it by this time next week." Eerily, Guiness said this on September 23, 1955, seven days before Dean's death.

Nick Adams was also shaky about the new car. "When I told him," Adams later recalled, "he said that his death in a speeding car was destined."

On September 30, 1955, Dean and Rolf Wueterich set off for the sports car race in Salinas. Originally, Dean intended to take the Porsche to Salinas by trailer, pulled behind his Ford Country Squire station wagon. At the last minute, Dean drove the Spyder, having decided that he needed more time to familiarize himself with the car. Two of his friends, Bill Hickman, and photographer Stanford Roth, who was planning a photo story of Dean at the races, followed with the trailer. Dean and Wueterich stopped for gas and then sped north on Highway 99 with the Ford following behind.

As the two vehicles continued on, Donald Gene Turnupseed, a student from California Polytechnic, was driving home for the weekend in his old Ford sedan. Turnupseed, who, like Dean, was 24 years old, had hoped to arrive in his hometown of Tulare by dark. He had no idea that he was on a collision course with death.

At 3:30 p.m., Dean was ticketed in Kern County for doing 65 in a 55 mph zone. Hickman and Roth were also ticketed for traveling 10 mph over the limit, with the speed limit for vehicles towing trailers at 45 mph. Dean turned off U.S. 99 and headed west toward Lost Hills on Route 466 (now State Highway 46). The highway was a straight line without a curve for 12 miles across the Antelope Plain. It is not known what speed Dean's car attained along this straightaway, but it had the capability to travel at more than 150 mph.

Just 60 miles to the west, Turnupseed had left

THE "REBEL WITHOUT A CAUSE" CURSE?

"Rebel Without a Cause" is considered one of the original "cursed" Hollywood films. Four of the actors in the film – James Dean, Natalie Wood, Sal Mineo, and Nick Adams – died violent deaths, well before their time.

On September 30, 1955 Dean was killed in a horrific traffic accident while driving his sleek silver Porsche Spyder. Dean's speech to an empty banquet hall in the 1956 release of the film "Giant," had to be later redubbed by his friend Nick Adams, another victim of the "Rebel Without a Cause" curse. He was the next star of the movie to die. An alcoholic, Adams succumbed to a mysterious drug overdose in 1968. The death of Sal Mineo eight years later was equally untimely. Mineo was stabbed to death in the empty garage of his home just off Santa Monica Boulevard. Mineo managed to crawl up an adjacent set of steps before bleeding to death in the middle of the street.

Natalie Wood also died a terrifying death. During the making of the film "The Star" in 1952, with Bette Davis, Wood had to jump out of a boat and swim to a raft some distance away. She didn't want to do it because she was terrified of the water. Bette Davis witnessed the scene and reportedly bawled out the director, "I'm not going to stand here while you throw some screaming kid into the ocean! If you want a goddamned swimmer, you should get Johnny Weissmuller!"

Suffering from a lifelong fear of water, Wood was discovered drowned at the age of 43 in what many consider to be suspicious circumstances off Catalina Island. At the time of her death, she was three days from the end of shooting for "Brainstorm," a film she was working on with Christopher Walken and her husband, Robert Wagner. She was last seen climbing into a yacht's small rowboat and rowing herself out into the tide in the middle of the night. Some have claimed that her drowning was no accident, but a suicide, but it will never be known for sure.

Paso Robles and was driving east on Route 466. Driving conditions were ideal along the two-lane highway. Oil rigs dotted the landscape, tractors worked slowly in nearby fields, and patches of desert pine were scattered here and there, catching the last rays of the sun as it dipped down toward the horizon. As Turnupseed moved in one direction, the Spyder ate up the highway in another, roaring along toward the Diablo Range of mountains in the hazy distance.

As Dean approached Blackwell's Corner, a two-structure settlement where route 466 intersected with 33, Dean slowed down to admire a car that was parked on the side of the road. He wheeled into the parking lot of a combination gas station, grocery store, restaurant, and beer joint to have a closer look at a gray Mercedes-Benz 300 SL gull-wing sports car that was parked in the lot.

Lance Reventlow, owner of the Mercedes and son of Woolworth heiress Barbara Hutton, came outside when he saw the Spyder. Reventlow, who was also heading to the races in Salinas, later became a sports car racer of great renown. The two men discussed cars and mutual acquaintances for several minutes until Hickman and Roth caught up in the station wagon. They made plans to meet for dinner that night in Paso Robles and Dean and Wueterich climbed back into the Spyder. As he was about to start up the engine, Dean paused, got out of the car and went into the store to purchase a six-pack of beer. This delay at Blackwell's Corner guaranteed his rendezvous with destiny, as Turnupseed's Ford sedan was still moving eastward along Route 466.

The air was getting cooler as the Porsche sped along the highway. Wueterich reached behind his seat for Dean's red jacket, which he put on. The station wagon was now far behind them. They roared up the grade toward Polonio Pass, which took Route 466 through the Diablo Range.

Donald Turnupseed's Ford had passed through the town of Shandon and was nearing Cholame, which consisted of little more than a gas station, a restaurant, a post office, and a population of five lonely souls.

Contrary to popular belief, Dean may not have been speeding as he traveled along Antelope Grade toward where Route 466 met 41, which connected that junction with Tulare to the northeast. Although he may have slowed down just before the accident, police reports later stated, "The wreckage and the position of Dean's body indicated his speed was more like 55 mph," and not the 85 mph that has been widely reported. Ironically, perhaps if he had been going faster, the collision might never have occurred.

As Dean continued along the Antelope Grade, Turnupseed was passing through Cholame, just one mile away from his turnoff onto Route 41.

Dean neared the bottom of the grade. The road ahead was straight and empty. Just before 6 p.m., the Spyder and the Ford came into view of each other. Dean's foot remained steady on the accelerator. The Ford moved slowly across the center line of the roadway. Turnupseed was getting ready to make his left turn onto Route 41 at the Y-shaped intersection. The distance between the two cars was shrinking quickly – and Turnupseed never saw the Spyder coming.

Dean's last known words, uttered right before the impact, were said to have been, "That guy's gotta stop! He'll see us!"

There was an explosion of shattering metal and flying glass as the two cars collided almost head-on. Turnupseed lay across the front seat of his car with severe head and facial lacerations. Wueterich was thrown 20 feet from the wreck with a fractured jaw, a broken leg, and internal injuries. The Spyder, crumpled like a tin can, was nearly torn in two. The steering wheel and driver's seat were shoved over so far that the car appeared to be driven from the right-hand side. James Dean, his neck broken and his body shattered, was slung over the passenger's door. He was pronounced dead when he arrived at the Paso Robles War Memorial Hospital.

Turnupseed received a gashed forehead and bruised nose and was not cited by police for the accident. He was treated and released from the hospital. Rolf Wueterich was hospitalized for many months after the accident and when he recovered, he returned home to Germany and went to work in a Porsche factory. He later died in a road accident in 1981, after surviving several suicide attempts.

Word of Dean's death hit Hollywood like a bomb. Elizabeth Taylor and several members of the "Giant" cast were in the screening room looking at rushes when the telephone rang. Taylor later recalled, "I heard George Stevens answer it and say, 'Oh God! No, when? Are you sure it was him?' He hung up the phone, stopped the projector, and turned on the lights. He turned to us and said, 'I've just been told the news that Jimmy Dean has been killed.'"

While completing "Giant," and to promote "Rebel Without a Cause," a cowboy-hatted Dean filmed a short interview with actor Gig Young for an episode of "Warner Brothers Presents" in which Dean, instead of saying the popular phrase: "The life you save may be your own" instead ad-libbed: "Take it easy driving. The lives you might save might be mine." Dean's sudden death prompted the studio to re-film the section, and the piece was never aired, although in the past several books and articles have referred to the footage, mistakenly identifying it as a public service announcement.

Many attributed Dean's death to his driving habits, pointing to his earlier speeding ticket on the

Dean's crumpled Porsche Spyder after the fatal accident that claimed his life. The car, which some claimed was "cursed", was displayed for several years and then vanished without a trace between Florida and L.A.

day of his death, his obsession for racing, and his need for great speed. Others, however, were not so sure. Many came to believe that the ominous Porsche Spyder was somehow cursed. Many of Dean's friends and acquaintances believed there was "something wrong" with the car, but what? Could the car have had something evil in its background? As silly as it sounds, could something have happened at the factory where it was made? Could a car actually leave the showroom floor with a jinx?

If superstitious friends didn't believe this before Dean died, they became believers soon afterward.

George Barris, Dean's friend who claimed to be nervous every time he was around the "Little Bastard," bought the wreck from the insurance underwriters for $2,500. It was a rare car and he purchased it for parts since some of the components were not easy to come by. He soon regretted his decision. He said, "I wish I'd sent to the junkyard and had it shredded."

After the wrecked Porsche arrived at his garage, some of his mechanics were unloading it from the truck when suddenly the car slipped and fell on one of them, breaking both his legs. A short time later, Barris sold the car's engine to Dr. Troy McHenry, a Beverly Hills physician who raced sports cars as a hobby. Another physician, Dr. William F. Eschrid of Burbank, bought the drive train. Both doctors were preparing their cars for a race to be held at the Ponoma Fair Grounds on October 24, 1956. During the race, McHenry was killed when his car went out of control and crashed into a tree. Eschrid was seriously injured when his car rolled over. He later said that he had no idea what happened – just that when he went into a curve, the car suddenly locked up and rolled over.

"After that race, I knew the car carried a curse," George Barris said.

People began coming to Barris' lot to see the remains of "James Dean's Death Car." One teenager, while trying to steal the steering wheel as a souvenir, slipped and cut his arm badly on a jagged piece of metal. Someone else got hurt trying to rip out a bloodstained piece of upholstery.

Barris reluctantly sold two of the car's undamaged heavy-duty racing tires to a sports car buff. Less than two weeks later, the young man called Barris and told him that he had run off the road and nearly wrecked his car when the two tires from Dean's car blew out simultaneously. After that, Barris decided to put the car away in storage in one of his garages so that it couldn't hurt anyone else.

Soon afterward, though, the California Highway Patrol approached him and asked to use the car in a traveling safety exhibit that would be aimed at young people. Barris figured that maybe the remains of the car would help save lives instead of taking them, so he welded the pieces of the car together so that they wouldn't fall apart and turned the wreck over to the California Highway Patrol. In this way, he hoped that the curse on the car might be lifted.

That turned out to be too much to hope for. After being shown twice without incident, the car was taken to Fresno one evening to be displayed the following day. It was stored for the night in a California Highway Patrol garage. Four hours later, the garage caught on fire and it was destroyed, along with an adjacent building. Every vehicle in the garage was burned beyond repair - except the Spyder, which was only slightly scorched. No cause was ever determined for the fire.

The Spyder was then taken to Sacramento, where it was again put on display. While a group of high school students were gathered around it, the car inexplicably fell off its display pedestal and broke the hip of one of the bystanders.

Several weeks later, George Barkuis, a California state employee, was transporting the car to Salinas on a flatbed truck, but the trip went horribly wrong. Barkuis lost control of the truck and was thrown from the cab. The Spyder tore loose from the truck's bed and crashed down on Barkuis, killing him instantly.

Two years later, near Oakland, the Porsche broke in two and fell from a truck on the freeway, causing an accident.

In 1958, the truck that was carrying Dean's car was parked on a hill in Oregon. The truck's emergency brake slipped, causing it to roll backward and crash through the window of a store. Fortunately, no one was injured in this mishap. In 1959, while the car was on display in New Orleans, it suddenly broke apart into 11 pieces while sitting on its display stand. When Barris got it back, he could find no reason why the car would have fallen apart.

In 1960, the "Little Bastard" was loaned to the Florida Highway Patrol for a safety exhibit in Miami. After the showing, it was crated up, loaded on a truck and sent back to Los Angeles. Barris awaited its arrival because he had to get it ready for the National Safety Council, which wanted to put the car on display. After a week, the car still had not arrived. Barris called Miami and was told that the Spyder was definitely on its way - but James Dean's car simply never arrived. Somewhere between Miami and Los Angeles, it vanished without a trace.

In 2005, a car museum in Volo, Illinois offered $1 million to anyone that could produce the car. In commemoration of the 50th anniversary of Dean's death, the museum planned to display artifacts from the crash, including a passenger-side door of the car. The money was offered to try and convince whoever had the vehicle to come forward with it - no questions asked. Once the car was authenticated by George Barris, the money would be given to the seller. But the anniversary came and went and no word about the fate of the car was ever spoken.

To this day, no one has ever been able to discover what happened to it.

THE "SWEATER GIRL" & THE GANGSTER
HOLLYWOOD'S BIGGEST SCANDAL OF THE 1950S

"I find men terribly exciting," Lana Turner once said, "and any girl who says she doesn't is an anemic old maid, a streetwalker, or a saint." There was no question that Hollywood star and pin-up girl Lana Turner had no problem attracting men - lots of men. In fact, she probably attracted far too many. Later in life, even Turner herself admitted that her eight marriages to seven different men were a bit excessive. She did it, she said, because she was old-fashioned: she usually married every man she thought she was in love with.

One of Turner's lovers became, along with Turner and her daughter, Cheryl, part of one of the biggest Hollywood scandals of the 1950s. His name was Johnny Stompanato and he was a handsome, well-endowed, and dangerous member of Mickey Cohen's L.A. outfit. Her relationship with Stompanato eventually soured and when it did, it turned deadly and resulted in a very public scandal. On April 4, 1958, Stompanato was stabbed to death in Lana's Beverly Hills home and it was alleged that 14-year-old Cheryl was the one holding the bloody knife. But was she really? The jury remains out on that particular question to this day.

Lana was born Julia Jean Mildred Frances Turner on February 8, 1920 in Wallace, a bleak mining town in the rough mountains of Idaho. Her father, Virgil J. Turner, who went by his middle name of John, was an itinerant farm worker from Alabama who met her mother, 16-year-old hairdresser Mildred Frances Cowan, in Wallace. They eloped and soon became parents to Julia, who everyone called "Judy" before her film career took off. Hard times eventually forced the family to re-locate to San Francisco, where John and Mildred soon separated.

On December 14, 1930, John Turner won a bit of money at an all-night dice game and headed for home. He was later found dead on the corner of Minnesota and Mariposa streets, on the edge of Potrero Hill and the Mission District in San Francisco. His killer and his winnings were never found. Soon after, Mildred Turner developed health problems and was advised by her doctor to move to a drier climate. She and her daughter moved to Los Angeles in 1931. By the time that Judy started high school, she already had a stunning figure and soon, her discovery at Schwab's Drug Store became one of Hollywood's most enduring show-business legends.

As a 16-year-old student at Hollywood High School, Turner decided to skip class one day and buy a Coke at the Top Hat Café, located on the southeast corner of Sunset Boulevard and

Lana Turner

McCadden Place. There, she was spotted by William R. Wilkerson, publisher of the *Hollywood Reporter*. Wilkerson was attracted by her beauty, and referred her to the actor, comedian, and talent agent Zeppo Marx. Marx's agency immediately signed her on and introduced her to film director Mervyn LeRoy, who cast her in her first film, 1937's "They Won't Forget." He was so impressed with her that he signed her to a $50 a week personal contract. When the producer and director joined with MGM in 1938, Judy went along with him. At MGM, she became Lana Turner and first sported bright, red hair. Her debut there was in "Love Finds Andy Hardy" in 1938 and the picture's star, Andy Rooney, enjoyed a brief fling with the newcomer, which allegedly led to her first abortion.

Lana met famous bandleader Artie Shaw

when they made "Dancing Co-Ed" in 1939. The two did not hit it off at first but one night, to make her current boyfriend jealous, she agreed to have dinner with Shaw, who had a reputation for being a notorious ladies man. During that evening in 1940, the couple impetuously flew to Las Vegas and got married. Within seven months, the marriage was over.

In the early 1940s, Lana became an increasingly important star at MGM and one of Hollywood's leading party girls. She earned the nickname "The Sweater Girl" for her often form-fitting attire and during World War II Turner became a popular pin-up girl after films such as "Ziegfeld Girl," "Johnny Eager," and four films with MGM's most respected star, Clark Gable. Lana even had a B-17 bomber named after her, the "Tempest Turner." After the war, Lana's career hit a new high with the 1946 classic film-noir "The Postman Always Rings Twice," with John Garfield.

Lana, who admitted to have a voracious sexual appetite, dated regularly – and ended up marrying whatever current "man of her dreams" wandered into her life. She and Stephen Crane, a restaurant owner, married in 1942 but the marriage was annulled when it was discovered that his divorce from his prior wife was not final. They wed again in 1943 and that July their daughter, Cheryl, was born. The couple split in 1944. Lana's next great romance was with "Zorro" star Tyrone Power. However, he was still married at the time and didn't want to commit to Turner.

She married again, this time to Henry J. Topping, the heir to a tinplate fortune. Topping proposed to Lana at the 21 Club in Los Angeles by dropping a diamond ring into her martini. Lana became pregnant, but gave birth to a stillborn baby in early 1949. Lana then returned to film making after a two-year absence. Although worth millions when they married, Topping suffered heavy financial losses due to poor investments and excessive gambling. Lana finally divorced Topping when she realized he could no longer afford to keep them in the lavish lifestyle to which they had grown accustomed. She always said that, "a successful man is one who makes more money that a wife can spend. A successful woman is one who can find such a man." Topping no longer fit the role of a "successful man."

Lana's next husband was brawny "Tarzan" actor Lex Barker, whom she married in 1953. The stormy union lasted for four years and in her divorce papers, Lana cited his "cruel and inhuman conduct." This was spelled out later when it was learned that Cheryl Crane claimed that Barker had repeatedly molested and raped her.

During the 1950s, Lana starred in a series of films that bombed at the box office, a situation that MGM tried to fix by casting her in musicals. The first, "Mr. Imperium," was a flop, but "The Merry Widow" was more successful. Lana garnered praise in the 1952 film, "The Bad and the Beautiful" and later starred with John Wayne in the adventure film "The Sea Chase." She bombed again in "The Prodigal" and after the 1956 film "Diane," MGM opted not to renew her contract.

Turner's career recovered briefly after appearing in the hugely successful big-screen

Hollywood goombah, Johnny Stompanato

adaptation of Grace Metalious's best-selling novel, "Peyton Place," for which she was nominated for an Academy Award for Best Actress. More box-office failures followed, but it was the 1958 scandal surrounding the murder of Johnny Stompanato that threatened to derail her career completely.

The affair with Stompanato began in the spring of 1957. Lana began receiving telephone calls, flowers, and messages from a "John Steele" who wanted to meet her. She kept saying no, but the man persisted. One day, he simply showed up at the front door of her house. She was angry at first, no matter how good-looking he was, but she was soon flattered his attentions, his gifts, and knowledge about her favorite foods. "Steele" next went to work on Cheryl, suggesting that the young woman might like to try out the new horse that he had just purchased. The flirtation continued as Lana filmed "Peyton Place" and around this time, learned that "Steele" was really Johnny Stompanato, a mobster who worked for L.A. crime boss Mickey Cohen. For the sake of her career, Lana knew that she should steer clear of the handsome wiseguy, but she didn't.

Stompanato had been born in Woodstock, Ill., the son of a barbershop owner. He had served in the Marines during World War II and after his discharge, remained in China, where he opened a nightclub and married a Turkish woman. After the club closed down, the couple returned to Illinois with their baby boy. Stompanato worked as a bread salesman for a few months before abandoning his family and moving to Los Angeles, where he met Cohen. The mobster hired Stompanato as a bouncer, enforcer, and personal bodyguard and when not working as an underworld gunman, he used his good looks to score on the Hollywood club circuit. He was married briefly to actress Helen Gilbert and later married another screen star, Helene Stanley. That marriage lasted three years.

After a brief, stormy fling, Lana decided to cool things off with Stompanato. She began dating other people, but Johnny's jealous behavior made any sort of relationship impossible. One night, he broke into her house and almost smothered her in her sleep with a pillow. She threatened to call the police if he didn't stay away from her, but Stompanato knew this was an idle threat. Lana valued appearances above all else.

When a film deal arose to make "Another Time, Another Place" in England, Lana jumped at the chance to act again. Stompanato demanded that he be allowed to accompany her, but she refused. Then, for whatever reason, she relented and arranged for him to fly to England. He moved into her rented house in Hampstead Heath, just outside of London. One has to wonder how long it took for Lana to regret this rash decision. Stompanato was bored with London within a few days and decided

Stompanato (with hairy chest and gold chains) with Lana Turner and her daughter, Cheryl Crane. This photo was taken in happier times.

that he wanted to hang out with Lana on the set. She was fearful that his presence at the soundstage would not only distract her, but might alert the media about her disreputable boyfriend. A confrontation occurred and Johnny attempted to strangle her when she tried to call the police. Only the intervention of her maid saved her. Another time, Lana's co-star, Sean Connery, came to her rescue. Stompanato was convinced that Connery and Lana were having an affair (no evidence of this exists) and stormed onto the movie set brandishing a gun. Connery landed a single punch to Stompanato's jaw and handily took the gun away from him. Lana managed to get Stompanato deported by Scotland Yard after this incident, leaving her to finish the film in peace.

But incapable of doing anything other than using her same bad judgment, Lana was soon talking to Stompanato again, who was back in L.A. She mention that she planned to vacation in Acapulco after her film wrapped and when her plane stopped over in Copenhagen, Johnny was already there with a ticket on the same flight to Mexico. During their holiday together, Lana again regretted the decision to let the gangster back into her life. She decided to bide her time, though, believing that she could shake him once they got back to Los Angeles. Lana was still in Mexico in February 1958 when her agent called to tell her that she had been nominated for an Academy Award for Best Actress for "Peyton Place."

Once back in Hollywood, Lana knew that her career had been revived. She rented a fully furnished house on North Bedford Drive in Beverly Hills, with a lease that began on April 1. Until then, she stayed in her favorite bungalow at the Bel-Air Hotel. Despite Stompanato's demands, she refused to let him accompany her to the Academy Awards on March 26. She took her mother and daughter with her instead. Although Lana did not win an Oscar, she was pleased to be the center of attention at the event. She invited Cheryl to spend the night with her at the Bel-Air bungalow, where they stayed up most of the night talking. When Lana finally told her daughter good night, she found Stompanato was waiting for her in an outer room. They had another heated argument and Johnny slapped her around, leaving her with a number of bruises. This was bad, but things got much worse on the night of April 4, 1958 – a night that Lana later always referred to as "the happening."

As Lana and Cheryl prepared to move into the Beverly Hills house, Stompanato stalked Turner and was a constant presence in her life, following her to the hardware store, a kitchen store, and even to pick up some groceries. On April 4, Lana went shopping and when she returned home, two of her friends stopped by for drinks. Johnny had "accompanied her" to the grocery store and after he left, one of the guests mentioned that he and Stompanato had attended the same military academy. At this point, Lana discovered that Johnny was seven years younger than he claimed to be, embarrassing her yet again because she didn't want to be seen dating a younger man.

That evening, Stompanato returned in a foul mood. Lana was frightened, but was also determined to get Stompanato out of her life for good. She knew that the evening was going to turn nasty, so she ordered 14-year-old Cheryl to her room. Things were bad from the start, as Lana told Stompanato that their relationship was over for good. As things accelerated and turned physical, Johnny chased Lana into her bedroom. At one point, he reportedly threatened to cut Lana up and disfigure her face. By then, a hysterical Cheryl was shouting for her mother to let her into the room. Lana, thinking that Stompanato would calm down in front of the girl, unlocked the door and let her in. At that moment, according to Lana's account, Johnny was standing in front of the door. He had just gathered some of his clothing from the closet. Some of the clothing was draped over his shoulder, held in place with one hand, and he was using his free hand to take some hangers from the closet.

While the fight had been going on, Cheryl had run downstairs into the kitchen and, in what was referred to as a both a "panic" and a "trance," grabbed a large knife. Returning upstairs, she went to her mother's door with the knife in her hand and begged to be let inside. Later, she claimed that her arm involuntarily went forward when the door opened – and the blade plunged into Stompanato's stomach. As the teenager backed away in shock,

Johnny stepped away from the girl gasping, "What have you done?" He fell to the floor, bleeding badly. The long blade of the knife had sliced a kidney, struck his spine, and punctured his aorta.

Panicked and hysterical, Lana tried to stop Stompanato's bleeding and calm down Cheryl, and at the same time called a physician, whose answering service said that he would call back, and tried to contact her mother, who did not answer. She did not call the police. Later, the doctor arrived, as did Lana's mother and Stephen Crane, whom Cheryl had called. When the doctor could not revive Johnny, he advised her to call Jerry Giesler. The famous Hollywood attorney hurried to the scene and it was he who finally telephoned the Beverly Hills Police Department.

Later that same night, Mickey Cohen heard rumors that Stompanato had been killed at Turner's house. He rushed over and encountered Giesler at the door. The lawyer told him, "If Lana sees you, she's gonna fall out all together. John's dead; the body's at the morgue." Cohen, who never liked Lana, insisted later, "I don't believe Cheryl killed him. I don't want to outright accuse anyone, but I don't believe it was Cheryl or Lana who done this thing. Someone must have come in somehow and stabbed him."

Cohen announced his theory in the press, which covered just about everything he ever did, but despite his public rumblings about the murder, Lana was terrified that he would seek reprisals against her and Cheryl. Cohen did make a move, but not in the way that she suspected. Angered that Hollywood closed ranks to try and protect one of their own, he made sure that everyone knew that she and Stompanato had been romantically

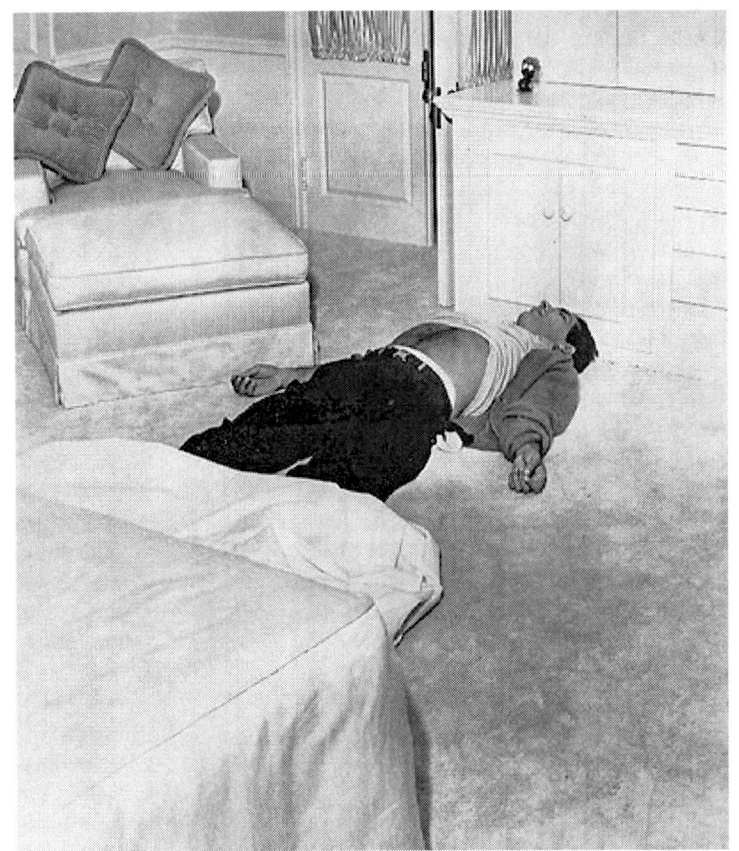

Stompanato died on the floor of Lana's master bedroom
(LAPD crime scene photograph)

involved, and that Johnny had not been some hoodlum who broke into her house. He turned a dozen love notes that Turner had written to Stompanato over to the press, hoping to set the record straight. When this didn't win his dead pal any sympathy (the media was in favor of the seemingly vulnerable Lana), Cohen allegedly tried to blackmail Lana with nude photos that Stompanato had taken of her when she was sleeping. Jerry Giesler managed to get a hold of the negatives, however, ruining Cohen's plan.

Within a few days of the killing, Los Angeles County D.A. William B. McKesson held a press conference to assure the public that, despite their being a celebrity involved in the case, it would be handled just like any other. Cheryl, a juvenile who had been held in the Beverly Hills jail overnight, was placed at the county's juvenile hall as a material witness. At a hearing, she was detained so that no one could influence her testimony in the case. Stompanato's body was flown back to Illinois, where he was buried with full military honors as a World War II veteran.

At the coroner's inquest that was held a week later, Cheryl was never called to testify because it was feared that she would be further traumatized. Instead, Lana took the stand and emotionally told the story of Cheryl stabbing Stompanato. She made a dramatic appearance in the courtroom, mirroring the courtroom scene in "Peyton Place" in which she tearfully took the witness stand on behalf of her teenage daughter. Lana answered questions for the jury, occasionally wiping her face and twice, breaking down as she tried to reply to the jury's inquiries. When the press later surrounded her, the emotionally drained woman almost fainted.

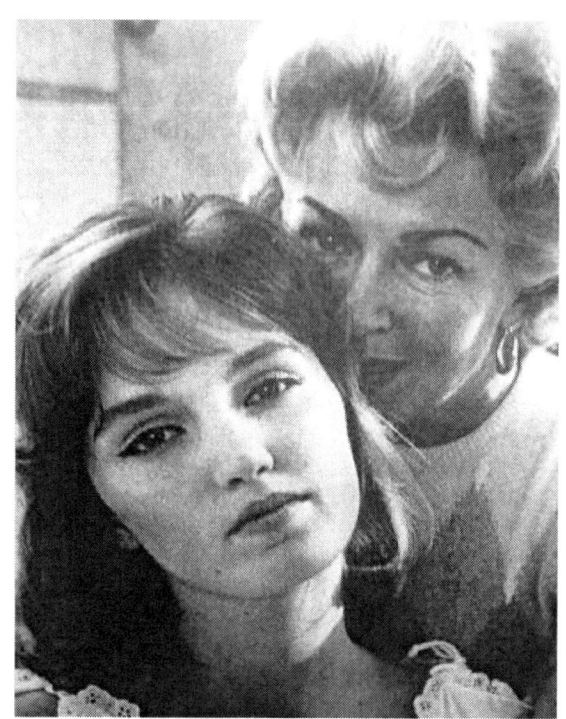

Lana & Cheryl

In later testimony, police investigators brought up questions about the weapon that was used, including why a supposedly new knife was scratched and chipped. They also wondered why there were no fingerprints on the knife, nor any blood splashed around the room, or on Lana. All of these questions remained unanswered.

In less than 30 minutes, the jury reached a unanimous decision. It was a case of justifiable homicide, in which Cheryl had used deadly force because she feared for her and her mother's lives. The prosecutor chose not to pursue criminal charges in the case, although Stompanato's family later filed a civil suit, which was settled out of court.

District Attorney McKesson did hold legal hearings to determine Lana's fitness as a parent and Cheryl became a ward of the juvenile court. For the next two years, she lived with Lana's mother and after that, her parents, with the court's permission, had her transferred to the El Retiro Institution in the San Fernando Valley. Lana stated that this was done to help Cheryl recover from the severe shock she had sustained at the time of Stompanato's death. She said, "This institution is to help girls who need that extra bit of help." During her stay there, Cheryl twice escaped from the facility. Later, as an adult, Cheryl worked for her father for several years and then opened her own business. Cheryl had one more brush with the law in 1969 when three half-grown cannabis plants were discovered in her car. She was on good terms with her mother for the rest of Lana's life and when she came out to her that she was a lesbian, Lana took the news well. She said she regarded Cheryl's partner, Jocelyn Roy, as a "second daughter." In 1988, Cheryl wrote an autobiography, *Detour: A Hollywood Story*, in which she publicly discussed the Stompanato killing for the first time, and admitted to stabbing him. She currently lives in the Palm Springs, California, area, where she works as a real-estate agent.

After the publicity of the Stompanato scandal, Lana feared that she would never work again, so she was thrilled when she was offered the lead role in a re-make of "Imitation of Life." Universal Studios capitalized on her recent notoriety and the film became one of the biggest hits of 1959, not to mention the biggest of Turner's career. Since Turner had accepted a percentage of the box-office receipts in lieu of salary, she was paid handsomely for the role. Critics and audiences couldn't help noticing that the film borrowed from Turner's private life — a single mother coping with a troubled teenage daughter.

In 1961, she made her last film appearance under her old contract with MGM, starring with Bob Hope in "Bachelor in Paradise." Other highlights of this era include two Ross Hunter productions, "Portrait in Black" and "Madame X," which proved to be her last major starring role.

Unfortunately, her choices of men didn't improve after the Stompanato disaster. She was briefly married to a rancher named Fred May until 1962. Three years later, she married Robert P. Eaton, who later went on to write "The Body Brokers," a behind-the-scenes look at the Hollywood movie world, featuring a character named Marla Jordan, based on Turner. They divorced in 1969 and soon after, she married a nightclub hypnotist named Ronald Pellar, who used the stage names of Ronald Dante, or Dr. Dante. The couple met in a Los Angeles club and married that same year. After about six months of marriage, Pellar disappeared a few days after she had written a $35,000 check to him to help him in an investment. The marriage broke up after Lana learned that he used it for other purposes. She also accused him of stealing $100,000 worth of her jewelry.

In the 1970s and 1980s, Lana appeared in several television roles, most notably the 1982-1983 season of the series "Falcon Crest" as Jacqueline Perrault. The majority of her final decade was spent out of the public eye. She died at the age of 74 in 1995 of complications from throat cancer, which was diagnosed in 1992 and which she had been battling ever since. She was, until her death, a very heavy smoker. She was survived by her only child, Cheryl Crane, and Cheryl's life partner Jocelyn LeRoy. They inherited some of Lana's sizeable estate, built through shrewd real estate holdings and investments. However, the majority of her estate was left to her maid, Carmen Lopez Cruz.

GHOST OF THE PINK PALACE
JAYNE MANSFIELD & THE DEATH CURSE

On June 29, 1967, the woman who was one of America's top pinup girls died a horrible and violent death along a lonely roadway near Biloxi, Miss. Her death had a sobering effect on the Hollywood film community and also strange repercussions in the occult community of the time, as well. Jayne's death was said to have been caused by a curse gone awry and the tragic event opened up a side of the actress' life that few were aware of. Could her mysterious death be the reason that her former home was rumored to be haunted by her restless spirit until it was destroyed in 2002?

She was born Vera Jayne Palmer in Bryn Mawr, Pa., on April 19, 1933 and spend most of her childhood in Phillipsburg, N.J. When she was three years old, her father, Herbert, died of a heart attack while driving in a car with his wife and daughter. After his death, her mother worked as a schoolteacher and in 1939, Vera Palmer re-married and the family moved to Dallas, Tex. Jayne's desire to become an actress started at an early age and after high school, she studied both drama and physics at Southern Methodist University.

In January 1950, Jayne was secretly married to Paul Mansfield and the couple of married in a public ceremony a few months later. Jayne's show business aspirations were put on hold with the birth of her first child, Jayne Marie Mansfield, in November of that same year. Jayne was 17 at the time. She juggled motherhood and university classes and spent the summer at Camp Gordon, Ga., during her husband's service in the Army. She attended UCLA in the summer of 1953 and then went back to Texas for the fall quarter at Southern Methodist University. In Dallas she became a student of actor Baruch Lumet, father of director Sidney Lumet and founder of the Dallas Institute of the Performing Arts. On October 22, 1953, she first appeared on stage in a production of Arthur Miller's "Death of a Salesman."

Jayne won several beauty contests while living in Texas, but few had any idea about just

Jayne Mansfield

talent scouts and seen her in a production at the Pasadena Playhouse. Jane got small roles in "Female Jungle" and "Pete Kelly's Blues" and then in 1955, Paul Wendkos offered her the dramatic role of Gladden in "The Burglar," his film adaptation of David Goodis' novel. The film was done in film noir style, and Mansfield appeared alongside Dan Duryea and Martha Vickers. "The Burglar" was released two years later when Mansfield's fame was at its peak. She was successful in this straight dramatic role, though most of her subsequent film appearances would be either comedic in nature or take advantage of her sex appeal.

Her next role was on the stage, in which she first appeared wearing nothing but a towel, in "Will Success Spoil Rock Hunter?" After that, she starred in the camp, comic film "The Girl Can't Help It" in 1956. Her first real starring role featured her as an outrageously voluptuous, tone-deaf girlfriend of a retired racketeer. The film features some early performances by Fats Domino, The Platters and Little Richard, successfully introducing rock-n-roll to many movie audiences.

In May 1956, Jayne signed a long-term contract with 20th Century Fox and then played a straight dramatic role in "The Wayward Bus," a 1957 film based on the book by John Steinbeck. She tried to move away from her "dumb blonde" image in this film and establish herself as a serious actress. The cast also included Dan Dailey and Joan Collins and enjoyed reasonable success at the box office. Jayne's performance in this film earned her a Golden Globe for New Star of the Year – Actress, and she beat out Carroll Baker and Natalie Wood.

In 1957, Hayne reprised her role in the movie version of "Will Success Spoil Rock Hunter?" co-starring Tony Randall and Joan Blondell. This film, along with "The Girl Can't Help It," remains the most beloved films among Jayne's fans. They were popular and successful in their day and remain classics of the era. Jayne's fourth starring role was in "Kiss Them For Me," in which she received prominent billing with Cary Grant. However, her part is little more than the usual "dumb blonde"

how smart she was. Her IQ was said to be 163, she spoke five languages, and she was a classically trained pianist and violinist. But she admitted later in her career that the public didn't care about her brains, they were more interested in her looks and the size of her breasts.

Paul Mansfield had hoped that the birth of their daughter would discourage his wife's interest in acting. When he realized that it hadn't, he agreed to move to Los Angeles with her in late 1954 to help her start a movie career. Between working at a variety of odd jobs, Jayne studied drama at UCLA. Her film career began with bit parts at Warner Brothers, which had signed her after one of its comic relief. The movie turned out to be a box office disappointment and would prove to be her final starring role in a mainstream Hollywood film. Unfortunately, she missed out on a part opposite Jack Lemmon in "Bell, Book, and Candle" because she was pregnant at the time.

Jayne had divorced Paul Mansfield on January 8, 1958 and five days later, she married actor, bodybuilder and Mr. Universe titleholder Mickey Hargitay. Their marriage lasted for just five years and Jayne got a Mexican divorce in Juarez in May 1963. The divorce was initially declared invalid in California, and the two reconciled in October 1963. After the birth of their third child, Mansfield sued for the Juarez divorce to be declared legal and won. Their acrimonious divorce battle had the actress accusing Hargitay of kidnapping one of her children to force a more favorable financial settlement. During this marriage, she had three children — Miklós Jeffrey Palmer Hargitay, Zoltán Anthony Hargitay, and Mariska Magdolina Hargitay, an actress currently known for her role as Detective Olivia Benson in "Law & Order: Special Victims Unit."

At the time of her divorce from Mansfield and her marriage to Hargitay, Jayne's career was still at its height. In addition to her movie roles, she also gained a lot of publicity for her repeated successful attempts to expose her breasts in carefully staged "accidents." Her breasts had become a huge part (pardon the pun!) of her public persona and once when she appeared on "The Tonight Show," host Jack Parr introduced her by saying, "Here they are, Jayne Mansfield!" Early in her career, the prominence of her breasts was often problematic, leading her to be cut from her first professional assignment, an advertising campaign for General Electric, which depicted several young women in bathing suits relaxing around a pool.

A photo taken during the "Sophia Loren Incident"

In April 1957, her breasts were part of a notorious publicity stunt that was intended to deflect attention from Sophia Loren during a dinner party in the Italian star's honor. Photographs of the encounter were published around the world. One image showed Sophia Loren raising an eyebrow at Jayne, who was sitting between Loren and Clifton Webb, as she leaned over the table, allowing her breasts to spill out of her low-cut dress and exposing a nipple.

A similar incident, this time revealing full exposure of both breasts, occurred during a film festival in West Berlin. Jayne was wearing a low-cut dress and Mickey Hargitay picked her up so that she could bite a bunch of grapes that were hanging overhead at a party. The movement caused her breasts to spring out of her dress. The photograph of the incident became a sensation, appearing in newspapers and magazines all over the world with the word "censored" hiding the actress' exposed and ample breasts.

Throughout her career, Jayne was compared to the reigning sex symbol of the period, Marilyn Monroe. Of this comparison, she said, "I don't know why you people [the press] like to compare me to Marilyn or that girl, what's her name, Kim Novak. Cleavage, of course, helped me a lot to get where I am. I don't know how they got there." Even as her film roles began to fade, Jayne was still considered to be Marilyn's primary rival in a field that had become too crowded with "dumb blondes" like Mamie Van Doren (who Jayne considered her real nemesis), Diana Dors, Barbara Nichols, Joi Lansing, and Sheree North.

Despite all of the publicity that she garnered, and her popularity with the public, good roles dried up for Jayne after 1959. She still managed to keep busy making a series of low-budget films, mostly in Europe. In 1960 Fox loaned her out to appear in two independent gangster thrillers in England, "Too Hot to Handle" and "The Challenge." Fox also lined up "It Happened in Athens," an Olympic-themed movie that was filmed in Greece. Despite receiving top billing in the film, Jayne was relegated to a colorful, scantily clad supporting role. Jayne still commanded high prices as live performer during this time, though she yearned to establish a more sophisticated image. She announced that she planned to study acting in New York, hoping this would rejuvenate her career, but it was too late. Her reliance on racy publicity had brought her fame, but it also proved to be her downfall. Fox did not renew its contract with her in 1962.

But Jayne continued to work. In 1963, Tommy Noonan persuaded her to become the first mainstream American actress to appear nude with a starring role in the film "Promises! Promises!" Photographs of a naked Mansfield on the set were published in *Playboy* magazine. The sold-out issue resulted in an obscenity charge for Hugh Hefner, which was later dropped. "Promises! Promises!" was banned in Cleveland, but it enjoyed box office success elsewhere and managed to land Jayne a spot on the Top 10 list of Box Office Attractions for that year. Later that year, she also appeared in the low-budget West German movie "Homesick for St. Pauli." She played Evelyne, a sexy American singer who traveling to Hamburg by ship. She sang two German songs in the movie, though her speaking voice was dubbed.

Jayne remained a highly visible personality, despite her film career setbacks and publicity antics. However, good movie roles were getting harder and harder to find. Toward the end of her life, she appeared in a number of low-budget, dismal films like "Let's Go Bust," "The Las Vegas Hillbillys," and "Panic Button." Her personal life was not going very well, either. In 1963, she had a well-publicized relationship with singer Nelson Sardelli, whom she planned to marry once her divorce from Hargitay was finalized. This marriage never took place but in September 1964, Jayne married Matt Cimber (whose real name was Matteo Ottaviano, né Thomas Vitale Ottaviano), an Italian-born film director. The couple was together less than a year and was divorced by July 1966. Jayne had worked with Cimber before, when he directed her in a widely praised stage production of "Bus Stop." He also worked with her on her last film, "Single Room Furnished," but work was suspended when their marriage collapsed. The film was later released posthumously in 1968.

In the middle 1960s, faced with a flagging career, Jayne began supporting herself doing burlesque and dinner theater. In late 1966, she took another step to revive her career, which many dismiss as nothing more than another of her infamous publicity stunts – Jayne joined the newly created Church of Satan, founded by Anton LaVey. According to the late church leader, Jayne had a very real interest in exploring the philosophies of satanism, although friends claim that she was simply curious about it. Others more cynically believed that she was merely attaching herself to LaVey for the publicity and the attention. The Church of Satan had recently been making headlines and appearing in magazines and LaVey himself cut a sinister and dashing figure. He had become quite notorious in a short time and even those who disliked him respected him as being a great showman and promoter. Other celebrities, like Sammy Davis, Jr., were photographed with the country's leading satanist and Jayne may have been looking to get a little free publicity for herself.

Two photographs from the notorious photo session with Church of Satan founder, Anton LaVey. Both Jayne and LaVey were likely looking for some free publicity from the meeting.

In November 1966, Jayne met LaVey for the first time. She and her current boyfriend and attorney, Sam Brody, drove with a press agent of the San Francisco Film Festival to meet with LaVey at his home. While the reasons for Jayne's visit may vary, one thing that all of the accounts agree upon is that LaVey and Sam Brody took an instant dislike to one another. It was said that while Jayne was touring LaVey's home and church, Brody purposely touched a skull and two candles that LaVey stated were cursed. Brody laughed at the foolishness and LaVey grew angry and asked them to leave.

Nevertheless, Jayne returned and while some say that it was in an effort to placate LaVey, others say that it was at the satanist's invitation. She was hungry for the publicity that the Church of Satan could offer her and LaVey saw the chance to publicize himself through the actress, whether her career was on the downslide or not. Apparently, Jayne agreed to pose for a photo layout with LaVey as an apology for Brody's earlier offenses. LaVey brought out skulls, candles and trappings of the church and asked Jayne to pose in a bikini. She refused but wore a dress instead and copies of the photo taken do survive, showing Jayne drinking from a chalice with LaVey looming behind her in a black cloak.

Brody, who had accompanied Jayne to the photo session, had opposed her posing with LaVey but he promised to be on his best behavior. Then, he allegedly began fondling a statue of a nude woman and making jokes and LaVey grew furious with him again. When he ordered Brody to leave, the attorney instead laughed at the High Priest and began blowing out the black candles that were placed around the room. Infuriated, LaVey pronounced a curse on Brody and told him that he would be dead within a year. Jayne's friend, May Mann, later recalled that LaVey warned Jayne that if she continued to see Brody, she too could face a tragic death.

Anton LaVey recalled the incidents with Brody and the curse a little differently than other accounts. According to his story, Jayne became an active member of the Church of Satan and the curse had been one that had been placed to protect Jayne, rather than because LaVey was simply angry. In an interview, LaVey said that the curse was placed on

Dead Men Do Tell Tales: Bloody Hollywood - Page 183

Sam Brody because, "He'd been giving her [Jayne] a rough time and even embarrassing her in public. At the San Francisco Film Festival, he threw liquor all over her dress. He had blackened her eyes and beaten her up on many occasions."

He tried to protect Jayne, LaVey claimed. "Brody followed Jayne everywhere she went, despite her attempts to shake him. Jayne unloaded her problems with Brody on me daily. When she returned home from San Francisco, furniture would be missing from her home or she'd find bills for services that had not been authorized or in some cases not even performed. Brody padded his statements and sometimes double-billed her. He had her in a very delicate position. Supposedly, he represented her legally but he had her so compromised that she couldn't leave him. He arranged it so that she was so deeply in debt to him for legal services that if he had demanded payment, the consequences would have been terrible. And if she didn't conform to his personal wishes, he threatened to have custody of her children withdrawn and have her declared an unfit mother."

According to LaVey, the incidents that provoked the curse were different than in other accounts. One night, Jayne had telephoned LaVey, screaming and crying because Brody had been beating her. She was calling for help and weeping. Brody took the phone away from her and ordered LaVey to never speak to Jayne again. He said that if the church leader continued to befriend her, then Brody would see that he was exposed as a charlatan and instigate legal actions against the church.

At this point, LaVey had finally had enough of Brody's abuse. "I warned him that he was dealing with greater powers than he had ever dreamed of and that all of his threats would amount to nothing," LaVey recalled. "I told him to go ahead, expose and attack me because in one year, you'll be dead." Brody slammed down the phone without saying another word.

Jayne called back a few minutes later to plead with LaVey to remove the curse, but he refused. "I warned her to stay away from him," LaVey said. "I explained that Brody was traveling under a dark cloud and there was no way that he could escape. But she wouldn't listen... she just wouldn't listen."

Not long after, Jayne and Brody were involved in two separate auto accidents. The first occurred at the intersection of Sunset and Whittier in Beverly Hills. Although Jayne was not injured, Brody suffered a broken leg, a broken elbow and thumb and two cracked teeth. His late-model Mercedes was destroyed. A few weeks later, when Brody's arm and leg were still in casts, they were involved in another accident. This time they were in San Francisco and Brody refused to let Jayne ride in LaVey's Jaguar, insisting that she ride with him instead. Neither of them was injured in this mishap and Jayne still refused to heed LaVey's warning to stay away from the attorney.

About a month later, Jayne's 5-year-old son, Zoltan, accompanied Jayne to Jungleland, in Thousand Oaks, where she had agreed to pose for publicity photos. While she looked on in horror, a supposedly tame lion suddenly jumped onto the little boy and began mauling him. As the boy underwent several emergency surgeries, Jayne flew to San Francisco to plead with Anton LaVey to try and help her son. According to friends, LaVey donned a ceremonial robe and climbed to the top of Mount Tamalpais, outside of the city, in the driving rain to perform a ceremony that would provide assistance for Jayne's son. Whether you believe in such things or not, Zoltan survived and Jayne credited LaVey for saving the boy's life.

And while the children may have been able to avoid the curse that hung over the heads of the actress and her attorney, Jayne's troubles were just beginning. A short time later, while on tour in Japan, a collection of prized diamonds that Jayne had bought at the height of her career were stolen. Soon after, in Britain, she was publicly humiliated and her performance canceled when she was falsely accused of skipping out on her hotel bills. She was also hit by a charge of income tax evasion from the Venezuelan government, robbed in Las Vegas and attacked at Carnival in Rio de Janeiro by a crazed mob that stripped her of her clothing.

On June 22, Sam Brody was on his way to pick up Jayne for a charity luncheon when his vehicle was stuck by another car. It was badly damaged and Brody was again hospitalized with a broken leg and cracked ribs.

A week later, in the early morning hours of June 29, Jayne left Gus Steven's Supper Club in Biloxi, Miss., to drive to New Orleans, where she was scheduled to appear on a television talk show later that morning. Jayne was accompanied by Sam Brody, the supper club's 19-year-old driver, Ron Harrison, and three of her children, Miklos, Zoltan, and Mariska.

According to those who were on the scene, Jayne stood nearby as the kids and her trademark pink luggage were loaded into the car. She looked tired and haggard as she climbed in next to Brody in the front seat. The attorney sat in the middle next to Ron Harrison and Jayne sat next to the door. The children were all sleeping in the back seat as they started driving west on Route 90. The road was shiny and slick from a light rain that had fallen earlier. Ahead of the car, Harrison spotted a white cloud that was coming from a mosquito-spraying truck ahead of them on the highway. He slowed down and followed the truck for several minutes but then became impatient, accelerated and drove around the truck into the fog. It was now 2:25 a.m.

Harrison did not know that a slow-moving trailer truck was ahead of the mosquito truck until the front of the supper club's Buick slammed under it. The metal was sheared off and rolled backwards like an opened can. Sam Brody died instantly when he was thrown from the car and Harrison suffered the same fate. The children, lying down in the back, sustained injuries, but they survived the crash.

When the truck driver, who was unhurt, jumped down from his cab, he immediately spotted the bodies of the two men on the pavement. Glancing back through the Buick's windshield, he saw the battered body of a woman in blood-soaked clothing. Legends state that Jayne was decapitated

The wreckage of the car that Jayne was riding in when she was killed.

in the crash, but later reports from police officers who investigated the scene discovered that what the truck driver thought was her severed head was actually one of Jayne's blond, and now bloody, wigs.

Anton LaVey later declared that, "Jayne was a victim of her own frivolity" and California occultists were of the opinion that the satanist's curse killed both the believer and the victim alike. Shortly after Jayne's death, a memorial service was held at the Church of Satan in Jayne's honor. About 30 people were present and saw several amber-colored bulbs suddenly flare up without explanation. The sudden glare lasted for less than a minute but left the bulbs undamaged, something considered impossible at the time. One of the bulbs remained with its filaments in the shape of a heart, Jayne's favorite design. Many of the possessions in her home, including the swimming pool, bathtubs and pieces of furniture were heart-shaped. LaVey denied causing the bizarre light show. "Anyone can rig bulbs to flare like that, but to do so without damaging them is impossible," he said. "I think that Jayne wanted to let us know that she was still with us."

After Jayne's horrible death, her estate became the subject of considerable legal dispute for family members, would-be heirs and freeloaders.

Everyone wanted a piece of it, from those who truly deserved it, like her children, to her estranged husband, her ex-husband, business associates, Brody's wife, and countless attorneys and creditors.

Like Anton LaVey, others connected to Jayne began to experience strange happenings. Linda Mudrick, Jayne's personal maid for many years, often heard Miklos, who had been injured in the accident that took his mother's life, talking to someone when she knew he was alone in his room. He told her that he had been talking to his mother and Mudrick believed that Jayne was somehow communicating with the boy from the other side.

Other weird happenings were taking place in and around the Pink Palace, Jayne's former home in Beverly Hills. She had bought the house, a 40-room, Mediterranean-style mansion that had once belonged to singer Rudy Vallee, in November 1957. Jayne had the house painted pink, with cupids surrounded by pink fluorescent lights, pink furs in the bathrooms, a pink heart-shaped bathtub, and a fountain spurting pink champagne. Her husband, Hargitay, was a plumber and carpenter before getting into bodybuilding, and he built a pink heart-shaped swimming pool. Mansfield decorated the Pink Palace by writing to furniture and building suppliers requesting free samples. She received over $150,000 worth of free merchandise while paying only $76,000 for the mansion itself.

Mickey Hargitay was involved in a bad car accident just after driving out of the gate of the Palace. Third husband, Matt Cimber, also began having his share of troubles. His father had a heart attack, legal problems were wreaking havoc on his newly opened nightclub, and his best friend was killed. Victor Huston, a young man who worked as Jayne's road manager and who was a constant visitor at the Pink Palace, died suddenly. Linda Mudrick was also involved in a terrible car accident. It was almost as if the curse that killed Jayne and Brody was still out there looking for places where it could unleash its fury.

Two of Jayne's children, Miklos and Jayne Marie, who had survived the car accident, were playing in a toy electric car one afternoon on the mansion's playground. Jayne Marie leaned back and somehow, her long black hair became entangled around an axle. All of the hair on the back of her head was torn out by the roots.

Bursting water pipes ruined many pieces of furniture and plumbers who came to repair the damage were allegedly frightened off by moving objects. One painter said that when he was working in Jayne's old room, he felt that someone was watching him and several times he felt someone touch him on the shoulder. Eerie moaning sounds were often reported and servants refused to stay on. New ones were hired, but often left after only a few days in the house. Even Linda Mudrick, Jayne's long-time companion, finally quit, stating that, "I never want to go in that house again." Many came to believe that Jayne was still around, perhaps haunting

Jayne's Pink Palace -- was it true that it was haunted by her ghost for decades after her death?

the house because of what was happening with her estate and her children's inheritance.

According to a 1978 article, the Pink Palace was finally sacked by Matt Cimber, Jayne's estranged husband, and his attorneys. They locked out the children and Jayne's parents and then sold the place. The first occupants of the house were a bank president and his family. Right after they moved in, the banker's son found a pink Honda that the late actor Nick Adams had given to Jayne during a brief affair. The boy started it up and took it for a spin around the estate and then decided to try it out on the road. Just as he was roaring out of the gates and onto Sunset Boulevard, he was struck by an oncoming car and was killed. The banker and his family allegedly moved out the same day.

The singer Cass Elliot, of the "Mamas & the Papas," later bought the house and moved in with her husband. She went to London to record some television commercials and left her husband behind to oversee the redecorating of the mansion. Mama Cass's death occurred while she was away. Was it also linked to the curse and the Pink Palace?

Another occupant of the house also claimed to experience strange phenomena, as well as the urge to dye her hair blond and to dress in clothing that had once belonged to Jayne and which she had found in storage. After going to a plastic surgeon for a breast enlargement, she was questioned by concerned friends, but could give no explanation for her strange behavior. She became obsessed with Jayne Mansfield and began spending thousands of dollars to purchase any memorabilia of the actress that she could find. She didn't stay in the house for long, though. One night she claimed that she heard a woman's voice begging her to "get out." Aware of the fate that had befallen the two previous tenants she packed up her belongings and fled the Pink Palace.

The next occupant of the mansion was Beatle Ringo Starr, who had been a fan of Jayne when she was alive and had been a good friend of hers. Although Ringo mostly used the house for parties and only actually lived in it for a short while, he had the exterior of the pink mansion repainted white. Soon though, the house began turning pink again. Some said that this was because pink was a hard color to cover, but others claimed that it was Jayne's presence making herself known. The house was repainted again, using a sealer and two coats of paint, but it turned pink once more - much to the bewilderment of paint consultants and chemists. Eventually, though, the house was successfully repainted and remained white until it was torn down.

The singer Englebert Humperdinck, who had once been romantically involved with Jayne, purchased the house in 1977. Before moving in, he had the house blessed by a Catholic priest and issued a statement about the haunting in 1980. He did not believe that the house was haunted any longer, but he did admit to a few unsettling moments. Once, after an earthquake, he discovered a section of the yard had settled into the shape of a heart -- Jayne's favorite design! Although he first believed that perhaps Jayne had returned after all, it was discovered that the heart was a filled-in wading pool that Jayne had built for the children.

In 2002, Humperdinck sold the house to developers, and it was demolished in November of that year. Since that time, there have been no further reports of Jayne's ghost and it seems that the haunting, like many memories of the vivacious actress, has faded away.

4. NO REST FOR THE WICKED
HOLLYWOOD MURDERS & UNSOLVED MYSTERIES

A stunning blonde stands up to a vicious gangster when he tries to take over her seaside restaurant and turn it into a casino. When she turns down his offer, he has her killed in retaliation. A famous director is shot to death in his L.A. bungalow and the most popular suspect is a Hollywood starlet. A beloved television actor is beaten to death in a sleazy hotel and his killer is never prosecuted. A would-be actress is brutally killed and her decapitated body is found dumped in an empty lot, creating one of the most famous unsolved murders of all time.

Are these plots from Hollywood films? Not even close – these are real murders and mysteries that have plagued the American public, as well as Los Angeles cops, for decades. Not only are all of the cases that you are about to read in the pages ahead some of the greatest unsolved mysteries in Hollywood's tarnished history, but a number of them have left behind whispers in their wake – tales of ghosts, hauntings, and restless spirits.

HOLLYWOOD'S ORIGINAL UNSOLVED MYSTERY
THE MURDER OF WILLIAM DESMOND TAYLOR

Early in the morning of February 2, 1922, William Desmond Taylor, one of the most famous movie directors of the day, was found dead in his bungalow in the Westlake District of Los Angeles. At first, it was assumed that he died of natural causes – until someone discovered that he had been shot in the back by a .38-caliber revolver.

Taylor's murder became one of the most sensational cases in the annals of Hollywood crime and one that has never been close to being solved. The coroner's jury, at a crowded inquest, had no choice but to return an open verdict. Fantastic rumors made the rounds of the film colony. There was an entire "cast of killers" blamed for his death and the gossips named suspects that ranged from an actress who had killed him in a jealous rage over another actress, the husband of a woman Taylor had elevated to stardom on the proverbial "casting couch, and even a butler with whom the director was having a homosexual affair.

Taylor's murder continues to be talked about today, largely because of the many bizarre facts that were uncovered by investigators as they tried to piece together what really happened in the case. Taylor was known in Hollywood as a man of many romances. Was he murdered by a jealous rival, either a man or woman? Was he killed by some figure from his past, which the investigation discovered was more than a little disreputable? Was he killed by someone who broke into his bungalow to rob the place and was caught in the act? Were two of Hollywood's most beloved celebrities, Mabel Normand and Mary Miles Minter, who were labeled by the press as "rival lovers" of the dead man, somehow involved in the crime?

None of these questions have ever been answered, largely thanks to representatives from Paramount Pictures (which employed both Taylor and Minter) and their deliberate tampering with the murder scene evidence. It was no secret at the time that the LAPD was under the thumb of Adolph Zukor, the powerful head of Paramount, and the investigation, which had already been bungled by careless police work, was further hampered by his efforts. Paramount could hardly be blamed for attempting some damage control in this latest disaster. It was already trying to cope with the fallout from the Roscoe "Fatty" Arbuckle scandal in 1921. To counter the sordid reputation that had befallen the industry, Hollywood (led by Adolph Zukor) had hired U.S. Postmaster General Will Hays to introduce the Production Code, which would censor Hollywood products and publicly keep the morality of the industry in check. Now, with the facts in the Taylor case pointing to sex, alleged drug dealing, and more, the world was stunned, horrified, and of course, fascinated by every lurid development that came along.

Taylor was born William Cunningham Deane-Tanner on April 26, 1872 in Carlow, Ireland, located south of Dublin. He was the second of four children born to a British army officer and his Irish society wife. His father ran the household like a military barracks and father and son quarreled

William Desmond Taylor

often. When William was 15 years old, he left home and went to England. By 1890, using the name Cunningham Deane, he began performing on the stage. When his father learned of this dishonor to his family name, he demanded that William enroll at Runnymede, an establishment in Kansas that turned disreputable and wealthy young men into respectable farmers. William traveled to the Midwest and remained at the institution for 18 months. After the school went bankrupt and closed down, he decided to stay in America.

He traveled to New York and earned a living as a manual laborer, a magazine salesman, a gambler, and as the modestly successful owner of a small restaurant. Soon, however, he returned to the stage. In 1895, he went to work on Broadway and then toured with actress Fanny Davenport and her company. That position ended when Davenport died in 1898.

By that time, William had met Effie Hamilton, a pretty young chorus girl from a wealthy family.

The couple was married in December 1901 and the following year, their daughter, Ethel Daisy, was born. Effie never returned to the stage and William decided to take up a new line of work to support his family. With a $25,000 loan that he acquired from his in-laws, he bought out two eastside Manhattan antique stores. He was a great success in this new trade and the family lived well in suburban Larchmont.

In 1908, though, everything fell apart. There was gossip that several vintage items sold in his shops were fakes. A planned inheritance from Effie's uncle never materialized after the elderly uncle married, then died, leaving everything to his new spouse. William began drinking heavily and then it was discovered in the summer of that year that he took a vacation trip to the Adirondacks with a woman who was not his wife. Unable to pay a sizable hotel bill, he gave the owner a diamond ring as security.

In September 1908, William vanished from New York after pilfering $600 from one of the antique stores. He sent $500 of it to Effie and used the rest to start a new life. He never returned to his family and in 1912, Effie filed for divorce. She later married a wealthy restaurant owner. Her former husband, meanwhile, re-created himself as William Desmond Taylor and began working with an acting troupe in New Jersey. Never more than a workman-like performer, he soon turned to other employment, like factory work and gold mining in Colorado, the Yukon, and northern California. He gained a reputation as a ladies' man and a hard drinker and his years on the road were certainly colorful ones. Eventually, he ended up back on the stage and was performing in San Francisco when he was hired by filmmaker Thomas Ince to appear in silent pictures.

Taylor moved to Southern California and began working at Ince's studio in Santa Monica. By 1914, he was working for Vitagraph and starring in "Captain Alvarez." As a side note, this film was re-issued in 1918 and was seen by Taylor's daughter, Ethel Daisy, in New York, which is how she learned of his new profession. This led to a good relationship between Taylor and his daughter.

By this time, Taylor was in his mid-40s and knew that he would never make much of a success for himself on the screen. He decided to switch to directing. He was working for the Balboa Amusement Producing Company in Long Beach when he met and fell in love with leading lady Neva Gerber. Unfortunately, Neva was 20 years old, married, and had a child and a much older husband who refused to divorce her. She got involved with Taylor anyway, but learned that Taylor was subject to bouts of great melancholy. Sometimes, after completing a new picture, he left on trips to Northern California, and always remained vague about where he was going and what he was doing there. Later, when Neva was single again, she decided that the troubled director was not good marriage material. However, the two remained close friends.

Taylor's career continued to advance and in the middle 1910s, he switched studios again. Taylor was brought to Pallas Pictures by Julia Crawford Ivers, a screenwriter, producer, and director. When Pallas was bought out by Paramount, Julia and Taylor often worked together and maintained a close friendship that might have been spurred on by romantic hopes on her part. At Paramount, Taylor became very successful, directing a steady stream of major pictures.

In the fall of 1917, Taylor was allowed time off from Paramount to join the Canadian Army and serve in World War I. By August 1918, he was based in Nova Scotia for military training and then shipped out to England. Although the war was over by the time he arrived, the filmmaker asked to be stationed in France until his discharge. By the spring of 1919, he had risen to the rank of major.

Taylor returned to Hollywood later that year and got right back to work for Paramount. One of his first major films was "Anne of Green Gables" starring Mary Miles Minter. He was named to the position of president for the Motion Pictures Directors Association and settled into an affluent Hollywood life. He moved from the Los Angeles Athletic Club to one of eight bungalows that made up Alvarado Court, located in a pleasant section of L.A. and favored by movie industry insiders. Among those living at Alvarado Court was comedy actor Douglas MacLean, and his wife, members of

Taylor's elite social circle. Taylor hired staff to run his household, including Edward F. Sands as a combination secretary, valet, and cook and Earl Tiffany, who often worked as his driver.

During the spring of 1921, Taylor had surgery and went abroad in June to recover. While he was away, he loaned out his bungalow to playwright Edward Knoblock in exchange for the writer's London apartment. To make sure that his guest was comfortable, Taylor foolishly left a signed blank check for Edward Sands to use in case of an emergency. While his employer was away, Sands not only cashed the check in the amount of $5,000, but he also forged a number of smaller checks from Taylor's accounts. A week before Taylor returned home, Sands vanished. When he arrived, Taylor discovered that, in addition to the missing funds, Sands had also stolen much of his wardrobe, some jewelry, a number of personal items, and an automobile, which was later found wrecked. Taylor filed a report with the police and then, a few months later, he received a letter from Sands, half-heartedly apologizing for what he had done. The note also contained two pawn tickets for diamond cuff links that Mabel Normand had given to the director. Sand's job at Taylor's home was taken over by Henry Peavey.

Mabel Normand, then 27, had built her career as the "Queen of Comedy" working for Keystone Studios, which was run by her mentor and close friend, Mack Sennett. In 1918, she signed with producer Samuel Goldwyn to make features and during this time, the popular actress developed a serious cocaine habit. Later, she became romantically involved with Taylor, who was sympathetic to her drug problem. He tried to get her off the drugs and keep her away from the dealers who were feeding her dangerous and, if the public found out, scandalous habit.

Taylor's Alvarado Court Bungalow

Another woman in Taylor's complicated life was Mary Miles Minter, then 19 years old, whom he had directed in three 1920 features. Under the watchful eye of her controlling stage mother, Charlotte Selby, doe-eyed Minter looked on Taylor as both a father figure and a dashing hero. She fantasized about marrying and continually pursued him, despite his efforts to dissuade her.

On Wednesday, February 1, 1922, Taylor spent the evening at his bungalow, working on income tax reports from the previous year at his desk in the living room. Henry Peavey, Taylor's cook and valet, later told the police that he summoned Taylor to dinner at around 6:30 p.m. The director was eating his solitary meal when he received a telephone call. He was still engaged in this conversation (no one knows who the call was from) when Mabel Normand stopped by Taylor's bungalow to pick up two books that he had recently purchased for her. Peavey let Mabel into the house as Taylor hung up the telephone, and then proceeded to mix a couple of drinks.

Peavey left the house about 7:30 p.m. after

Two of the women in Taylor's life: (Left) Mary Miles Minter, the young actress with a crush on the handsome director and (Left) Mabel Normand, one of Hollywood's most infamous cocaine addicts. Both of them became suspects in Taylor's murder.

first going out to chat with Mabel's driver. When he wished Taylor good night, he and Mabel were sitting on the sofa sipping cocktails. According to Mabel, she left the bungalow at a little before 8 p.m. Taylor walked the actress to her car, leaving the front door standing open behind him. She waved as her driver pulled away from the curb and Taylor returned to the house. At midnight, actress Edna Purviance, who also lived at Alvarado Court, returned home and noticed that all of the lights were still on at Taylor's home, but she thought it was too late to stop for a visit.

The following morning, Peavey reported to work at 7:30 a.m. and let himself into the house with his own key. He walked into the living room and found the director's body sprawled out, face-up, on the living room floor. He looked as though he had fallen and an overturned chair was across his legs.

As news spread around Alvarado Court, several of the residents hurried over and entered Taylor's home, contaminating the crime scene. When Taylor's new driver, Howard Fellows, arrived at the house, he telephoned the news to his brother. The brother, Harry, was an assistant director who worked with Taylor at Paramount. He contacted Charles Eyton, Paramount's general manager, and told him of Taylor's death. Eyton ordered Harry, along with Julia Crawford Ivers and her son James (Taylor's cinematographer), to rush to Taylor's home. Their instructions were to remove any incriminating evidence that could damage the filmmaker's reputation --- which would look bad for the studio.

At this point, no one had yet called the police.

Julia, James, and Harry Fellows hurried to the bungalow and gathered up anything they could find that might shed a bad light on Taylor. They took letters to Taylor from Mabel Normand, Mary Miles Minter, and Neva Gerber, as well as notes from Ethel Daisy to her father. They also removed bootleg liquor from the house, just minutes before the police finally arrived.

As law officers were starting to take statements from the Taylor's staff, and from the neighbors, Charles Eyton arrived. Because of his importance in Los Angeles, the police did not stop him from going into the house for a look around. They also didn't question him when he came back out, checking to see if her had moved anything or had taken anything from the scene.

A short time later, the deputy coroner and his assistant arrived and it was only then that it was discovered that Taylor had been shot in the back. This was a surprise to everyone at the scene, and the homicide squad was called in to handle the case. The revelation came as such of a shock because the first officers at the scene believed that Taylor had died of a stomach hemorrhage. They came to this conclusion because a doctor had earlier been in the neighborhood making a house call and came by to see what all of the excitement was about. Without turning the body over, the doctor offered his snap diagnosis. The cops made a note of it, but failed to obtain the doctor's name. The physician left the scene and was never heard from again.

A horde of reporters soon descended on Alvarado Court and a flurry of wild accusations, rumors, crazy theories, and outright lies began to be published all over the country. Some newspapers insisted that the killer had to be the missing Edward Sands, a theory that was eventually dismissed. For a time, journalists also suggested that Henry Peavey was the culprit. Since he was African-American and a homosexual, he was the natural culprit. On the day after the murder, Taylor had been scheduled to appear in court on Peavey's behalf in a sexual misconduct allegation. Because of this, it was hinted by the media that Taylor might have been a "gay bird" and that this "fact" might have something to do with his murder. Peavey was cleared of murder, but rumors that Taylor may have been gay, or at least bisexual, have remained ever since.

With these kinds of stories, rumors, and innuendoes running rampant, it was hard to tell where the truth ended and fantasy began. Taylor's closest neighbors, the MacLeans, told the police that their maid heard someone in the alley between their house and Taylor's after 7 p.m. on the night of the murder. Later, when Mrs. MacLean heard a noise that sounded like a car backfiring, she had looked outside and saw a person leave Taylor's bungalow and walk calmly away. She described this person as a "roughly dressed man," wearing a cap and a scarf. However, it was later learned that a friend of Taylor's had borrowed his car for the evening and had returned it to his house that same night. After parking it in the garage, he went to the door, but when he got no reply, he left. The police believed that he was the figure seen by Mrs. MacLean that night.

Mystery was added to the mystery and the investigation was certainly not helped by L.A. District Attorney Thomas Woolwine, who had close ties to major players in the movie industry. One newspaper accused the district attorney of

> Early in the investigation, authorities cleared Taylor's valet, Henry Peavey, of any involvement in the slaying. However, a reporter named Florabel Muir was convinced that he was the killer. She believed she could trick Peavey into a confession – and get a great scoop for herself. She enlisted two men, Frank Carson and Al Weinshank, in her plan. Muir went to Peavey and offered him $10 to guide her to the location of Taylor's grave at Hollywood Memorial Park. Peavey agreed and he rode along with Muir and Frank Carson to the cemetery. They found Taylor's gravesite and got out of the car. As they did, Weinshank, who was covered with a white sheet, came running toward them and shouted, "I am the ghost of William Desmond Taylor. You murdered me. Confess, Peavey!" Peavey burst out laughing. Then, realizing what the trio had tried to do to him, he loudly and furiously denounced them all.
> On a side note, Al Weinshank later became one of the gangsters killed during the infamous St. Valentine's Day Massacre in Chicago.

"erecting a barricade of silence between the searchers for truth and the truth itself." The investigation was being badly handled, even hamstrung, in an effort to protect Taylor and the studio, but some of the witnesses hindered things even further by withholding information in an effort to protect their own reputations. When Mabel Normand was questioned by the police, she did her best to downplay her romantic relationship with Taylor. She was also deliberately vague on other issues involving herself and the director, especially when it came to her drug problem and Taylor's efforts to help her break the habit.

The newspapers continued to hamper the investigation, as well. In a rush for lurid headlines, journalists were quick to report the discovery of Mary Miles Winter's monogrammed pink "lingerie" at Taylor's house. The young actress denied this and the "lingerie" turned out to be a monogrammed handkerchief that she had once loaned him. However, the initial distorted information suggested to the public that the supposedly demure Mary and the much-older Taylor were having a clandestine romance. This theory was given further credence by a note that was discovered tucked inside a book of erotic writing that was on the shelf in Taylor's well-stocked library. On the stationary were the initials M.M.M. The letter read:

**Dearest, I love you. I love you. I love you.
XXXXXXXXXXXXXXXX
Yours always, Mary**

When Mary was questioned about this, she admitted, "I did love William Desmond Taylor, I loved him deeply and tenderly, with all of the admiration that a young girl gives to a man with the poise and position of Mr. Taylor." Those who knew Taylor were well aware that he had tried to discourage Mary from the crush that she had on him and no proof was ever brought forward to show that they truly were having a sexual relationship.

But this didn't stop Mary from dreaming about it. At Taylor's garish, crowded funeral, Mary approached the director's casket and kissed his corpse full on the lips. She then caused a stir in the room as she loudly announced that the corpse had spoken to her! "He whispered something to me," she said, "it sounded like 'I shall love you always, Mary!'"

This bit of theatrics, along with the scandal itself, helped to destroy her film career.

The coroner's inquest was held on February 4, 1922 and lasted for less than an hour. Not all of the witnesses on hand were called to testify. The coroner's jury quickly concluded that the director's death had been caused by a gunshot wound "by some person or persons unknown to this jury." To many observers, the murder investigation appeared to be a series of contrivances used to hush up potential scandals. A *Chicago Tribune* article stated, "Twenty people are said to be under suspicion. Twenty thousand theories of the crime are being aired, but there has not been one arrest and not one clue. It is believed that movie interests would spend a million not to catch the murderer, to prevent the real truth from coming out." To battle such sentiment, the film studios established a special committee, allegedly to help the press deal with the case, which the studios wanted forgotten as quickly as possible. A few reporters who did not bow to pressure from the special committee claimed to be intimidated by the Los Angeles police.

The case was never officially resolved and as the years passed, bits of truth continued to emerge amidst the stories, rumors, and Hollywood legends. Speculation included the idea that Taylor was murdered by a hired killer who was working for one of the drug dealers servicing Mabel Normand. Friends of Taylor knew that he had appealed to the U.S. Attorney a short time before his death to try and combat the narcotics ring that was selling cocaine to Normand. A dozen known addicts and dealers were questioned and detectives even traveled to Folsom Prison to question two convicts that the warden implicated in Taylor's murder. One of them said that the other had killed the director at the urging of "a well-known actress" who resented Taylor for interfering with her dope supply. After an exhaustive investigation, detectives became convinced the convicts were lying in hopes of getting transferred to a minimum-

District Attorney Thomas Woolwine

security facility.

Another theory surmised that Taylor had been killed by a disgruntled World War I veteran who blamed him for his court-martial, then waited a few years to carry out his revenge. The most popular murder theories have involved Mabel Normand and Mary Miles Minter, one or the other of whom murdered Taylor during a lover's spat. Another bit of guesswork suggests the killer was Mary's manipulative mother, who was also a jealous rival for the director's love.

Mabel Norman's career was destroyed by the Taylor scandal, as well as by another incident that occurred shortly afterward involving her chauffeur and the murder of a Hollywood playboy. She made a few additional films but by then, her drug abuse had ruined her health. She died in 1930 from tuberculosis and pneumonia. Mary Miles Minter retired permanently from the screen in 1924. She spent the next few decades feuding with her overbearing mother who finally died, leaving Mary in peace, in 1957. Mary died a recluse in 1984.

Weird stories continued to circulate about the case for years. District Attorney Woolwine, the man who probably knew more about the case than anyone else, resigned due to poor health and died soon after. In 1926, his successor, Asa Keyes, re-opened the Taylor case and announced that an arrest was imminent. Later, Keyes stated that certain vital evidence, kept in a locked cabinet in his office "mysterious vanished" and the case was allowed to lay dormant once more. Keyes later died after going to prison for accepting a bribe in a million dollar oil scandal.

In 1929, the mystery was resurrected again when F.W. Richardson, a former California governor, stated that back in 1926 he had received "positive information" that a "certain top screen actress" had killed Taylor, but he was unable to do anything about it because of the corrupt conditions that existed in L.A. at the time. Richardson implied that the film industry had bribed officials to "bury the investigation." But Richardson's startling announcement led to more dead ends.

In 1943, a man arrested on federal narcotics charges in Indiana offered to name William Desmond Taylor's killer in return for immunity. The government refused to make the deal and the man remained silent and died of pneumonia in the prison hospital.

At that point, any real investigation into the case came to an end. From time to time, writers, reporters, and retired cops will come forward and state that the killer was indeed known to the authorities at the time, but no one could do anything about it. Some have spoken mysteriously of an "actress" or an "actor" who was involved, but no definitive proof has ever been offered. The spectacular William Desmond Taylor case will continue to fascinate for many years to come as a classic Hollywood murder mystery, although it's one that will never be solved in the last pages of the book or in the film's final scenes.

THE "CREEPY LITTLE MAN"
THE STRANGE DEATH & GHOSTLY SIGHTINGS OF PAUL BERN

Jean Harlow was one of Hollywood's true comedians, but like so many other comic actors, she found little happiness in her personal life. During her short career, she gained screen fame for not only her attractive figure and striking platinum hair, but for her sassy personality, as well. But it was the drama in her private life that made her a legend, even before her untimely death in 1937, at the age of only 26.

Jean had a disastrous record of marriages. She divorced two of her three spouses, and her second husband, MGM executive Paul Bern, died under suspicious circumstances in 1932, placing his complicated private life under intense scrutiny. Although Bern's death was officially listed as a suicide, many believe that it was actually murder – a murder that remains unsolved today.

Whatever the case, the explosive facts surrounding his death led to one of Hollywood's most celebrated cover-ups. As in the case of William Desmond Taylor, studio executives descended on Bern's home after his death and boldly tampered with evidence before summoning the police. MGM also manage to rearrange the chronology of "facts" and the "testimony" of crucial witnesses to protect their investment in Jean

Jean Harlow

Harlow's career. With the evidence in the case of Paul Bern muddled beyond repair, the mystery of his death remains a bizarre riddle in Hollywood's murky history.

But none of it could have happened without Jean Harlow. She was born Harlean Harlow Carpenter on March 3, 1911 in Kansas City, Mo. Her adoring father, Mont Clair Carpenter, was a prominent dentist and her mother, Jean, was an unhappy homemaker. Her parents divorced in 1922 and the next year, Harlean and her mother moved to Hollywood, hoping to get lucky in the movies. After two frustrating years, they reluctantly returned to the Midwest. Harlean's grandfather, prominent real estate agent Skip Harlow, had demanded that Harlean be returned to Kansas City or her mother would be disinherited.

Harlean was spoiled and pampered as she grew up, attending private schools and leading a privileged life. By then, her mother had met Marino Bello, a dapper, married slick-talker who had charmed his way into her life. While Harlean barely tolerated the man, Skip Harlow hated him. However, he preferred that his daughter marry the scheming Bello than continue her unseemly affair with him. After Bello's first wife filed for divorce, she married him in early 1927.

By this time, the stunning Harlean was attending a private girls' academy in Lake Forest, Ill. On a blind date, she met Charles Fremont McGrew II, the heir of a wealthy local family. For the bored young woman, marriage to the rich young man seemed preferable to continuing her academic life. Charles and 16-year-old Harlean eloped to Waukegan, Ill., in September 1927.

A few months later, Charles came into a portion of his inheritance and the newlyweds departed for L.A. They bought a home in Beverly Hills and settled down to enjoy their lavish lifestyle in Southern California. Much to the couple's chagrin, Harlean's mother and her slick husband also moved to the West Coast, hoping to share in Harlean's affluent new life.

Although she was content, fate intervened in Harlean's life. Through a friend, she was introduced to executives at Fox Films and it was suggested that she try her hand at movie acting. Her friends wagered that she would be too shy to give it a go. To prove them wrong, she registered at Central Casting using her mother's maiden name of Jean Harlow. She made her movie debut in a bit part in 1928. Sensing an opportunity, her mother and Bello persuaded the young woman to seek a movie career. Jean was soon appearing in small roles for Paramount and other studios, but was relieved to learn, in the spring of 1929, that she was pregnant. This would allow her to give up acting, something she enjoyed but that she had been pushed into. Her mother was furious and demanded that Jean have an abortion, which Bello arranged. Heartbroken, the young girl went along with it, only to suffer another loss a short time later. She and Charles separated, and in 1930 they divorced. He could no longer stand his meddling and intrusive in-laws.

Jean was now stuck with supporting herself, along with her mother and her stepfather. She began to get more serious about her career. She had a small role in Clara Bow's "The Saturday Night Kid" but her big break came about thanks to

Howard Hughes' fascination with Tinseltown. His film productions were well received in the movie colony and when he discovered Harlow, he already had a movie in the works called "Hell's Angels," starring Greta Nissen. Then, overnight, talking pictures became all the rage and "Hell's Angels" had to be re-made as a talkie. Jean Harlow won the lead in the new picture and she quickly skyrocketed as an overnight sensation. The Hollywood publicity machine went into overdrive for Harlow. She soon became known for her signature look of platinum blond hair and her notable, low-cut necklines.

Meanwhile, fed up with being controlled by her mother and Bello, Jean became involved in several unrealistic love affairs. One of them was with an L.A. stockbroker and another was with a New Jersey gangster named Abner "Longy" Zwillman, a date that was arranged by Bello. The homely Zwillman was obsessed with Jean and he lavished her with gifts and paid for a new, more upscale home for Jean and her parasitic family.

Jean may have been amused by the attention lavished on her by Zwillman, but she was more intrigued by MGM executive Paul Bern, who had been taking a strong interest in her career. He had arranged for her to come to MGM on loan, which he did again for "Beast of the City," released in 1932. He also used his influence at the studio to get MGM to buy Jean's contract from Howard Hughes.

It would have been hard to find two people more incompatible than Jean Harlow and Paul Bern. Most of Bern's contemporaries considered him a genius – although a rather strange one. He was born in Germany with the name Paul Levy in 1889 and he came to New York with his parents when he was 9 years old. He originally planned to study psychiatry but that costly dream ended when his father died in 1908. He supported his family and later enrolled at the American Academy of Dramatic Arts, graduating in 1911. By then, he had adopted the less ethnic stage name of Paul Bern and went to work acting, stage managing, and writing scripts for silent films. His mother committed suicide in 1920 and Bern was so ashamed of this that he often told others that her death was accidental. For the rest of his life, he feared that he had inherited her mental instability.

Paul Bern

Bern later took a job in Toronto with a fledging film company and then moved west to California when he realized the potential for movies. After landing in Hollywood, he worked as a film cutter and a script editor before directing a few pictures and ending up as a supervisor at MGM. In 1928, Irving C. Thalberg appointed Bern his second in command.

During his time in Hollywood, Bern became infatuated with several beautiful actresses, including Joan Crawford and the tragic Barbara La Marr, who died from drug addiction in 1926. However, none of these infatuations actually led to romance and rumors circulated that Bern had some issues when it came to women. His problems ranged from impotence to severe mood swings that left his ecstatic one moment and deeply depressed the next. While always kind toward women, he also had a fascination with them that reportedly fueled a pretty dark fantasy life, which be barely kept under control. With a list like this of his romantic shortcomings, it was no surprise that most women tended to avoid him when it came to relationships. However, he did gain a reputation in Hollywood as a sensitive and compassionate person (a rare thing in Tinseltown) and he began to be called "Hollywood's Father Confessor." Everyone took his troubles to Bern for advice, help, and sympathy.

In May 1932, Jean was filming "Red Headed Woman" and was being taken out on the town by Bern. He had never been much for public life and was something of a mystery man to those who craved the spotlight and the lure of Hollywood's legendary nightlife. No one said much when he began appearing in some of the local clubs with Jean because it was assumed it would never last. Soon, though, Bern began telling his associates that he and Jean were going to be married. This was shocking enough, but gossips were genuinely stunned when Jean confirmed it. Everyone seemed amazed that Jean would consider marrying this physically nondescript little man who was 22 years older than she was. It was assumed that the marriage was one of convenience, to simply further her career. Even Jean's mother was worried about her daughter and this strange man, but she kept silent. Jean's former boyfriend, Longy Zwillman did not. He confronted her and told her that Bern was reputed to be a homosexual, but his warning did not change her mind.

Little planning went into the nuptials and, in fact, Jean did not even have time to purchase a real wedding gown. She simply went into a dress shop that she frequented and bought an off-the-rack white dress and matching shawl. They were married on Saturday, July 2, 1932 in a small ceremony at Bern's home in Beverly Hills. To Jean's bewilderment, they did not consummate their wedding that night and she accepted this as another sign of his tremendous respect for her. At a reception at the Bellos' house on Sunday, the bride seemed very happy.

But that would all soon change.

During the rest of the summer of 1932, there were delays on Jean's next picture, "Red Dust." Bern attempted to wean Jean away from the negative influences of her mother and stepfather. Failing in this regard, he became angry when she gave them money or invested in another of Bello's schemes. She even asked him if they could give Bern's home to her family so that she and Paul could move closer to civilization. The house was set in the midst of five acres of ground in Benedict Canyon and Jean didn't like the place. Bern refused and argued that he wanted it to be their home together. As the weeks passed, Bern became more and more depressed, distraught, and haggard looking. This melancholy state was so prolonged that he consulted a physician about impotence and took to heavy drinking. Meanwhile, Jean seemed buoyant, even telling friends that she hoped to adopt a child.

On Friday and Saturday, September 2 and 3, Jean was at work on the set of "Red Dust," while Bern was busy developing "China Seas," an

The Harlow - Bern wedding. Jean is at left, Bern at right and actress Norma Shearer stands between them. Irving Thalberg stands over Jean's shoulder.

upcoming Harlow picture. On Saturday night, because Jean was delayed at the studio, Bern canceled plans for them to attend a celebrity party. Instead, he dined at a bungalow at the Ambassador Hotel with married MGM producer Bernard Hyman and his mistress, actress Barbara Barondess. Bern then went home, read for a while, and went to bed. Jean stayed at her mother's house that evening because it was closer to the studio and she had to go back early in the morning.

On Sunday, Paul worked at home and Jean went back to the studio. She promised to stay with her mother again that night, since Bello had planned a weekend holiday with Clark Gable. When Jean talked with Paul that night, she tried to convince him to come over to her mother's for dinner. He refused, because he disliked the Bellos so much. When Jean suggested that she would stay home with him, he reportedly insisted that she go as planned, which makes something that he wrote to her in his final correspondence all the more puzzling.

On Monday morning, September 5, 1932, the Berns' cook and butler arrived at the house to find Bern's nude body in a pool of blood, sprawled out in front of the dressing room mirror. He was supposedly drenched in Jean's favorite perfume and had been shot in the head with a .38-caliber revolver, which was still lying by his side. After discovering Bern's body, the butler went running to find his wife, the cook for the household. She called the Bello home and told Jean's mother the bad news. In turn, Jean Bello contacted Louis B. Mayer, head of

Paul Bern's body was it was when the police finally arrived at the house. The authorities were not summoned until hours after his death, giving studio bosses the chance to clean up the scene.

MGM, without, allegedly, telling Jean that her husband was dead. Mayer called MGM's security chief, W.P. "Whitey" Hendry, who was at home in Santa Monica, enjoying the Labor Day weekend, and Howard Strickling, the head of MGM's publicity department and ordered both men to the

Culver City lot. When they arrived, they met Virgil Apger, the company's still photographer. Hendry and Apger went to the death scene, where photographs were taken for future reference.

Not surprisingly, no one called the police

Strickling soon arrived at the Bern house. He spotted the deceased's guest book lying on a table. Flipping through the pages, he came across a puzzling entry:

Dearest Dear,
Unfortunately, this is the only way to make good the frightful wrong I have done you and to wipe out my abject humiliation.
I love you. Paul
You understand last night was only a comedy.

When Mayer arrived at the house, Strickling prevented him from removing the guest book, suggesting that without it, the authorities might believe that Jean had killed her husband. Mayer agreed with this line of reasoning and when Thalberg arrived, he also agreed to leave the book where it was. It was not until three hours after the body was discovered that the police were alerted to Bern's death. Just what happened in those two hours will never be known.

When detectives arrived, they discovered a .38 that had been fired in the dead man's right hand. Another .38, which had not been fired, was on a nearby table, next to the guest book. Meanwhile, Thalberg had gone to the Bellos' house to finally tell Jean about Bern's death. The detectives looked over the note that Bern had scrawled in the guest book, but failed to understand its meaning. The case appeared to be a suicide and after speaking with the butler and the staff, they went to Jean's mother's house to talk with the actress. Jean's mother turned them away at the door. She told them Jean was "too hysterical to undergo questioning at this time" and she had been sedated by her doctor. News of Bern's strange death was soon reported in the press.

The next day, the powers at MGM concluded that they needed to force Jean's mother to let the young woman talk to the police. Continued refusal would make the distressed movie star look bad to the public, who, at that moment, were blaming Jean for somehow causing Bern's suicide. On Tuesday, detectives interviewed Jean, but she insisted, "There was nothing between us that would have caused him to do this." Louis B. Mayer was on hand for the questioning and, later, conferred with Jean upstairs. Insisting that she needed to do something to gain public sympathy for the tragedy, he told her to tell the authorities about the sexual problems in her marriage. Jean refused and was said to have tried to throw herself over the balcony, but Mayer managed to stop her.

On September 7, MGM asked Tallulah Bankhead to replace the still-inconsolable Harlow in "Red Dust," but she refused. An inquest followed and the authorities began to piece together Bern's final hours. Jean had stayed with her mother on Saturday night and then again on Sunday. She had reportedly asked Bern if he wanted her to come home but he told her that he planned to stay up late reading scripts. She did not hear from him again and assumed that he had fallen asleep. She heard nothing else until being told that he was dead on Monday afternoon. Needless to say, the inquest brought many unanswered questions, like what was Bern referring to in the note that he wrote to Jean saying, "You understand last night was only a comedy"? Did he meet with someone else that night? And what was the motive for his suicide? The coroner's inquest ended with a verdict that Bern had committed suicide for undetermined reasons.

There was a lot of speculation about Bern's "comedy" and the nature of the sexual problems in the marriage. Some believed that Bern was impotent, or a latent homosexual who was unable to perform sexually with Jean. Others believed that he was suffering from a physical infirmity (either chronic impotence or an unusually small penis) that made it impossible for him to have intercourse with his wife. The "comedy" referred to in the suicide note was Bern's attempt to overcome his problem and carry out his marital obligations to Jean with a realistic, phony phallus. The night ended in disaster and Jean fled back to her mother's house. She refused to admit that she was at home to spare Bern's reputation any further damage.

By this time, Bern's brother, Henry, had arrived in L.A. and he was angry about the rumors going around about Paul's sexual inadequacies. He insisted that the gossip was wrong – Paul Bern had lived normally with another woman for many years. Strangely, the woman had vanished on the same day that Bern's body had been found and was found dead one week later.

The woman's name was Dorothy Roddy and under the stage name of Dorothy Millette, she was working as a struggling actress in New York when Paul Bern met her. They lived together in both New York and Toronto and she often referred to herself as "Mrs. Paul Bern." Under New York law at the time, living together transformed Dorothy into Bern's common-law wife. Tragically, Bern's mother, who wanted to be the only woman in her son's life, committed suicide when she learned of her "rival." Not long after, the guilt-stricken Dorothy was institutionalized after a nervous breakdown. Bern paid for all of her expenses. After he moved to L.A., he kept the information about Dorothy hidden from all but his closest friends. Those who did hear about her, including Jean, had no idea of the whole story.

After being released from the mental hospital, Dorothy moved into the Algonquin Hotel in New York. She lived quietly, spending most of her time reading and walking in Central Park. Bern paid her a monthly stipend, sent occasional letters, and always visited her when he was in New York. His 1920 will, in fact, left everything he owned to Dorothy. However, this was changed in a later will, which bequeathed his estate to Jean.

On March 17, 1932, Paul received a letter from Dorothy stating that she was moving to San Francisco. He suggested to her that she stay at the Plaza Hotel, which offered an "attractive rate" and that if she did decide to stay somewhere else, he would "find some way of supplying you with funds in a manner convenient for you."

On September 6, the day after Bern died, Dorothy checked out of the Plaza and boarded a river steamer that journeyed back and forth between San Francisco and Sacramento. An officer later found a woman's coat and shoes next to the

Although devastated by Bern's death, Jean's career continued on until her own untimely death a few years later.

ship's railing. Dorothy Millette was not on board when the ship docked at Sacramento. Fishermen found her body one week later. Her death was ruled a suicide.

On September 9, a funeral was conducted for Bern at Inglewood Park Cemetery, with Jean sobbing through the entire service. Bern's body was cremated at its conclusion. On Monday, September 12, Jean returned to work on the set of "Red Dust," the studio having decided that public sentiment had turned in her favor.

Jean Harlow's career continued and she married MGM cinematographer Hal Rosson in September 1933, but divorced him two years later. She later became romantically involved with actor

William Powell.

Although no records exist, it is rumored that in the early part of 1937, Harlow fell ill with influenza. If so, even after she recovered, the attack would have weakened her body against the kidney disease that eventually killed her. In the days before kidney dialysis and transplants, this condition was usually fatal.

In the spring of 1937, Jean began making her final film, "Saratoga," with Clark Gable. Jean began having problems getting to the set on time and was perspiring heavily during the filming. On May 29, she collapsed on the set and was rushed to the hospital, where she was diagnosed with uremic poisoning. She was cared for at home for the next eight days and was given constant medical attention. Nonetheless, her condition worsened. On June 6, she was rushed back to the hospital, where she died the following morning. She was 26.

Strangely, the story of Paul Bern's "suicide" was not over yet.

A strange series of circumstances shed new – and more mysterious-- light on the case a year after the inquest. At that time, a grand jury had been impaneled to investigate District Attorney Buron Fitts, who had handled the original Bern inquest. The jury foreman insisted that they were only interested in Fitts' expenditures in the case and yet new revelations came to light because of it.

Important information came from Davis, the gardener, and Irene Harrison, Bern's secretary. Davis believed that he "thought it was murder. I thought so from the beginning." He believed that the butler had lied about what happened. He testified that the butler told the police that Bern and Harlow were always hugging and kissing and that he sometimes overheard Bern talking of suicide. The gardener said that the opposite was actually true. He never thought that the couple got along that well and he had never once heard Bern talk about killing himself. He also said that he didn't believe the suicide note was even in his employer's handwriting.

Irene Harrison confirmed this and she also added that Jean Harlow, not Bern, had been the pursuer in the relationship. She also added that she didn't think that Bern looked particularly happy at the reception after the wedding ceremony.

The most intriguing testimony came from Winifred Carmichael, Bern's cook. She stated that the household staff had seen a strange woman at the house on Sunday evening. The cook stated that a woman's voice, which was unfamiliar to her, was heard. The woman screamed once. She also said that she later found a wet woman's bathing suit on the edge of the swimming pool and two empty glasses nearby. There is no record of whether or not the police ever checked the glasses for fingerprints or whether or not they followed up on further testimony from Davis, who said that he told detectives of finding a small puddle of blood near Bern's favorite chair by the swimming pool.

Even after all this, Bern's death was still considered a suicide. It remained that way until 1960 when writer Ben Hecht published an article that stated Bern's death was actually a murder. "Studio officials decided," Hecht wrote, "sitting in a conference around his dead body, that it was better to have Paul Bern as a suicide than as a murder victim of another woman." He wrote that it would be better for Jean Harlow's career that she not seem like a woman who couldn't hold a husband.

The L.A. District Attorney got in touch with Hecht, who told him that director Henry Hathaway had told him about the tragedy. But Hathaway, who was living in New York, claimed to have no first-hand knowledge of the case. He had no information to say that the suicide note was not real or that it had been planted by the studio heads.

Still, many believed that Bern might have been murdered. But if he was, who killed him? Could it have been Dorothy Millette? There are many who believe that Dorothy came to Los Angeles the night before Labor Day to confront Bern about his marriage to Jean. They believe that Jean was at the house that night and encountered Dorothy arguing with Bern, which might explain Bern's reference to a "comedy." Both women left the house – but what if one of them returned? Could Dorothy or Jean have murdered Paul and then arranged it to look like a suicide?

The idea of Dorothy being the killer is problematic. In those days, the fastest transportation between Los Angeles and San Francisco was the Southern Pacific daylight train or the overnight Lark. Either method of transportation took almost 10 hours and Dorothy was back in San Francisco to check out of her hotel the next morning. For Dorothy to make it, she would have had to catch the 10 p.m. train, meaning that a cab would have had to have picked her up from Bern's isolated home by at least 8 p.m. However, no trace any such call or taxi driver was ever located.

But if Dorothy did kill Bern, was she the woman who was heard in the house and left a wet swimsuit behind? If so, why did she bother to go all the way back to her San Francisco hotel after a ten-hour train ride, pack her things, board the river boat and after all of that effort, commit suicide? If this was a crime of passion, why didn't she just kill herself there, next to the body of her dead lover?

Unfortunately, Jean is a more likely culprit if Bern's death was indeed a murder. The emotional actress could have become distraught over finding out the extent of Paul and Dorothy's relationship, returned to the house and killed him. There are many who believe that Jean already knew that Bern was dead when Thalberg arrived at her mother's house on Monday afternoon. In this scenario, the note that was found in the guest book was intended to accompany flowers to Jean at her studio dressing room. But Bern was dead before any flowers could be ordered. There seems to be little question as to whether or not studio executives would have covered for Harlow is they even suspected that she was involved – they would have!

Or could there have been another woman involved? If not Dorothy, then who did the wet swimming suit belong to? The staff said that they heard a woman's voice that they did not recognize, which seems to rule out Jean. Whose blood was on the tiles near the swimming pool? Who did the second glass belong to? Why was it never checked for fingerprints?

These questions remain unanswered and for

Sharon Tate with Jay Sebring, who lived in Paul Bern's former home in Benedict Canyon

many crime buffs, the death of Paul Bern remains unsolved. Could this be why his ghost is still reportedly haunting the Harlow House? Perhaps, but many believe that Bern's first otherworldly appearance in the house was actually meant as a warning. It was a premonition for another beautiful blond actress that, if she had heeded it, might have saved her life. That woman's name was Sharon Tate.

In 1969, Sharon was a victim of the most savage slayings in Hollywood history. But three years before she was brutally murdered at the hands of the Charles Manson "family," she glimpsed a ghostly image of the horrific fate that awaited her. Could the glimpse into the future have been provided by the phantom of Paul Bern?

Sharon was a struggling actress, hoping to make a name for herself, when she met Jay Sebring, who would soon become known as the premier men's hair stylist in Hollywood. The two dated for three years and even announced their engagement at one point, but Sharon broke it off with him in 1966, when she met her future husband, Roman Polanski. The break-up was not bitter and the two of them stayed very close friends. In fact, it was Jay who was keeping Sharon company at the Cielo Drive house while Roman was away filming. And it was Jay who died trying to protect her from the Manson clan.

Jay lived in Benedict Canyon in the former home of Jean Harlow. He loved the house but was always concerned about the fact that it was supposed to be "jinxed." He knew the stories about Paul Bern's death and he also learned that two people had drowned in the swimming pool, as well.

One night in 1966, Sharon stayed alone at Jay's house. Unable to sleep, she lay awake in Jay's room with all the lights on. She was very uncomfortable, although she couldn't explain why. She felt "funny," she later told reporter Dick Kleiner, and was frightened by every little sound that she heard.

Suddenly, a person that she described as a "creepy little man" came into the bedroom. She was later convinced that this man was Paul Bern. He ignored her and wandered about the room, apparently looking for something. Sharon put on her robe and hurried out of the bedroom.

What happened next would be especially chilling in light of events to come. Sharon started down the stairs but halfway down them, froze in shock. There was a figure tied to the staircase posts at the bottom of the steps. She couldn't tell if it was a man or a woman. However, she could clearly see that the figure's throat had been cut. Then, the apparition vanished.

Shaken, Sharon went into the living room to pour herself a drink, but she couldn't find where Jay kept the alcohol. She felt an inexplicable urge to press on a section of the bookcase and it opened to reveal a hidden bar. As she reached for a bottle to pour herself a drink, she accidentally tore a small piece of wallpaper at the base of the bar. She swallowed a strong glass of liquor and then went back to bed.

In the morning, Sharon was convinced the whole episode had been a terrible nightmare -- until she saw the wallpaper that had been torn away from the bar. At that point, she realized that she indeed seen the ghost of Paul Bern, the "creepy little man." She had also, unknowingly, seen a vision of her own fate, a macabre message that was too subtle to save her just a few years later.

"HOT TODDY!"
THE MYSTERIOUS DEATH OF THELMA TODD, THE ICE CREAM BLONDE

The ghost of Thelma Todd still walks in Hollywood, or at least that's what the owners of a building on the Pacific Coast Highway have claimed for years. It was in this building where Todd's "Roadside Rest Cafe" was once located and it's not far from the house where she met her mysterious end. This is a house where the ghostly elements of her demise are still repeated today. But what strange events have caused this glamorous ghost to linger behind in our world? The official

Thelma Todd

cause of Thelma's death was said to be an accidental poisoning from carbon monoxide, but the true facts in this sensational case remain unresolved to this day. Perhaps this is why Thelma still lingers, looking for someone to uncover what really happened on the night of December 16, 1935.

Thelma Todd was born on July 29, 1905 in Lawrence, Mass., and was the first of two children of John and Alice Todd. Thelma's father was a former police officer who had entered politics and had little time for his family. Because of this, her frustrated mother channeled all of her energy into Thelma and her younger brother, William. By the time Thelma was 10, her father had become the director of public health and welfare for the state of Massachusetts, a position that kept him away from home even more. Thelma was an exceptional student and did very well in school. She had also turned into a very pretty young woman. In 1932, she enrolled at the Lowell State Normal School, intent on become a teacher. In 1925, her brother was killed in an accident and engulfed by this family tragedy, Thelma began dreaming of moving away and making a life away from her oppressive home.

Fate intervened when a local boy submitted her high school picture into a statewide beauty contest and she won. This led to a talent scout from Famous Players-Lasky (later Paramount) inviting Thelma to screen test for the studio's first film school. She passed the audition and became one of the 16 attendees, on the condition that she lose 10 pounds before arriving at the facility in Astoria, N.Y.

During her training, Thelma fell in love with a classmate, Robert Andrews, but the studio nipped the romance in the bud, fearing gossip would somehow taint the new school. This led the always-rebellious Thelma to seek revenge by being extra sexy and flirty around studio executives. It was this aspect of her nature that led to her nickname of "Hot Toddy." With her classmates from the film school, Thelma made her screen debut

Thelma in one of her comedy shorts with Zasu Pitts

Thelma with Groucho Marx in "Horse Feathers"

in the silent feature "Fascinating Youth" in 1926.

Initially, Thelma's mother had been thrilled by her daughter's career opportunities, but she had doubts when she saw a publicity photo of the pretty girl in a flimsy costume. Alice Todd rushed to New York to voice her moral objections to studio executives. Already at wit's end with Thelma's rebellious behavior, Paramount gave her an ultimatum – relocate to Paramount's studio in Hollywood, or go home. Thelma packed up and moved to California.

Thelma went to work under a five-year, $75-per-week contract with Paramount and throughout 1927 she was given small parts in a number of feature films like "Rubber Heels" with Ed Wynn and "Nevada," a western with Gary Cooper. Then, Al Jolson spoke a few words onscreen in "The Jazz Singer" and motion pictures were changed forever. The industry went through a terrifying series of changes as the "Talkies" became the new medium of choice. The old silent films were gone for good and with them went some of the biggest stars of the era. The careers of screen legends like John Gilbert, Clara Bow, Norma Talmadge and many others were suddenly over. They were forced into retirement when the public did not respond to the sound of their voices. For Thelma, the coming of sound motion pictures could not have occurred at a better time. She was now able to develop her wisecracking persona and the demise of many screen veterans made room for newcomers and little-known actors like Thelma. A new generation of screen stars was born. However, Paramount discharged her in 1929.

A short time later, Thelma was approached by Hal Roach, who offered her a new movie deal that would also allow her to freelance for other studios. Roach planned to feature Thelma with comedy actress Zasu Pitts in a series of two-reel comedies. A former director at Essanay, Roach persuaded Pathe to sponsor him in his own studios and he soon emerged as a comedic talent, envisioning hilarious situations and translating them to film. Roach concentrated more on story than slapstick and audiences loved him at the box office. His biggest stars became Laurel and Hardy, Charlie Chase and Thelma Todd. She proved to be a real asset to Roach, not only appearing in her own films but as a female foil to Stan and Ollie and others.

At first, Thelma was reluctant to take the deal with Roach because the requirement came with conditions. The first was that she had to bleach her hair platinum blonde and the second required her to abide by the "potato clause." This meant that she was being signed at a certain weight, and if she gained more than five pounds, it was cause for instant dismissal. Thelma's mother, widowed since 1925, was in Hollywood for one of her frequent visits and she urged Thelma to take the deal. Before reporting to the Roach lot for her first shoot, Alice Todd supervised the bleaching of her daughter's hair and helped her to arrange a stringent diet.

In addition to Thelma's comedies for Hal Roach, Thelma also played major roles in films for other studios. They were mostly comedies in which she portrayed the sarcastic and wisecracking blonde role that most suited her. She appeared in two different films with the Marx Brothers, "Monkey Business" and the classic "Horse Feathers." Stan Laurel always wanted Thelma as the female lead in the Laurel and Hardy films, but her personality didn't always mesh with the two comedians on screen. She and Laurel became close friends and he often found work for her in other films when she wasn't working for Roach. He loved her bawdy sense of humor and when she suffered from boyfriend problems, she always confided in Stan.

Thelma was always up for partying when she was not at work and found it difficult to avoid liquor and foods, both of which were fattening. Friends on the Roach lot introduced her to diet pills, and she soon became hooked on the tablets.

By 1930, Zasu Pitts had moved on to other work and Thelma was often joined on screen by Patsy Kelly. They were still going strong in 1935 and her professional career was filled with high spots. Always restless in her personal life, though, Thelma was pleased when director Roland West started showing an interest in her, even though the unattractive older man was already married to silent screen actress Jewel Carmen. West was one of the most respected directors in Hollywood during the 1920s and early 1930s. While his output of films was small, his work was appreciated by studios and audiences alike. His greatest success came in 1926 with "The Bat," an atmospheric thriller starring Jack Pickford and Jewel Carmen. His visually astounding 1928 film, "The Dove," won an Academy Award for art direction. In 1931, he created one of the most extraordinary chillers of the time, "The Bat Whispers" with Chester Morris. West and Thelma began a romance, with West promising her the lead in Howard Hughes' "Hell's

Director Roland West and an advertisement for one of his most famous films, "The Bat Whispers". West and Thelma were involved for some time and "separately shared" an apartment behind the restaurant they owned together.

Angels," but that role went to Jean Harlow instead.

To make amends, West cast Thelma as the lead in "Corsair," a new film that he was producing and directing for United Artists. When released, the film bombed and Thelma returned to her heavy work schedule. Although she was no longer romantically interested in West, they remained friends. By then, he had lost interest in making movies and suggested that they open a restaurant that catered to the film colony. Thelma promised to consider the idea.

Around this same time, Thelma met Pasquale DiCicco, a handsome New York playboy who associated with gangsters for the thrill of it. The suave Pat, new to Hollywood, promoted himself as a talent agent and began making the rounds of the L.A. restaurant and nightclub circuit. Movie industry people knew that he associated with Charles "Lucky" Luciano, the Syndicate gangster who was based out of New York, which, of course, made him an intriguing character. Thelma was also amused by DiCicco and dating him gave her life a touch of danger – although it would prove to be more danger than she could have ever wanted.

Thelma and DiCicco had a whirlwind romance and, despite his violent temper and a number of beatings, the couple eloped on July 10, 1932 to Prescott, Ariz. The happy marriage did not last long. DiCicco refused to settle into married life and often left his new wife alone at their Brentwood home while he was out on the town. Frustrated, Thelma began drinking heavily, always relying on her faithful diet pills to keep the weight off. One night when Thelma convinced Pat to take her out with him to the clubs, DiCicco introduced her to Lucky Luciano, who was in town for a visit. Thelma was excited to be in the presence of the famous mobster, although DiCicco was unnerved by the gangster's obvious interest in his wife.

By 1933, DiCicco was frequently away on business in New York and Thelma was continuing to churn out films, including her popular shorts with Patsy Kelly. Reportedly, she was seen out on the town several times with Luciano during this period. By February 1934, Thelma filed for divorce from DiCicco. That August, she began making plans with Roland West to open their restaurant on the beach. With funding from West's wife, supervision by West himself, and Thelma's name to lure in the film crowd, Thelma Todd's Sidewalk Café opened for business.

Located under the palisades of what is now Pacific Coast Highway (then known as Roosevelt Highway), the restaurant occupied the ground floor along with a drug store. On the second level were a bar, lounge, and West's business office, as well as two apartments, one of which West and Todd shared "separately." Nearby, at 17531 Posetano Rd, was the grand house where West's wife, Jewel, sometimes lived, along with her brother (the café's business manager), and his wife. Thelma stored her car in one of the garages of the Posetano Road house. To reach the garage from the restaurant required an arduous climb of 270 concrete steps. The café opened to good business. Many of West's and Thelma's famous friends began frequenting the place and it became popular with actors and star-struck fans alike.

In mid-1935, Thelma was spending much of her spare time operating the café. She was still

Dead Men Do Tell Tales: Bloody Hollywood - Page 207

(Left) Thelma Todd's Sidewalk Café (Left) The stairs behind the restaurant that led up to the apartment, Jewel Carmen's house, and the garage where Thelma stored her car.

working hard, drinking, and keep up her steady run of diet pills. Her hectic life was further complicated by several threatening letters demanding a sizable blackmail fee. They proved to be the work of a deranged stalker in New York and while this bit of strangeness worked itself out, it was not the most frightening thing that Thelma had to deal with that summer.

Her most disconcerting problem was the pressure that she was receiving from Luciano to turn over the café's third story storage room (used unofficially as a gambling parlor for wealthy customers) to him as a Syndicate operation. At that time, organized crime was starting to appear in California, moving west from places like New York and Chicago. Bootlegging and drug trafficking had long been a part of Hollywood, but in the middle 1930s, Luciano was making an attempt to penetrate California with his illegal gambling enterprise. He already had casinos all over the country and with so much money flowing in and out of Hollywood, he was looking for a way to get a piece of the action. Thelma kept refusing Luciano's request and he eventually became violent, causing her to break off all contact with him.

Their final confrontation came one night in late November at the Brown Derby in Beverly Hills. According to witnesses, the pair had a brief exchange in the restaurant:

Thelma Todd: "You'll open a gambling casino in my restaurant over my dead body!"
Luciano: "That can be arranged."

Thelma threatened to take her problems with Luciano to L.A. District Attorney Buron Fitts and made an appointment at his office for December 17, 1935. To spite Luciano, she began converting the third-floor café space into a steakhouse. Meanwhile, Pat DiCicco showed up one day at the restaurant and asked her about the possibility of managing the place. Thelma didn't know if he was trying to get back into her life – or if he was on a mission from Luciano.

Thelma's film work continued to thrive. In 1935, she appeared with Bing Crosby in the Paramount musical "Two for Tonight" and in November, she began working with Laurel and

Hardy again in the feature-length musical "The Bohemian Girl." This film was also based on an operetta and Stan found an unusual part for Thelma to play. She appeared as a gypsy's daughter, wearing a black wig to cover her blond curls. She continued to work on the film well into December.

On December 14, Thelma received an invitation to a Hollywood party. A few years earlier, she had made a film with Stanley Lupino, the British stage comedian and father of actress Ida Lupino. Stanley and his wife were in town, and Ida was hosting a dinner party for him at the Café Trocadero. When Thelma informed West about the party, he was irritated with her that she would not be at their own restaurant on such a busy night before the holidays. But this was not the worst thing to come that night. A few days earlier, Pat DiCicco had run into Ida Lupino at the Trocadero and she had unknowingly invited him to the party.

On the afternoon of December 14, Thelma and her mother went out Christmas shopping, driven by her chauffeur, Ernest Peters. Later, she returned home to change clothes while her mother continued with her errands. At 7:30 p.m., Peters, along with Mrs. Todd, picked up Thelma. The actress was wearing a blue satin evening gown with lace and sequins, expensive jewelry, and a luxurious mink coat. Before leaving, she and West argued again about the café, but the still-rebellious Thelma slammed the door in his face and walked out. After dropping Thelma off at the Trocadero, Peters took Mrs. Todd home and then made himself available to drive Thelma home after the party.

The party was a great success and Pat DiCicco showed up later in the evening with actress Margaret Lindsay, a subtle way of snubbing his ex-wife. During the dinner, Thelma left the group to make a telephone call and use the restroom. When she returned, she seemed moody, but did not say why. Around midnight, DiCicco also made a mysterious phone call, which left him jittery. He refused to comment on it and left with Lindsay at about 1:15 a.m. without saying good night to anyone.

While Thelma waited for her driver to arrive, she asked her friend, theater owner Sid Grauman, to call Roland West and tell him that she was on her way home. Sid made the call, telling West that Thelma should be back at the apartment by 2:30 a.m., although a half-hour after that, she was still waiting at the restaurant. The car reached its destination about 3:30 a.m. As usual, Peters offered to escort Thelma to the door, but she told him that it wasn't necessary. She gathered her coat around her and walked off into the dark – and this was the last time that Thelma Todd was ever seen alive.

At 10 a.m. on Monday morning, December 16, Thelma's maid, Mae Whitehead, entered the garage

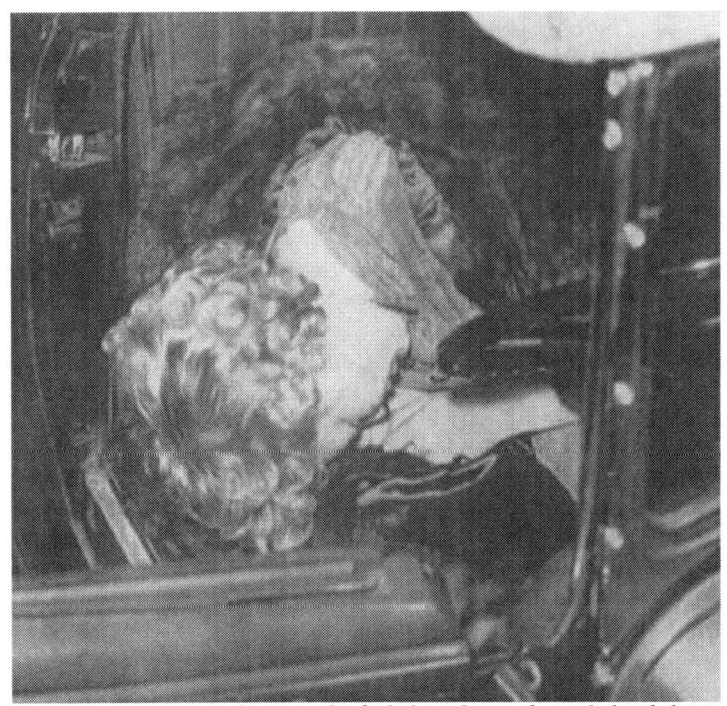

Police crime scene photograph of Thelma slumped over behind the wheel of her car. Suicide could not explain the beating that she had taken before her death.

of the Posetano House and found the body of Thelma Todd. She was lying face down on the front seat of her Packard convertible. Her blond hair was matted and her skin was pale. She was still wearing her clothes from Saturday night. A porcelain replacement tooth had been knocked out of her mouth and blood was spattered on her skin, her evening gown, and on the mink coat. The police were summoned at once and the shoddy investigation – or cover-up, depending on what you believe – began.

Thelma died from carbon monoxide asphyxiation, but how she managed to get locked into her garage, by her own hands or by someone else's, was a matter of conjecture. The investigation into her death revealed more questions than answers. Some suggested that Thelma might have committed suicide. It was not an uncommon method for such an act, but then murders had been committed in a similar fashion. In addition, if she had killed herself, where had the blood on her face and clothing come from? To make matters more suspicious, an autopsy had revealed that Thelma had suffered a broken nose, several broken ribs, and enough bruises to suggest that she had been roughed up. This seemed to rule out suicide.

As the investigation continued, some nervous witnesses claimed to receive ominous threats and, in turn, recanted part, or all, of their original statements. In another weird twist, when Thelma's mother first arrived at the scene, she insisted that someone had murdered her daughter. Later, she said that she believed Thelma's death had been accidental. Then, still later in life, she changed her story again and once more said that Thelma had been murdered. Did someone lean on Thelma's mother during the investigation and convince her that voicing suspicions of murder was a bad idea?

But if Thelma had been murdered, who had killed her? Roland West seemed to be the likely suspect and witnesses from the party, including Ida Lupino, said that she had been uneasy after making a telephone call. All agreed that she had been drunker than usual when she went home and Sid Grauman told the police about his telephone call to West. Also, witnesses from the neighborhood told the court how they had seen Thelma, still in her evening gown and mink coat, screaming obscenities and kicking at the door of the apartment. Apparently, she may have made it to the top of the concrete stairs, but could not get into the apartment.

Throughout the investigation, West contradicted himself several times, changing his story about his activities over the weekend several times. West admitted that instead of helping Thelma into bed on Sunday morning, he had locked the door to the apartment. After their fight earlier on Saturday, West had warned her that if she was not home by 2 a.m., he was going to lock her out. Some have surmised that Thelma's telephone call during the party had been to West, hoping for a reprieve. When it didn't come, she had asked mutual friend Sid Grauman to call for her later. But West remained adamant and said that after Thelma got home, they had another fight through the door. However, he added a strange contradiction to his story. He stated that he had later been awakened by his dog barking and was sure that he heard water running in the apartment. He assumed that Thelma had somehow gotten into the house.

An examination of the door did reveal marks where it was apparently kicked. Police were baffled though as to how Thelma could have gotten inside when it was bolted shut on the other side. This made them even more suspicious of West. Someone raised the incredible theory that West had hired an actress to pretend to be Thelma beating on the door while he was actually beating the real woman to death inside. The idea of the look-alike aside, West had a strong alibi against murder. Although his statement was contradictory, there was no evidence to tie him to the murder scene. He was, by his own admission, the last person to speak with Thelma on Sunday morning, just a short time before she died.

Another strange twist came from West's wife, Jewel Carmen. She claimed that she had seen Thelma on Sunday morning, after the sun was up, driving her Packard past the intersection of Hollywood and Vine. At her side was a handsome stranger. This testimony was very bizarre because the coroner and the police believed that Thelma was already dead by then. They were sure that she had died during the early morning hours of Sunday and was not discovered until the following day.

But how reliable was Jewel Carmen? She was West's wife and he was the prime suspect in the case. If she were lying, why would an estranged wife protect her unfaithful husband? Some suggested that perhaps if West did kill Thelma, perhaps Carmen hoped to get back into his good graces by providing an alternate killer in the form of the "handsome stranger." She could also put Thelma in another place far from the early morning argument with West. All of the confusing stories, combined with no hard evidence, eventually cleared West of Thelma's murder.

Years later, sources who have studied the case have pointed out West's close ties to industry mogul Joseph M. Schenk and believe that it's possible that Schenk may have used his major clout to help his friend get away with murder. Regardless, West never directed another film in Hollywood. He and Jewel Carmen divorced shortly after Thelma's death and later, he sold the café. In 1950, he suffered a debilitating stroke and endured an emotional breakdown. On his deathbed in March 1952, he confessed to Chester Morris that he had always been haunted by Thelma's death and felt that he was in some way responsible for it.

At the inquest that was held into Thelma's death, the jury ruled that she had died accidentally from carbon monoxide poisoning. They had been confused by all of the complicated testimony and, lacking any real evidence of murder, had no choice but to conclude that it had been an accident.

But Thelma's attorney, who attended the inquest, was sure that the police had been on the wrong track all along. He requested a second inquest, in which he would be able to prove his theory. He believed that he could pin her murder, not accidental death, on Lucky Luciano. He was sure that when Thelma had turned down the gangster's offer to take over the gambling at her café, she had unknowingly signed her own death warrant. The attorney was convinced that Luciano, or someone who worked for him, had beaten Thelma, put her in the car unconscious, and then started the engine. With the garage door closed, she had been poisoned by the fumes.

The district attorney agreed to the idea and a second inquest was scheduled. However, when Hal Roach learned of the plans for the second inquest, he begged the D.A. to drop the matter. Terrified at the thought of crossing Luciano, he urged the District Attorney to reconsider. Reluctantly, he agreed and the case was closed for good. As a result, the murder of Thelma Todd was never solved.

Although the case was wrapped up as far as the law was concerned, there were just too many unanswered questions and, as usual, involvement in the affair was enough to bring on the Hollywood style of retribution. In the past, Hollywood circles had ruined the careers of many popular stars and the death of Thelma Todd brought on the destruction of Roland West, who never worked again. No one else wanted to join him in his descent into obscurity.

The mystery over the unsolved death of Thelma Todd has lingered for decades. Some believe this may be why her spirit is so restless. Her ghost is still frequently seen and encountered at the building where the Roadside Rest Cafe was once located. Staff members at the production company that took over the space a few years ago stated that they often saw a filmy apparition that resembled Thelma. It was often seen near the concrete steps leading to the garage and also outside, in a small courtyard area. Was she replaying the events that occurred on the night of her death?

But the café is not the only spot connected to Thelma Todd's death where ghostly events have occurred. In the garage of the house on Posetano Road, people have complained about the sound of a spectral engine running when the space is actually empty. Others say they have smelled, and have been nearly overwhelmed, by noxious exhaust fumes in the garage, even when no car was present. Apparently, the terrible events of that long-ago night in December have left an indelible impression on the place.

Will Thelma Todd ever rest in peace? It's not likely. Unless new evidence could somehow come to light, her murder will always remain unsolved --- perhaps resulting in a tragic spirit that will continue to walk for many years to come.

Elizabeth Short - The Black Dahlia
(Wide World Photos)

WHO KILLED THE BLACK DAHLIA?
THE TRAGIC LIFE & DEATH OF ELIZABETH SHORT

The lobby of Hollywood's Biltmore Hotel is crowded on a warm and sunny afternoon in early spring. A man crosses the room and taps on the call key for an elevator. As the door opens, he steps inside and presses the number 8 button for his floor. He glances down as he does so and he sees that the number 6 is already illuminated. With a quick glance to his left, he realizes that he is not alone in the elevator. A dark-haired young woman stands in the corner and as he looks at her, she offers a faint smile.

The man smiles back at her and then looks up as the numerals above the door light up with the passage of each floor. He glances at the reflection of the woman in the polished steel of the doors. Even in this blurred view, she is stunning. Her dark, nearly black hair is swept back and up in the outdated style of the 1940s, although it is very becoming on her. Her skin is pale, perhaps looking even more so against her jet-black dress. The shiny material clings to her every curve. She makes no sound other than the soft rustle of her dress.

Finally, the elevator reaches the sixth floor and with a soft chime, the doors slide open. The man steps aside to let her pass and notices that she is not moving. She continues to stand in the corner, seemingly unaware that the lift has reached her floor. He finally speaks up and his voice seems to startle the girl. He says, "This is the sixth floor."

She steps forward and moves past him off the elevator. As she does, the man trembles involuntarily. A wave of chilled, ice cold air seems to brush past him as the girl departs. Gooseflesh appears on his arms as he watches the shapely young woman walk past the doors. Then, just as she steps out onto the sixth floor, she turns back to look at the man inside the elevator. She does not speak, but there is no mistaking the look of urgency in her eyes. She is begging him for help, the man realizes, but it's almost too late. The elevator doors have started to close, cutting off the young woman as she tries to re-enter the elevator. The man frantically pushes the button that will open the door again and just before they close completely, they slowly start to slide open again.

But the girl in black is gone!

Confused, he leans out into the lobby of the sixth floor. He looks quickly in both directions, but the small lobby and the hallways in either direction are empty and deserted. Where could she have gone so quickly? He calls out, but his voice echoes in the stillness of the corridor. The young woman had vanished, as if she had never existed at all.

Two days later, the man is browsing in a local bookshop and happens to pick up a book about true, unsolved mysteries. As he flips through it, he is startled by a face that he recognizes: it's the girl from the elevator! He looks at the photograph and is convinced that it is the same young woman in black. Then, he realizes such a thing is impossible. Scanning through the text, he sees that the girl died years before. How could she have been at the Biltmore Hotel just two days ago?

How indeed? Could this young woman who was killed in 1947 still be lingering at the last place that she was seen alive? Is she still looking for help – from the other side?

The face that the young man, and many others just like him, recognized once belonged to a beautiful young woman named Elizabeth Short. In death, she would come to be known by a more colorful nickname, the "Black Dahlia." Her tragic murder would forever leave a mark on Tinseltown. She came in search of stardom but only found it in death, becoming lost in the netherworld that is the dark side of Hollywood.

On January 15, 1947 a housewife named Betty Bersinger left her home on Norton Avenue in the Leimert Park section of Los Angeles, bound for a shoe repair shop. She took her 3-year-old daughter with her and as they walked along the street, coming up on the corner of Norton and 39th, they passed several vacant lots that were overgrown with weeds. Bersinger couldn't help but feel a little depressed as she looked out over the deserted area. Development had been halted here, thanks to the war, and the empty lots had been left looking abandoned and eerie. Betty felt slightly disconcerted but then shrugged it off, blaming her emotional state on the gray skies and the cold, dreary morning.

As she walked a little farther along, she caught a glimpse of something white over in the weeds. She was not surprised. It wasn't uncommon for people to toss their garbage into the vacant lot and this time, it looked as though someone had left

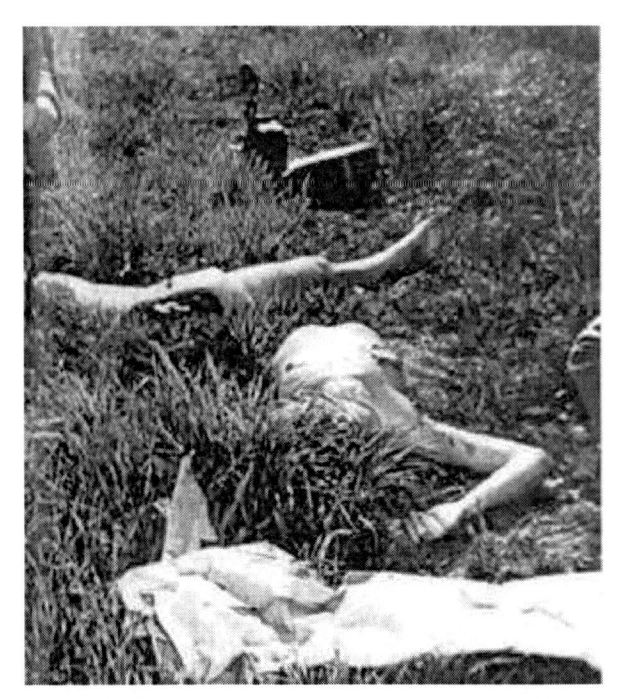

(Top) Elizabeth Short's severed remains were found by a housewife walking past an empty lot. (Below) Newspapers doctored the covered remains to make the photograph less horrifying.

a broken department store mannequin there. The dummy had been shattered and the two halves lay separated from one another, with the bottom half

Dead Men Do Tell Tales: Bloody Hollywood – Page 213

lying twisted into a macabre pose. Who would throw such a thing into an empty lot?

Betty shook her head and walked on, but then found her glance pulled back to the ghostly, white mannequin. She looked again and then realized that this was no department store dummy at all – it was the severed body of a woman! With a sharp intake of breath and a stifled scream, she took her daughter away from the gruesome sight and ran to a nearby house. Sobbing, she telephoned the police.

The call was answered by Officers Frank Perkins and Will Fitzgerald, who arrived within minutes. When they found the naked body of a woman who had been cut in half, they immediately called for assistance. The dead woman, it was noted, seemed to have been posed. She was lying on her back with her arms raised over her shoulders and her legs spread in an obscene imitation of seductiveness. Cuts and abrasions covered her body and her mouth had been slashed so savagely that her smile extended grotesquely from ear to ear. There were rope marks on her wrists, ankles and neck and investigators later surmised that she had been tied down and tortured for several days. Worst of all was the fact that she had been sliced cleanly in two, just above the waist. It was clear that she had been killed somewhere else and then dumped in the vacant lot overnight. There was no blood on her body and none on the ground where she had been left. The killer had washed her off before bringing her to the dump site.

The horrible nature of the case made it a top priority for the LAPD. Captain John Donahoe assigned his senior detectives to the case, Detective Sergeant Harry Hansen and his partner, Finis Brown. He also added Herman Willis, a bright young cop from the Metro Division, to help follow up on the leads that were sure to come in.

By the time the detectives were contacted and could get to the scene, it was swarming with reporters, photographers and a crowd of curiosity seekers. Hansen was furious that bystanders and even careless police personnel were trampling the crime scene. Evidence was being destroyed, he knew, and he immediately cleared the scene. Then, while he and his partners examined the scene, the body of the woman was taken to the Los Angeles County Morgue. Her fingerprints were lifted and with the help of the assistant managing editor of the *Los Angeles Examiner*, the prints were sent to the FBI in Washington using the newspaper's "Soundphoto" equipment. The newspaperman had, of course, asked for information in exchange for the use of the equipment.

Meanwhile, an examination of the corpse was started at the coroner's office. It began to detail an incredible and horrifying variety of wounds to the young woman's body, although the official cause of death was "hemorrhage and shock due to concussion of the brain and lacerations of the face." An autopsy revealed multiple lacerations to the face and head, along with the severing of the victim's body. It also appeared that the woman had been sodomized and her sexual organs abused but not penetrated. There was no sperm present on the body and most of the damage appeared to have been done after she was dead. The coroner also noted that her stomach contents contained human feces. Even the hardened doctors and detectives were shocked at the state of the girl's corpse.

The doctor also revealed to Detectives Hansen, Brown and Willis an important piece of evidence and one that would have a huge bearing on the case as more of the victim's past was later revealed. He told the detectives, "It is impossible to tell you if she was raped because traces of spermatozoa are negative, and she did not have fully developed genitals... The area is shallow indicating that she did not have a completed vaginal canal." According to the coroner, the young woman's vagina was almost child-like and normal sex for her would have been impossible.

This information would have an important impact on what they would learn about the victim and Hansen immediately decided not to make this information public. In fact, only a few detectives working the case would know about it. Hansen's decision was the right one and he must have known how much newspaper coverage such a bizarre murder would get. Soon, tips, calls and false confessions would come pouring into police headquarters. More than 50 people would eventually confess to the killing!

Shortly after receiving the fingerprints, the

FBI had a match for the Los Angeles detectives. The victim of the brutal murder was Elizabeth Short, 22, who originally came from Massachusetts. During World War II, she had been a clerk at Camp Cooke in California, which explained why her fingerprints were on file. Once the detectives had this information, they went to work finding out who knew Elizabeth Short, believing that this would lead them to her killer. What they discovered was a complex maze that led them into the shadowy side of the city in search of a woman called the "Black Dahlia."

Like all the other pretty girls before and since, Elizabeth Short (who preferred the name Beth) came to Hollywood hoping to make it big in the movie business. She was smart enough to know that looks weren't everything and that to break into films, she had to know the right people. So, she spent most of her time trying to make new acquaintances that she could use to her advantage and to make sure that she was in the right nightspots and clubs. Here, she was convinced she would come to the attention of the important people in the business. Beth's pretty face got her noticed. She had done some modeling before coming to Hollywood and men couldn't keep their eyes off her. She created a character for herself, dressing completely in black, which emphasized her pale beauty.

In Hollywood, Beth roomed with a hopeful dancer who introduced her to Barbara Lee, a well-connected actress for Paramount. Lee took Beth to all of the right places, including the famous Hollywood Canteen, where Beth always hoped she would be discovered. Beth loved to socialize, loved the Hollywood nightlife and loved to meet men. Despite the rumors, Beth was never promiscuous and she did not work as a prostitute. Considering the findings of the coroner, it isn't likely that sex with men involved normal penetration. Beautiful, lively and seductive, Beth was sometimes referred to as a "tease" as her boyfriends never had any idea that romance could only go so far.

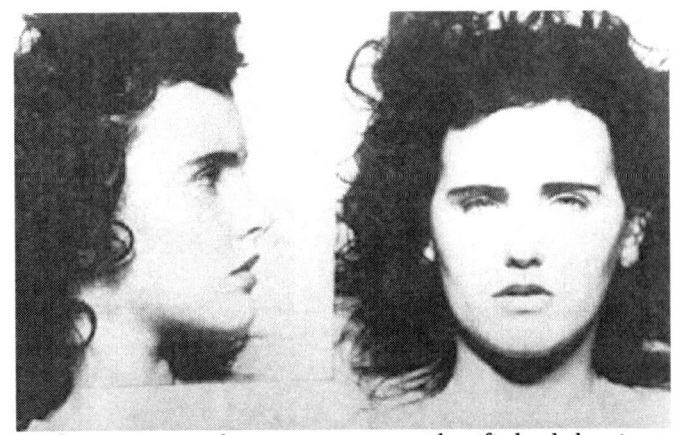

The fingerprints on the corpse were soon identified as belonging to Elizabeth Short. This photo is not a "mug shot" as some have identified it, but rather the photos taken for Beth's civilian ID at Camp Cooke. (Wide World Photos)

One of the men who befriended Beth was Mark Hansen, a nightclub and theater owner who knew many important show business people. He eventually moved her into his house, along with a number of other young actresses who roomed there and who entertained guests at Hansen's clubs. On any given day, a visitor to Hansen's house could find a number of beautiful actresses and models sunning themselves by the swimming pool. Beth soon became a part of this group, although her prospects for film work remained non-existent. She didn't have much of an income and only seemed to eat and drink when others, usually her dates, were buying. She shared rooms with other people and borrowed money from her friends constantly, never paying it back. She never seemed to appreciate the hospitality given to her by others, either, rarely contributing to where she was living and staying out most of the night and sleeping all day. She became known as a beautiful freeloader.

Around this same time, the film "The Blue Dahlia," starring Veronica Lake and Alan Ladd was released. Some of Beth's friends starting calling her "the Black Dahlia," thanks to her dark hair and back lacy clothing and the nickname stuck. It fit well with the mysterious and glamorous persona that Beth had already created. Tragically, it may have also led to her death.

Beth in Hollywood

Although she is remembered today as the Black Dahlia, Elizabeth Short did not start out as a sexy vamp who "haunted" the nightclubs of Hollywood. She was born on July 29, 1924, in Hyde Park, Mass. Her parents, Cleo and Phoebe Short, moved the family to Medford, a few miles outside of Boston, shortly after Elizabeth was born. Cleo Short was a man ahead of his time, making a prosperous living designing and building miniature golf courses. Unfortunately, the Depression caught up with him in 1929 and he fell on hard times. Without a second thought, he abandoned his wife and five daughters and faked his suicide. His empty car was discovered near a bridge and the authorities believed that he had jumped into the river below.

Phoebe was left to file for bankruptcy and to raise the girls by herself. She worked several jobs, including as a bookkeeper and a clerk in a bakery shop, but most of the money came from public assistance. One day, she received a letter from Cleo, who was now living in California. He apologized for deserting his family and asked to come home. Phoebe refused his apology and would not allow him to come back.

Beth (known as Betty to her family and friends) grew up to be a very pretty girl, looking older and acting more sophisticated then she really was. Everyone who knew her liked her and although she had serious problems with asthma, she was considered very bright and lively. She was also fascinated by the movies, which were her family's main source of affordable entertainment. She found an escape at the theater that she couldn't find in the day-to-day drudgery of ordinary life.

While she was growing up, Beth remained in touch with her father (once she knew he was actually alive). They wrote letters back and forth and when she was older, he offered to have her come out to California and stay with him until she was able to find a job. Beth had worked in restaurants and movie houses in the past but she knew that if she went to California, she wanted to be a star. She packed up and headed out West to her father.

At that time, Cleo was living in Vallejo and working at the Mare Island Naval Base. Beth hadn't been staying with her father long before the relationship between them became strained. Cleo began to launch into tirades about her laziness, poor housekeeping and dating habits. Eventually, he threw her out and Beth was left to fend for herself. Undaunted, she went to Camp Cooke and applied for a job as a cashier at the Post Exchange. It didn't take long for the servicemen to notice the new cashier and she won the title of "Camp Cutie of Camp Cooke" in a beauty contest. They didn't realize that the sweet romantic girl was emotionally vulnerable, though, and desperate to marry a handsome serviceman, preferably a pilot. She made no secret of wanting a permanent relationship with one of the men with whom she constantly flirted. The word soon got around that Beth was not an easy girl and pressure for more than just hand-holding kept Beth at home most nights. Several encounters made her uncomfortable at Camp Cooke and she left to stay with a girlfriend who lived near Santa Barbara.

During this time, Beth had her only run-in with the law. A group of friends that she was with got rowdy in a restaurant and the owners called the police. Since Beth was underage, she was booked and fingerprinted, but never charged. A kind policewoman felt sorry for her and arranged for a trip back to Massachusetts. After spending some time at home, she came back to California, this time to Hollywood.

At the Hollywood Canteen, Beth met and fell in love with a pilot named Lieutenant Gordon Fickling. He was exactly what she was looking for and she began making plans to ensnare him in matrimony. Unfortunately, though, her plans were cut short when Fickling was shipped out to Europe.

Beth took a few modeling jobs but became discouraged and went back East. She spent the holidays in Medford and then went to Miami, where she had relatives with whom she could live for a while. Beth began dating servicemen, always with marriage as her goal. She fell in love again on New Year's Eve 1945 with a pilot, Major Matt Gordon. A commitment was apparently made between them after he was sent to India. Beth wrote to him constantly and Gordon remained in touch with her. As a pre-engagement gift, he gave Beth a gold wristwatch that was set with diamonds and spoke about her (and their engagement) to family and friends. Best of all, as far as Beth was concerned, he respected her wishes about waiting until their honeymoon to consummate their love. They would get married and have a proper honeymoon, he promised her, after he returned from overseas. One has to wonder how Beth planned to deal with the physical problems they would encounter once the relationship turned sexual, but perhaps she was too caught up in the moment to worry about it at that time.

Beth went back home to Massachusetts and

Beth met & fell in love with a pilot, Major Matt Gordon, but when he was killed in a plane crash, her life began to spiral out of control

got a job, dreaming of her October wedding. Her friends often commented on how happy she was and after the war ended in Europef she became ecstatic about Gordon returning home. A short time later, she received a telegram from Gordon's mother. As soon as it arrived, Beth tore the message open, believing that it was about plans for the upcoming wedding. Instead, Mrs. Gordon had written, "Received word War Department. Matt killed in plane crash on way home from India. Our deepest sympathy is with you. Pray it isn't true."

Tragically, it was true and Gordon's death left Beth a little unbalanced. After a period of mourning, during which Beth told people that she and Matt had been married and that their baby had died at birth, she began to pick up the pieces of her old life and started contacting her Hollywood friends. One of those friends was former boyfriend, Gordon Fickling, whom Beth saw as a possible replacement for her dead fiancée. They began to write to one another and then got together briefly in Chicago when Fickling was in town for a couple of days. Soon, Beth was in love with him again. She agreed to come to Long Beach and be with him, happy and excited once again. A short time later,

Beth was back in California.

Her excitement over the new relationship didn't last long. She had to stay in a hotel that was miles from the base where Fickling was stationed and he constantly pressured Beth for sex. She had no intention of giving herself to a man except in marriage, she told a friend, and Fickling had no intention of making such a commitment. She began dating other men and when Fickling found out, he ended their relationship.

In December 1946, Beth took up "temporary" residence in San Diego with a young woman named Dorothy French. She was a counter girl at the Aztec Theater, which stayed open all night, and after an evening show, she found Beth sleeping in one of the seats. Beth told her that she had left Hollywood because work was hard to find due to the actors' strikes that were going on. Dorothy felt sorry for her and offered her a place to stay at her mother's home. The invitation was intended to last only for a few days, but Beth ended up sleeping on the Frenchs' couch for more than a month.

As usual, she did nothing to contribute to the household and she continued her late-night partying and dating. One of the men she dated was Robert "Red" Manley, a salesman from Los Angeles with a pregnant young wife at home. He admitted being attracted to Beth, but later claimed that he never slept with her. They saw each other on and off for a few weeks and then Beth asked him for a ride back to Hollywood. He agreed and on January 8 picked her up from the French house and paid for a motel room for her that night. They went out together to a couple of different nightspots and returned back to the motel. He slept on the bed, while Beth, complaining that she didn't feel well, slept in a chair.

Red had a morning appointment but came back to pick her up around noon. She told him that she was going back home to Boston but first she was going to meet her married sister at the Biltmore Hotel in Hollywood. Manley drove her back to Los Angeles. He had an appointment at the home of his employer that evening, so he didn't wait around for Beth's sister to arrive. Manley said Beth was making phone calls in the hotel lobby when he saw her last, becoming, along with the hotel employees, the last person to see her alive. As far as the police could discover, only her killer ever saw her after that. She vanished for six days from the Biltmore before her body was found in the empty lot.

The investigation into the Black Dahlia's murder was the highest profile crime in Hollywood of the 1940s. The police were constantly harassed by the newspapers and the public for results. Hundreds of suspects were questioned. Because it was considered a sex crime, the usual suspects and perverts were rounded up and interrogated. Beth's friends and acquaintances were questioned as the detectives tried to reconstruct her final days and hours. Every lead that seemed hopeful ended up leading nowhere and the cops were further hampered by the lunatics whose crazed confessions were still pouring in.

As the investigators traced Beth's activities, they discovered their strongest suspect, Robert Manley. He became the chief target of the investigation. The LAPD put him through grueling

A dramatic newspaper photo of Robert "Red" Manley. He later became a suspect in Beth's murder but was eventually cleared.

Tragically, Beth achieved the fame in death that she never found in life. Soon, newspapers were printed with banner headlines about her murder and her photo (Left) was seen everywhere.

The police dealt with thousands of "confessions" to Beth's murder but also received several letters (mailed to the Los Angeles Herald-Examiner newspaper) that might have been sent by the killer.

interrogations and even administered two different polygraph tests, both of which he passed. He was released a couple of days later but the strain on him was so great that he later suffered a nervous breakdown.

While the police worked frantically, Beth's mother made the trip to Los Angeles to claim her daughter's body. Her father, who had not seen her since 1943, refused to identify her. Sadly, Phoebe Short had learned of her daughter's death from a newspaper reporter who had called her, using the pretext that Beth had won a beauty contest and the paper wanted some background information about her. Once he had gleaned as much information as he could, he informed her that Beth had actually been murdered

A few days after Beth's body was found, a mysterious package appeared at the offices of the *Los Angeles Examiner*. An envelope contained a note that had been cut and pasted from newspaper letters. It read:

Here is the Dahlia's Belongings – Letter to Follow

Inside the small package was Beth's social security card, birth certificate, photographs of Beth with various servicemen, business cards and claim checks for suitcases she had left at the bus depot. Another item was an address book that belonged to club owner Mark Hansen. The address book had several pages torn out.

The police attempted to lift fingerprints off the items but found that all of them had been washed in gasoline to remove any trace of evidence. The detectives then began the overwhelming task of tracking down everyone in the address book and while Mark Hansen and a few others were singled out for interrogation, nothing ever came of it. In addition, the promised "letter to follow" never arrived.

All of the leads in the Black Dahlia case came to dead ends and the investigation fizzled, and then came to a halt. The murder remains unsolved today, although it's possible that the killer may have actually been identified by one investigator in the case. The possible killer first came to the attention of John St. John, a respected investigator for the LAPD who eventually took over the Dahlia case. St. John had worked many of the city's most notorious murders and was the basis of the book and television series "Jigsaw John." He had been in charge of the Dahlia case for about a year when a confidential informant came to him with a tape recording that implicated a suspect in the murder. The suspect had also shown the informant some photos and personal items that he claimed had belonged to the Black Dahlia.

The suspect turned out to be a tall, thin man with a pronounced limp who went by the name of Arnold Smith. On the recording, Smith claimed that a character named "Al Morrison" was the violent sexual deviant who had killed and mutilated Beth Short. St. John suspected that Arnold Smith and Al Morrison were actually the same person. The tape was a chilling and detailed account of how Beth had come to Al Morrison's Hollywood hotel room because she didn't have anywhere else to stay. According to Smith, Beth refused both liquor and sex with Morrison and became upset when he drove her to a house on East 31st Street, near San Pedro and Trinity streets. Here, he assaulted her and prevented her from escaping by beating her into submission. Even though Beth fought back, he was able to overwhelm her with his superior strength. While she was on the floor, Morrison stated that he planned to sodomize her and Beth began struggling once again. This time, he hit her so hard that she passed out.

The tape then went on the describe how Morrison had gotten a paring knife, a large butcher knife and some rope and had returned to the room to find Beth conscious again. She tried to scream, but he stuffed her underpants into her mouth and tied her up. While she was naked and bound, he began jabbing her over and over again with the knives, cutting and slashing her. One of the lacerations even extended from both sides of her mouth and across her face. By this time, the girl was dead.

Morrison then laid boards across the bathtub and cut Beth in half with a butcher knife, letting the blood drain into the tub. He wrapped the two pieces of the body in a tablecloth and a shower curtain and put it into the trunk of his car. From there, he drove to the vacant lot and left the body to be found later that morning.

St. John discovered that this same suspect, Al Morrison, had also come to the attention of Detective Joel Lesnick of the sheriff's department for another brutal murder. Lesnick had learned that both Al Morrison and Arnold Smith were aliases of a man named Jack Anderson Wilson, a tall and lanky alcoholic with a crippled leg and a record for sex offenses and robbery. Lesnick guessed that, "As the years went on, Smith's ego drew him closer, not to confessing, but wanting to tell someone in a roundabout way what he got away with primarily through luck."

After hearing the record of events on the tape recordings, St. John became determined to track down "Arnold Smith." He checked into the story of "Al Morrison," the alleged violent pervert, and could find no proof that he existed, thus confirming the idea that Smith (Jack Wilson) was actually the killer. St. John began to leave no stone unturned in his pursuit to link Jack Wilson to Elizabeth Short.

In the midst of the investigation, word came that the press had gotten wind of the fact that a new suspect had emerged in the Dahlia case. Even after all of the years (at this point the mid-1980s) that had passed, interest in the case was still strong. At this point, St. John realized that it was imperative that he move quickly before Wilson/Smith became spooked. The informant did not know where Smith lived but he left messages for him in a café. Several messages were left but Smith never returned them, possibly because he found out about the police surveillance of the restaurant. Finally, the informant received a reply and a meeting was set with Smith. The police made plans to pick him up for questioning.

Unfortunately, just before the meeting took place, Smith passed out while smoking in bed at the Holland Hotel, where he was staying. He was burned to death and the flames destroyed the photos and belongings that supposedly belonged to Beth Short – and possibly all hope that her murder would ever be solved.

A short time after Wilson's body was released to the county for cremation, the Los Angeles District Attorney's office was presented with a file on the matter. The prosecutor's office summed up the case by saying, "The case cannot be officially closed due to the death of the individual considered a suspect. While the documentation appears to link this individual with the homicide of Elizabeth Short, his death, however, precludes the opportunity of an interview to obtain from him the corroboration…Therefore, any conclusion as to his criminal involvement is circumstantial, and unfortunately, the suspect cannot be charged or tried, due to his demise. However, despite this inconclusiveness, the circumstantial evidence is of such a nature that were this suspect alive, an intensive inquiry would be recommended. And depending upon the outcome of such an inquiry, it is conceivable that Jack Wilson might have been charged as a suspect in the murder of Elizabeth Short – also known as the Black Dahlia."

Since the time of her death in 1947, many books have been written and many theories have been expressed about who killed Elizabeth Short. But no matter the number of theories, books and documentaries on the case, to this date it remains unsolved. No one has ever been charged with her murder and, as far as we know, her death has never been avenged. She remains an elusive mystery from the dark side of Hollywood – and the even darker side of the American landscape.

Perhaps this is why her ghost still walks at the Biltmore Hotel and her specter still looms over the shadowy streets of Hollywood. Even today, an occasional man who stays at the Biltmore encounters the spectral image of a woman in a black dress, sometimes in the lobby, waiting in the corridors or even riding to the sixth floor on the elevator. What is she trying to tell us? Are there still clues to the identity of her killer that have never been found?

Or does the Black Dahlia simply wish to continue the mystery that was created more than 60 years ago? For sadly, Beth found the fame in death that she never managed to achieve in life.

VANISHED!
THE UNSOLVED DISAPPEARANCE OF JEAN SPANGLER

Jean Elizabeth Spangler was one of the many hundreds of pretty, talented girls who come to Hollywood hoping for their big break in the movies. While she waited for it, Jean studied, worked hard, and acted regularly in the movies as a bit player and an extra. Jean had been with the Earl Carroll Theatre and Florentine Gardens as a dancer, earning money to support her mother and 5-year-old daughter, Christine, who had been born during World War II. Jean's marriage broke up soon after the war ended.

In 1949, Jean was 27 years old, a tall brunette with an oval-shaped face, large dark eyes, and a wide, sensuous mouth. She had been raised in Los Angeles, attended Franklin High School, and got a job after graduation as a legal secretary, but gave that up to try and make it in the movie business. She was a beautiful young woman but, unfortunately, had little to set her apart from the other beautiful young women who arrived in Hollywood every day – until the unthinkable happened. Jean Spangler vanished without a trace one day and the short period of fame that followed turned out to be tragically more than she ever found on the silver screen.

On October 7, 1949, Jean left her home in Los Angeles around 5 p.m., leaving her daughter with her sister-in-law, Sophie Spangler, who lived with Jean, her mother, daughter, and her brother. She told Sophie that she was going to meet her former

Pretty Hollywood showgirl Jean Spangler

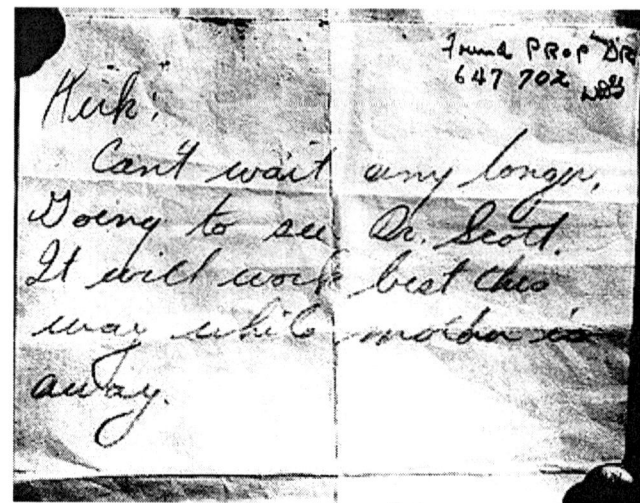

(Left) Jean's purse was found in Griffith Park and contained the mysterious letter to "Kirk". No trace of this man -- or of Jean Spangler -- was ever found.

husband to talk about his child support payment that had been due a week before, then go on to work on a movie set. Jean had recently finished work on a small role in the film "The Petty Girl" and had been in a good mood. She seemed nervous as she kissed her daughter goodbye and left the house. She was wearing a wool blouse, green slacks, and a while coat.

That was the last time that Jean's family ever saw her alive.

When Jean failed to return home that night, Sophie became worried. Jean had a number of friends and went out a great deal, but she never before failed to telephone home, much less stay out all night. Jean's mother was visiting family in Kentucky at the time, so Sophie went to the police and filed a missing person report the next day.

Jean had told Sophie that she was going to work on a movie set after she met with her former husband, but the police checked and found that none of the studios had any work in progress or were even open on the evening of October 7. They next checked into her story about meeting her ex-husband. Jean had been through a long custody battle with him, and won custody of Christine in 1948. Dexter Benner, her former husband, had been awarded custody in 1946 at the time of the divorce. Police questioned Benner about her statement to her sister-in-law that she was going to meet him about the overdue child support payment. He said that he had not seen his former wife for several weeks before Spangler disappeared. His new wife, Lynn Lasky Benner, stated that he was with her at the time of Jean's disappearance.

Two days after she vanished, on October 9, Jean's purse was found near the entrance gate to Griffith Park in Los Angeles with both of the straps on one side torn loose as if it had been ripped from her arm. There was no money inside (Sophie told the police that Jean had no money when she left the house, ruling out robbery as a motive in her disappearance), but it did contain her membership cards in the Screen Actors Guild, the Screen Extras Guild, her driver's license, and a curious note. The note read:

Kirk – can't wait any longer. Going to see Dr. Scott. It will work out best this way while mother is away,

The note ended with a comma and was apparently unfinished. A police handwriting expert was able to determine that the note was in Jean's handwriting.

More than 60 police officers and over 100 volunteers searched the sprawling park, but no other clues were found. Detectives began working to track down any leads they could find about Jean's life and an all-points bulletin was issued. Photographs of the young woman were sent to newspapers and soon, witnesses began to come forward, disclosing the secrets of the aspiring actress' tangled and complicated life.

One of those witnesses was Hollywood attorney Albert Pearlson, who had employed Jean as a legal secretary for a short time. He told the police that Jean had met Dexter Benner in high school and the mismatched couple became romantically involved. Jean was outgoing and her boyfriend was an introvert. They were married in 1942, shortly after Jean started working at Pearlson's law firm. He told detectives that about six months after the wedding, Jean came to him looking for a divorce. Pearlson tried to talk her out of it, but Jean was insistent. A complaint was filed, but the couple reconciled and the divorce hearing was removed from the calendar. Benner went into the Army during the war and about six months after he left, Christine was born. Then, after she had broken into the movies as a bit player, Jean began to be seen around the Hollywood nightspots.

In 1944, Benner was discharged from the military and he sent word to Jean that he was coming home. Even though she no longer worked for the attorney, Jean came to Pearlson and pleaded with him for help. She had apparently fallen in love with a first lieutenant in the Air Corps. Benner was under the impression that she had saved the money he had been sending to her, and that she owned a car. However, Jean had spent all of the money and had wrecked the car months before. Pearlson agreed to help her and when Benner returned to L.A., Jean met him when he arrived and brought him straight to Pearlson's office to tell him that she wanted a divorce. Benner agreed and custody of Christine was given to him.

Four days later, Jean returned to Pearlson's office with a black eye and a bruised face. She said that her boyfriend had beaten her and threatened to kill her if she ever left him like she had her husband. The lawyer called him and issued him a warning, but didn't hear from Jean again until a year later. By that time, she had broken off the affair with the Air Corps officer and wanted Pearlson to help her file suit to regain custody of her daughter. She lost the initial suit, but sued again in May 1948 and won. Benner decided not to fight the second time after Pearlson convinced him that Jean was a troubled young woman and having Christine might help her.

Other witnesses came forward, including the owner of a store near where Jean lived. A cashier at the store, Lillian Marks, said that Jean had wandered around the place for a few minutes around 5:30 p.m. on October 7, as if waiting, or looking, for someone. She saw no one approach her and she did not notice when Jean actually left.

The only definite clue that the police had to work with was the mysterious note, but neither Jean's family nor her friends knew anyone by those names. Jean's mother, Florence, returned to Los Angeles and told police that someone named Kirk had picked up Jean at her house twice, but he stayed in his car and didn't come in. Police searched for Kirk and the only person in the Hollywood community that they could think of with that name was Kirk Douglas, who had starred in a recent film "Young Man With A Horn" in which Jean had a small part. Douglas was vacationing in Palm Springs and heard about the disappearance. He called the police and told them he was not the Kirk mentioned in the note. Douglas was interviewed by the head of the investigating team and stated that he had heard the name and that Spangler had been an extra in his new film, but he didn't know her personally. He said that he didn't remember her at all until a friend reminded him that she had been in the film. He told the detectives, "If she's the one I'm thinking about, I remember talking to her. But I never saw her before or since and I never went out with her."

Exhausting their leads in the search for "Kirk," the police turned to finding "Dr. Scott." They contacted and questioned every doctor with the last name Scott in L.A., but none of them had a patient with the last name Spangler or Benner. Attorney Pearlson recalled that Jean had called her

Air Corps officer boyfriend "Scotty," but the lawyer said that she not seen him since 1946.

Some of Jean's friends told the police that they suspected that she had been pregnant when she disappeared and that she had talked to one or two of them about getting an abortion, which was illegal at that time. The police talked with several people who frequented the same nightclubs and bars that Jean did who told them they had heard that there was a former medical student known as "Doc," who had said that he would perform abortions for money. Police searched for "Doc" with the idea that Jean had gone to him to have an abortion and died as a result, but they not could locate him or anyone who would say that they had actually met him. The idea of her getting an abortion while her mother was out of town did seem to make sense in conjunction with the note that had been found in her purse, but nothing solid ever came from this line of investigation.

As the investigation was running into dead ends in Los Angeles, tips began coming in from places that kept the investigators busy. Each one of them was checked out over the weeks and months that followed, no matter how flimsy or strange. Rumors had her in Mexico City, the San Fernando Valley, Yuma, Ariz., San Francisco, and Fresno. A psychic contacted the police and offered her services and another man claimed that he could locate her body with a radar gadget.

One of the most reliable sightings paired Jean with Davy Ogul, an associate of Mickey Cohen, in Palm Springs, Calif. (Jean was connected to Cohen in other ways, too. She had allegedly once dated Johnny Stompanato) Ogul, who was under indictment for conspiracy, had disappeared two days before Jean did. This led police to investigate the possibility that Jean had left town and met Ogul in Palm Springs, then left California with him. In 1950 a customs agent in El Paso, Tex., had reported seeing Ogul and a woman who looked like Jean in a hotel in El Paso. But neither Davy Ogul nor Jean Spangler's name appeared on the hotel register and she could not be located in El Paso.

All of the leads and angles in the case eventually reached a dead end. The police were never able to identify any secret boyfriend, or the mysterious doctor. It seemed likely that at some point, Jean had gotten mixed up in something that probably led to her death. The authorities continued the search and circulated Jean's picture for several years in an unsuccessful attempt to find her, but nothing turned up. Most veteran detectives came to believe that she was dead.

Following Jean's disappearance, a bitter custody battle for Christine began between Dexter Benner and Jean's mother, Florence Spangler. The courts awarded the child to her father, but Florence was given visitation rights, which Benner fought against. He claimed in his suit that Christine had been "abandoned" by her mother and that Florence was a negative influence on her. The case wore on until 1953, when Benner suddenly vanished with his wife and the child. He was never found.

Not every detective gave up on the idea of finding Jean Spangler alive. Nationwide bulletins were still issued for years after she vanished and Florence Spangler periodically appealed to the press for information about her daughter's fate. She even enlisted the aid of gossip columnist Louella Parsons, who appeared on television with photos of Jean and offered a $1,000 reward for information. But no information ever came and Florence, who hung onto the desperate hope that Jean might still be alive, eventually resigned herself to the fact that her daughter had been murdered.

To this day, Jean Spangler is still listed as a missing person with the Los Angeles Police Department and her case file remains open.

THE UNSOLVED MURDER OF HELENE JEROME

One of the strangest – and least remembered – unsolved murders in Hollywood history occurred in August 1958, in a hotel apartment just a few steps away from the bright lights of Hollywood Boulevard. The victim was Helene Adele Jerome, once a well-known British stage star who had been dreaming of making a comeback in Hollywood. Tragically, that comeback was not meant to be.

Helene Jerome was born in New York, but was raised in England. She studied at London's famous Royal Academy of the Dramatic Art, which

(Left) Helene Jerome's hotel at the time of her death. The killer gained access to her room using a ground floor entrance that was not seen by the desk clerk.

Hollywood Boulevard in 1958

spawned some of the most recognized actors in the world, including Sir Laurence Olivier and Paul Robeson. For many years, Helene enjoyed a successful stage career, touring the world with many British companies and achieving considerable fame in the 1930s. In her prime, she was a tall, striking woman with an aristocratic air about her. Helene had appeared in a few films during her career, including "The Bitter Tea of General Yen" with Barbara Stanwyck and "Klondike Annie" with Mae West. At a very young-looking 50, she hoped to find some new, more substantial roles on the Hollywood screen.

In the years before her death, Helene had been separated from her husband, Edwin Jerome, a character actor on stage and in a few Hollywood films, like "The Man Who Understood Women" and "The Three Faces of Eve." However, the couple had remained on good terms and the elderly actor (Jerome was 20 years older than his wife), worried about her constantly and devoted himself to her well-being. He worked hard, using his industry contacts, to try and find some roles for her in new productions. He hoped, according to friends, that he and Helene would eventually reconcile.

On Wednesday morning, August 27, 1958, Jerome called the hotel where Helene was staying, but there was no answer on her line. He checked with the hotel operator and learned that her extension had been off the hook for quite some time. Jerome was immediately worried. Helene's health had been up and down for several years and recently, she had been under a doctor's care. After several more attempts to reach her by telephone, Jerome went to her hotel at 1738 North Las Palmas Ave., shortly after 1:30 p.m. on a sweltering Southern California afternoon, one of the hottest days of the year.

Instead of passing through the lobby, Jerome approached Helene's ground floor rear apartment, which had its own private entrance, by way of a garden path. He found the screen door unlatched, noting that the screen itself had been torn. The inner door stood slightly open. When he pushed it open and entered the apartment, he was stunned to see his wife dead, lying completely naked on the bed, only partially covered with the edge of a blanket. Helene was stretched out on her back with her head against the headboard, face turned toward the wall, her left arm and leg dangling a little over the edge of the bed.

Jerome ran from the room, dashed to the hotel lobby, and immediately called the police. An ambulance and a police car arrived almost simultaneously and medical officers quickly confirmed that Helene was dead. Her body was stiff and cold, as both the air conditioner and an electric fan in the bedroom had been turned on high.

Edwin Jerome was questioned by LAPD officer Jerry Jacobsen. The actor sat huddled in a chair, obviously in shock over what the police first believed was a natural death, or at worst, a suicide. Jerome told the officer that he had last seen Helene the previous night, when she seemed to be fine. She had been under the weather, but not seriously ill, and her death came as a total shock to him. Officer Jacobsen noted the array of pill bottles next to the bed, which matched those found in the bathroom medicine cabinet, and asked Jerome if it was possible that his wife might have taken her own life. Jerome sadly shrugged, "Poor Helene wasn't herself at times."

Still believing that Helene might have died of natural causes, or overdosed on pills, her body was examined and one of the officers noted a slight bruise on the dead woman's neck. As this was being discovered, Jerome was telling Jacobsen that he had never known his wife to sleep in the nude. When he had left her the night before, she was wearing blue flowered pajamas with a robe over them. He was also certain that a brassiere and panties had been resting on a chair, when she had placed them after getting ready for bed. The pajamas and the underwear were now tossed on an overstuffed chair and the robe was in a crumpled heap in the corner. Jacobsen also noted the torn screen in the door, and found another torn screen in the bathroom window. After that, the young patrolman called the Hollywood detective bureau to report that, while the death might still be routine, there were some circumstances that needed to be checked out by the homicide squad.

When the homicide detectives, Robert Beck and James Close, arrived Helen's doctor, who had been summoned by Edwin Jerome, was examining the body as Jacobsen stood by watching. The doctor clearly seemed puzzled by the death. He said that he had been treating the actress for asthma and some other minor ailments, but that Helene's heart had been in good condition. The doctor found no indications of an overdose and, while he also noted the bruise, it seemed very slight. However, Edwin Jerome did say that he had not seen the bruise while he was visiting her on the previous evening. Finally, the doctor stated that the coroner needed to be called. He was unable to sign a death certificate under those conditions.

Detectives questioned the night clerk at the hotel, Orio Janes, who further complicated the case. He told the officers that he had seen Helene come home, alone, fully dressed and slightly intoxicated, about 3 a.m. About an hour later, he noted that Helene's telephone was off the hook, so he walked around the garden path and looked into her apartment to make sure that she was all right. According to his story, he saw a man in bed with Helene in the well-lighted room. Both were naked and the clerk, not wanting to interrupt anything or be seen, hurried back to his desk in the lobby. About a half-hour later, he said he saw a tall, bushy-haired, neatly dressed man walking quickly away from the apartment. Janes also added that a man of similar description had phoned Helene from the hotel desk earlier in the evening and had given his name as "George" when her husband had answered. Edwin Jerome had apparently told him that Helene was sleeping and couldn't be disturbed. Later, a neighbor had seen the man around 2 a.m., knocking on Helene's door and calling her name.

Beck and Close realized that the situation sounded a lot like two other current cases, unsolved sex killings of lone women in their apartments. The possible murder of Helene Jerome was shaping up as another one. The detectives reported the case to their commanding officer as a possible homicide and crime lab technicians began to arrive at the apartment. Meanwhile, Beck and Close questioned Edwin Jerome more closely as he filled them in on his wife's background.

Edwin said he and Helene had been married for about 15 years, but had been separated "on and off" for the past two or three years. Jerome had been living in Hollywood for about five years, but his wife had only recently moved there. He insisted that they had been on close and friendly terms. He paid his wife's rent, gave her money for groceries, and there had never been any discussion of divorce. They simply never lived together because of what he called Helene's "vile temperament," which he explained was caused by a long history of alcoholism and emotional problems. It was these two factors that contributed to the failure of her stage career. Helene had been treated in various institutions over the years and had attempted suicide several times. He had tried to help her find work in Hollywood, but no producer or director wanted to work with her because her reputation for being undependable had preceded her.

Jerome assured the detectives that there was no other man in her life and that while he had not been sexually involved with her in at least seven years, he didn't believe that anyone else had either. Of course, the detectives knew that this was wishful thinking on the part of the aging actor, but they kept that information to themselves. Jerome did admit that from time to time, Helene had taken a "motherly interest" in some young actor or writer and recently, there had been a young actor and producer that had been visiting her that Helene called her "protégé."

Beck and Close went back to the night clerk, and also spoke to a number of the hotel's staff, who gave a different description of Helene's life than her estranged husband had. They recalled that Helene had lived a very active nightlife. She stayed out late almost every night, leaving after Jerome had come and gone. She met various men and was spotted in bars up and down Hollywood Boulevard. The night clerk described Helene's last early morning visitor as about 25 to 30 years old, tall, slim and very dark complexioned, possibly a Latino, with a full head of dark hair and prominent ears. He had been wearing a dark sports coat and dark slacks. Was he her killer? Or had Helene actually died from natural causes?

The next morning, the suspicions of the two detectives were confirmed when Dr. Frederick D. Newbarr of the L.A. coroner's staff reported that Helene had died at the hands of a strangler. An autopsy revealed that the cartilage in her neck was fractured and her windpipe had been crushed. The report also stated that the dead woman's body contained a high alcohol level.

Detectives brought all of the witnesses in the case to the station, questioned then further, and then fingerprinted them for comparison with the prints founds in the murder room. Helene's young "protégé," whom the police were anxious to speak with, couldn't be located right away. No one knew his name or where he worked, but detectives began canvassing taverns and cocktail lounges in the vicinity of the hotel in hopes of tracking him down and picking up Helene's trail during her last night among the living.

In the meantime, detectives decided to fill in Edwin Jerome on his wife's nocturnal activities. He nearly collapsed in shock, perhaps more shaken by the fact that his wife was out late at night picking up strange men than by the fact that she was a murder victim. He had no idea who these men might be, who "George" might have been who telephoned from the hotel lobby, or how he could have missed the warning signs in Helene's behavior. At least now he understood, he told detectives, why she always insisted that he call her first before coming over to her apartment. She always got angry and upset if he dropped in unexpectedly.

Bob Beck and Jim Close pounded the pavements along Hollywood Boulevard and Highland Avenue, locating a score of bartenders and tavern regulars who knew Helene and had seen her regularly. They soon caught up with the slain woman's 26-year-old "protégé," a communications technician for a recording company. He was shocked to learn that Helene had been murdered and swore that he could offer no information about the crime. He referred to Helene as "just a good friend" and said that he had not seen her in a few days. On Tuesday night, he said he and a friend had dropped in at the apartment of one of Helene's neighbors and shared a bottle of wine with her. They left at about 9:30 p.m. and the technician said he returned to his own apartment and stayed there the rest of the night.

The "protégé" didn't fit the description of the man who had been seen by the desk clerk, but he seemed nervous and evasive, which interested the detectives. He denied that he had ever had sex with Helene, whom he said was too old for him, although he described her as "practically a nymphomaniac, especially when she was drinking." He confided that he had once saved Helene's life when she had attempted suicide with sleeping pills, because another young man had spurned her sexual advances. The technician insisted that he had no idea who might have killed Helene and knew only the first names of a few of her other male friends – although he knew no one named "George." He also didn't recall seeing the man, based on the description the desk clerks had given the police. After the detectives checked the young man's alibi, he was released, but warned not to leave town until the investigation was completed.

Investigators continued to try and find the dark complexioned man who had been seen at the hotel, and "George," who might have been the same man. Witnesses supplied descriptions of him and LAPD techs managed to find a set of partial fingerprints in the room that didn't match Helene, Jerome, or any of the staff at the hotel. The technicians believed that they might belong to the killer.

At 1 a.m. on the Saturday after the murder, a patrolman named Adam Saifan picked up a frightened 25-year-old man from Texas. He was a tall, dapper, mustached young man who, after initially denying it, admitted that he had left a bar with Helene on the night she had been killed. However, he swore that he had parted company with her at the corner of Yucca and Las Palmas. He stated that he had romanced Helene in the bar, and bought her drinks, hoping that she would go home with him. When they left the bar, though, she claimed that she was not feeling well, that the hot weather was bothering her asthma. The young man stated that he walked her most of the way to her hotel, hoping to convince her to change her mind, but that he left her to walk the last block or so by herself. He arrived back at his own apartment at around 2:30 a.m., a fact that his roommate could confirm.

The suspect consented to a polygraph test, but he was so nervous during the test (as well as badly hung over from a long night of drinking), that it turned out to be inconclusive. His roommate, who had a police record, was picked up and he substantiated his friend's story. Staff members from Helene's hotel were brought in to try and identify the suspect, but they didn't recognize him. After several more days of questioning, as well as a fingerprint comparison, the young man was released. He immediately returned home to Texas.

Two more suspects were questioned and released. One was the night manager of a nearby business who reportedly bragged about having sex with Helene and the other an ex-convict from Ohio who also claimed to have slept with Helene. He had a record of breaking and entering but, like the night manager, was able to supply an alibi for the night of the murder. The frustrated detectives questioned a score of men whose names appeared in Helene's address book. Several of the potential suspects offered to undergo a lie detector test, as did Edwin Jerome and Helene's "protégé." All of them were cleared.

Edwin Jerome never recovered from the shock of his wife's murder. His health began to fail a short time later and he died in September 1959 from natural causes. From time to time, the homicide squad reopened the file on the case, based on tips and leads, but the killer that the night clerk saw in bed with the British actress was never identified. All of the leads in the case eventually dried up and the slaying of Helene Jerome remains to this day, and probably always will, another of Hollywood's unsolved mysteries.

FASTER THAN A SPEEDING BULLET?
THE UNSOLVED MYSTERY OF GEORGE REEVES

Superman died at 1:59 am on June 16, 1959. Not the comic book character, of course, but the man who personified the "real" Superman for an entire generation of television fans. George Reeves, it was discovered, was not faster than a speeding bullet after all. Even though the initial coroner's report listed Reeves' death as an "indicated suicide," after nearly five decades there are many who do not believe that he killed himself. The death of George Reeves remains one of Hollywood's most compelling unsolved mysteries, combining rumors of murder, conspiracy, cover-ups – and a lingering ghost.

He was born George Keefer Brewer in Woolstock, Iowa, the son of Don Brewer and Helen

Lescher, just five months into his parents' marriage. The pair separated soon afterward, and Helen moved back home to Galesburg, Ill. A short time later, George's mother moved to Pasadena, Calif., to stay with her sister and there, she met and married Frank Bessolo. In 1927, Frank adopted George as his son, and the boy took on his new stepfather's last name to become George Bessolo. Helen's marriage to Frank lasted 15 years and ended in divorce while George was away visiting relatives. Helen told George that Frank had committed suicide. It would not be until George joined the Army during World War II that he discovered a number of things that his mother had hidden from him. She had concealed his true birth date and the fact that Bessolo was still alive and that he was actually George's stepfather, not his biological father. This information disturbed Reeves so much that he did not speak to her through most of the 1940s.

Growing up, George was an accomplished athlete and in 1932, entered the Golden Gloves boxing competition against his mother's wishes. He did well in the event and went to the Olympics in L.A. in 1932. After having his nose broken nine times, he hung up his gloves and decided to pursue acting. He had started acting and singing in high school and continued performing on stage as a student at Pasadena Junior College. Accepted by the Pasadena Playhouse, Reeves had prominent roles. His film career began in 1939, when he was cast as Stuart Tarleton, one of Vivien Leigh's suitors in "Gone with the Wind." It was a minor role, but he and Fred Crane, both with brightly dyed red hair as "the Tarleton Twins," were in the film's opening scenes. He was contracted to Warner Brothers at the time, and the actor's professional name became "George Reeves." He married actress Ellanora Needles in 1940, but had no children with her during their nine-year marriage.

Reeves starred in a number of two-reel short subjects and appeared in several low budget pictures, including two with Ronald Reagan and three with James Cagney. Warner Brothers loaned him out to co-star with Merle Oberon in "Lydia," a box-office failure. After his Warner Brothers contract expired, he signed on with Twentieth Century-Fox but was released after only a handful of films. He freelanced, appearing in five Hopalong Cassidy westerns before he was cast as Lieutenant John Summers, opposite Claudette Colbert, in "So Proudly We Hail!" The war drama for Paramount won him critical acclaim for the role and considerable publicity.

George Reeves

Reeves was drafted into the Army about 18 months after the Japanese attack on Pearl Harbor. In late 1943, he was transferred to the U.S. Army Air Forces (USAAF) and assigned to the Broadway show "Winged Victory," produced by and for the USAAF. A long Broadway run followed, as well as a national tour and a movie version of the play. He was later transferred to the USAAF's First Motion Picture Unit, where he made training films.

After the war ended, Reeves returned to Hollywood but many studios had slowed down their production schedules and others had shut down completely. He took work where he could

(Left) A publicity shot for the "Superman" Series (Right) The cast of "Superman" in a happy moment

find it, including in some outdoor thrillers with Ralph Byrd and a serial called "The Adventures of Sir Galahad." These were low-budget films for which Reeves simply fit the rugged casting requirements and, with his retentive memory for dialogue, could do well under rushed production conditions. He also played against type with one villainous role as a gold hunter in a Johnny Weissmuller "Jungle Jim" film, which turned out to be a moderate success for a B-picture.

In the autumn of 1949, Reeves (whose divorce had recently become final) decided to move to New York. While there, he performed on several live television anthology programs, as well as on radio. Reeves returned to Hollywood in April 1951, specifically for a role in a Fritz Lang film, "Rancho Notorious."

In June 1951, Reeves career permanently changed when he was offered the role of Superman in a television series. He was initially reluctant to take the role because, like many actors of his time, he considered television to be unimportant and believed that few would see his work. He worked for low pay, even as the star, and was only paid during the weeks of production. The half-hour films were shot on tight schedules of at least two shows every six days.

His career as Superman began with "Superman and the Mole Men," a film that was designed to be a theatrical picture and the pilot for the television series. Immediately after it was completed, Reeves and the crew began production of the first season's episodes, shot over 13 weeks during the summer of 1951. The series began airing in 1952 and Reeves was astonished when he became a national celebrity in his role as newspaper reporter Clark Kent, who was really Superman. In 1957, the struggling ABC Network picked up the show for national broadcast, which gave him and the rest of the cast even greater visibility. His portrayal of the character became wildly popular and everywhere he went, children and adults alike clamored to meet him and obtain his autograph.

Reeves never resented doing personal appearances as Superman, especially since they paid money beyond his meager salary, and his affection for young fans was genuine. Reeves took his role model status seriously, avoiding cigarettes where children could see him, eventually quitting smoking altogether, and keeping his private life very discreet. But Reeves loved women and many who were close to him stated that he broke the hearts of many of the actresses that he worked with. In 1951, he had begun a romantic relationship with a married ex-showgirl, Toni Mannix, wife of

MGM general manager Eddie Mannix. Some believe this affair may have cost Reeves his life.

Whether or not Reeves resented being typecast as Superman, he played the heroic role to the hilt, and sometimes not just on screen. With Toni Mannix, Reeves worked tirelessly to raise money to fight myasthenia gravis, a neuromuscular disease leading to fluctuating muscle weakness and fatigue. He served as national chairman for the Myasthenia Gravis Foundation in 1955. During the second season, Reeves appeared in a short film for the US Treasury Department, in which he caught some crooks and told kids why they should invest in government savings stamps.

George Reeves and Toni Mannix. Many believe that Reeves' affair with the studio bosses' wife may have cost him his life.

Jack Larson, who played Jimmy Olsen in the series, recalled that Reeves was always a gentleman to the other actors in the show, although he loved to play practical jokes on the cast and crew. He insisted that the original Lois Lane, Phyllis Coates, be given equal billing in the credits in the first season. When Coates was replaced by Noel Neill, Reeves quietly defended her nervousness on her first day when he felt that the director was being too harsh with her. He also stood by Robert Shayne (who played Police Inspector William "Bill" Henderson) when Shayne was subpoenaed by FBI agents on the set of Superman. Shayne's political activism in the Screen Actors Guild in the 1940s was used by his bitter ex-wife as an excuse to lie and say that he was a member of the Communist Party. On the other hand, Reeves delighted in standing outside camera range, making faces at the other cast members to see whether he could break them up. By all accounts, there was a strong camaraderie among the principal actors.

After two seasons, though, Reeves began to get tired of both the Superman role and the low salary he was receiving. He was now 40 and he wanted to move on with his career. He established his own production company and conceived a television adventure series called "Port of Entry," which would be filmed on location in Hawaii and Mexico. He wrote the pilot script himself and prepared to start pre-production work when the producers of "Superman" offered him a large salary increase. Not wanting to turn it down, he returned to the role.

In 1957, there was talk of producing a new theatrical Superman film and possibly discontinuing the series, but this never happened. Instead, another season of the show was developed. By mid-1959, contracts were signed, costumes re-fitted, and new scripts were assigned to the writers. Noel Neill was quoted as saying that the cast was ready to do a new season of the still-popular show. Producers reportedly promised Reeves that the new programs would be as serious and action-packed as the first season, guaranteed him creative input, and slated him to direct several of the new shows, as he had the final three episodes of the 1957 season.

In between the first and second seasons of "Superman," Reeves got sporadic acting assignments on television and in two feature films,

"Forever Female" and "The Blue Gardenia." But by the time the series was airing nationwide, Reeves found himself so associated with Superman and Clark Kent that it was difficult for him to find other roles. He also sang on the "Tony Bennett Show" in August 1956 and appeared in an episode of "I Love Lucy" as Superman. His good friend Bill Walsh, a producer at Disney Studios, gave Reeves a prominent role in "Westward Ho the Wagons," in which Reeves wore a beard and mustache. It was to be his final feature film appearance.

In spite of his sporadic film and television work, and Superman appearances, Reeves was not doing well financially. In 1958, he broke off his affair with Toni Mannix and announced his engagement to society girl, Leonore Lemmon. He complained to friends, columnists, and his mother of his financial problems. The royalties that he was receiving from the syndication of "Superman" were insubstantial, especially in view of his lifestyle. Apparently, the planned new season of the show, as well as his appearances were a much-needed lifeline. Reeves needed money and the only option that he had to make any was by portraying Superman, which he reluctantly agreed to do.

Just three days after his death, he was to have returned to the boxing ring with light heavyweight champion Archie Moore. The exhibition match was to be played on television so that viewers across the country could tune in to see Superman beat the champ. Reeves told reporters, "the Archie Moore fight will be the highlight of my life."

After the fight, he and Leonore were to be married. They planned to honeymoon in Spain and then go to Australia for six weeks, where Reeves would pick up over $20,000 for appearances as Superman. The series had just been sold to an Australian television network and local viewers were clamoring to meet the "Man of Steel."

Reeves would then return to Hollywood later in the year to star in a feature film that he was putting together, which he would also direct. He was then scheduled to shoot new episodes of "Superman" and receive another hefty salary increase. Things seemed to being going well for Reeves, even while being stuck playing Superman, and some said that he seemed to have everything to live for.

But all was not perfect in his life. In the three months before his death, Reeves was involved in three mysterious automobile mishaps that almost cost him his life. The first time, his car was nearly crushed by two trucks on the freeway. Another time, a speeding car nearly killed him, but he survived thanks to his quick, athletic reflexes. The third time, Reeves' brakes failed on a narrow, twisting road. All of the brake fluid, it was discovered, was gone from the hydraulic system, in spite of the fact that an examination by a mechanic found the system was in perfect working order.

"When the mechanic suggested that someone had pumped out the fluid, George dismissed the notion," said Arthur Weissman, Reeves' best friend and business manager. Weissman always remained convinced that his friend had been murdered. He

George Reeves with his car. In the months before his death, the actor was involved in three suspicious car accidents, leading many to believe that someone was trying to kill him.

tried to convince Reeves that he needed to be careful, but Reeves brushed off the warnings.

About a month later, he began to receive death threats on his unlisted telephone line. Most of them came late at night and there were sometimes 20 or more each day. Often, the anonymous caller wh would simply hang up when Reeves answered. They said nothing, but after a few graphic and detailed threats, Reeves knew it was the same person. Nervous after the near misses in his car, Reeves filed a report with the Beverly Hills Police Department and a complaint with the L.A. District Attorney's Office. He even went so far as to suggest a suspect, his former lover, Toni Mannix.

It was never explained why Reeves openly pointed the finger at Toni Mannix. Their relationship had never been a public one but it was a badly kept secret in Hollywood. Eddie Mannix was likely aware of the situation and didn't like it. According to Reeves' friend Arthur Weissman, Mannix was a disliked, but feared, member of the Hollywood movie industry. Weissman believed that the executive was responsible not only for the threats that Reeves received, but also for the attempts on his life.

The D.A.'s office investigated the complaint filed by Reeves, including his accusations of Toni Mannix's involvement, but soon discovered that both Reeves and Toni were receiving telephone threats and crank calls. When that was disclosed, many people assumed that it was Eddie Mannix who had instigated the calls through employees or hired thugs.

Weissman believed that Mannix was behind Reeve's near-fatal auto crashes, as well. In the film and theater business, Mannix had access to a lot of people outside of the general public. For a price, these men could maneuver two trucks close together on the highway, or could drain the brake fluid from someone's car. Furthermore, he was sure that Mannix also had access to someone who could arrange a murder, too.

On June 16, 1959, Lenore Lemmon served dinner at around 6:30 p.m. at Reeves' Benedict Canyon home. She had prepared the meal for Reeves and guest Robert Condon, a writer who

The modest home where George Reeves died. Was it suicide or murder?

was there to do an article on Reeves and his upcoming bout with Archie Moore. After dinner, they settled down in the living room to watch television. Around midnight, everyone went to bed. Around 1 a.m., a friend named Carol Von Ronkel came by the house with another friend, William Bliss. Even though the house was the frequent scene of parties and entertaining, Reeves did not want guests after midnight. However, Von Ronkel and Bliss banged on the door until Leonore got up and let them in. George also came downstairs in his bathrobe and yelled at them for showing up so late. After blowing off steam, he stayed with the guests for a while, had a drink, and then retired upstairs again. When he left, Leonore turned to the others who were present and said something along the lines of, "Well, he's sulking, he'll probably go up to his room and shoot himself."

The houseguests later heard a single gunshot. Bliss ran into the master bedroom and found George Reeves dead, lying across his bed, naked and face-up, his feet on the floor. This position has been attributed to Reeves sitting on the edge of the bed when he shot himself, after which his body fell back on the bed and the 9mm Luger pistol fell between his feet.

Superman was dead.

The Beverly Hills police report of the incident states that, while entertaining his fiancée and three others in his home, Reeves suddenly, without any explanation, left the room and impulsively committed suicide. The statements made to the police and the press by those at the house that night essentially agree. Quite some time passed before the police were summoned to the scene, although neither Leonore nor the other witnesses made any explanation for the delay. They claimed that the shock of the death, the lateness of the house, and their intoxication caused the delay – they had nothing to hide. Detectives did say that all of the witnesses were extremely inebriated, and that their coherent stories were very difficult to obtain.

In the press, Leonore attributed Reeves's apparent suicide to depression caused by his "failed career" and inability to find more work, which was clearly not the case. The witness statements and examination of the crime scene led to the conclusion that the death was self-inflicted. A more extensive official inquiry concluded that the death was indeed suicide. Reeves's will bequeathed his entire estate to Toni Mannix, much to Lemmon's surprise and devastation.

Many people at the time, and many more in later years, have refused to believe the idea that George Reeves would kill himself. Even though he believed his friend was murdered, Arthur Weissman surprisingly did not dispute the sequence of events offered by Leonore Lemmon and the other witnesses. He said that this was just how it happened, but that Reeves did not intend to kill himself. He explained that Reeves was just playing his favorite morbid game, a practic with a gun that was loaded with a blank. According to Weissman, that was why Leonore said what she did. All of Reeves' friends knew that when he was drinking, he would sometimes fire a blank at his head in a mock suicide attempt, making certain that his arm was far enough away so that he didn't get powder burns on his face. Weissman claimed that, unknown to Reeves, the blank was replaced by a real bullet by someone hired by Eddie Mannix.

Reeves' clandestine former girlfriend, Toni Mannix, was madly in love with him and according to Weissman, their relationship was an open Hollywood secret. It continued for years and then came to an end when George announced that he was marrying Leonore Lemmon. Friends said that Toni was "enraged" over this development and began bombarding Reeves with phone calls, making all sorts of threats. It was believed that both she and her husband, who was openly humiliated by Reeves over the affair, had the perfect opportunity to seek revenge, especially since Toni possessed a key to the Reeves house. The police never looked deeply into Weisman's claims of the switched bullet, believing instead that Reeves' death had been self-inflicted.

Among those who were unhappy with the findings of "indicated suicide" were Reeves' mother, Helen Bessolo. She retained the Nick Harris Detectives of Los Angeles to look into the case. At that time, a man named Milo Speriglio was a novice investigator at the firm and played a small role in the investigation. "Nearly everyone in Hollywood has always been led to believe that George Reeves' death was a suicide," he said in a later interview. "Not everyone believed it then, nor do they believe it now. I am one of those who does not." And neither did Helen Bessolo. She went to her grave in 1964 convinced that her son was murdered.

The Nick Harris Agency, which had been founded in Los Angeles before the FBI was even in existence, quickly came to believe that Reeves' death had been a homicide. Even based on the fact that many of the witnesses that night were intoxicated and incoherent, the detectives felt that they could rule out suicide. Unfortunately, though, the Beverly Hills Police investigators chose to ignore their findings. A review of the facts seemed to indicate the agency's suspicions were well founded. They also ruled out the idea of Reeves' "suicide game" as his cause of death – they believed that someone else was in the house at the time he died.

For one thing, the absence of powder burns

on Reeves' face showed that he did not hold the gun to his head, as the police report stated. For the weapon to have not left any facial burns, it had to have been at least a foot and a half away from Reeves' head, which is totally impractical in a suicide attempt. In addition, Reeves was discovered after his death on the bed, lying on his back. The single shell was found under his body. According to experts, self-inflicted gunshot wounds usually propel the victim forward and away from the expended bullet casing.

Speriglio made a careful examination of the police report and noticed that the bullet wound was described as "irregular." So, the agency reconstructed the bullet entry and exit. The slug had exited Reeves' head and was found lodged in the ceiling. His head, at the moment of death, would have had to have been twisted, making a self-inflicted shot improbable. Speriglio suspected that an intruder had entered Reeves' room and that the actor had found his gun. A struggle had followed and Reeves was shot. The intruder then escaped from the house unnoticed.

While interesting, this theory does not explain why the gun (normally loaded with blanks) had a bullet in it and how the intruder escaped from the house with other people inside.

Regardless of whether or not he killed himself, it was obvious that Reeves' death was never properly investigated. Police investigators never even bothered to take fingerprints at the scene and people like Arthur Weissman believed they were pressured to make it an "open and shut" case. George Reeves, according to the official findings, had committed suicide. But did he really?

We will never know for sure. In 1961, Reeves' body was exhumed and cremated, forever destroying whatever evidence was left behind. The death of George Reeves will always remain another unsolved Hollywood mystery.

Could this be why ghostly phenomena has been reported at the former Reeves house ever since his death? Many believe that the ghostly appearances by the actor lend credence to the idea that he was murdered. Over the years, occupants of the house have been plagued by not only the sound of a single gunshot that echoes in the darkness, but strange lights, and even the apparition of George Reeves.

After Reeves' death, real estate agents attempted to sell the house to settle the actor's estate. Unfortunately, though, they had trouble. Occupants would not stay long because they would report inexplicable noises in the upstairs bedroom where Reeves died. When they would go to investigate the sounds, they would find the room was not as they had left it. Often, the bedding would be torn off, clothing would be strewn about, and some reported the ominous odor of gunpowder in the air. One tenant also noticed that his German Shepherd would stand in the doorway of the room and bark furiously as though he could see something his owners could not. The phenomenon in the house was so widely witnessed that at one point, two L.A. County deputies were assigned to watch the place because neighbors had reported screams, gunshots, and lights going on and off in the empty house during the night.

New occupants moved out quickly, becoming completely unnerved after encountering Reeves' ghost, decked out in his Superman costume! The first couple that spotted him was not the last to see him either. Many later residents also saw the ghost and one couple became so frightened that they moved out of the house that same night. Later, the ghost was even reported on the front lawn by neighboring residents.

In the 1980s, while the house was being used as a set for a television show, the ghost made another startling appearance. He was seen by several of the actors and crewmembers before abruptly vanishing, furthering the mysterious elements of this strange and complicated case.

BIRTH OF A LEGEND
THE MYSTERIOUS DEATH OF MARILYN MONROE

There are few personalities of the Twentieth Century that have inspired as much enthusiasm and worship as Marilyn Monroe. She is one of Hollywood's greatest icons and the facts, rumors, and legends about her life and mysterious death are an integral part of Tinseltown's lore. Unquestionably, a portion of Marilyn's enduring fame stems from her sudden death at the age of 36. At first, most people agreed with the official verdict that her death was likely by suicide. But as the years have passed, he persistent questions about her demise have refused to go away. An increasing number of researchers have come to believe that her romantic relationships with the Kennedy clan, both John F. Kennedy and Robert Kennedy, might well have been the cause of her "suicide." Many of those who believe that she was murdered also believe in a conspiracy that was created to cover up the secret homicide. These lingering questions, doubts, and theories have turned the death of Marilyn Monroe into one of Hollywood's greatest unsolved mysteries.

She was born Norma Jeane Mortenson on June 1, 1926. Her mother, Gladys, had previously been married to a businessman, John Baker. She then wed a gas company meter man named Martin Mortenson. However, they had separated in 1925 and he had filed for divorce many months before Gladys became pregnant with Norma Jeane, making the baby's father one of a number of different candidates. During much of Norma Jeane's youth, the erratic Gladys was often institutionalized, which mean that Norma Jeane lived in foster homes and later, an orphanage.

In June 1942, to prevent being sent off to stay in another foster home, the 16-year-old Norma Jeane married James Doughtery, a 22-year-old aircraft factory worker. Doughtery was drafted and sent overseas during the war and Norma Jeane worked in a factory, inspecting parachutes. In 1944, she was photographed by the Army as a promotion to show women on the assembly line contributing to the war effort. One of the photographers asked to take further pictures of her and by the following spring, she had appeared on the covers of 33 national magazines. In July 1946, the would-be actress screen-tested for Twentieth Century Fox and was soon signed to a $75-per-week contract. The studio selected a new name for her, Marilyn Monroe, and gave her a minor part in the film "Scudda-Hoo! Scudda-Hay!" In September, she was granted her first divorce.

Marilyn only had a few small roles at Fox and after six months, her newcomer's option was dropped. She ended up over at Columbia Pictures (reportedly after being forced to work the "casting couch" option) where she signed a new contract for $125 per week. There, she earned a part in the musical "Ladies of the Chorus." Rumor has it that she ruined her chances on the lot because she refused to do special favors for studio mogul Harry Cohn. At this time, naïve Marilyn was involved with vocal coach and music arranger Fred Karger. When he dropped her for another girlfriend, Marilyn was devastated.

In 1949, she met agent Johnny Hyde of the William Morris Agency. He was married, short, unattractive, and 31 years older than Marilyn. Nevertheless, the high-powered agent became her mentor and her lover. She also agreed to pose nude for a calendar that year and her career was on its way. Her first major role came in 1950 in "The Asphalt Jungle," which earned her great reviews. This was followed by "All About Eve" and others. Hyde died in 1950, but by then Marilyn was coming into her own at Fox and became the studio's new blonde bombshell. Her rapid rise to fame, though, seemed to exacerbate her many insecurities and that made her temperamental both on and off the set. As a marquee attraction, she indulged her newfound power by rejecting studio projects, especially those that would further showcase her as a dumb blonde, an image that she hated. Her pleas to be given more substantial roles were virtually ignored, which only increased her frustration and added to her lack of self confidence.

In 1952, Marilyn met and fell in love with Joe DiMaggio, the famous baseball player. That same year, she began filming "Niagara" with Joseph Cotten, a film that would establish her stardom, although "Gentlemen Prefer Blondes" with Jane Russell would make her a legend.

On January 14, 1954, Marilyn and DiMaggio were married. The wedding made headlines all over the world, but the "dream romance" was never meant to last. Joe was a jealous type who thought that Marilyn was going to drop out of the movie business and become a housewife, something that she was never destined to be. In the fall of 1954, they separated and were later divorced. Despite this personal crisis, Marilyn's stardom continued to

Marilyn in one of her most classic poses

skyrocket as she filmed her classic role in "The Seven Year Itch."

In early 1955, Marilyn rebelled further against the studio, went to New York, and joined the Actors Studio, intent on becoming known as a serious actress. Here, she renewed her acquaintance with playwright Arthur Miller and the two of them began an affair that would later lead to marriage. To Marilyn, Miller represented the serious theater and a keen intellect that she found very attractive.

Marilyn returned to Hollywood in February 1956, after a yearlong absence, to film "Bus Stop."

Marilyn and Joe DiMaggio

She earned solid reviews for the picture, which prompted her demand for greater control over her films, wishes that the studio ignored because she was difficult on the set and resistant to guidance. As the conflicts with her bosses intensified, so did her consumption of drugs and alcohol.

Marilyn sought relief from her problems by

Marilyn and Arthur Miller

getting married again. She returned to New York in June and she and Arthur Miller were married on June 29. She hoped that this older, kind, and intellectual man would smooth over her escalating problems. Months later, Marilyn suffered a miscarriage, as would happen again in 1957 and 1958. During this emotionally draining period, she flew to England to star opposite Sir Laurence Olivier in "The Prince and The Showgirl." It was an unhappy shoot and the film failed with both audiences and critics. After London, she returned to Hollywood to make "Some Like It Hot" with Jack Lemmon and Tony Curtis.

It was around this time when her health began to deteriorate thanks to her increased dependency on drugs, especially sleeping pills. She was often late arriving on the set and was unable to remember her lines. In 1960, she began seeing Dr. Ralph Greenson, the so-called "psychoanalyst to the stars." As was common during this time, he relied heavily on prescribing barbiturates and tranquilizers to accompany his therapy.

July 1960 marked the start of filming for "The Misfits." The movie was based on a short story by Arthur Miller but while on location, he and Marilyn lived in separate quarters and were hardly speaking. Drugs were flown in for Marilyn from her doctor, but somehow she managed to give an exceptional performance. The shoot would be marked with tragedy, though. On the day after filming was completed, co-star Clark Gable would suffer a serious heart attack and die. Marilyn felt a tremendous amount of guilt over his death, further aggravating her depression.

By late 1960, her marriage with Arthur Miller had completely fallen apart. Their divorce became final in Juarez, Mexico, in January 1961. During the filming of "The Misfits," Marilyn was often out of control. At one point, she was hospitalized to detoxify and regain a degree of emotional stability. After her divorce from Miller, Marilyn spiraled even further down and began displaying suicidal behavior. In February, her analyst convinced her to enter the psychiatric ward of the Payne Whitney Clinic, where was confined for seven horrifying days. Subjected to a locked, padded cell, Marilyn, now even more distraught, called Joe DiMaggio and asked him to rescue her. He immediately arranged for a discharge.

In October 1961, Marilyn had her first meeting with President John F. Kennedy at a dinner party that was hosted by his sister, Pat, and his brother-in-law, actor Peter Lawford, at the couple's home in Santa Monica, Calif. A few months later, Marilyn and Kennedy met again at a New York dinner gathering. Their third meeting occurred in late March 1962 at the Palm Springs home of Bing Crosby, where she and Kennedy were both houseguests. Reportedly, this is when the president and the movie star began their short-lived affair.

Meanwhile, in 1962, Marilyn purchased the first house that she had ever owned, a Spanish-style home in the Brentwood section of Los Angeles. At Greeson's urging, she hired Eunice Murray as housekeeper. Murray called herself a nurse but had neither the training nor any credentials. Strangely, it is believed that Murray was essentially a "spy" for Greenson, who continued to have more and more control over Marilyn's life. He saw her almost daily when she was in Hollywood.

After a long period away from the soundstages, Marilyn returned to the studio in April 1962 to begin a romantic comedy called "Something's Got To Give" with Dean Martin. Although Marilyn looked wonderful, she was an emotional wreck and on the days that she bothered to show up on the set, she was often struggling to remember her dialogue. No one at the studio was very happy, especially in light of the debt that had been recently created for the studio by the schedule and cost overruns on the set of "Cleopatra," starring Elizabeth Taylor and Richard Burton. As the budget for that film climbed out of control, harried executives decided that by canceling Marilyn's film, with a lower budget and fewer actors, they could save enough money to finish the filming of "Cleopatra."

In mid-May 1962, during one of her many absences from the lot, Marilyn went to New York to sing "Happy Birthday" to the president at a Madison Square Garden party. Because Marilyn so brazenly defied the studio with her well-documented absence, her bosses became even angrier. Perhaps realizing that she had gone too far, Marilyn was much more cooperative when she returned to L.A. But by then it was too late. On June 1, Marilyn turned 36 and celebrated with a small party on the set. Six days later, Fox fired her for "unprofessional antics." The studio also filed a $750,000 lawsuit against their former star and attempted to re-cast her part in the film. However, Dean Martin refused to work with anyone else but Marilyn. Cooler heads soon prevailed and the studio suggested a compromise: after Martin completed other film commitments, the movie would restart with Marilyn again as the leading lady.

In the meantime, Marilyn was contemplating

Bobby and Jack Kennedy. How involved were the famous brothers in Marilyn's life -- and her death?

other movie and stage offers, including some in Las Vegas, as well as the possibility of a layout in *Playboy* magazine. After short visits to New York and Mexico City, the actress returned home. On August 1, Marilyn was signed to a new $250,000 contract to complete "Something's Got To Give."

On Saturday, August 4, 1962, Marilyn was at home all day. Her only guest was her publicist, Pat Newcomb. Later reports would claim that Robert F. Kennedy visited the house that day. Around 5 p.m., Greenson, came over for their usual therapy session. Marilyn retired to her bedroom around 8 p.m. and took the telephone from the hall into the room with her. She made several phone calls that night, including one to Joe DiMaggio's son, Joe Jr., who had recently broken up with his girlfriend. Marilyn called to console him.

She also called Peter Lawford to cancel a dinner invitation. Marilyn allegedly said to Lawford, "Peter, I don't think I'm going to make it tonight because I don't feel well. Will you say goodbye to Pat [Lawford's wife] and to Jack and to yourself, because you're a nice guy?" Lawford supposedly became concerned about the "goodbye" portion of her call and wanted to rush over to check on her, but was advised not to. As the president's brother-in-law, it could generate adverse publicity for everyone if there was actually something amiss. Lawford later claimed that he contacted Marilyn's agent and had that person call the house. Mrs. Murray answered the call at 9:30 p.m. and said that the telephone extension was still in Marilyn's room, so she must be fine. She always placed the telephone outside her room at night so that her troubled sleep would not be disturbed if it rang. It is unknown if any other calls came into, or were made from, Marilyn's house that night. The telephone records for the night of August 4 mysteriously disappeared after being obtained by the authorities from the phone company.

According to the "official" account of Marilyn's death, Eunice Murray noticed a light shining under her bedroom door at about midnight (later revised to 3:25 a.m.). When Marilyn did not respond to Murray's knocking, the woman went outside and peered through the closed window. Her view of Marilyn on the bed looked "peculiar," so she telephoned Dr. Greenson. When he arrived, he broke a pane in the French window and opened the door, finding Marilyn on the bed, unconscious. Greenson then called Marilyn's personal physician, Dr. Hyman Engelberg, who pronounced Marilyn dead at the scene. A short time later, the police were summoned to the house.

When LAPD Sergeant Jack Clemmons arrived, he found several people there, including the two doctors and Mrs. Murray. Clemmons later said, "It looked like a convention" and added something "wasn't kosher." Clemmons affirmed that he found Marilyn lying naked, facedown, and at an angle on the bed in the sparsely furnished master bedroom. He noted that her arm seemed to be reaching out for the nearby telephone. An empty bottle of sleeping pills was found next to the bed. There were 10 to 14 other bottles on the nightstand, including one that contacted 10 capsules of chloral hydrate, used as a hypnotic. Marilyn's body was taken to the Westwood Village Mortuary and the house was sealed and placed under guard.

Later, the body was taken to the county morgue, where Los Angeles County Deputy Medical Examiner Thomas T. Noguchi conducted the high-profile autopsy. Noguchi would claim that his youth and relative inexperience caused errors in the case, but later, claimed to have been pressured by his superiors to sign his original autopsy report on Monroe's death. The official investigation attributed Marilyn's death to "acute barbiturate poisoning, ingestion of overdose" -- namely Nembutal and chloral hydrate. It was determined to be a suicide. However, a strong forensic doubt can be cast on this conclusion since no barbiturates were actually found in Marilyn's body, despite the blood and liver levels and the empty bottle of Nembutal found next to the bed.

After the autopsy, Joe DiMaggio came to Marilyn's rescue once more. He flew from San Francisco to supervise the funeral arrangements. Marilyn was buried at Westwood Memorial Park, where for the next several decades, red roses were delivered to her crypt each week, courtesy of DiMaggio. Joe died at the age of 85 in 1999 and until the day he died, he regretted losing Marilyn and told friends that he had hoped to remarry her.

Reportedly, not long before his death, Joe told his longtime attorney and friend, Morris Engelberg, "I'll finally get to see Marilyn."

Marilyn's life was over, but she was certainly not being allowed to rest in peace. Controversy and conspiracy theories ran rampant after her death and many refused to believe that she had actually committed suicide. The most popular theories claimed that she had been silenced to protect the reputation of the Kennedy family, as revenge against the Kennedys, or worse.

The inconsistencies were so strange that they prompted a 1985 investigation into Marilyn's death. According to Walter Schaefer, owner of the Schaefer Ambulance Company, he received a call at about 2 a.m. on the night of Marilyn's death. He picked her up at her home and delivered her to Santa Monica Hospital, where she died in the emergency room. Inexplicably, though, she was found back at her house, naked, prone on the bed, reaching for the telephone. Deborah Gould, former wife of Marilyn's friend Peter Lawford, insisted that Lawford and an investigator went to Marilyn's house to "clean things up" and that Lawford destroyed a note she had written. Gould also stated that Lawford told her, "Marilyn took her last big enema." At the time of her death, the actress had been taking enemas to facilitate bowel movements, but Gould interpreted this comment to mean something else – namely an enema filled with an overdose of drugs.

Most conspiracy theories about Marilyn's death seem to connect to her alleged affair with John F. Kennedy. According to a number of accounts, they were attracted to one another after they met yet opinions vary as to just how serious the affair actually was. White House telephone logs show that they spoke on the phone numerous times, yet proving the two had an actual affair has been problematic. Somewhere along the line, the president's brother, Robert Kennedy, was added to the mix.

According to the stories, Robert Kennedy arrived in L.A. on August 1, 1962 to give a speech to the Bar Association. Apparently, he met Marilyn later that evening at Peter Lawford's house for an impromptu dinner. Some have speculated that Marilyn organized the dinner herself, while others claim that Bobby arranged the evening, primarily to tell her to stay away from his brother. In any case, the two supposedly ended up making love that night, further complicating matters. Days later, Bobby allegedly rejected Marilyn and warned her again about staying away from the Kennedy family. That forced Marilyn, who was already emotionally distraught, to threaten to expose the contents of her diary – contents that allegedly contained some pretty unsavory information regarding her affair with the president, and about the Kennedys' collusion with organized crime. As the theory goes, Robert then had to have her silenced – or did someone do it for him?

Another popular theory describes Marilyn's death at the hands of the mob. As many writers have suggested, the Mafia had a long-standing relationship with the Kennedy family, dating all the way back to Joseph Kennedy and his days as a bootlegger. Underworld legend has it that during the 1960 election, the mob put their muscle behind John Kennedy, especially in Chicago, to insure that he won the presidency. In return, they were given assurances that mob activities would be untouched during the Kennedy administration. But by 1962, it had become painfully obvious that the Kennedys had no intention of keeping up their end of the bargain. In 1960, for example, a mere 19 organized crime figures had been indicted, but within the first two years of the Kennedy administration, 121 Mafia characters were indicted, thanks to Robert Kennedy's efforts as Attorney General. That left the mob with only one solution – to get the Kennedys out of the way. They tried to do this by first revealing the president's messy affair with Marilyn, then arranging her death so that the Kennedys appeared to be involved. Unfortunately, for the mob's efforts anyway, the possible connection between Marilyn and the Kennedys would not really become a part of popular culture until long after almost everyone involved was dead.

If there was a conspiracy behind Marilyn's death, then based on the contradictions in the case, it would seem to have had to involve her analyst, Dr. Ralph Greenson. He was the man who provided Marilyn with her drugs in the first place.

Apparently, on August 4, the day of her death, Greenson gave her a fresh prescription for nembutal. Yet when her body was found in the early morning hours, all 50 pills were gone. Those who believed that she committed suicide have suggested that she simply swallowed all 50 of them. Yet, Noguchi failed to find any trace of drugs in her stomach or intestinal tract when he performed the autopsy. That means that Marilyn had to administer the pills – all 50 of them – rectally. Of course, she could have done this on her own, but if she was trying to kill herself it certainly seems more plausible that she would have just swallowed them with a glass of water. In other words, it seems very possible that someone helped her.

At least one neighbor claimed to have seen Greenson arrive at Marilyn's house in the early evening with a man who looked like Bobby Kennedy. And if Kennedy was there, he probably came to warn Marilyn away from the family once and for all, and did so with Dr. Greenson's help. That may have unhinged Marilyn completely, perhaps to the point of hurting herself. That, in turn, may have forced everyone out of the room so that Greenson could administer a sedative. There are accounts that Greenson then left and met up with the rest of the group for dinner at a nearby restaurant. And there are also accounts of Marilyn trying to make a number of frantic calls to Peter Lawford around the same time. In any case, the group apparently returned to her house a few hours later and that's when she was found unconscious, or even perhaps dead. This may explain why an ambulance driver claimed to take her to the hospital and if a Kennedy really was present, why her body was returned to the house so that it could be "discovered" there.

Regardless, in spite of the hundreds of books written on the subject, no one has ever really been able to solve the mysteries surrounding Marilyn's death. Part of this has to do with a very real, documented cover-up involving destroyed phone records, a missing diary, and invented alibis. In addition, in the intervening years, almost everyone involved with the case has died, including Peter Lawford, L.A. Police Chief William H. Parker, John F. Kennedy, and Robert Kennedy. In 1985, a Los Angeles grand jury was asked to re-examine Marilyn's death, but they recommended against reopening the still-controversial case – there was simply not enough hard evidence to suggest that she had been murdered. Even so, the question remains.

Could this be why Marilyn's ghost is still rumored to linger in Tinseltown? Perhaps – although, as it is in the case of Valentino, one has to wonder just how many places Marilyn's spirit can haunt? Perhaps the most likely spot to find her ghost would be her former home in Brentwood. Rumor has it that her spirit has been encountered many times in the room where she died. The late Anna Nicole Smith lived in Marilyn's former home for a time, and she claimed to frequently see and feel Marilyn's spirit in the house.

One of the most famous locations where Marilyn's ghost has been encountered has been at the Hollywood Roosevelt Hotel. A hotel employee named Suzanne Leonard was the first to encounter Marilyn's spectral image in a mirror that was hanging in a hotel office, but she has not been the last. It was later learned that the hotel once hung in Marilyn's favorite suite, which she

Marilyn's crypt in Westwood Village Memorial Park. Joe DiMaggio had flowers delivered to her grave until his death.

often used when she wanted to escape from the pressures of her career. Apparently, Marilyn has been encountered in other ways at the hotel, too. Singer Nick Lachey told a friend in 2006 that he had entered an elevator in the hotel and was stunned to see a gorgeous blonde dressed in sexy 1950s-style evening wear. When he pressed the button for his floor and then turned around for a better look, the woman had vanished. Lachey was convinced that the phantom was Marilyn Monroe.

Marilyn's ghost has also supposedly been seen at her crypt in the Westwood Village Memorial Park. This haunting is reportedly connected to DiMaggio's weekly delivery of roses to her grave, which ended with the slugger's death in 1999. Other admirers still leave flowers and other items at her grave today, but it's Joe's roses that Marilyn's specter allegedly waits for. A number of people claim that they have spotted her as a filmy cloud, hovering nearby as she waits for her roses to be delivered to her tomb.

NOTE FROM THE AUTHOR:

I saved this final unsolved Hollywood mystery for the end of the book for a couple of reasons. The first is that, in almost every case, I have tried to recount the compelling ghost stories and mysteries of Hollywood in chronological order, picking and choosing the cases that most interested me from the early days of Hollywood to more modern times.

However, I always intended to save my recounting of Bob Crane's murder for last because this was the case that probably had the most impact on me personally. It's not because I knew Bob Crane, although it certainly seemed like I did. As a small child in the early 1970s, I was what came to be known as a "latchkey kid." I walked home from school each day, let myself into the house, grabbed a snack, and sat down to watch a succession of re-runs on the television that I had in my room. "Gilligan's Island" and "The Munsters" were always a treat for me, but there was no show that I liked as much as "Hogan's Heroes." While it might seem strange for a 7-year-old kid to be fascinated with a comedy about POW's in a German prison camp during World War II, I simply loved the show and most of all, I loved Bob Crane. There was just something about the handsome, wisecracking actor that appealed to me as a kid and I never forgot my fondness for him and the show that brought me so much entertainment every afternoon.

I was only 12 years old when Bob Crane was murdered, but I certainly understood that the kinky actor was certainly no Colonel Hogan. As I learned more and more about his strange private life, I learned not to just enjoy his onscreen work, but sympathized with his personal demons. He was a man who was driven by something that I didn't understand, but could certainly accept. Unfortunately for Bob, it led to his death – and to an enduring mystery that will probably never be solved.

This ends my introduction to the story. It's an unprofessional interruption to the book I hope that you'll forgive and if you do, save a little of that forgiveness for Bob Crane (and so many other tragic figures in this book). Like all of us, they certainly had their problems – problems that couldn't always be solved by the bright lights of fame and fortune.

THE FALL OF A "HERO"
THE UNSOLVED MURDER OF BOB CRANE

The death of a celebrity is, without a doubt, always an object of morbid curiosity in America. It is always followed by television accounts, newspaper stories, and tributes by peers and admirers from every walk of life. However, when the Hollywood notable dies under strange or bloody circumstances, then the death remains curious, and gains bigger headlines, for an even longer period of time. Should the murder go unsolved, the death becomes a legend, often unfortunately defining that performer's place in history and overshadowing the accomplishments that earned them a place as a celebrity in the first place. As the reader has noted, this has been the case with many notables from Hollywood's past, including William Desmond Taylor, Thelma Todd, Marilyn Monroe, George Reeves, and others.

In the case of Bob Crane, however, there was an added element to the mystery, making it even more lurid. It was not until his brutal murder in 1978 that the public learned that the seemingly wholesome disk jockey and television performer was leading a strange double life. It turned out that Crane was a convulsive sexual exhibitionist and swinger who devoted much of his time to picking up women he met on the dinner theater circuit, and then documenting his tireless sexual performances with photographs and videotapes. Another facet to his personality was his startling lack of shame about what he did. He often proudly showed his albums of pornographic photographs and tapes to anyone who stopped by his house, or even to his family. He seemed clueless as to how offensive his behavior might be to them and ignorant of the destructiveness of his compulsive womanizing.

Robert Edward Crane was born in July 13, 1928 in Waterbury, Conn. He grew up in a middle-class home, the younger son of Alfred and Rosemary Crane. His father was a furniture and floor-covering salesman as his career progressed he moved his family to nearby, upscale Stamford. As a child, Bob showed an affinity for music and by age 11, he was playing drums in his own band. At 16, he dropped out of high school and in 1944, became a percussionist for the Connecticut Symphony Orchestra. He was let go after two years because he couldn't stop "cutting up" during performances. After that, he toured the Northeast with several bands, finally getting out of music in the late 1940s as the era of the big swing bands began to fade.

In May 1949, he married Anne Terzian, whom he had been dating since he was 14 and she was 12. During their course of their 20-year marriage, the couple had three children: Robert David, Deborah, and Karen. For a time, they lived with Anne's family, but Bob was determined to find a dependable source of income. He began working in a jewelry store during the day and working band gigs at night. In 1950, he became a disk jockey and a radio host. He soon gained a solid reputation as a performer and became very popular for his on-air clowning around. He was hired by Los Angeles station KNX in 1956 and moved his family to California. His celebrity interview show quickly gained a huge audience and before long the "King of the L.A. Airwaves" was bringing home a $100,000 annual salary.

Always restless, though, Crane began dreaming of becoming an actor. To gain experience, he performed in local theaters and began winning guest spots on television and small movie roles in films like "Return to Peyton Place" and "Man Trap." For a short time, he substituted for Johnny Carson as the host of the daytime TV quiz show "Who Do You Trust?" After guest roles on shows like "The Twilight Zone" and "Alfred Hitchcock Presents," Crane landed a part on the popular sitcom "The Dick Van Dyke Show." Donna Reed saws the handsome actor in the episode and thought he would be perfect to play Dr. Dave Kelsey on "The Donna Reed Show." His role as the amiable next-door neighbor was only supposed to be featured in one episode, but it led to his becoming a regular on the show in 1963. Bob also continued with his daytime radio show and, with the added income, moved his family to a new home in Tarzana, in the San Fernando Valley.

Crane left "The Donna Reed Show" in 1965, reportedly because his feelings were hurt after he overheard some comments on the set about his performance. On the surface, Bob was confident and self-assured, but underneath, he was very sensitive. One day, he accidentally overhead Donna Reed's husband, the show's producer, say that he was unimpressed by Crane's acting in the show. Wounded, Crane left the show soon after.

As it turned out, though, Reed's husband was apparently the only producer unimpressed with Crane's work. His role in the earlier series led directly to his being cast as the clever American POW in "Hogan's Heroes," an offbeat sitcom that premiered in September 1965. Set in a German prisoner-of-war camp, the show pitted Crane's slippery officer and ingenious men against the incompetent Colonel Klink (played by Werner Klemperer) who ran Stalag 13 with his the help of the easily hoodwinked Sergeant Schultz and his bumbling troops.

A young Bob Crane in his early days as a disk jockey. His success on the radio would lead to television roles and then national stardom.

Part of the appeal of "Hogan's Heroes" was undoubtedly its star, Bob Crane, a handsome man with a broad, open face and twinkling eyes. The show made Bob Crane a household name, despite some of the controversy that it caused. Some Neo-Nazi groups were upset by the way the program lampooned their ideological fathers. Crane said he received threats from such extremist groups. Some Jews were offended by the almost "lovable jerk" treatment given to the Germans. However, Crane pointed out that the show had Jewish fans. Indeed, it had Jewish actors — including the two playing the top German characters, Colonel Klink and Sergeant Schultz.

The cast of the popular "Hogan's Heroes"

Werner Klemperer was born in Cologne, Germany, on March 22, 1929. He grew up in Berlin. His father, Otto, was Jewish by ethnicity, but had converted to Christianity. Such a conversion would not, of course, prevent persecution by the Nazis. In 1933, Otto and his family fled the country. They went to Switzerland, then Austria, and then sailed for America in 1935. John Banner took the role of the baffled and weak Sergeant Hans Schultz. On the program, the silly sergeant took bribes from Hogan's sly band, thus ensuring his reluctant complicity in their hi-jinks. Banner was Jewish, and his family had been victimized by Nazism. He was 28 and living in Austria when the Nazis took over. His family died in extermination camps. Banner fled to Switzerland and then he headed for America in 1939. He often played Nazis, remarking, "Who can play Nazis better than us Jews?" As Sergeant Schultz, he was especially popular with children who loved his trademark statements, "I know NO-thing! I see NO-thing!"

Many in the program feared offending soldiers who had actually lived through the experience of being prisoners of Germany during World War II.

However, as Crane pointed out, many such ex-POWs were fans. "Ex-POWs are our greatest boosters," Crane once proudly noted. "The ex-POWs in Albuquerque, New Mexico, have an association. They had a convention and invited me."

Despite the risky premise of setting a comedy in a Nazi prison camp, the show became a huge success and ran for 168 episodes over six seasons. During the show's run, Crane found time to do summer stock theater, talk show appearances, and movies.

Crane's success in the movie business seemed to escalate his need for sexual encounters and led to a series of extramarital affairs. But, despite what some sources claim, his success was not what started his extreme behavior. According to his son from his second marriage, Crane was having sexual encounters and photographing naked women as far back as the 1940s. He began experiments with sex at the age of 14, when he began sleeping with a neighbor's wife and he also began making amateur porn films in the 1950s. His need to have, and record, multiple sexual partners did not begin with his television success; it likely just made it easier for him to find willing partners.

The recurrent problems in their marriage led his wife to divorce him in May 1969, a short time before their twentieth anniversary. The divorce was a bitter one and led to a long and drawn out fight over finances. Regardless, in October 1970, Crane wed actress Patricia Arnette Olsen on the set of "Hogan's Heroes." Under her professional name of Sigrid Valdis, Olsen played Hilda, the shapely German secretary in Colonel Klink's office. The next year, the Cranes had a son, Robert Scott.

Bob with his second wife, Patricia Olsen, who played Hilda on "Hogan's Heroes"

After the end of "Hogan's Heroes," Crane made numerous guest appearances on television shows and appeared in several made-for-television movies and the Disney film "Superdad." He rejected several sitcom pilots, claiming they were weak follow-ups to his earlier success. In 1974, he passed on a $300,000 job as the host of an L.A. radio show that would require him to work on-air just four hours a day. Instead, he chose to do the "The Bob Crane Show," an uninspired sitcom that only lasted for one season. This failure left Crane bitter and without direction and he wound up with a secondary role in the Disney football film "Gus," about a donkey that kicked field goals, and as a guest star on shows like "The Love Boat." Some reports say that word was starting to spread in the industry about the actor's penchant for hanging out in topless bars and lounges and that this was so much the opposite of Crane's clean-cut image that producers were worried about hiring him.

By 1978, Crane and Patricia were in the process of getting a divorce and their now seven-year-old son, Scotty, went to live with his mother. To stay active and make a living, Crane began headlining romantic comedies at dinner theaters all over the country. One of his favorite productions was "Beginner's Luck," a light sex comedy with a small cast. In June, Bob was starring in this play at the Windmill Dinner Theater in Scottsdale, Ariz.

At this point in his life, Bob had developed the habit of getting together during his road trips with John Henry Carpenter, a video equipment salesman and repairman from Los Angeles. The pair had initially become friends after being introduced by Crane's "Hogan's Heroes" co-star, Richard Dawson. Bob wanted to tape his sexual escapades and needed recommendations on what kind of equipment to buy. Video was still in its infancy at the time, and was very expensive. However, it offered Crane much more than mere photographs, which he still used. Carpenter found that his much better looking friend had an easy way with women and he used Crane's celebrity to pick up the actor's cast-offs. Typically, during their nights on the town, Crane and his hanger-on would visit local bars, meet willing young women, and escort them back to their hotel room for a sex and sessions with Bob's video equipment.

Dead Men Do Tell Tales: Bloody Hollywood - Page 247

Some reports say that prior to, or during, Bob's stay in Scottsdale, he had reconsidered his compulsive lifestyle and was thinking of trying to deal with, or at least cut back on, his sexual addiction. Part of this plan called for him to stop associating with his tawdry, needy sidekick. Some believe that it was this resolution that may have gotten the actor killed.

On Wednesday, June 28, 1978, after a performance of "Beginner's Luck," Crane and Carpenter went to several different Scottsdale bars. Later, witnesses recalled pieces of their conversation and remembered that Bob seemed upset about a recent encounter with his estranged wife. A few days before, Patricia and Scotty had traveled to Scottsdale to see Crane, but the visit had resulted in a heated argument. In addition, several others recalled that there seemed to be problems between Crane and Carpenter. Purportedly, Crane had already told his slimy friend that they would be going their separate ways. Nevertheless, the pair had drinks with two women and then was later seen with them in a local coffee shop. After that, Carpenter allegedly left to pack for his return trip to L.A. and later, from his Sunburst Motel room, he telephoned Bob.

The next afternoon, just after 2 p.m., Victoria Berry, a member of the cast of "Beginner's Luck," came by the star's place at the Winfield Apartments. Crane had failed to show up for a lunch that was being used to promote the show. Earlier, she had arranged to come by his apartment and pick up a copy of a tape of her stage performance, which she hoped to use in her résumé. When she arrived at apartment 132A, the door to his ground-floor residence was unlocked. Victoria went inside and as she walked through the place calling for Bob, no one answered. When she reached the bedroom, she spotted someone under a sheet on the bed. Startled, she looked up and saw a crimson spatter all over the walls and on the bed. The person under the sheet, she realized, was lying in a pool of blood. Panicked, she pulled back the sheet and saw that the figure was a man, although his face was so damaged that she was unsure whether or not it was Bob Crane. She immediately called the police.

Officers arrived at 2:20 p.m. and it was soon determined that the victim at the scene was Crane. His head had been beaten in by an unidentified blunt object and there was no sign of a struggle, or a forced entry to the apartment. The coroner later determined that Crane had been struck twice while sleeping, although the first blow had likely killed him. The police investigation determined that two separate parts of a camera tripod struck Crane's head, inflicting two separate wounds. An electrical cord, taken from a video camera in his bedroom, had been tied in a bow around the victim's neck after he was dead. Paulette Kasieta, the first Scottsdale police officer to arrive on the scene, immediately secured the area and a short time later Scottsdale's Police Lieutenant Ron Dean arrived at the apartment and took over.

News quickly spread about the murder, stunning his friends and former "Hogan's Heroes" cast mates. Werner Klemperer learned of the murder from a television newscast and later said, "I almost had a heart attack." While the homicide was being investigated, Crane was buried on July 5, 1978 at Oakwood Memorial Park in Chatsworth, Calif. More than 200 mourners attended the burial mass at St. Paul the Apostle Catholic Church in Westwood, including his first wife and their three children, his widow and son, Victoria Berry, friends and former cast mates, and John Carpenter.

Meanwhile, Scottsdale investigators were hard at work on the case. Their working theory was that the killer was someone that Crane knew, a person who before the homicide had left the apartment, but then returned through the front door or a window that he or she had left unlocked earlier. They came back while Bob was sleeping and struck the actor a heavy blow on the left side of his head with the video tripod. A second, lighter blow crushed Crane's skull. The killer tied the electrical cord tightly around Crane's neck, but by that time, he was already dead. Before fleeing, the killer pulled the sheet up around the victim's head. Cash was found in Crane's wallet, which eliminated robbery as a motive.

Thanks to the high-profile coverage of the crime (especially by the tabloids) and the ongoing police investigation, Bob's secret sex life came to light. Approximately 50 pornographic videotapes were found at the Winfield apartment, as well as professional photography equipment in the bathroom for developing and enlarging still shots. A large album of pornographic pictures that Crane possessed was missing from the crime scene.

The initial suspect in the case was Crane's long-time friend John Carpenter. On the evening before Crane's murder, Carpenter sat with Victoria Berry at the Windmill Dinner Theatre while she wasn't onstage. She later saw the two men leave the theater together. While Berry was writing out her witness statement in the kitchen of Crane's apartment, the phone rang. Police Lieutenant Ron Dean told her to answer the phone, but not to say anything about Crane. The call was from John Carpenter, who was back in L.A. The police lieutenant took the phone, identified himself, and told Carpenter that the police were at Crane's apartment investigating "an incident."

Carpenter told Dean he had been out with Crane until around 1 a.m. but later changed the time to 2:45 a.m. He then said he'd driven by himself to the airport later in the morning for his return flight to Los Angeles. Dean said later that he found it strange that Carpenter had not asked him why the police were in Crane's apartment, or where Crane was.

Later that day, police interviewed some of Crane's colleagues and friends, discovering that though Crane was personable, charming, and fun to be around, he had made enemies, including an actor that he had worked with at a dinner theater in Texas who had argued with Crane and threatened him. Inevitably, given Crane's reputation with the ladies, there were numerous angry husbands and boyfriends.

Still, Carpenter remained the prime suspect. Some witnesses claimed there was a strain in their relationship, but no actual evidence of a disagreement existed between the two men. Any physical evidence that might have tied Carpenter to the crime was also scarce, as was the motive that would have compelled him to murder his friend. Rumors surfaced, though, claiming that Crane might have loaned Carpenter $15,000 that his friend was unable to pay back. This may have also have been what caused the strain in their relationship, or it simply could have been that Carpenter was angry because he would no longer have access to Crane's rejected women if the two stopped going out together.

Perhaps even more compelling than the rumors was the discovery of a small blood smear on the passenger side door of Carpenter's rented vehicle. Scottsdale Detective Darwin Barrie inspected the vehicle and found a small amount of dried blood on the door. The car was examined and photographed but the blood turned out to be inconclusive. It was tested and determined to be Type B -- the same blood type as Crane. Carpenter had the far more common Type A blood. Though its presence in Carpenter's car was suspicious, the police, in these pre-DNA testing days, had no way of positively identifying the blood as Crane's. Thanks to this, no formal charges were filed at the time because of insufficient evidence.

Because of the continuing popularity of "Hogan's Heroes" in re-runs, and thanks to the unsolved murder, Bob Crane's name remained in the news in the years that followed. In May 1992, after a change in prosecutors in Scottsdale, the Crane case was re-opened. This time, John Carpenter was named as the defendant and arrested. However, because of charges pending against Carpenter in California (sexual misconduct with a minor), the trial in the Crane case did not begin until September 1994. Despite the district attorney's best efforts, which included DNA testing, the evidence from the crime scene and Carpenter's rental car had been too compromised over the years. As it was in 1978, the case turned out to be stronger in theory than it was in actual evidence. On September 4, 1998, John Carpenter died, maintaining his innocence to the end. The full truth about the unsolved murder will probably never be known.

The ongoing mystery and a feature film about the case, "Auto Focus," have helped keep Bob Crane's recognizable one over the years. These things may also have contributed to the presence of Crane's ghost, which is reportedly still active. Surprisingly, though, the spirit of the tormented actor is not connected to the place where he died, but rather to a location where he found several years of happiness during his life.

The haunting is believed to occur at CBS Columbia Square, where Bob worked as an on-air personality for CBS's original radio station, KNX. Located on Sunset Boulevard in Hollywood, the Square was home to both radio and television stations for decades, although all of them have since moved to other facilities in the L.A. area. The Square fell into disrepair in recent years, although the National Trust for Historic Preservation and Los Angeles Conservancy have been actively engaged in efforts to preserve the Hollywood landmark.

Bob Crane's ghost was spotted for many years by various witnesses at the CBS Columbia Studios, perhaps recapturing those days when his life was still uncomplicated by television fame and overwhelmed by his personal demons.

BLOODY HOLLYWOOD BIBLIOGRAPHY & RECOMMENDED READING

Agan, Patrick - *The Decline and Fall of the Love Goddesses* (1979)
Alexander, Paul - *Boulevard of Broken Dreams: The Life, Times, and Legend of James Dean* (1994)
American Hauntings website (Haunted Hollywood section – www.americanhauntings.org / 1997)
Anger, Kenneth – *Hollywood Babylon* (1975)
Anger, Kenneth – *Hollywood Babylon 2* (1984)
Arnold, William - *Shadowland* (1978)
Austen, John – *Hollywood's Unsolved Mysteries* (1970)
Barlett, Donald L. and James B. Steele - *Empire: The Life, Legend and Madness of Howard Hughes* (1979)
Bast, William - *James Dean: A Biography* (1956)
Berger, Robert & Anne Conser – *The Last Remaining Seats* (1997)
Bingham, Joan & Dolores Riccio – *More Haunted Houses* (1991)
Blanche, Tony & Brad Schreiber – *Death in Paradise* (1998)
Brooks, Marla – *Ghosts of Hollywood* (2008)
Brown, Peter Harry and Pat H. Broeske - *Howard Hughes: The Untold Story* (1996)
Bruck, Connie - *When Hollywood Had a King* (1998)
Bugliosi, Vincent with Curt Gentry - *Helter Skelter: The True Story of the Manson Murders.* (1974)
Carlo, Philip - *The Night Stalker* (1996)
Churchwell, Sarah - *The Many Lives of Marilyn Monroe* (2004)
Dywer, Jeff – *Ghost Hunter's Guide to Los Angeles* (2007)
Eames, John Douglas, with additional text by Robert Abele - *The Paramount Story: The Complete History of the Studio and Its Films* (2002)
Edmonds, Andy - *Frame-Up!: The Untold Story of Roscoe "Fatty" Arbuckle* (1991)
Edmonds, Andy – *Hot Toddy: True Story of Hollywood's Most Sensation Murder* (1989)
Eghigian, Jr., Mars – *After Capone: Life & World of Chicago Mob Boss Frank "The Enforcer" Nitti* (2006)
Epstein, Daniel Mark - *Sister Aimee: The Life of Aimee Semple McPherson* (1994)
Evans, Robert - *The Kid Stays in the Picture* (1994)
Flynn, Errol - *My Wicked, Wicked Ways: the Autobiography of Errol Flynn* (1959)
Gabler, Neal - *An Empire of Their Own: How the Jews Invented Hollywood* (1988)
Ghosts of the Prairie Magazine (Haunted Hollywood series by Troy Taylor / 1997-1998)
Gilmore, John - *Live Fast-Die Young: Remembering the Short Life of James Dean* (1998)
Gilmore, John - *Manson: The Unholy Trail of Charlie and the Family* (2000)
Gilmore, John - *Severed: The Real Story of the Black Dahlia* (1994)
Giroux, Robert - *A Deed of Death* (1990)
Global Book Publishing – *Cut! Hollywood Murders, Accidents & Other Tragedies* (2005)
Graysmith, Robert – *The Murder of Bob Crane* (1993)
Guiles, Fred Lawrence - *Norma Jean: The Life of Marilyn Monroe* (1993)
Hauck, Dennis William – *Haunted Places: The National Directory* (1996)
Heimann, Jim – *Sins of the City* (1999)
Henderson, Jan Alan & Randisi, Steve - *Behind the Crimson Cape* (2005)
Henderson, Jan Alan - *Speeding Bullet* (1999)
Higham, Charles - *Murder in Hollywood* (2004)
Holley, Val - *James Dean: The Biography* (1996)
Jacobson, Laurie & Marc Wannamaker – *Hollywood Haunted* (1994)

Jewell, Richard B.; Harbin, Vernon - *The RKO Story* (1982)
Kashner, Sam & Nancy Schoenberger - *Hollywood Kryptonite* (1996)
Kirkpatrick, Sidney D - *A Cast of Killers* (1992)
Koszarski, Richard - *An Evening's Entertainment: The Age of the Silent Feature Picture* (1994)
Lamparski, Richard – *Lamparski's Hidden Hollywood* (1981)
Leider, Emily - *Dark Lover: The Life and Death of Rudolph Valentino* (2003)
Lewis, Brad - *Hollywood's Celebrity Gangster: The Incredible Life and Times of Mickey* Cohen (2007)
Luijters, Guus - *Sexbomb: The Life and Death of Jayne Mansfield* (1988)
Macklin, John – *The Strange & the Uncanny* (1967)
Marx, Samuel and Joyce Vanderveen - *Deadly Illusions* (1990)
Masek, Mark J. – *Hollywood Remains to be Seen* (2001)
May, Antoinette – *Haunted Houses of California* (1990)
Miller, Frank - *Censored Hollywood* (1994)
Miller, R. DeWitt – *Impossible! Yet it Happened* (1947)
Mordden, Ethan - *The Hollywood Studios* (1989)
Munn, Michael – *Hollywood Murder Case Book* (1987)
Nash, James Robert – *Bloodletters and Bad Men* (1995)
O'Brien, Darcy – *Two of a Kind: The Hillside Stranglers* (1985)
Parrish, Michael – *For The People: Inside the Los Angeles County District Attorney's Office* (2001)
Parrish, James Robert – *The Hollywood Book of Death* (2002)
Parrish, James Robert – *The Hollywood Book of Scandals* (2004)
Phelan, James - *Howard Hughes: The Hidden Years* (1976)
Rue Morgue Magazine (issue #77 – Hollywood Forever Cemetery)
Sanders, Ed - *The Family* (2002 edition)
Saxton, Martha - *Jayne Mansfield and the American Fifties* (1976)
Schatz, Thomas - *The Genius of the System* (1989)
Senate, Richard – *Ghost Stalker's Guide to Haunted California* (1998)
Senate, Richard – *Hollywood's Ghosts* (2003)
Siakis, Carl – *The Mafia Encyclopedia* (1987)
Sifakis, Carl – *The Encyclopedia of American Crime* (1982)
Sklar, Robert - *Movie-Made America* (1994)
Smith, Barbara – *Ghost Stories of Hollywood* (2000)
Sperling, Millner, and Warner - *Hollywood Be Thy Name* (1988)
Spoto, Donald - Rebel: *The Life and Legend of James Dean* (1996)
Spoto, Donald - *Marilyn Monroe: The* Biography (2001)
Steiger, Brad & Sherry – *Hollywood & the Supernatural* (1983)
Strait, Raymond - *Here They Are Jayne Mansfield* (1992)
Taylor, Troy – *Dead Men Do Tell Tales* (2008)
Taylor, Troy – *Ghosts by Gaslight* (2007)
Taylor, Troy – *No Rest for the Wicked* (2002)
Tyler, Parker – *Magic & Myth of the Movies* (1947)
Walker, Alexander - *Rudolph Valentino* (1976)
Wallace, David – *Lost Hollywood* (2001)
Ward, Elizabeth & Alain Silver – *Raymond Chandler's Los Angeles* (1987)
Wayne, Jane Ellen *The Golden Girls of MGM: Greta Garbo, Joan Crawford, Lana Turner, Judy Garland, Ava Gardner, Grace Kelly and Others* (2003)
Wikipedia Website (www.wikipedia.com)
Wilkerson III, W.R. - *The Man Who Invented Las Vegas* (2000)

Winer, Richard – *Houses of Horror* (1983)
Winer, Richard & Nancy Osborn – *Haunted Houses* (1979)
Winer, Richard & Nancy Osborn Ishmael – *More Haunted Houses* (1981)
Wride, Tim B. (Essay / Introduction by James Ellroy) *Scene of the Crime* (2004)
Young, Paul – *L.A. Exposed* (2002)
Zukor, Adolph, with Dale Kramer. *The Public Is Never Wrong: The Autobiography of Adolph Zukor* (1953)

Special Thanks to:
Jill Hand -- Proofreading & Editing Services
Mike & Sandra Schwab
Robert & Anne Wlodarski
John Winterbauer
Lori Jacobson
Kenneth Anger
John Gilmore
Larry Harnisch
James Ellroy

& Haven Taylor

Note: Although Whitechapel Productions Press, Troy Taylor, and all affiliated with this book have carefully researched all sources to insure the accuracy and completeness of all of the information contained here, we assume no responsibility for errors, inaccuracies or omissions.

About the Author:

Troy Taylor is the author of nearly 60 books about history, hauntings and the unexplained in America. He is also the founder of the American Ghost Society and the American & Illinois Hauntings ghost tour companies. Along with writing about the unusual and hosting tours, Taylor is also a public speaker on the subject of ghosts and hauntings and has spoken to literally hundreds of private and public groups on a variety of paranormal subjects. He has appeared in newspaper and magazine articles about ghosts and has also been fortunate enough to be interviewed hundreds of times for radio and television broadcasts about the supernatural. He has also appeared in a number of documentary films, several television series and in one feature film about the paranormal. He is currently the executive producer of the iClips series, "Cringe".

Troy is constantly at work on other books about crime and the supernatural and he can be contacted through his website at **www.americanhauntings.org**

He currently resides in Central Illinois with his wife, Haven, in a decidedly non-haunted house.

COMING SOON FROM THE "DEAD MEN DO TELL TALES" SERIES

WITHOUT A TRACE:
The Mystery of History's Unexplained Disappearances

NO MAN KNOWS MY GRAVE:
History & Hauntings of the American Tropics

BLOODY NEW ORLEANS:
History & Hauntings of Murder & Mystery in the Crescent

BLOODY NEW ENGLAND: History & Hauntings of New England Crime & Mystery
BLOODY SOUTH: History & Hauntings of Murder, Crime & Mystery in the American South

ABOUT WHITECHAPEL PRESS

Whitechapel Productions Press is a division of Dark Haven Entertainment and a small press publisher, specializing in books about ghosts and hauntings. Since 1993, the company has been one of America's leading publishers of supernatural books and has produced such best-selling titles as "Haunted Illinois", "The Ghost Hunter's Guidebook", Ghosts on Film, Confessions of a Ghost Hunter, Resurrection Mary, Bloody Chicago, The Haunting of America, Spirits of the Civil War and many others.

With nearly a dozen different authors producing high quality books on all aspects of ghosts, hauntings and the paranormal, Whitechapel Press has made its mark with America's ghost enthusiasts.

Whitechapel Press is also the publisher of the acclaimed **Ghosts of the Prairie** magazine, which started in 1997 as one of the only ghost-related magazines on the market. It continues today as a travel guide to the weird, haunted and unusual in Illinois. Each issue also includes a print version of the Whitechapel Press ghost book catalog.

You can visit Whitechapel Productions Press online and browse through our selection of ghostly titles, plus get information on ghosts and hauntings, haunted history, spirit photographs, information on ghost hunting and much more. by visiting the internet website at:
WWW. DARK HAVEN ENTERTAINMENT.COM